Trends in Wheat Breeding

Trends in Wheat Breeding

Sultan Singh
Former Professor

I.S. Pawar
Wheat Breeder

CCS Haryana Agricultural University,
Hisar - 125 004

CBS

CBS PUBLISHERS & DISTRIBUTORS
NEW DELHI • BANGALORE

Paperback ISBN : 81-239-1380-X
Hardcover ISBN : 81-239-1384-2

First Edition : 2006

Copyright © Authors and Publisher

All rights reserved. No part of this publication may be reproduced, stored in a retrieval system, or transmitted in any form or by any means, electronic, mechanical, photocopying, recording, or otherwise, without written permission from the authors and publisher.

Publishing Director : Vinod K. Jain

Published by :
Satish Kumar Jain for CBS Publishers & Distributors,
4596/1-A, 11 Darya Ganj, New Delhi - 110 002 (India)
E-mail: cbspubs@vsnl.com • Website: www.cbspd.com

Branch Office :
2975, 17th Cross, K.R. Road, Bansankari 2nd Stage, Bangalore-70
Fax : 080-26771680 • E-mail : cbsbng@vsnl.net

Printed at :
Asia Printograph, Delhi

Preface

In the recent past, there has been a spectacular advancement in the breeding methodology of wheat and some other important food crops. For example, hybrid rice has become a commercial proposition in China. Efforts are also being made for making hybrid wheat a reality. After going through the book **"Trends in Wheat Breeding"**, the readers will feel that they are in close touch with what has so far happened in the field of wheat breeding.

Chpater 1 deals with the origin and evolution of wheat and also gives information about the tribe *Triticeae*. The second chapter provides details of cytogenetic and genetic aspects of wheat. The objectives of wheat breeding have been discussed in Chapter 3.

The Chapters 4-7 deal with conventional and unconventional approaches being used in wheat improvement programmes. Hybrid wheat is gaining importance in India and many other countries of the world. This important aspect of wheat breeding has been discussed in Chapter 8.

Development of wheat varieties resistant/tolerant to biotic and abiotic stresses is one of the major objectives of every wheat improvement programme. This aspect has been discussed in Chapter 9. Similarly, improvement in quality traits of wheat is a must for any successful wheat breeder. Chapter 10 deals with this aspect.

The use of biometrical genetic techniques helps the wheat breeder in choosing appropriate parents for hybridization and shaping and finalizing his breeding programme. The uses of biometrical methods in wheat breeding have been discussed in detail in Chapter 11.

A detailed information regarding wheat breeding in India is given in Chapter 12.

The present book will not only keep the readers informed about the present status of research in wheat crop and keep them in touch with the latest insights into wheat breeding methodology but will also be an enriching experience.

In the preparation of this book, the authors have consulted many books and journals on the subject (Wheat by B.P. Pal; Wheat Breeding–Its Scientific Basis by F.G.H. Lupton; Wheat and Wheat Improvement (2nd Edition) by E.G. Heyne; Breeding Field Crops : Theory and Practice by V.L. Chopra; Wheat : Research Needs Beyond 2000 AD by S. Nagarajan, G. Singh and B.S. Tyagi;

Wheat In A Global Environment by Z. Bedo and L. Lang; Wheat : Technologies for Warmer Areas by V.S. Rao, G. Singh and S.C. Misra; etc.) and owe sincerely to the writers of these books.

    The authors are thankful to the Vice-Chancellor, CCS Haryana Agricultural University, Hisar for granting permission for getting the book published by an outside agency.

    The authors are also thankful to CBS Publishers & Distributors, New Delhi for their keen interest shown in the publishing of the book.

    We are thankful to our family members, friends and colleagues who inspired us to write this book.

Sultan Singh
I.S. Pawar

Contents

Preface v

Chapter 1 **Origin and Evolution** 1-24
    The tribe *Triticeae* 1
    Origin of diploid wheats 16
    Origin and evolution of tetraploid wheats 18
    Origin and evolution of hexaploid wheats 20
    Ancestral diploid's differentiation hypothesis 21
    Diploidization in polyploid wheats 23

Chapter 2 **Cytogenetics and Genetics** 25-53
    Cytogenetics 25
    Aneuploid studies 25
    Aneuploidy in hexaploid wheat 26
    Aneuploidy in tetraploid wheat 28
    Genetics 30
    Qualitative characters 31
    Quantitative characters 40

Chapter 3 **Breeding Objectives** 55-68
    Increasing yield potential 55
    Stabilizing yield levels 59
    Improving product quality 66
    Mutual exclusiveness of the three major objectives 68

Chapter 4 **Breeding Methods** 69-86
    The wheat plant 69
    Breeding procedures 73
    Comparison between breeding procedures 85

Chapter 5 Mutation Breeding 87-96
Mutant varieties produced 87
When to use mutation breeding 88
Selection and use of mutagens 89
Mutagenic effect and pioidy level 93
Spontaneous mutations in wheat 94
Induction of desired mutants 94
Concluding remarks 96

Chapter 6 Alien Gene Transfers 97-115
Production of amphidiploids 98
Production of alien chromosome addition lines 100
Production of alien chromosome substitution lines 102
Classification of wild relatives of bread wheat 103
Transfers from primary gene pool 105
Transfers from secondary gene pool 106
Transfers from tertiary gene pool 107

Chapter 7 Biotechnology and Wheat Breeding 117-136
Production of haploids 118
Production of somaclonal variants 126
Use of biochemical markers 130
Use of molecular markers 132
Application of recombinant DNA technology 134

Chapter 8 Hybrid Wheat 137-154
Some important considerations 138
Essential pre-requisites for hybrid wheat 142
Level of heterosis in wheat 142
Cytoplasmic male sterility 144
Male fertility restoration 145
Photoperiod sensitive cytoplasmic male sterility 147
Genetic male sterility 147
Chemical hybridizing agents 148
Apomixis 150
Making hybrid wheat a commercial proposition 152

Chapter 9 Resistance Breeding 155-175
Biotic stresses 155
Breeding for disease resistance 155
Breeding for resistance to insect pests 168
Weed control 170
Abiotic stresses 171
Breeding for drought tolerance 171

	Breeding for salinity tolerance	172
	Breeding for lodging resistance	173
Chapter 10	**Breeding for Quality**	**177-187**
	Criteria for assessing wheat quality	177
	Botanical criteria	177
	Subjective criteria	178
	Objective criteria	178
	Quality of hard wheats	181
	Quality of soft wheats	182
	Quality of durum wheats	183
	Breeding for quality traits	184
Chapter 11	**Biometrical Genetics and Wheat Breeding**	**189-195**
	Biometrical genetic techniques in wheat	189
	Role of additive variation	194
	Role of dominance variation	194
	Role of epistatic variation	195
Chapter 12	**Wheat Breeding in India**	**197-224**
	Introduction of wheat in India	198
	Scientific wheat breeding in India	198
	Role of All India Coordinated Wheat Improvement Project	201
	Problems and objectives	213
	Breeding methodology	215
	Future strategies	223
References		225-290
Subject index		291-294

CHAPTER 1

Origin and Evolution

Wheat is the leading cereal grain crop in terms of production, consumption, nutritive value, storage qualities, adaptation and trade, and has been intimately linked with the development of both agriculture and civilization over a long period of time. Because of its wide usage in the form of human food (65 per cent), feed for livestock (21 per cent), seed (8 per cent) and industrial and other products (6 per cent), wheat has played a significant role in establishing permanent settlements, fostering the development of human civilization through cultural/religious development, and in continuing population growth all over the world. This cereal is expected to play a greater role in future in those regions of the world where there is an increasing preference for wheat products (especially developing countries). Furthermore, humans are becoming increasingly health conscious and shifting their non-vegetarian food habits to vegetarian diets.

Although wheat is called a cool-season crop, its cultivation is done in large areas of the world representing different agroclimatic conditions. As a result, harvesting of this cereal is done almost throughout the year. Of course, maximum harvesting is done between April and September (Temperate zone of Northern Hemisphere) and rest of the wheat crop is harvested between October and January (Southern Hemisphere).

The quality of wheat flour is chiefly determined by the amount and the quality of gluten, a large complex of polymeric and monomeric endosperm proteins. The elasticity, viscousness and extensibility properties of these proteins (also called as dough strength) cause a remarkable rise in the dough through the formation of minute gas cells and help in retaining the CO_2 formed during chemical leavening or yeast formation.

The Tribe *Triticeae*

Wheat belongs to the tribe *Triticeae* (Dumort; *Hordeae*, Benth.) and subtribe *Triticinae* of the grass family *Poaceae* (*Gramineae*), one of the largest families of Angiosperms (flowering plants) including

600-700 genera and approximately 10000 species. According to Levy and Feldman (2002), all major types of polyploids (autopolyploids, allopolyploids and segmental polyploids) are the members of this family. The main characteristics of *Triticeae* (a festucoid tribe) are :

1. Inflorescence is a compound spike (i.e., spike of spikelets).
2. Spikelets are laterally compressed and each spikelet is surrounded by two bracts, the glumes.
3. The chromosome number is seven or its multiple.
4. The tribe has very wide adaptability and its members (both annual and perennial forms) are found in a large range of habitats.

Triticeae contains a large number of genera (*Triticum, Hordeum, Secale, Aegilops, Agropyron, Elymus, Eremopyron, Haynaldia, Henrardia*, and many others). However, the genera *Triticum, Aegilops, Agropyron, Haynaldia* and *Secale* possess some common characteristics and constitute a separate group called subtribe *Triticinae*. Based on the knowledge presently available, only two of these genera, *Triticum* and *Aegilops* (goat grasses), were certainly involved in the evolution of common hexaploid wheat possessing AABBDD genomes. However, the genus *Secale* has been used as a parent in the development of the man-made cereal *Triticale* or *Triticosecale* or *Tritosecale* (Wittmack), a synthetic amphidiploid between wheat and rye. Whereas both *Triticum* and *Aegilops* have three ploidy levels (2x, 4x and 6x), *Secale* has only 2x ploidy level.

However, a great confusion exists among the scientists about the taxonomy, nomenclature and classification of the tribe *Triticeae* and this confusion could not be fully resolved till today. A number of attempts were made during the twentieth century (Bowden, 1959; Morris and Sears, 1967; Kihara and Tanaka, 1970; Sakamoto, 1973; Baum, 1977, 1978a, 1978b; Kimber and Sears, 1983; Love, 1984; and others) to classify this tribe into different subtribes and genera, but with different views and with different bases. As a result, the positions of some species of this tribe have been frequently oscillating between different genera. For example, according to some scientists (Bowden, 1959; and some others), the genus *Aegilops* (goat grasses) should be merged into the genus *Triticum* (wheats) and thus all the species of *Aegilops* genus should have their generic name as *Triticum* (*Triticum speltoides, T. squarrosum*, etc.). On the contrary, some other scientists (Miller, 1987; and some others) do not agree with this merger of the two genera and have retained *Aegilops* as a separate genus. Miller (1987) has largely followed the classification and nomenclature suggested by Kihara and Tanaka (1970). According to Miller, making of *Triticum-Aegilops* complex may be correct from a taxonomic viewpoint, but from a practical point of view, it has no justification. However, the authors of the present book agree with the merger of *Aegilops* into the genus *Triticum* and, therefore, in subsequent chapters, the species of *Aegilops* genus will have their generic name as *Triticum*. The botanical names, common names and main characteristics of different species of the genus *Triticum* are given in Table 1.1. For the convenience of the readers, synonyms of these species (wherever necessary) are also given in this table. Since both the genera, *Triticum* and *Aegilops*, have contributed towards the evolution of polyploid wheats, Bowden's suggestion has a special significance for the wheat breeders.

Some similar suggestions about the merger of some genera into larger groups have been made by different scientists from time to time. According to Sakamoto (1973), the four genera, namely, *Agropyron, Elymus, Elytrigia* and *Sitanion*, may be combined together to form a single group. Similarly, Baum (1978a) suggested a combination of the genera *Leymus, Clinelymus, Aneurolepidium* and *Terrellia* with *Elymus*. Also, the genus *Critesion* may be combined with *Hordeum*. In this way,

Table 1.1. Different species of *Triticum*

Botanical name	Common name	Main characteristics
Diploid Species (2n=2x=14)		
Triticum urartu (Tum.)	Einkorn wheat or Small spelt wheat	Wild diploid wheat with AA genome, long fragile ears (brittle rachis) with awns, each spikelet contains two fertile florets.
T. boeoticum (Boiss.) sub-species *aegilopoides* OR *T. aegilopoides* (Link.) Bal.	-do-	Wild diploid wheat with AA genome, long fragile ears usually with single awn per spikelet, each spikelet contains one fertile floret.
T. boeoticum (Boiss) sub-species *thaoudar* OR *T. thaoudar* (Reut.)	-do-	Wild diploid wheat with AA genome, long fragile ears usually with two awns per spikelet, each spikelet contains two fertile florets.
T. monococcum (L.)	-do-	Cultivated diploid wheat with AA genome, resembles to wild diploid wheats, medium long, more dense and broader ears with small awns, less brittle ears usually with single awn per spikelet, each spikelet contains one fertile floret, but in some forms each spikelet conntains two fertile florets.
T. sinskajae (A. Filat. & Kurk.)	-do-	Cultivated diploid wheat with AA genome, similar to *T. monococcum* for most characteristics except that it has free-threshing habit, has shorter ears than *T. monococcum*.
T. caudatum (L.) Godr.× Gren. OR *T. dichasians* (Zhuk.) Bowden OR *Aegilops caudata*	Goat grass	Wild annual diploid grass with CC genome, long ears with two long awns on the top of the spike.

Contd.

Botanical name	Common name	Main characteristics
T. tauschii (Cosson.) Schmal OR *T. squarrosum* (Raspail) OR *T. aegilops* (P. Beauv ex Ri & S) OR *Ae. tauschii* (Cosson) OR *Ae. squarrosa* (L.)	-do-	Wild annual diploid grass with DD genome, long ears with small to medium long awns.
T. comosum (Sibth. & Sm.) Richter OR *Ae. comosa* (Sibth. & Sm.)	-do-	Wild annual diploid grass with MM genome, medium long ears with several long awns on the top of the spike.
T. uniaristatum (Vis.) Richter OR *Ae. uniaristata* (Vis.) OR *Ae. notarisii* (Clem.)	-do-	Wild annual diploid grass with $M^U M^U$ or Un Un genome, small ears with medium long awns on the top of the spike.
T. muticum (Boiss.) Hackel OR *T. tripsacoides* (Jaub. & spach) Bowden OR *T. emarginatum* (Godr.) OR *Ae. mutica* (Boiss.) OR *Ae. tripsacoides* (Jaub & Spach) OR *Ae. loliaceae* (Jaub. & Spach)	-do-	Wild annual diploid grass with Mt Mt genome, very long awnless ears.

Contd.

Botanical name	Common name	Main characteristics
T. speltoides (Tausch) Gren. ex Richter OR *T. ligusticum* (Bert.) OR *T. obtusatum* (Godr.) OR *Ae. speltoides* (Tausch) OR *Ae. ligustica* (Savign) Cosson OR *Ae. macura* (Jaub. & Spach.) OR *Ae. tournefortii* (Savign) OR *Ae. agropyroides* (Godr.) OR *Agropyron ligusticum* (Savign)	-do-	Wild annual diploid grass with SS genome, long ears with medium to long awns on each spikelet.
T. bicorne (Forsk.) OR *Ae. bicornis* (Forsk.) Jaub. and Spach	-do-	Wild annual diploid grass with S^bS^b genome, long ears with few awns on the top of the spike.
T. longissimum (Schweinf. & Muschl.) Bowden OR *Ae. longissima* (Schweinf. & Muschl.)	-do-	Wild annual diploid grass with S^lS^l genome, small ears with some small to medium long awns.
T. searsii (Feld.& Kis) OR *Ae. searsii* (Feld.& Kis.)	-do-	Wild annual diploid grass with S^sS^s genome, long ears with few long awns on the top of the spike.

Contd.

Botanical name	Common name	Main characteristics
T. umbellulatum (Zhuk.) Bowden OR *Ae. umbellulata* (Zhuk.)	-do-	Wild annual diploid grass with UU genome, very small ears with small awn on each spikelet.
Tetraploid Species (2n=4x=28)		
T. dicoccoides (Korn) Schweinf OR *T. turgidum* (L.) Thell sub-species *dicoccoides* (Korn) Thell OR *T. vulgare* (Vill.) var. *dicoccoides* (Korn)	Emmer wheat	Wild tetraploid wheat with AABB genomes, fragile ears with awns, ears laterally compressed.
T. dicoccum (Schrank) Schubl OR *T. turgidum* (L.) Thell sub-species *dicoccum* (Schrank) Schubl OR *T.dicoccum* (Schrank) OR *T. farrum* (Bayle-Barelle) OR *T. amyleum* (Seringe) OR *T. vulgare dicoccum* (Alef.) OR *T. sativum dicoccum* (Hack.)	Emmer wheat	Cultivated tetraploid wheat with AABB genomes, less fragile ears with awns, ears are often laterally compressed.
T. turgidum (L.) OR *T. turgidum* (L.) Thell sub-species *turgidum* OR	Cone wheat OR Rivert wheat OR Pollard wheat	Cultivated tetraploid wheat with AABB genomes, compact ears with strong constitution, usually awned ears, each spikelet often contains four or five fertile florets.

Contd.

Botanical name	Common name	Main characteristics
T. vulgare turgidum (Alef.) OR *T. sativum turgidum* (Hackel)		
T. durum (Desf.) OR *T. turgidum* (L.) Thell sub-species *Turgidum* conv. *durum* (Desf.) Mk. OR *T. vulgare durum* (Alef.) OR *T. sativum durum* (Hackel)	Macaroni wheat OR Durum wheat	Widely cultivated tetraploid wheat with AABB genomes, laterally compressed ears with awns, endosperm is hard and translucent.
T. paleocolchicum (Men.) OR *T. turgidum* (L.) Thell sub-species *paleocolchicum* (Men.) Mk OR *T. dicoccum* (Schrank) variety *chvamlicum* (Supat.) OR *T. georgicum* (Dek.)	—	Monomorphic cultivated tetraploid wheat with AABB genomes, laterally compressed compact small ears with awns, zigzag rachis.
T. carthlicum (Nevski) OR *T. turgidum* (L.) Thell sub-species *carthlicum* (Nevski) Mk. OR *T. persicum* (Vav.) OR *T. ibericum* (Men.) OR *T. paradoxum* (Parodii)	Persian wheat	Cultivated tetraploid wheat with AABB genomes, presence of awn on lemma as well as on the outer glume, a wheat with free threshing characteristic, long ears.

Contd.

Botanical name	Common name	Main characteristics
T. polonicum OR *T. turgidum* (L.) Thell sub-species *turgidum* conv, *polonicum* (L.) Mk. OR *T. levissimum* (Haller) OR *T. glaucum* (Moench)	Polish wheat	Cultivated tetraploid wheat with AABB genomes, large ears, glumes are long, narrow and empty.
T. turanicum (Jakubz) OR *T. turgidum* (L.) Thell sub-species *turgidum* conv. *turanicum* (Jakubz) Mk. OR *T. orientale* (Perc.) OR *T. percivalii*	Khorasan wheat	Cultivated tetraploid wheat with AABB genomes, very loose ears with scabrous awns.
T. araraticum (Jakubz.) OR *T. timopheevii* (Zhuk.) sub-species *araraticum* (Jakubz.) Mk. OR *T. dicoccoides* sub-species *armeniacum* (Jakubz.) OR *T. armeniacum* (Mak.) OR *T. montanum* (Mak.) OR *T. chaldicum* (Men.)	Emmer wheat	Wild tetraploid wheat with AAGG genomes, medium long ears with awns.
T. timopheevii (Zhuk.) OR *T. timopheevii* (Zhuk.)	Timopheevi wheat	Cultivated tetraploid wheat with AAGG genomes, wide and laterally compressed ears with awns.

Contd.

Botanical name	Common name	Main characteristics
sub-species *timopheevii* OR *T. dicoccum dicoccoides* (Korn.) var. *timopheevii* (Zhuk.)		
T. militinae (Zhik. & Migusch)	A derivative of timopheevi wheat	Cultivated tetraploid wheat with AAGG genomes, ears are wide, dense and short with black colour, free-threshing characteristic, each spikelet contains one extra awn on its outer bract.
T. cylindricum (Ces, Pass & Gb.) *Ae. cylindrica* (Host.) OR *Ae. caudata* (L.) var. *cylindricum* (Fiori.) OR *Ae. nova* (Win.)	Goat grass	Wild annual tetraploid grass with CCDD genomes, long ears with some short awns on the top of the spike.
T. crassum (Boiss.) Aitch. & Hemsl. OR *Ae. crassa* (Boiss.) 4x	-do-	Wild annual tetraploid grass with DDM^{cr} M^{cr} or DDMM genomes, wide long ears with very short awns on spikelets and some medium long awns on the top of the spike.
T. ventricosum (Ces., Pass. & Gib.) OR *T. fragile* (Parlat.) Ces., Pass. & Gib. OR *Ae. ventricosa* (Tausch) OR *Ae. fragilis* (Parlat.) OR *Ae. subulata* (Pomel.)	-do-	Wild annual tetraploid grass with DDM^{V}M^V or DDUnUn genomes, medium long ears with short awns.

Contd.

Botanical name	Common name	Main characteristics
T. triunciale (L.) Raspail OR *Ae. triuncialis* (L.) OR *Ae. elongata* (Lamarck) OR *Ae. persica* (Boiss.) OR *Ae. croatica* (Gdrg.) OR *Ae. bushirica* (Rosh.) OR *Ae. echinata* (Presl.)	-do-	Wild annual tetrapliid grass with UUCC genomes, medium long ears with few medium long awns on the top of the spike.
T. kotschyi (Boiss.) Bowden OR *T. triunciale* (Godr. & Gran.) var. *kotschyi* (Achers.) OR *T. perigrinum* (Hackel) OR *Ae. variabilis* (Eig.) OR *Ae. kotschyi* (Boiss.) OR *Ae. triuncialis* sub-species *kotschyi* (Boiss.) OR *Ae. triuncials* (L.) sub-species *brachyathera* (Boiss.) OR *Ae. triuncialis* (L.) var. *leptostachya* (Bor.) OR *Ae. caudata* var. *polyathera* (Post.) OR	-do-	Wild annual tetraploid grass with UUSS genomes, very small ears with small horizontal awns.

Contd.

Botanical name	Common name	Main characteristics
Ae. perigrina (Hack.) Mairs & Weill OR *Ae. geniculata* (Fig.& Nat.)		
T. biunciale (Richter) OR *T. machrochaetum* (Shuttl.& Huet.) Richter OR *T. lorentii* (Hochst.) Zeven OR *Ae. biuncialis* (Vis.) OR *Ae. machrochaetum* (Shuttl.) & Huet.) OR *Ae. lorentii* (Hochst.) OR *Ae. ovata* var. *biuncialis* (Vis.)	-do-	Wild annual tetraploid grass with UUM^{b}M^b or UUMM genomes, very small ears with short and medium long awns.
T. columnare (Zhuk.) Morris & Sears OR *Ae. columnaris* (Zhuk.) OR *Ae. neglecta* (Req.) OR *Ae. mixta* (Sennen)	-do-	Wild annual tetraploid grass with UUM^{c}M^c or UUMM genomes, long ears with medium long awns.
T. ovatum (L.) Raspail. OR *Ae. ovata* (L.) OR *Ae. echinum* (Godr.) OR *Ae. geniculata* (Roth.) OR	-do-	Wild annual tetraploid grass with UUM^{o}M^o or UUMM genomes, small wide ears with short awns on spikelets.

Contd.

Botanical name	Common name	Main characteristics
Ae. fausii (Sennen.) Etc.		
T. triaristatum (Willd.) Godr. & Gren. OR *Ae. triaristata* (Willd.) 4x OR *Ae. neglecta* (Req.)	-do-	Wild annual tetraploid grass with UU$M^t M^t$ or UUMM genomes, very small ears with short to medium long awns.
HEXAPLOID SPECIES (2n=6x=42)		
T. aestivum (L.) OR *T. aestivum* (L.) Thell sub-species *vulgare* (Vull.)Mk. OR *T. vulgare* (Vill.), Hopt.) OR *T. sativum* (Lamk.), (Pers.) OR *T. hybericum* (L.)	Common wheat OR Bread wheat	Most widely grown hexaploid wheat with AABBDD genomes, tough rachis, free-threshing characteristic.
T. spelta (L.) OR *T. aestivum* (L.) Thell. sub-species *spelta* (L.) Thell. OR *T. vulgare spelta* (Alef.) OR *T. sativum spelta* (Hackel) OR *Spelta vulgaris* (Seringe)	Spelt wheat (Dinkel)	Cultivated hexaploid wheat with AABBDD genomes, long loose fragile ears, awns present or absent, grains tightly invested.
T. sphaerococcum (Perc.) OR *T. aestivum* (L.) Thell sub. species *sphaerococcum* (Perc.) Mk.	Shot wheat Or Indian dwarf wheat	Cultivated hexaploid wheat with AABBDD genomes, main crop of northwest India and parts of Iran, short dense ears, awns present or absent, grains small with nearly hemispherical shape.

Contd.

Botanical name	Common name	Main characteristics

T. compactum (Host.)
    OR
T. aestivum (L.) Thell. sub-species *compactum* (Host.) Mk.
    OR
T. vulgare compactum (Alef.)
    OR
T. sativum compactum (Hackel.)
	Club wheat	Cultivated hexaploid wheat with AABBDD genomes, a wheat with free-threshing characteristic, ears are short and uniformly thick with oblong or oval shape, awns present or absent.

T. macha (Dek. & Men.)
    OR
T. aestivum (L.) Thell. sub-species *macha* (Dek. & Men.)
    OR
T. tuballicum (Dek.)
    OR
T. imereticum (Dek.)
	Spelt wheat (western Georgia)	Cultivated hexaploid wheat with AABBDD genomes, a polymorphic wheat, ears are wide, fragile and laterally compressed, awns present or absent.

T. vavilovi (Tum.) Jakubz. OR *T. aestivum* (L.) Thell. sub-species *vavilovi* (Tum.) sears	Spelt wheat (Armenia)	Cultivated hexaploid wheat with AABBDD genomes, ears are branched because of elongated rachilla, awns are short.
T. zhukovskyi (Men & Er.)	Zhukovsky wheat	Cultivated hexaploid wheat with AAAAGG genomes, grown in the same area of western Georgia where *T. timopheevii* is grown, has slightly longer and less compact ears than *T. timopheevii*.
T. crassum (Boiss.) Aitch. & Hemsl.) OR *Ae. crassa* (Boiss.) 6x	Goat grass	Wild hexaploid grass with $DDD^2D^2\ M^{cr}M^{cr}$ or DDDDMM genomes, long wide ears with very small awns on spikelets and some medium long awns on the top of the spike.
T. syriacum (Bowden) OR *Ae. vavilovi* (Zhuk.) Chem.	-do-	Wild hexaploid grass with DDMMSS genomes, large ears with medium long awns on the top of the spike.

Contd.

Botanical name	Common name	Main characteristics
OR *Ae. crassa* sub-species *vavilovi* (Skuk.) OR *Ae. crassa* sub-species *palaestrina* (Eig.)		
T. juvenale (Thell) OR *T. turcomanicum* (Rosh.) Bowden OR *Ae. juvenalis* (Thell.) Eig. OR *Ae. turcomanica* (Rosh.)	-do-	Wild hexaploid grass with DDMMUU genomes, wide medium large awnless ears.
T. trianstatum (Willd.) Godr. & Gren. OR *Ae. triaristata* (Wild.) 6x OR *Ae. recta* (Zhuk.) Chenn	-do-	Wild hexaploid grass with $UUM^tM^tM_2M_2$ or $UUMMU^nU^n$ genomes, small ears with short to medium long awns.

Note: The authors have largely followed the classification given by Miller (1987) except that they support the merger of the genus *Aegilops* into *Triticum*.

the number of genera coming under the tribe *Triticeae* may be considerably reduced. Baum (1977, 1978a, 1978b) has discussed the classification and nomenclature of this tribe in detail. Nevertheless, such a detailed information regarding the classification and nomenclature of *Triticeae* is of little importance to the wheat breeders.

A similar confusion exists about the classification of and the genome assignment to the different species falling under the genus *Aegilops*. Kihara (1954) classified nine diploid species (excluding *Aegilops searsii*) of this genus into three groups. Group 1 with C genome included *Ae. caudata* (CC) and *Ae. umbellulata* (C^uC^u); Group 2 with M genome had *Ae. comosa* (MM), *Ae. mutica* (M^tM^t), *Ae. uniaristata* (M^uM^u) and *Ae. squarrosa* (DD); and Group 3 with S genome included *Ae. speltoides* (SS), *Ae. bicornis* (S^bS^b) and *Ae. longissima* (S^lS^l) species. Several points were raised against this classification. For example, *Ae. umbellulata* is not related to *Ae. caudata* and, therefore, these two species should not be put under the same group. Later on, it was felt that *Ae. umbellulata* should be assigned UU genome instead of C^uC^u genome. Similarly, inclusion of *Ae. squarrosa* and *Ae. mutica* in the second group is not justified. Also, a change in the genome of *Ae. uniaristata* from M^uM^u to Un Un was suggested by Kimber *et al.* (1983). However, Kihara and Tanaka (1970) classified all the diploid and polyploid species of *Aegilops* into six groups as **Cylindropyrum** (*Ae. caudata* and *Ae. cylindrica*), **Vertebrata** (*Ae. squarrosa, Ae. crassa* 4x and 6x, *Ae. ventricosa, Ae. vavilovii* and *Ae. juvenalis*), **Comopyrum** (*Ae. comosa* and *Ae. uniaristata*), **Ambylopyrum** (*Ae. mutica*), **Sitopsis** (*Ae. speltoides, Ae. bicornis, Ae. longissima* and *Ae. searsii*) and **Polyeides** (*Ae. umbellulata, Ae. biuncialis, Ae. columnaris, Ae. ovata* and *Ae. triaristata* 4x and 6x). In many cases, the geographic distribution of the polyploid species of this genus is wider than that of their diploid parent species.

The nomenclature of wheats (*Triticum* spp.) like that of goatgrasses (*Aegilops* spp.) is hopelessly confused (Percival, 1921). If we look at the classifications given for the *Triticum* species by different scientists (Bowden, 1959; Mac Key, 1966; Morris and Sears, 1967; Dorgleev and Korovina, 1979; and others), there is no similarity in the nomenclature. Not only different names have been given to the same form, but the same name has been assigned to different forms. Till today, we do not have any classification which is universally accepted. In fact, the readers need a classification which is free of nomenclature ambiguity and has a practical value.

Miller (1987) suggested a practical scheme for classifying different species of the genus *Triticum* without combining this genus with *Aegilops*. According to Miller, this scheme has no taxonomic basis nor it follows any specific rule of nomenclature, but it is a step forward towards simplifying the problem of nomenclature. According to this scheme, there are four diploid species (*Triticum urartu, T. boeoticum* with two subspecies *aegilopoides* and *thaoudar, T. monococcum* and *T. sinskajae*), eleven tetraploid species (*T. dicoccoides, T. dicoccum, T. turgidum, T. durum, T. paleocolchicum, T. carthlicum, T. polonicum, T. turanicum, T. araraticum, T. timopheevii* and *T. militinae*) and seven hexaploid species (*T. aestivum, T. spelta, T. sphaerococcum, T. compactum, T. macha, T. vavilovi* and *T. zhukovskyi*) under the genus *Triticum*.

Of the four diploid species, two (*T. urartu* and *T. boeoticum*) are wild and the rest are cultivated. The two subspecies of *T. boeoticum* can be differentiated on the basis of the number of fertile floret(s) per spikelet. Whereas the subspecies *aegilopoides* contains only one fertile floret in each spikelet (i.e., single seeded), *thaoudar* has two fertile florets per spikelet (i.e, double seeded). For convenience, these two subspecies may be called as *T. aegilopoides* and *T. thaoudar*. All these diploid species contain the same AA genome. This genome is also found in all the eleven tetraploid and the seven hexaploid species of *Triticum* mentioned above.

Out of the 11 tetraploid species, only two (*T. dicoccoides* and *T. araraticum*) are wild and the remaining nine species are cultivated. Further, eight tetraploid species (except *T. araraticum, T. timopheevii* and *T. militinae* which all have AAGG genomes) have AABB genomes. The two wild species are though morphologically similar and have overlapping geographic distribution, are genetically different.

On the contrary, all the seven hexaploid species are cultivated. However, six out of total seven 6x species contain AABBDD genomic constitution except *T. zhukovskyi* which contains AAAAGG genomes.

Except the three species which contain AAGG genomes, all the tetraploid species can be put under a single major group *T. turgidum*.

T. turgidum subspecies	*turgidum*	convariety	*turgidum*
-do-	-do-	conv.	*durum*
-do-	-do-	conv.	*polonicum*
-do-	-do-	conv.	*turanicum*
-do-	ssp.	*dicoccoides*	
-do-	ssp.	*dicoccum*	
-do-	ssp.	*paleocolchicum*	
-do-	ssp.	*carthlicum*	

Similarly, except the species *T. zhukovskyi* which contains AAAAGG genomes, all the hexaploid species may be put under one major group *T. aestivum*.

T. aestivum
T. aestivum subspecies *spelta*
T. aestivum ssp. *sphaerococcum*
T. aestivum ssp. *compactum*
T. aestivum ssp. *macha*
T. aestivum ssp. *vavilovi*

Therefore, the species of the genus *Triticum* have been classified in different ways. However, as mentioned earlier, we have classified the species combining the genus *Aegilops* with *Triticum* (Table 1.1).

Origin of diploid wheats

As mentioned earlier, the four diploid species of the genus *Triticum* which contain AA genome are *T. urartu*, *T. boeoticum*, *T. monococcum* and *T. sinskajae*. The first two species are wild and the last two are cultivated. The geographical distribution of 14 wild species (12 diploid and 2 tetraploid) of *Triticum* is given in Table 1.2. The geographical distribution of these 14 wild species has been diagrommatically shown by Miller (1987). The species *T. boeoticum* has a much wide distribtion as compared to that of *T. urartu* with some common regions (particularly northern Syria, parts of Turkey, northern Iraq and north western Iran). However, the two wild species are genetically different. *T. monococcum* resembles to wild diploids (*T. urartu* and *T. boeoticum*) for several characters but has broader and more dense spikes. The awns of ears are also relatively shorter. Like *T. boeoticum* subspecies *aegilopoides*, *T. monococcum* has one fertile floret per spikelet. These two species (*T. monococcum* and *T. aegilopoides*) also show similarity for isozyme pattern and seed storage proteins. It, therefore, seems that *T. aegilopoides* is the progenitor of *T. monococcum* and latter is the result of artificial selection for cultivation from the former. The more recent cultivated form *T. sinskajae* appears to be a mutant form of *T. monococcum*. Perhaps the mutation occurred for free threshing characteristic.

However, a strong morphological similarity for several characters between *T. monococcum* and the tetraploid *T. turgidum* and the extent of chromosome pairing shown by their hybrids indicate that A genome present in polyploid wheats has come from *T. monococcum*. But, the archaeological records (Helback, 1959) clearly show that *T. turgidum* is as old cultivated wheat (about 8000 B.C.) as is *T. monococcum*. Thus, archaeologically, *T. monococcum* cannot be the contributor of A genome, rather some wild diploid form might be the donor of this genome. According to Riley (1965), the

Table 1.2. Geographic distribution of wild species of the genus Triticum

Species	Geographical distribution
T. urartu	Northern Syria, south-eastern Turkey, northern Iraq, north-western Iran and Transcaucasia.
T. boeoticum	Widely distributed including south-eastern Europe, Turkey, north-western Syria, northern Iraq, north-western Iran, Armenia and Georgia.
T. caudatum	Wide distribution including south-eastern Europe, Turkey, Syria.
T. squarrosum	Very wide distribution starting from Turkey to central China including major part of Turkey, small part of south eastern Russia, Georgia, Armenia, north eastern Syria, northern Iraq, major part of Iran (entire north Iran), north western Afghanistan, Turkmanistan, Uzkebistan, and central China.
T. comosum	South eastern Europe and western part of Turkey.
T. muticum	Restricted mainly to north Turkey.
T. uniaristatum	South eastern Europe.
T. speltoides	Turkey (mainly central region), north western Syria.
T. bicorne	North African region, Israel, Jordan.
T. longissimum	Lebanon, Israel, Jordan and touching north eastern Africa.
T. searsii	Very restricted distribution, part of Syria and upper region of Jordan.
T. umbellulatum	Wide distribution, Turkey, Syria and northern regions of Iraq and Iran.
T. dicoccoides	Palestine, Syria, Turkey (south eastern region), western Iran.
T. araraticum	North eastern part of Asia Minor, Transcaucasia, northern region of Iraq and north western part of Iran.

contributor of A genome to the tetraploid wheats is either *T. aegilopoides* or *T. thaoudar*. The recent molecular approaches to this problem indicate that *T. aegilopoides* is the progenitor of *T. monococcum* and that *T. urartu* has contributed A genome to *T. dicoccum, T. timopheevii* and *T. aestivum* (Dvorak, 1988; Dvorak *et al.*, 1990). Rudnoy *et al.* (2004) also found that *T. urartu* is the donor of A genome to *T. aesticum*. The current evidence also indicates that *T. dicoccoides* is the result of amphidiploidy between *T. urartu* and an unknown diploid or diploids having genomes similar to the Sitopsis section of *Aegilops* (*Ae. speltoides, Ae. bicornis, Ae. longissima* and *Ae. searsii*), that is, the A genome of *T. dicoccoides* has come from *T. urartu*. Furthermore, it appears that A genome of *T. araraticum* (another wild tetraploid emmer wheat with AAGG genomes) has come from *T. baeoticum*. It has also been indicated by the current evidence that the origin of 4A chromosome is still unknown and that the A genome progenitor had contributed only six chromosomes of this genome to *T. aestivum* (Kimber and Sears, 1987). It means that during the process of hexaploidy, there was considerable modification in the chromosomes of the A genome.

Origin and Evolution of Tetraploid Wheats

The cultivated tetraploid wheats can be broadly classified into two groups : (1) Those species which contain AABB genomes (*T. dicoccum, T. turgidum, T. durum, T. paleocolchicum, T. carthlicum, T. polonicum* and *T. turanicum*); and (2) those species which have AAGG genomes (*T. timopheevii* and *T. militinae*). It means cultivated 4x wheats have diphyletic origin. In one evolutionary path, the A genome donor diploid species hybridized with another diploid species having B genome, whereas in another evolutionary path the A genome donor species hybridized with another species containing G genome. As mentioned earlier, the A genome donor species in these two evolutionary paths may not be the same.

In addition to tetraploid cultivated wheats, the wild tetraploid species *T. dicoccoides* also contains AABB genomes. Similarly, the wild tetraploid *T. araraticum* has AAGG genomes. Also, there are several tetraploid wild species of *Triticum* (belonging to the old *Aegilops* group) with different genomic constitutions (CCDD, DDMM, UUCC, UUSS, etc.).

A number of suggestions have been made regarding the source of B genome. However, the origin of this genome still remains controversial and unsolved (Miller, 1987; Kimber and Sears, 1987; Poehlman and Sleper, 1995; Feldman, 2001; Rao, 2001; Rudnoy *et al.*, 2004; and many others). A widely accepted theory was proposed by Pathak (1940), Sarkar and Stebbins (1956) and Riley *et al.* (1958) that *T. speltoides* (*Ae. speltoides*) was the donor of B genome or donor of a substantial part of this genome. Cytoplasmic studies (Tsunewaki *et al.*, 1980) also supported this theory and showed that *T. speltoides* was the donor of cytoplasm to the tetraploid wheats containing AABB and AAGG genomes. However, the cytological (chromosome pairing) studies of Kimber and Athwal (1972), chromosome banding studies of Shands and Kimber (1973) and of Hadlaczky and Belea (1975), *in situ* hybridization studies of Gerlach *et al.* (1978), isozyme studies of Belea and Fejer (1980) and the results of the phylogenetic analysis based on the internal transcribed spacer (ITS) sequences carried out by Rudnoy *et al.* (2004) did not support this theory. These discoveries, therefore, reopened the issue of the source of B genome. Another suggestion about the source of B genome came from McFadden and Sears (1946). According to them, *Agropyron triticum* (*Eremopyron triticum*) was the contributor of B genome. But this suggestion did not get support from other scientists and Sears in 1956 gave an altogether different opinion and said that the source of B genome was *T. bicorne* (*Ae. bicornis*). Johnson (1975) proposed a new theory and opined that it was a case of autoploidy in *T. urartu*, that is, *T. uratu* was also the donor of B genome. However, according to Chapman *et al.* (1976) and Dvorak (1976), this theory has no cytological (chromosome pairing) basis. Nevertheless, Feldman (1979) proposed that on geographical, morphological and cytological bases, *T. searsii* (separated from *T. longissimum* and given a species status by Feldman and Kislev in 1977) is a more probable source of B genome. This belief of Feldman got a strong support from Nath *et al.* (1983, 1984) based on their DNA-hybridization studies. These studies also ruled out the probability of *T. longissimum* as the donor of B genome.

Miller (1987) has discussed the B genome issue in detail. In fact, there may be several possibilities for the origin of this genome :

1. The original donor species now does not exist, that is, the original donor might have extinct after contributing this genome to the tetraploid wheat,
2. the original donor species may exist but its identification may not be possible because of a considerable change which may have occurred in the arrangement of its DNA after the incorporation of this genome into the tetraploid (significant intraspecific differentiation),
3. the original donor may exist but it is still an unidentified species, or
4. there may be a mixed origin of B genome, that is, more than one species may be responsible for the contribution of this genome (genome mosaicity).

According to Zohary and Feldman (1961), hybridization between two or more allotetraploids possessing the same A genome could give rise to a B genome due to the rearrangement and reassortment of the second genome. Further, according to Maan (1975) and Miller et al. (1982), the results of some studies have shown that there are chromosomes in the Sitopsis group of *Aegilops* (*Ae. speltoides*, *Ae. longissima*, *Ae. searsii* and *Ae. bicornis*) which have a tendency of preferential transmission, becoming a part of the chromosome complement, and thus enhancing the possibility of obtaining a mixed genome.

Like the origin of B genome, the origin of G genome is also not yet fully known. There are two contradictory hypotheses about the origin of the G genome. According to Wagenaar (1961), there is no essential difference between the B and G genomes rather G genome is a modified form of B genome and the differences between the two genomes in terms of poor chromosome pairing (asynapsis) and sterility are only due to a genetic mechanism. However, this theory could not be confirmed (Feldman, 1966; Miller, unpublished). The second hypothesis was that the genomes B and G were contributed by two different species. Feldman and Miller supported this second theory. According to Shands and Kimber (1973), *T. speltoides* (*Ae. speltoides*) was the contributor of G genome. Their suggestion was based on the pairing between the chromosomes of *T. speltoides* and those of G genome. The proposal got strong support from the results of seed protein studies (Caldwell and Kasarda, 1978) and cytoplasmic studies (Tsunewaki *et al.*, 1980) and a partial support from chromosome banding studies (Gill and Kimber, 1974). Although the chromosome banding pattern of *T. speloides* did not completely match with that of G genome, the two genomes showed more similarity than was shown by the genomes of *T. speltoides* and the B genome. However, like the origin of B genome, the origin of G genome may have different possibilities.

It is appropriate to mention here that the results of isoenzyme studies have shown that the A genomes of two tetraploid groups (one with AABB genomes and the other with AAGG genomes) have come from different sources. The studies of Gubareva *et al.* (1975), Caldwell and Kasarda (1978) and Jaaska and Jaaska (1980) showed that the A genome of AABB group was similar to the genome of *T. urartu*, whereas the A genome of AAGG group was similar to the genome of *T. boeoticum* and to that of *T. monococcum*.

On the basis of the current evidence available, it can be said that amphidiploidy between *T. urartu* and an unknown diploid species (most probably a member of the Sitopsis group of *Aegilops*) gave rise to the wild tetraploid *T. dicoccoides*. Similarly, at about the same time, amphidiploidy between *T. boeoticum* and a wild diploid or diploids (very close or similar to *T. speltoides*) resulted in the origin of *T. araraticum*. The geographical distribution of these two tetraploid wild species (*T. dicoccoides* and *T. araraticum*) is given in Table 1.2. Archaeological evidence (though not very decisively) has shown that there was no likelyhood of *T. monococcum* being the donor of A genome to the wild tetraploid. Archaeological records show that the establishment of *T. dicoccoides* and *T. araraticum* probably took place between 8000 and 10000 B.C. (Helback, 1969; Hopf, 1969; Van Zeist, 1972; Dennell, 1973a,b; Mellaart, 1975; Van Zeist and Bakker-Heeres, 1979). However, there is no record of the existence of *T. monococcum* before the establishment of the two wild tetraploids mentioned above.

The cultivation of tetraploid wheats probably started with the evolution of *T. dicoccum* from *T. dicoccoides* and the evolution of *T. timopheevii* from *T. araraticum*. However, there could be some wild species in between *T. dicoccum* and *T. dicoccoides* and the former was the result of selection from the wild form. Similarly, there could be some wild species in between *T. timopheeii* and *T. araraticum*. The other cultivated tetraploids evolved due to modification/mutation/selection in these cultivated forms. For example, *T.durum* and other cultivated tetraploids of AABB group evolved from *T. dicoccum*. The cultivated tetraploid *T. militinae* of AAGG group is a selection of a mutant of *T. timopheevi* for free threshing characteristic.

Origin and Evolution of Hexaploid Wheats

Like tetraploids, cultivated hexaploid wheats also fall in two separate groups : (1) Those which contain AABBDD genomes; and (2) the only one species *T. zhukovskyi* which contains AAAAGG genomes (Table 1.1). Since none of the species belonging to these two groups (AABBDD and AAAAGG) is found in wild form, all these hexaploid wheats should have evolved in cultivation. It is now fully confirmed through geographical, archaeological, phylogenetic analysis based on ITS sequences, and through other proofs that *T. tauschii* (*Ae. squarrosa*) is the donor of the D genome or Dinkel genome (Pathak, 1940; Kihara, 1944; McFadden and Sears, 1946; Riley and Chapman, 1960; Rudnoy et al., 2004; and others). Kihara (1924) proposed the letter D for the third genome of 6x wheat. This theory is supported by the fact that *T. tauschii* is found as a common weed in wheat fields in Middle East and Transcaucasia. Also, the archaeological records show that the establishment of hexaploid wheat took place about 7000 B.C. (Hillman, 1972).

The hypothesis that hexaploid wheats arose in cultivation, is supported by the fact that some genes which are found in AABB genomes of hexaploid wheats, are absent in the present form of *T. dicoccoides* (Kihara and Tsunewaki, 1963). Therefore, it is more likely that *T. dicoccum* rather than *T. dicoccocides* was the tetraploid parent in the evolution of hexaploid wheats. Again, according to Tsunewaki et al. (1980), the tetraploid wheat was the female parent during amphidiploidy between an AABB tetraploid and the wild diploid *T. tauschii* containing D genome because the cytoplasm of hexaploid wheat is similar to that of *T. speltoides* (*Ae. speltoides*) rather than to that of *T. tauschii*.

Now the basic question arises that which of the hexaploid wheats was first evolved? The answer of this question is not easy. However, single-gene differences found among the five hexaploid species (except *T. vavilovi* which has a two-gene difference from other hexaploids) belonging to AABB group (Table 1.3), may help in finding the answer of this important question. In fact, mutations have played an important role during the evolution of different wheat species. Three types of mutations, namely, at q-Q locus on chromosome 5A (where the speltoid gene q mutated to Q responsible for free-threshing quality and tough rachis), at c-C locus on chromosome 2D (where c allele mutated to C responsible for compact ear), and at S-s locus on chromosome 3D (where S allele mutated to s responsible for spherical grain shape), help in characterizing various hexaploid species of AABBDD group (Swaminathan and Rao, 1961). The genotypes and characteristics of the five hexaploid species (except *T. vavilovi*) are given in Table 1.3. The alleles C and s were not present in the original D genome. Therefore, both *T. compactum* and *T. sphaerococcum* are mutant forms and none of these two can be the primitive hexaploid wheat. Similarly, *T. aestivum* is also a mutant form of hexaploid wheat and thus the possibility of this species as the primitive hexaploid wheat is also ruled out. According to Morris and Sears (1967) and Kuckuck (1979), *T. compactum* and *T. sphaerococcum* acquired free-threshing quality through introgression from *T. aestivum*. On the basis of this viewpoint, *T. compactum* and *T. sphaerococcum* are more recent than *T. aestivum*. *T. vavilovi* has a two-gene difference from other hexaploid wheats and has only a restricted cultivation in Armenia, it cannot be the primitive hexaploid wheat. This species may be a variant of *T. spelta*. On the basis of the presence of C allele in *T. macha* and a restricted cultivation of this species in recent times, it seems that *T. spelta* is the primitive species. But, since *T. macha* is a polymorphic hexaploid and was grown in wide areas in prehistoric times (Dorofeev, 1972), this species may be considered as the primitive hexaploid wheat.

Table 1.3. Genotypes and characteristics of five hexaploid wheats

S. No.	Species	Genotype	Characteristics
1.	*T. compactum*	QQCCSS	Free-threshing, compact ears
2.	*T. macha*	qqCCSS	Polymorphic wheat
3.	*T. spelta*	qqccSS	Loose fragile ears
4.	*T. aestivum*	QQccSS	Free-threshing, tough rachis
5.	*T. sphaerococcum*	QQccss	Free-threshing, small spherical grains

The evolution of *T. zhukovskyi* appears to be very simple. According to Upadhya and Swaminathan (1965), this species is the result of amphidiploidy between *T. timopheevii* and *T. monococcum*.

Ancestral Diploid's Differentiation Hypothesis

Earlier wheat workers (Sakamura, 1918; Kihara, 1919, 1924; Sax, 1922; and several others) were of the opinion that the cultivated tetraploid and hexaploid wheats were allopolyploids. Several wheat scientists believed that differentiation in the genome of an unknown diploid ancestor was the cause of the origin of various diploids (with AA, BB, GG and DD genomes). Then natural hybridization between diploids with different genomes followed by diploidization gave rise to different polyploid wheats. The whole scheme can be shown as given in Figure 1.1. According to diploid ancestor's differentiation hypothesis, first there was origin of a diploid species with AA genome after genome differentiation in the unknown ancestral diploid. Then a second diploid species with BB genome originated from the same diploid ancestor due to much large differentiation in its genome. Parallelly, there was origin of a diploid with GG genome in the same way. The occurrence of amphidiploidy between diploids with AA and BB genomes resulted in the evolution of tetraploid with AABB genomes. Similarly, amphidiploidy between diploids with AA and GG genomes resulted in the evolution of tetraploid with AAGG genomes. Then amphidiploidy between the tetraploid with AABB genomes and a diploid containing highly differentiated genome DD from the ancestral diploid resulted in the evolution of hexaploid with AABBDD genomes. Similarly, amphidiploidy between the tetraploid with AAGG

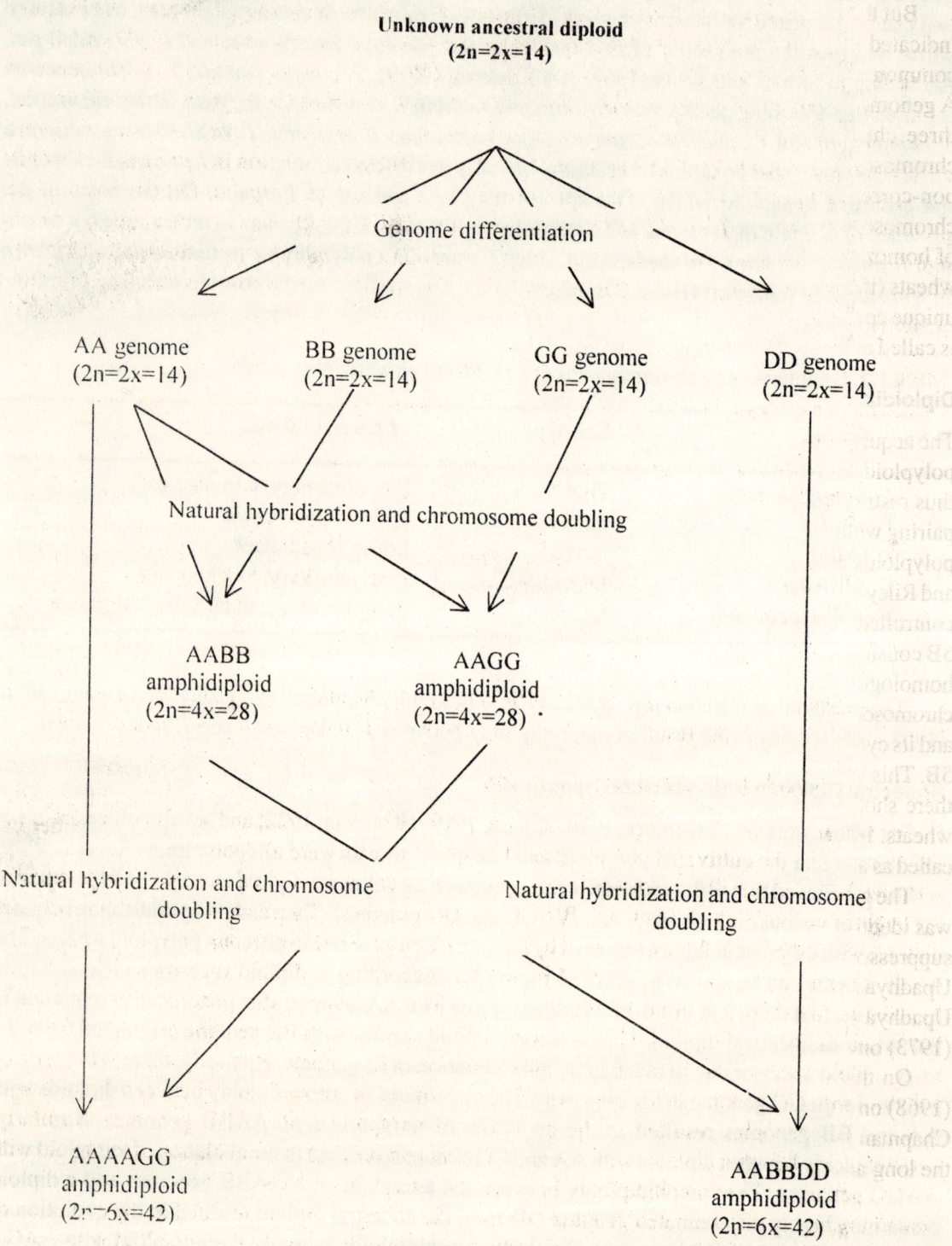

Figure 1.1. Ancestral diploid's differentiation hypothesis for the evolution of wheats

genomes and a diploid with AA genome resulted in the origin of the hexaploid with AAAAGG genomes.

But the results of the studies carried out by Sears and Okamoto (1956) and Sears (1966) clearly indicated that the differences between the chromosomes of the three genomes (A, B and D) of common wheat (*T. aestivum*) were not so big as were supposed earlier, rather each chromosome of A genome has a homeologous chromosome in each of the remaining two genomes (B and D) and the three chromosomes of each homeologous set are closely related genetically. Homeologous chromosomes have some corresponding genetic regions for which they are homologous and some non-corresponding genetic regions for which they are non-homologous, that is, homeologous chromosomes are partly homologous and partly non-homologous and thus present a unique condition of homozygosity within each genome and heterozygosity between different genomes of polyploid wheats (if corresponding genetic regions of homeologous chromosomes have different alleles). This unique condition allows advantage of heterozygous condition in homozygous (pure line) varieties and is called as **homozygous genomic heterosis**.

Diploidization in Polyploid Wheats

The acquisition of diploidizing mechanism was the major factor in the successful establishment of the polyploid wheats. This mechanism does not allow pairing between homeologous chromosomes and thus restricts chromosome pairing to homologous chromosomes only, that is, there is chromosome pairing within each genome but no pairing between genomes. Therefore, because of this mechanism, polyploids behave like diploids as regards pairing between chromosomes. However, Okamoto (1957) and Riley and Chapman (1958) found that the diploidizing mechanism in hexaploid wheat is genetically controlled. Accoding to them, the presence of some gene or genes on the long arm of chromosome 5B considerably affects the meiotic pairing in hexaploid wheat by restricting chromosome pairing to homologues only. The absence of 5B chromosome causes considerable pairing between homeologous chromosomes. This discovery indicated that hexaploid wheat is more autopolyploid than an allopolyploid and its cytological behaviour like diploids, high level of fertility and stability are due to the presence of 5B. This view is, therefore, against the earlier view that cultivated wheat is allopolyploid. However, there should be no confusion or controversy about the kind of polyploidy in tetra- and hexaploid wheats. In fact, the polyploid wheats are segmental polyploids and these wheats should neither be called as allopolyploids nor as autopolyploids.

The gene responsible for the suppression of chromosome pairing between homeologues in wheat was identified by Wall *et al.* (1971) and designated as *Ph* (later modified to *Ph 1*). In addition to 5B suppressor system, other suppressor systems (with minor suppressing effect) have been found by Upadhya and Swaminathan (1967) and Driscoll (1973) on the short arm of 3A and called as 3AS; by Upadhya and Swaminathan (1967), Mello-Sampayo (1968, 1971) and Mello-Sampayo and Canas (1973) on the short arm of 3D and called as 3DS; and by Driscoll (1973) on 4D.

On the contrary, some chromosome pairing promotor systems have been found by Feldman (1968) on the long arm of 5A called as 5AL; by Feldman and Mello-Sampayo (1967) and Riley and Chapman (1967) on the short arm of 5B called as 5 BS; by Feldman (1966) and Riley *et al.* (1966) on the long arm of 5D called as 5 DL; and by Feldman (1968) on the short arm of 5D called as 5DS.

The presene of several pairing suppressor and promotor systems in wheat indicates that the meiotic pairing in polyploid wheats is controlled by a complex genetic process and the degree of pairing would depend on the balance between these systems (Feldman, 1968). However, the pairing suppressor system under the control of *Ph1* gene on 5 BL is the major pairing control system and thus this gene is called as the *pairing-control gene*. The remaining suppressors, in the absence of *Ph1*, act as a balancing force against the promotors.

The stage (diploid or tetraploid) at which the *Ph1* gene came into existence is not yet fully known. However, it is more likely that this gene was present in the raw AABB amphidiploid.

CHAPTER 2

Cytogenetics and Genetics

Sakamura in Japan and Sax in USA, in the year 1918, independently discovered that the genus *Triticum* contains three types of species : Diploids (2n=2x=14), tetraploids (2n=4x=28), and hexaploids (2n=6x=42). This discovery became a significant milestone in the history of wheat genetics (Kihara, 1958) and created curiosity in the minds of wheat geneticists about the probable origin of tetraploid and hexaploid wheats. As discussed in chapter 1, two of the three diploid progenitors of *Triticum aestivum* have been fully identified (Rudnoy *et al.*, 2004). These two diploid species are *T.urartu* (donor of A genome) and *T.tauschii* or *Aegilops squarrosa* (donor of D or Dinkel genome). However, the origin of B genome still remains debatable and unsolved (Feldman, 2001). There may be several possibilities about the origin of B genome (Chapter 1).

Cytogenetics

Although wheat is considered to be one of the best understood polyploids, chromosome pairing in tetraploid and hexaploid wheats is a complex phenomenon. As discussed in Chapter 1, the chromosomes of different genomes of wheat are neither completely homologous nor completely non-homologous but are homeologous. Therefore, it is better to call the polyploid wheats as segmental polyploids rather than as autopolyploids or allopolyploids.

Anenploidy studies

A change in chromosome number (increase or reduction) without involving an entire genome is termed as aneuploidy. This change varies from the loss or addition of a single chromosome arm (as in case of telosomics) to the loss or addition of a pair of chromosomes (as in case of nullisomics and tetrasomics). Various types of aneuploids (monotelosomics, ditelosomics, monosomics, trisomics, nullisomics, tetrasomics, nullisomic-tetrasomics, etc.) have been produced in wheat.

The uses of aneuploidy analysis are :
1. To know the position of genes on chromosomes;
2. to map distance between genes and centromere and between different genes;
3. to identify genes governing various characters;
4. to transfer chromosomes from one variety to another and from one species to another;
5. to develop addition and substitution lines; and
6. to determine homology between chromosomes which helps in defining relationships between chromosomes of different genomes regarding their function and origin.

Since polyploids have increased dosage of chromosomes and thus can more easily tolerate the loss of chromosome(s) than the diploids, the occurrence of aneuploidy is more frequent in polyploids than in diploids. Wheat is one of the best materials for aneuploidy studies. However, because of the following reasons, aneuploidy studies in hexaploids wheat were carried out earlier than in tetraploid wheats :
1. Hexaploid wheats can tolerate loss of chromosomes more easily than tetraploid wheats; and
2. hexaploid wheats are more widely grown (about in 90 per cent of area under wheat cultivation) than tetraploid wheats.

Whereas a large number of aneuploids were developed in hexaploid wheats in 1940s and 1950s, aneuploidy studies in tetraploid wheat could be effectively started in late 1970s only. Therefore, aneuploidy studies in hexaploid and tetraploid wheats will be discussed separately.

Aneuploidy in Hexaploid Wheat

Hexaplid wheat of AABBDD group contains $n=3x=21$ chromosomes (seven chromosomes belonging to each of the three genomes). Sears numbered the 21 chromosomes of variety Chinese Spring of *Triticum aestivum* as I-XXI. The chromosomes I-XIV belong to A and B genomes and the remaining seven chromosomes (XV-XXI) to D genome. Based on nullisomic-tetrasomic combinations (that is, homeologous groups where, within each group, one chromosome pair of a genome is able to compensate, at least in part, chromosome pair of another genome), Sears (1954, 1959, 1966) put the 21 chromosomes in seven homeologous groups as given in Table 2.1. As shown in this table, the

Table 2.1. Classification of T.aestivum chromosomes into homeologous groups

Homeologous group	A genome	B genome	D genome
1	XIV (1A)	I (1B)	XVII (1D)
2	II (2A)	XIII (2B)	XX (2D)
3	XII (3A)	III (3B)	XVI (3D)
4	IV (4A)	VIII (4B)	XV (4D)
5	IX (5A)	V (5B)	XVIII (5D)
6	VI (6A)	X (6B)	XIX (6D)
7	XI (7A)	VII (7B)	XXI (7D)

Note: Chromosome numbers in parentheses are according to new nomenclature.

chromosomes XIV, I and XVII fall in the first homeologous group; II, XIII and XX in the second; XII, III and XVI in the third; IV, VIII and XV in the fourth; IX, V and XVIII in the fifth; VI, X and XIX in the sixth; and the chromosomes XI, VII and XXI in the seventh homeologous group. However, the degree of compensation varies from one homeologous group to another. For example, tetrasomic-nullisomic combinations within homeologous groups 1, 3 and 7 show good compensation indicating that there is a good degree of genetic relationship between chromosomes within each of the three groups. The combinations within each of these three groups produce almost normal plants. But, the degree of compensation shown by combinations within homeologous groups 2, 4 and 6 is lower than that shown by combinations within groups 1, 3 and 7. In these three homeologous groups (2, 4 and 6), the degree of compensation is differentially affected by the members of homeologous pair, that is, one chromosome has greater effect on the degree of compensation than its homeologue. The chromosomes 2A, 4A and 6B have been found more important than their homeologues. Nevertheless, tetrasomic-nullisomic combination within homeologous group 5 show poor compensation. The probable cause of this poor compensation is the presence of speltoid-suppressing gene on chromosome 5A and that of vernalization requirement reducing gene Vrn 3 on chromosome 5D. The production of inter-homeologous group combinations did not give satisfactory results as the plants with such combinations were weak (Sears, 1966).

The production of a complete series of monosomics in the variety Chinese Spring by Sears (1939, 1944) may be considered as an important contribution towards the progress in wheat genetics. The aneuploid analysis in hexaploid wheat proved to be an elegant genetic tool, particularly for studying linkage groups in this group of wheats. The genetic studies in wheat were generally based on the differences in morphological characters between monosomics and normal diploid plants in the F_1 generation, identification of chromosome lines showing skewed ratios in F_2 generation, and the characteristics of nullisomics.

In fact, aneuploidy studies in hexaploid wheat began with the production of monosomics with meiotic configuration $20^{II}+1^{I}$. As mentioned earlier, the credit for producing all the 21 possible monosomics in hexaploid wheat goes to Sears. The principal sources of the production of the monosomics were haploid plants or the plants nullisomic for chromosome 3B (the chromosome responsible for reducing chromosome pairing at the time of meiosis). A large number of monosomic plants were produced by making backcrosses and all 21 types of monosomics were obtained through selection. The monosomics can be used for locating genes on specific chromosomes. Further, since the genes present on the univalent are in hemizygous condition, it is possible to know the position of recessive alleles. Since a monosomic has loss of one chromosome only and has presence of two of its homeologues belonging to the two other genomes, monosomics sometimes are not much different from diploid plants. However, the condition may vary from monosomic to monosomic.

The selfing of monosomics gives rise to nullisomics with meiotic configuration 20^{II} when the gametes with n-1 chromosomes unite with other similar gametes and produce nullisomic plants with 2n-2=40 chromosomes. The nullisomics are generally sterile and unstable and, therefore, are considerably different from diploids and monosomics. Only nine nullisomics, namely, for chromosomes 1A, 3A, 6A, 7A, 3B, 6B, 7B, 1D and 3D, are maintainable. Even the fertile nullisomics are mostly unstable and thus, manytimes, do not attain maturity. The three nullisomics of a homeologous group, manytimes, show great degree of resemblance. The nullisomics show highest degree of abonormality followed by tetrasomics, monosomics and trisomics, in order.

The trisomics with meiotic configuration $20^{II}+1^{III}$, show least degree of abnormality, rather their phenotype is almost similar to the phenotype of normal diploid plants. The sources of the production of trisomics, may be same as those of the monosomics. In addition, trisomics may also be obtained from the progeny of nullisomics if compensating trisomics are present in such progeny.

The selfing of trisomics gives rise to tetrasomics with meiotic configuration $20^{II}+1^{IV}$ when the gametes with n+1 chromosomes unite with other similar gemetes and produce plants with 2n+2=44 chromosomes. The frequency of the production of tetrasomics from trisomics is almost similar to the frequency of the production of nullisomics from monosomics. Tetrasomics are generally more abnormal than trisomics or monosomics but have better survival and fertility than nullisomics. Like nullisomics, the three tetrasomics of a homeologous group often show a high degree of resemblance. However, tetrasomic plants have a tendency to revert to the normal diploid condition and thus their maintenance sometimes becomes problematical. This problem can be solved by periodic cytological checking.

As dicussed earlier, all possible 42 nullisomic tetrasomic combinations with meiotic configuration $19^{II}+1^{IV}$ have been produced in hexaploid wheat to determine the compensation of a pair of chromosomes of a genome by a pair of chromosomes of the other genome (Sears, 1966). However, the degree of compensation varies from combination to combination. Also, addition lines have been produced in wheat. Inter-variety chromosome substitutions in wheat where a chromosome pair of a variety is substituted into another variety, are useful not only for the identification of genes controlling qualitative character but the effect and interaction of genes governing quantitative characters can also be studied with the help of these substitutions. Kuspira and Unrau (1957) substituted specific chromosomes of wheat varieties Hope, Thatcher and Timstein for their corresponding homologues in the lines of Chinese Spring and observed highly significant changes for plant height, earliness, lodging resistance and yield. Chromosome substitutions are not restricted to the wheat chromosomes only but chromosomes from other genera related to wheat may also be substituted for specific wheat chromosomes. For example, O'Mara (1947) substituted a specific chromosome pair (hairy-neck) from *Secale cereale* for the chromosome pair IX of *T.vulgare* and found that rye-wheat chromosome substitution proved better than the simple addition of a rye pair to the wheat chromosome complement. This finding of O'Mara opened new avenues for further chromosome substitutions from other genera related to *Triticum*.

In addition to the loss or addition of whole chromosomes, other aneuploid stocks which involve incomplete chromosome or chromosome arm with centromere or telocentric chromosome have been produced. Telocentric chromosomes arise due to the misdivision of the centrome. This division occurs at right angle (vertical) to the arms of the chromosome and divides the chromosome into two telocentric chromosomes rather than dividing it lengthwise. If the arm of the telocentric chromosome divides lengthwise, it gives rise to an isochromosome. Monotelosomics (with meiotic configuration $20^{II}+t^{I}$), ditelosomics (with meiotic configuration $20^{II}+t^{II}$), double monotelosomics (with meiotic configuration $20^{II}+t^{I}+t^{I}$), etc. have been produced. Telocentric chromosomes can be easily identified. Monotelosomics generally behave like monosomics.

Aneuploidy in Tetraploid Wheat

In general, addition of chromosome(s) to the chromosome complement is less harmful than the reduction of chromosome(s). Therefore, trisomics and tetrasomics are less abnormal than monosomics and nulisomics. Further, hexaploid wheat is a better tolerant of aneuploidy than tetraploid wheat, that is, aneuploidy induces greater degree of abnormality in case of tetraploid wheat than in case of hexaploid wheat. It has been found that 13-chromosome gametes have much low transmission rates than those of the 20-chromosome gametes (Mochizuki, 1968, 1970; Hanchinal and Goud, 1982). In addition to the low transmission rates, the vigour and fertility of the tetraploid monosomics is also low. As a result, the use of tetraploid monosomics for genetic analysis became difficult.

In view of the low transmission rates of 13-chromosome gametes and the low vigour and fertility of the tetraploid monosomics, some investigators (Allan and Vogel, 1960; Kuspira and Millis, 1967; Bozzini and Giorgi, 1971; Bozzini and Carluccio, 1973) tried to use hexaploid monosomics to carry out the genetic analysis of tetraploids. Instead of producing tetraploid monosomics directly, crosses were made between hexaploid monosomics for the A- and B-genome chromosomes and tetraploid durum wheat. On cytological basis, monopentaploid (with 34 chromosomes) and pentaploid (with 35 chromosomes) plants were indentified in F_1 generation of each cross. These two types of plants were compared to know the effect of chromosome belonging to A or B genome. Significant differences in terms of qualitative or quantitative trait between these two types of plants were attributed to the effect of missing A- and B-genome chromosome. However, the results of these studies were not very conclusive because of the difficulty in locating genes for specific characters.

To overcome this problem, hexaploid lines were developed by substituting individual pairs of chromosomes from tetraploid wheat into hexaploid. This approach proved more effective as it provided precise information about the effect of individual chromosomes on qualitative or quantitative traits. Some investigators (Snape et al., 1975; and others) used disomic-substitution lines and their intercrosses to determine quantitative inheritance and gene action on the basis of some elegant methods.

An alternative approach to overcome the deficiencies of tetraploid monosomics was suggested by Longwell and Sears (1963). The method was to develop mono-trisomic tetraploids where the plants are monosomic for one chromosome in one of the two genomes (A or B) and trisomic for the homeologous chromosome. For this purpose, crosses were made between multi-tetrasomics of Chinese Spring and durum wheat plants and mono-trisomics for the chromosomes 2A, 3A, 6A, 2B, 5B and 6B were produced. The approach was continued in durum wheat by Noronha-Wagner and Mello-Sampayo (1966). But three kinds of problems were faced :

1. Mono-trisomic plants had low fertility;
2. some of the trisomics were not simple primary trisomics but were tertiary trisomics; and
3. the translocated chromosome in such cases involved chromosomes not only of A and B genomes but in some cases, there was also involvement of the chromosome of D genome (Mello-Sampayo, 1972).

However, some mono-trisomics (eg., mono-5B-tri-5A) showed much higher transmission than durum wheat monosomics.

As mentioned earlier, the trisomics are generally as vigorous and fertile as the diploid plants and have been used for genetic analysis in several crop plant species. Simeone et al. (1983) produced a complete set of primary trisomics in the variety Cappelli of durum wheat by irradiating pollen or making crosses between nulli-tetrasomics of Chinese Spring and Cappelli and backcrossing the progeny of the cross to Cappelli. But, the use of these durum wheat trisomics has not yet been made for genetic analyses (Joppa, 1987). However, it should be possible to use these trisomics for genetic analysis in the same way as in other plant species.

In addition, a complete set of 14 disomic substitution lines (13 pairs of durum chromosomes + one pair of D-genome chromosomes) has been developed by crossing nulli-tetrasonics of Chinese Spring with Langdon variety of durum wheat (Joppa and Williams, 1983) and the possible uses of these substitution lines (to determine the location of genes on specific chromosome, develop inter-variety, homologous disomic substitutions, and to induce translocations between homeologous chromosomes) have been discussed (Joppa and Williams, 1979; Joppa *et al.,* 1983). Also, a complete set of double ditelosomics has been produced in Langdon. Joppa (1987) has discussed aneuploid analysis in tetraploid wheat in detail.

Genetics

Plant characters can be classified into two types : (1) **Qualitative characters** and (2) **quantitative characters**. Qualitative characters are governed by a single gene or a few major genes (oligo genes) and show a discontinuous or particulate variation. The mode of inheritance of such characters can be described on the basis of some genetic ratios (3:1, 9:3:3:1, 1:1:1:1, 9:7, 9:3:4, 15:1, etc.). Here, epistasis or non-allelic interaction or inter-allelic interaction can be accurately classified into different types (complementary, supplementary, duplicate, inhibitory, etc.). On the other hand, quantitative characters or metrical characters or continuously variable characters are governed by several or many genes called as polygenes or multiple genes or quantitative genes and show continuous variation. Though quantitative inheritance also has a Mendelian genetic basis, it is not possible to carry out accurate inheritance studies in case of metrical characters. In general, there is a considerable effect of environment on these characters. In fact, the large number of genes governing metrical characters and a considerable effect of environment on these characters are the two factors which change the discontinuties induced by individual genes into a continuous variation. Further, the classification of epistasis in case of quantitative variation is not so accurate as is possible in particulate variation. Here, the classification of epistasis is based on the signs of (h) and (l). If these two components have the same sign, it is complementary epistasis and if these components have different signs, the condition indicates duplicate epistasis. The component (h) is the summed dominance effect and the component (l) is the summed dominance × dominance epistatic effect (For details, see Singh and Pawar, 2005).

Nevertheless, the classification of plant characters given above is not so accurate as it is often supposed. There are cases where a character is governed by qualitative genes as well as by quantitative genes. For example, on the basis of plant height, wheat varieties are generally classified into tall, single dwarf, double dwarf and triple dwarf as if plant height in this cereal is governed by three major genes, that is, tall varieties possess all the three major genes responsible for more height, one-gene dwarf varieties contain two major gene for more height and one gene for dwarfness, two-gene dwarf varieties have one major gene for more height and two genes for dwarfness, and the three-gene dwarf varieties contain all the three genes for dwarfness. But, plant height in wheat is a continuously variable character and to describe it on the basis of three major genes only, is an oversimplification of the genetic control of this character. Certainly, there are some polygenes or modifying genes which are also involved in the control of plant height in wheat. Gruneberg (1952) called such variation as **quasi continuous variation**.

Whether a character is qualitative or quantitative can be determined on the basis of the type of variability observed for that character in segregating generations of a cross made between contrasting parents. If plants of a segregating generation can be divided into clear and discrete phenolypic classes according to some genetic ratio, the character showing such variability (that is, qualitative variability) is a qualitative character. On the contrary, if the phenotypic variation shown by a character is continuous, the character is quantitative.

Triticum aestivum (common wheat) is a segmental hexaploid species containing A, B and D genomes with homology of chromosomes within genome and homeology between genomes. However, because of diploidizing mechanism, this species behaves cytologically as a normal diploid and the occurrence of crossing-over is restricted to homologous chromosomes only, that is, there is no recombination between homeologous chromosomes. As a consequence, the segregation of **homeoalleles** (alleles on homeologous chromosomes) is independent of one another. Polyploidy in wheat though does not affect gene segregation, but it may affect gene expression, that is, the phenotypic expression of segregation at a locus may be affected by another allele present on a corresponding homeoallelic locus. This type of effect of homeoalleles is like an epistatic interaction which may cause disturbance in genetic ratios for major (qualitative) genes and may affect the magnitude of epistatic component of genetic variation for metrical characters. Such homeoallelic variation has been noted in a number of cases both for qualitative characters (e.g., photoperiodic response, dwarfism and vernalization requirement) and quantitative characters (yield, its component traits, plant height, etc.). However, the magnitude of this effect may vary from cross to cross for the same character. Therefore, it is not easy to carry out conventional genetic analyses in polyploid wheat.

Qualitative characters

Despite the polyploid nature of common wheat, a number of studies have been carried out to investigate the inheritance of qualitative characters on the basis of genetic ratios obtained from F_2 and backcross populations. These inheritance studies were carried out to determine the number of genes governing the character under study, the number of alleles present on each locus, and the dominance and epistatic properties of the alleles. The genetic ratios which form the basis of mode of inheritance, in fact, depend upon these properties of alleles. The genetic analysis can be pursued further to determine the location of genes on chromosomes, linkage relationships between different loci, genetic constitutions of different varieties, and to predict the frequencies of different phenotypes in specific crosses. Information about some characters is given below :

Ear shape : Three loci, namely, Q-q (on chromosome 5 AL) for good threshibility (sequare-headed ears) vs. poor threshibility, C-c (on chromosome $2D_\beta$) for compactoid ears vs. loose ears, and Sl-sl (on chromosome 3D) for elongated ears vs. rounded glumes and spherical grains, govern ear shape in wheat. Considering these three loci, the genotypes of *T.compactum, T. macha, T.spelta, T.aestivum* and *T. sphaerococcum* hexaploid wheats are QQCCSlSl, qqCCSlSl, qqccSlSl, QQccSlSl and QQccslsl, respectively. Free-threshing quality shows high positive correlation with size and shape of grains. Snape *et al.* (1985) studied pleiotropic effects of the gene Q and found that, in addition to threshibility, this gene also reduces ear length (with increase in the number of spikelets) and increases yielding potential.

Ear alignment : The alignment of ears (erect vs. drooping) is governed by a single gene (Prasad, 1959).

Awning : According to Evans and Rawson (1970), the presence of awns plays an important role in increasing surface area for both light interception and CO_2 uptake and thus may considerably increase the net photosynthetic rate of wheat ears. However, this significant increase in the photosynthetic rate (due to the presence of awns) can cause considerable increase in yield only under the condition of limited water supply (Evans et al., 1972). Awn is also called as beard.

According to Howard and Howard (1912, 1915), the development of awn in *T. aestivum* is governed by duplicate factors with an F_2 ratio of 15 awned : 1 awnless. Similar results were found by Sikka and Rao (1957) but with a different condition. They observed a 15 tipped : 1 fully awned F_2 ratio. Singh et al. (1957), Ghosh et al. (1958) and Prasad and Rao (1961) also reported the role of duplicate factors in the control of awn development. On the contrary, Abbasi (1949) and Sen and Joshi (1955) observed that awning in wheat was governed by a single gene pair. However, in the studies of Pal et al. (1956), the mode of inheritance of awn character differed from cross to cross. According to them, in one cross, awning was governed by duplicate factors whereas in the second cross this character was under the control of a single gene pair.

Nevertheless, aneuploid analyses carried out by Sears (1954) and Tsunewaki (1966) indicate that awning (presence or absence of awns) in wheat is governed by some promoting genes located on each of the group 2 chromosomes (2A, 2B and 2D) and by four suppressing genes, namely, Hd (on 4B chromosome), B_1 (on 5A chromosome), B_2 (on 6B chromosome) and B_3 (on 1D chromosome). The balance between the activities of these promotors and suppressors determines the degree of awning. Among the four suppressing genes, B_1 is strongest in action followed by B_2, Hd and B_3, in order. The homozygous condition of any two or all three dominant genes Hd, B_1 and B_2 is responsible for awnlessness, whereas homozygous condition of only one dominant gene makes the plant tip-awned (hooded). The homozygous recessiveness for all the three genes makes the plant fully awned.

Awn arrangement : According to Prasad (1959), the arrangement of awns (adpressed vs. spreading) is governed by a single gene pair.

Awn shedding : Like awn arrangement, this character is also under the control of a single gene (Prasad, 1959).

Awn colour : According to Howard and Howard (1912, 1915), black vs. white awn colour in wheat is under the control of a single gene. However, black vs. red awn colour is governed by two genes giving a 12 (black) : 3 (red) : 1 (white) ratio in F_2 generation (Kadam and Nazareth, 1931). Similar results were obtained by Ghosh et al. (1958).

Glume hairiness : Hairiness of glumes in wheat is a single-gene-determined expression which is dominant to the glabrous condition (Kadam, 1936; Pal et al., 1956; Singh et al., 1957; Ghosh et al., 1958; Sikka et.al.1960 a,b; Prasad and Rao, 1961; Maystrenko, 1976). The dominant allele Hg (found on the short arm of chromosome 1A) determines the dominant phenotype (hairiness) and shows a tight linkage with another dominant allele Bg, responsible for black glumes. Sikka and Rao (1957) also found almost similar results but some of the F_3 families of their material were less pubescent than their pubescent parents. This condition indicated that some minor genes or modifiers, in addition to the single major gene, are also involved in the control of glume hairiness in wheat.

Glume colour : Glume colouration is dependent on a single dominant allele. For example, dominant allele Bg (on chromosome 1A) determines black glume colour and the dominant allele Rg (on chromosome 1B) controls red colour of glumes. Similarly, a single gene (on chromosome 1D) is responsible for brown glume colour. Kadam (1936), Pal et al. (1956), Sikka and Rao (1957), Ghosh et al. (1958) and Prasad and Rao (1961) had found that a single gene governed the glume colour.

However, Ayad (1952) and Sen and Joshi (1955) found two genes and Sears (1948) found three genes responsible for the control of glume colour. According to Law and Chapman (1974), the presence of a gene or genes (on long arm of chromosome 1B) causes reduction in the intensity of glume colour.

Glume beak : According to Prasad and Rao (1961), two gene pairs determine obtuse (dominant) vs. accuminate beak in wheat.

Glume shoulder : This character is controlled by a single gene and square glume shoulder shows dominance over wanting glume shoulder (Prasad and Rao, 1960).

Grain colour : According to Howard and Howard (1912), the red grain colour may be governed by one, two or three independently inherited genes. Kadam (1936) found dominance of red grain colour over yellow grain colour. Similarly, Sikka and Rao (1957) observed dominance of red grain colour over amber colour. However, they found one, two and three gene pairs responsible for the control of grain colour in different materials. According to Ghosh et al. (1958), red colour of the grain was controlled by two genes.

In fact, grain colour in wheat is a complex character and is determined by pigments present in three different layers of the bran, namely, pericarp (the outermost layer), testa and the aleurone layer (Bradbury, Gill and McMasters, 1956). These three types of layers may carry purple, red and blue pigments, respectively. Whereas the pigments produced in pericarp and testa have maternal inheritance, the triploid endosperm determines the colour produced in the aleurone layer. According to Piech and Evans (1979), the purple grain colour in *T.durum* is governed by complementary dominant alleles found on 3A and 7B chromosomes. Sears (1954), Allan and Vogel, 1965) and Metzer and Silbaugh (1970a) found that the red grain expression which is dominant over white expression, is governed by three homeologous dominant alleles R_1, R_2 and R_3 found on the chromosomes 3D, 3A and 3B, respectively. The intensity of pigmentation (redness) depends upon the number of dominant alleles (one, two or all three) carried by red-grained varieties. According to Bolton (1968), the source of blue-grain genes found in triploid endosperm of hexaploid wheat is *Agropyron*. Since the blue pigmentation is determined by the triploid endosperm, within-ear segregation may be seen for grain colouration. Though the exact location of blue-grain genes is not fully known, these genes may be found on a group 4 chromsome (Metzer and Silbaugh, 1970b).

Grain texture : According to Prasad (1959), a single gene pair determines the hard vs. soft grain texture in wheat. The gene controlling grain texture is found on the chromosome 5D (Symes, 1965; Ausemus *et al.*, 1967; Mattern *et al.*, 1973). According to Law *et al.* (1978), the gene Ha responsible for grain hardness is found on the short arm of this chromosome (5D). However, Law and Krattiger (1987) noted that the removal of short arm of 5A also has an effect on the grain hardness. According to them, perhaps homeologous loci governing grain texture are found on the chromosomes 5A and 5B.

Grain hardness is an important character in wheat as it greatly affects the flour quality.

Grain shape : According to Ausemus *et al.* (1967), chromosome 4A contains the gene governing grain shape in wheat. However, in *T. sphaerococcum*, the gene controlling grain shape is found on chromosome 3D.

Grain lustre : Like grain texture, dull vs. lustrous grain lustre is governed by a single gene pair (Prasad, 1959).

Coleoptile and stem colours : According to Law (1966) and Sutka (1977), three genes Rc_1, Rc_2 and Rc_3 located on the 7A, 7B and 7D chromosomes, respectively, govern the red colour of coleoptiles. Also, the purple stem colour is determined by genes found on the chromosomes 7B and 7D. Therefore, these two characters (coleoptile colour and stem colour) are correlated.

Anthocyanin pigmentation of the rachis : This character is governed by a single dominant allele (Prasad and Rao, 1961). However, the presence of an inhibitor allele changes the colour of the rachis to normal colour.

Leaf blotching : The results of inheritance studies indicate that this character is controlled by a single recessive allele (Sikka and Jain, 1959; Prasad and Rao, 1960).

Anther colour : According to Sharman (1944), common wheat mostly has yellow anthers except a few lines which have purplish-pink anthers. He found that the character coloured vs. non-coloured anthers is governed by a single gene pair.

Anther size : Anther size has a special significance for those who are interested in developing hybrid wheat. Large sized anthers may cause opening of florets and thus may increase the degree of cross pollination. According to Sears (1954), chromosome 2A contains gene(s) controlling anther size.

Pollen lethality : Loegering and Sears (1963) found that a pollen killing gene Ki found on chromosome 6B is responsible for pollen lethality. This gene was linked with rust susceptibility.

Fertility and sterility : Information regarding male sterility and fertility restoration system is especially important for the development of hybrid wheat at commercial scale. Briggle (1963) has emphasized the importance of research on this topic.

Fertility of the wheat plant, more or less, is influenced by all chromosomes. The abortion or poor development of spikelets (usually of the basal ones) and deformation of some spikes may affect fertility of a plant. The plants nullisomic for effective chromosomes often show male and female sterility (Sears, 1954).

Kihara (1958) and co-workers were the first to report cytoplasmic-genetic male sterility in wheat by transferring *Triticum* nucleus into *Aegilops* cytoplasms. Wilson and Ross (1962) reported a similar type of male sterility by transferring *T.aestivum* nucleus into *T.timopheevii* cytoplasm.

According to Fukasawa (1958), at least two gene pairs govern effective male fertility restoration in the *ovatum* system. Livers (1964) and Schmidt and Johnson (1966) found a similar type of control of male fertility restoration by two major genes in the *timopheevii* system. Some modifying genes may also influence the expression of male fertility restoration.

Vernalization : Among the major cereal crops, wheat is the most widely adapted species and is grown all over the world. The exploitation of genes which control the time of flowering has played a considerable role in increasing the adaptation of genotypes to varying environmental conditions. The genes affecting adaptation of genotypes can be put in the following categories :

1. Genes governing vernalization;
2. genes governing photoperiodic response;
3. genes governing time to flowering; and
4. genes governing winter-hardiness.

Therefore, vernalization, photoperiodism and winter-hardiness fall under a common category, **adaptive**

characters. The genes governing adaptive characters protect the plants from the hazards of unfavourable temperature conditions.

Vernalization delays floral development until there are favourable temperature conditions for the plant. Vernalization is a more important requirement for winter wheats (grown in areas which face severe winter conditions). On the contrary, spring wheats are weakly sensitive or totaly insensitive to vernalization treatment. Insensitivity to vernalization treatment is dominant over vernalization sensitivity.

The major genes Vrn 1, Vrn 2, Vrn 3, Vrn 4 and Vrn 5 located on the chromosomes 5A, 2B, 5D, 5B and 7B, respectively, are said to govern vernalization in wheat. However, the description of the gene Vrn 2 is doubtful. It is suspected that either this gene governs photoperiodism (and should be called as Ppd 2) or affects developmental rate of the plant. The genes Vrn 1, Vrn 3 and Vrn 4 are identical and homeoalleles. According to Snape *et al.* (1976), multiple allelism at the loci Vrn 1 and Vrn 3 is also a cause of variation in vernalization requirement.

Photoperiodism : Genes for photoperiodism play an extremely important role in determining the adaptability of wheat under differing environmental conditions. Photoperiod-sensitive genes are being exploited to extend the growing season of winter wheats followed by delayed flowering and thus considerably increasing the yield potential of these wheats in United Kingdom and northwestern Europe. On the contrary, photoperiod-insensitive genes are being exploited to accelerate flowering in late flowering wheats to check desiccation and yield losses due to hot summer conditions of the Indian sub-continent, Australia, central and southern Europe and several other countries of the world.

Welsh *et al.* (1973) observed that two major genes Ppd 1 and Ppd 2 found on the chromosomes 2D and 2B, respectively, determine the day length insensitivity in the cultivar Sonora 64. According to Law *et al.* (1978), a third gene for photoperiodism Ppd 3 is found on chromosome 2A. Intervarietal chromosome substitution studies of Scarth and Law (1984) showed that there was presence of multiple alleles at the Ppd 1 and Ppd 2 loci. These multiple alleles actively promote photoperiod-insensitivity of genotypes.

Winter-hardiness : According to some scientists (Puchov and Zhirov, 1978; Sutka, 1981; and others), the genetic determination of winter-hardiness is relatively more complex and the cold resistance genes found on chromosomes, 5A, 5D, 5B, 4B, 4D and 7A also play a role in determining this character in wheat. As discussed earlier, the chromosomes 5A, 5D, 5B and 7A also contain major genes for vernalization. However, Cahalan and Law (1978), on the basis of the behaviour shown by group 5 aneuploids and intervarietal chromosome substitutions, demonstrated that freezing resistance and vernalization requirement were not correlated. They concluded that two independent genetic systems are operating on group 5 chromosomes. One of these systems provides resistance for frost and the other provides avoidance from frost. In addition, resistance to some diseases (e.g., snow mould) and the genes from specific cytoplasm(e.g., *T. ovatum* cytoplasm) may also affect winter-hardiness.

Like winter-hardiness, the genetic determination of floweing is also complex and genes found on most chromosomes contribute towards the control of this character.

Disease resistance : Disease resistance differs from morphological and physiological characters in two major ways : (1) Instead of one biologial organism (as in case of morphological and physiological characters), the researcher has to work on two biological organisms, the host and the causal organism (pathogen), while studying disease resistance; and (2) specialization goes on occurring in the pathogen due to the development of new physiological races from time to time. Both the biological organisms show heritable variation and disease intensity would depend upon the reaction conditioned by the heritable factors contained by the two organisms. Further, the same cultivar generally shows differential degree of resistance over sites and over years due to the differential reaction of different races. However, the basic principles to study disease resistance are similar to those used for studying morphological and physiological characters.

Although several diseases affect the wheat plant, our discussion will be restricted to the study of wheat rusts only. There are three types of wheat rusts : (1) Leaf rust or brown rust caused by *Puccinia recondita*; (2) stem rust or black rust caused by *Puccinia graminis*; and (3) stripe rust or yellow rust caused by *Puccinia striiformis*. Since last many years, the wheat breeders have been facing serious problems due to yield losses caused by rust diseases. However, the seriousness of the problem caused by a specific rust disease differs from region to region. Therefore, a particular rust disease has received maximum attention in the region where it has caused maximum destruction. For example, leaf rust and stem rust have caused maximum destruction in many parts of India and U.S., respectively, and thus have received maximum attention of researchers of these regions.

The inheritance of wheat rusts is complex. The results of inheritance studies show that the condition differs from cross to cross. In some cases, resistance is dominant, whereas in other cases, susceptibility is dominant. In some cases it has also been observed that neither resistance nor susceptibility is dominant but the offspring of the cross show intermediate effect.

Leaf rust : A large number of studies carried out on leaf rust show that resistance to specific races of this rust mostly depends on the parents involved in the cross. In most cases, one or two genes govern the resistance to specific races. Also, dominance and recessiveness of resistance varies from cross to cross. In some crosses, resistance is dominant, whereas in others it is recessive.

Abbasi (1949) found that resistance to leaf rust was governed by a single dominant allele in his material. According to Pal *et al.* (1956), the field reaction to brown rust was governed by two complementary genes in the cross NP 789 (resistant) × Frondoso (susceptible). Murty and Lakhani (1958) observed that resistance to brown rust in *aestivum* wheat was governed by two genes in some crosses and by one gene in others. According to Sikka *et al.* (1961a, b), resistance to brown rust was controlled by a single recessive allele in Frontiera and by two recessive alleles in La Prevision.

The seedling resistance to race 10 or brown rust was controlled by three genes (Bahl and Kohli, 1960).

The genes controlling leaf rust in wheat are located on the chromosomes 1A, 2A, 3B, 4B, 4D, 5A, 5D, 6B and 7B (Ausemus *et al.*, 1967).

Stem rust : Stem rust resistance has been studied in detail under field conditions as well as at seedling stage. However, the number of studies made under field conditions is much larger than the studies carried out at seedling stage. The studies on stem rust indicated that inkorn and some of durum and emmer wheats possess high resistance to stem rust. However, the common wheat is susceptible to this rust. The crosses between resistant and susceptible wheats were only partially successful as the hybrids showed sterility and the resistance was linked with some undesirable plant characters. Depending upon the cross, resistance to stem rust may show complete dominance, partial dominance or full recessiveness. However, the first two conditions are more frequently found.

Pal (1951) observed that field resistance to stem rust was dominant in some crosses but was recesisve in some others. Abbasi (1949) studied inheritance of resistance to stem rust in the wheat cross Premier × Kenya and found that the mature plant resistance to this rust was governed by two epistatic gene pairs. Of these two genes, one (dominant allele H) was present in Premier and other (dominant allele K) was carried by Kenya. According to Das (1954), field resistance to stem rust was governed by three complementary genes in the cross Ridley (susceptible) × NP789 (resistant). These complementary genes gave a 27 (resistant) : 37 (susceptible) F_2 ratio. Here, 27/64 offspring of F_2 generation had all the three genes enforcing resistance either in homozygous or heterozygous condition. Pal et al. (1956) also found that the resistance to most of the races of stem rust was governed by three complementary genes in the cross NP 784 (resistant) × Frondoso (susceptible). Sikka and Rao (1958) studied field resistance to stem rust in three wheat crosses, namely, NP 718 × NP 790, PbC 281 × NP 790 and PbC 591 × NP 790, by crossing NP 790 (resistant) to three susceptible varieties. Whereas resistance to stem rust was dominant and was conditioned by a single gene pair in the first cross, the resistance was recessive and was conditioned by three gene pairs in the last two crosses. According to them, the resistance of NP 790 in last two crosses was suppressed either by two inhibitory or two dominant genes for susceptibility carried by the varieties PbC 281 and PbC 591. Prasad and Rao (1960) confirmed the findings of Sikka and Rao on the basis of the results obtained from the crosses between NP 790 and other Punjab wheat varieties (PbC 273 and PbC 518). According to Sikka et al. (1961b), susceptibility to stem rust was dominant and the resistance was under the control of two recessive duplicate genes. Murty and Lakhani (1958) reported that resistance to black rust was conditioned by two genes in some crosses and by three genes in other crosses.

As regards the inheritance of seedling or physiologic resistance to different races of black rust, the reaction to different races in most of the cases was simply inherited by a single gene (Abbasi, 1949; Athwal, 1953; Sen and Joshi, 1955; and others).

The genes controlling resistance to stem rust are found on all the 21 wheat chromosomes except the chromosomes 1B, 7B and 4A (Ausemus et al., 1967).

Although the aneuploidy studies carried out by many researchers have greatly advanced the knowledge regarding the inheritance of wheat rusts, the inheritance of resistance to stem rust is not yet fully known because of the following reasons :

1. Difficulty in identifying a universally susceptible wheat;
2. since the genes for resistance to stem rust are located on almost all the 21 chromosomes, some of these genes may be homeoalleles and may complicate the inheritance;
3. some modifying genes may be involved in the inheritance of resistance and may influence the results;
4. sometimes, it is difficult to make a difference between closely linked genes and the alleles of the same gene; and
5. the host-gene-for-pathogen-gene relationship is complex as the number of genes for virulence in the pathogen appears to be greater than the loci for host reaction.

However, it appears that maximum efforts have been made to study the inheritance of stem rust.

Stripe rust : Although long back in the years 1905 and 1907, Biffen was able to show that host reaction to stripe rust was inherited in simple Mendelian fashion, our information regarding the genetics of resistance to this rust is still limited.

Different types of reports are available about the number of genes governing resistance to stripe rust in wheat. According to Ghosh et al. (1958), only one gene pair is responsible for conditioning resistance to stripe rust. However, results obtained by Bahl and Kohli (1960) and by Sikka et al. (1961a, b) from their studies on inheritance of resistance to stripe rust, indicated that two gene pairs were involved in the control of this disease. Pal *et al.* (1956) found that three gene pairs (two complementary genes and one independent gene) conditioned field resistance to stripe rust in the wheat cross NP 789 × Frondoso. Nevertheless, according to Lupton and Macer (1962), four genes were responsible for conditioning resistance to this rust in wheat.

Singh and Swaminathan (1959), on the basis of monosomic analysis in bread wheat, identified chromosomes carrying genes for resistance to two races of yellow rust. The genes conditioning resistance to stripe rust are located on the chromosomes 2A, 3B, 4A, 4B, 5A, 5B, 6A and 6B (Ausemus *et al.*, 1967),

Before we close our discussion on the inheritance of resistance to three rusts of wheat, it is necessary to clear one point regarding the resistance at the seedling storage and at mature plant stage. In many cases, there is a positive correlation between resistance at seedling stage and resistance at adult plant stage. However, in several other cases, the resistance at these two stages of plant growth, do not show any correlation, that is, resistance at seedling stage may completely vanish at adult stage and, similarly, plants showing absence of resistance at seedling stage, may show resistance at adult stage.

Grain storage proteins : The bread-making quality of wheat flour is determined by the quality and quantity of the proteins found in the wheat grain. Therefore, investigators have attached special importance to the study of grain storage proteins.

A number of loci controlling storage proteins have been identified. However, these loci seem to be genetically complex. Each locus mostly has two or more tightly linked genes which generally show no recombination. However, there is a large potential for allelic variation.

Most of the loci controlling grain storage proteins are located on the group 1 chromosomes. According to Payne *et al.* (1982), three loci Glu-A1, Glu-B1 and Glu-D1 found on 1AL, 1BL and 1DL chromosomes, respectively, encode the high-molecular weight (HMW) glutenin submits. Rybalka and Sozinov (1979) and Payne *et al.* (1984) found that low molecular weight (LMW) glutenin subunits are controlled by the loci Gli-A1, Gli-B1 and Gli-D1 located on the chromosomes 1AS, 1BS and 1DS, respectively. Three more genes, namely, Gld-2 1A (Sobko, 1984), Glu-B2 (Jackson *et al.*, 1985) and Gld-B6 (Galili and Feldman, 1984) have been identified to govern the synthesis of minor gliadin and glutenin submits. Furthermore, two genes, Tri-A1 and Tri-D1 located on 1AS and 1DS, respectively, have been recognized to control *triplet band proteins* (a minor group of proteins).

Plant height : As discussed earlier, plant height shows quasi-continuous variation, that is, this character is governed both by major genes and by minor genes. Therefore, this character will be discussed as a qualitative character as well as a quantitative character.

Aneuploid studies carried out in wheat (particularly the production of aneuploid monosomic series and intervarietal chromosome substitution lines and their comparisons with normal diploid plants and the recipient varieties, respectively) indicate that a large number of genes located on almost all the 21 chromosomes (except 5D and 7A chromosomes) govern plant height in wheat. In fact, almost all genes which are related to the growth, development and vigour of the plant have influence on plant height.

According to Law *et al.* (1978), plant height has a positive correlation with grain yield, that is, the genes causing reduction in plant height also generally cause reduction in grain yield. This is probably because that tall plants have longer ears than the dwarf plants. Pleiotropic effects of the same genes rather than linkage is the main cause of this positive correlation. However, this positive correlation between grain yield and plant height does not always hold true because of the following reasons :

1. Reduction in plant height helps in checking yield losses due to lodging; and
2. all dwarfing genes do not cause reduction in spike length.

For example, Norin 10 dwarfing genes Rht 1 and Rht 2 cause reduction in plant height by reducing stem internode lengths but have no adverse effect on spike length. The presence of these genes, therefore, helps in breaking the more-height-more-yield correlation, rather this correlation changes to less-height-more-yield correlation because of the reduction in yield losses due to lodging. However, tall-dwarf or semi-dwarf wheat varieties have given the best results (Gale and Law, 1977). The value of Norin 10 genes was reflected all over the world in 1960s when development of semi-dwarf wheat varieties resulted in phenomenal increase in wheat yields and played a significant role in green revolution.

Based on their reaction to exogenous gibberelic acid (GA), the Rht genes have been divided into two groups :

1. Genes insensitive to GA application; and
2. genes sensitive to GA application.

The symbol Rht has been used for all the alleles responsible for reduction in plant stature (relative to their rht alleles responsible for tallness). The capital letter has been used neither for dominance effect nor for increasing effect on plant height.

The Norin 10 genes, Rht 1, Rht 2, Rht 3 (extremely potent allele from Tom Thumb variety) and Rht 10 (from Ai-bian 1) and Saitama 27 gene (a gene found in Saitama 27 variety and is of less potency than Norin 10 genes), do not respond to GA application and thus fall under the first category mentioned above. The insensitivity of these genes to GA is due to the pleiotropic effect of the Rht genes and not due to linked genes Gai 1, Gai 2 and Gai 3. The genes Rht 1, Rht 3 and Saitama 27 are located on the short arm of the chromosome 4A, whereas the genes Rht 2 and Rht 10 are found on the short arm of the chromosome 4D.

If we look at the agronomic and physiological effects of the Norin 10 and Tom Thumb alleles, it seems that these alleles (semi-dwarf and dwarf, respectively) perform the function of restricting the active turnover of gibberellins in vegetative tissues. It has been found by Lenton et al. (1987) that the isogenic lines carrying Rht 1 and Rht 3 alleles show a proportionate increase in the levels of GA_1 and its precursor GA_{20} according to the stature-reducing effect of the two alleles. However, according to Lenton and Gale (1987), the presence of these alleles has no effect on the levels of GA_{56} (the prominant GA) in the developing grains. Also, the developing spikes and other developmental events (except reduced elongation growth in the stem) are uninfluenced by these alleles (Youssefian, 1986). Although the basis of these tissue specific effects of the GA-insensitive alleles is not yet precisely known, one important consequence of these effects is the increased availability of total assimilate to the growing ear (Brooking and Kirby, 1981). As a result, there is an increase in the number of grains per spike in plant materials grown under normal conditions followed by increased grain yield in semi-dwarf genotypes.

It is felt that the alleles Rht 3 and Rht 10 may be of greater use in the development of hybrid wheat varieties. According to Gale et al. (1987), the heterozygous combination Rht3/rht developed through the use of chemical hybridizing agent (CHA), has ideal plant height and shows higher magnitude of yield heterosis.

Adequate information is not available about the GA-sensitive Rht alleles. Only two alleles, Rht8 and Rht 9 are known to fall in this category. The allele Rht 8 is located on the chromosome 2DS, is closely linked with the photoperiod-insensitive allele Ppd 1, and causes 9% reduction in plant height and 5% reduction in grain yield. The allele Rht 9 is found on the chromosome 7BS.

Four more Rht alleles, Rht 4, Rht 5, Rht 7 and Rht 12, have been identified in hexaploid wheat. All the four are mutant alleles. The first three are recessive mutant alleles, whereas Rht 12 which is found on the chromosome 5A, is a dominant mutant allele. This allele came into existence due to X-ray treatment of the variety Karcag and is capable of causing 46% reduction in plant height. Among all the Rht alleles so far known in wheat, Rht 12 is the only dominant dwarfing allele.

Quantitative Characters

As mentioned earlier, quantitative characters show continuous variation and it is not possible to divide a segregating population into distinct phenotypic classes. Here, the mode of inheritance is not given on the basis of a genetic ratio, rather it is described in terms of *genetic architecture* of a character. Although quantitative inheritance, like qualitative inheritance, has a Mendelian basis, the approach to study quantitative variation is different from that used to study qualitative variation. The variation shown by a quantitative character is described in terms of statistical properties of the distribution of individuals and an appropriate scale is used for measuring the population. Unlike qualitative characters, quantitative characters are considerably influenced by environment. Therefore, it is necessary to know the relative contributions of genotype and environment towards a character and to assess the extent of genotype×environment (G×E) interaction. Further, it is equally important to partition the variation into different components and to know the relative contributions of additive effects, dominance effects, epistatic effects and linkage and relative influences of their interactions with environment (additive gene effects×environment, dominance gene effects×environment and epistatic gene effects × environment) at micro- and macro-environmental levels (See Singh and Pawar, 2005). Also, resemblance between relatives (measured in terms of heritability in broad sense as well as in narrow sense) provides additional information regarding phenotypic relationships between parents and their offspring. The relative contributions of fixable (additive and additive × additive) and unfixable (dominance, additive × dominance and dominance × dominance) components of genetic variation help the plant breeder in formulating and finalizing his breeding plans.

Although detailed information is available concerning the genetic control of a large number of qualitative characters in wheat, the most important characters of plant breeder's interest are the quantitative characters (especially grain yield and its component traits). In case of quantitative characters, the summed effect of all the genes controlling a character is studied on the basis of means (first degree statistics) or variances and covariances (second degree statistics). Therefore, two types of procedures, *methods based on first degree statistics* and *methods based on second degree statistics*, are used to study genetic architecture of populations. These two types of methods have their own advantages and disadvantages. The methods based on first degree statistics are easy and allow clearcut partitioning of various components of mean. But, these methods have the greatest disadvantage of the cancelling effect of genes. On the other hand, the analyses used in case of methods based on second degree statistics are generally cumbersome and, in several cases, do not provide a clearcut partitioning of variance or covariance. But, these methods are independent of the cancelling effect of genes.

The investigator should also have a clear idea about the method to be used (diallel, line × tester, triple test cross, etc. or any method based on first degree statistics) and the model to be followed that is, whether a fixed effects model (genotypes and block effects are both constants), a random effects model (genotype and block effects are both random varieables), or a mixed effects model (genotype effects are random but block effects are constants or genotype effects are constants and block effects are random variables) is to be used. The plant material should be prepared according to the method to be used and not *vice versa*. The test of significance of various items of analysis, information obtained and the genetic interpretation of results would vary according to the method and model used by the investigator.

Although it is not possible to determine exact locations of all the genes controlling a complex quantitative character, the production of aneuploid series in hexaploid wheat (production of full monosomic and nullisomic series by Sears *et al* in 1954 and later on production of full trisomic and tetrasomic series) has helped in detecting loci on the chromosomes which influence some quantitative characters. The production of complete telocentric series by Sears *et al.* (1973) has helped in identifying the specific arm (long or short arm) of the chromosome on which the genes influencing a quantitative trait are located. According to Mc Intosh (1973), the arms of the chromosomes possessing arms nearly of the same length, may be designated as α (on which the first locus was found) and β.

The genetic information about some quantitative characters of wheat is given below :

Grain yield : This character is the most important property of a variety and is influenced by some of its component traits like number of productive spikes per plant, grain weight, number of grains per spike and plant density (number of productive plants per unit area). Many plant breeders advocate that improvement in grain yield can be attained more easily by making selection for its component characters rather than making selection directly for this complex character.

The genes influencing grain yield are found on all the 21 chromosomes except the chromosomes 1A, 7A, 2B, 2D and 4D (Ausemus *et al.*, 1967). However, some geneticists feel that there are no separate genes for grain yield but the genes influencing component characters of yield also affect this complex character.

Grain weight : The genes governing grain weight are located on all the chromosomes except chromosomes 4A, 7A, 2B, 3D, 4D and 6D (Lelley, 1976).

Grains per spike : The chromosomes 5A, 1B, 6B, 7B and 7D contain genes for number of grains per spike (Lelley, 1976).

Spike length : The genes influencing spike length are found on all the chromosomes except 5A, 1B and 6D chromosomes (Ausemus *et al.*, 1967).

Spikelets per spike : Seven chromosomes (4A, 6A, 7A, 1B, 4B, 2D and 3D) contain genes for this character (Lelley, 1976).

Tillering ability and spikes per plant : According to Lelley (1976), the genes influencing tillering are found on the chromosomes 1B, 7B and 6D, whereas only two chromosomes (3A and 2B) contain genes for spike number. However, according to Ausemus *et al.* (1967), the genes influencing tillering in wheat are located on the chromosomes 2A, 4A, 6A, 1B, 2B, 4B, 1D, 2D, 3D, 4D and 5D,

Maturity period : The genes controlling maturity period in wheat are found on all the 21 chromosomes (Ausemus *et al.*, 1967; Lelley, 1976).

Protein content : According to Lelley (1976), the genes influencing protein content are located on all the chromosomes except the chromosomes 2D and 4D.

Plant height : The genes governing plant height are found on all the chromosomes except 7A and 5D (Ausemus et al., 1967). However, according to Lelley (1976), all the chromosomes except the four chromosomes (6B, 1D, 6D and 7D) contain genes for culm length in wheat.

Nevertheless, huge literature is available on the genetic architecture of wheat populations studied through the use of biometrical genetic procedures. Therefore, it is not possible to give all the references available on this aspect. Different situations regarding the relative contributions of various components of phenotypic variation have been observed. These relative contributions generally change not only for different characters but may also change from material to material for the same character. A summary of different situations for some important wheat characters is presented in Table 2.2. It can be seen from this table that the same reference is given for different situations of the same character. It is because of the fact that different crosses sometimes presented different situations. For example, Singh and Singh (1976) observed that additive component was relatively more important than dominance component for grain yield in the cross Kalyansona × Norteno 67, but the cross Norteno 67 × WL 212 presented a reverse condition for the same character. However, Singh and Pawar (1998) concluded that the use of triple test cross analysis in wheat populations leads to some important generalizations regarding the relative importance of different components of genetic variation and relative sensitivity of these components to environment. These generalizations are : (1) Additive gene effects are more important than dominance gene effects in governing quantitative characters; (2) dominance gene effects are less sensitive to environment change than additive gene effects; and (3) epistatic gene effets, in general, play an important role in the control of grain yield.

Table 2.2. Genetic architecture of wheat populations studied by different investigators for ten characters

Character	Condition	Author(s)
Total biomass	Additive component more important	Srivastava et al. (1981, 1992); Singh et al. (1986, 1988, 1989, 1992); Sarmah and Pawar (2000); Singh and Pawar (2000)
	Dominance component more important	Sharma and Singh (1982); Singh et al. (1984, 1986); Srivastava et al. (1992)
	Both components equally important	Yadav and Singh (1988)
	Epistasis present	Singh et al. (1985, 1986, 1988, 1989, 1992); ; Sarmah et al. (1997); Dhiman et al. (1999); Pawar et al. (1999); Sarmah and Pawar (2000); Singh and Pawar (2000)

Contd.

Character	Condition	Author(s)
	Fixable epistasis more important	Sarmah *et al.* (1997); Dhiman *et al.* (1999); Sarmah and Pawar (2000)
	Unfixable epistasis more important	Singh *et al.* (1986); Singh *et al.* (1988); Singh *et al.* (1989)
	Additive component more sensitive to environment	Singh *et al.* (1986, 1989, 1992); Sarmah *et al.* (1997); Singh and Pawar (2000)
	Fixable epistasis mor sensitive to environment	Singh *et al.* (1986)
	Unfixable epistasis more sensitive to environment	Singh *et al.* (1989); Sarmah *et al.* (1997)
Grain yield	Additive component more important	Singh and Singh (1976, 1978); Singh (1979, 1980, 1981, 1990); Singh and Dahiya (1984); Singh *et al.* (1985, 1986, 1988, 1989, 1995); Pawar *et al.* (1988a, 1994); Nanda and Singh (1989); Nanda *et al.* (1990); Singh *et al.* (1992); Srivastava *et al.* (1992); Sarmah and Pawar (2000); Yadav and Behl (2002)
	Dominance component more important	Singh and Singh (1976, 1978); Singh (1979, 1980, 1981, 1990); Sharma and Ahmad (1980); Nanda *et al.* (1983); Verma and Yunus (1986); Dasgupta and Mondal (1988); Pawar *et al.* (1988b); Singh and Singh 1992); Amawate and Behl (1995); Singh *et al.* (1995); Shekhawat *et al.* (2000); Dhayal *et al.* (2003); Prakash and Joshi (2003)
	Both components equally important	Singh and Dahiya (1984); Singh *et al.* (1984); Acharya and Singh (1986); Yadav and Singh (1988)
	Epistasis present	Singh and Singh (1976, 1978); Singh (1981, 1990); Singh and Dahiya (1984); Singh *et al.* (1985); Nanda and Singh (1989); Nanda *et al.* (1990); Singh *et al.* (1992);

Contd.

Character	Condition	Author(s)
		Srivastava et al. (1992); Pawar et al. (1994); Sarmah et al. (1997); Dhiman et al. (1999); Sarmah and Pawar (2000)
	Fixable epistasis more important	Singh and Singh (1976); Singh (1980); Singh and Dahiya (1984); Singh et al. (1986); Nanda et al. (1990); Pawar et al. (1994, 1996); Sarmah et al. (1997)
	Unfixable epistasis more important	Singh et al. (1988, 1989, 1995); Dhiman et al. (1999); Sarmah and Pawar (2000); Shekhawat et al. (2000)
	Both epistases equally important	Singh et al. (1995)
	Epistasis absent	Singh and Singh (1978); Singh (1990); Pawar et al. (1994); Amawate and Behl (1995); Singh et al. (1995)
	Additive component more sensitive to environment	Singh (1980, 1990); Singh and Dahiya (1984); Dhindsa and Bains (1986); Singh et al. (1989); Singh et al. (1992); Sarmah et al. (1997)
	Dominance component more sensitive to environment	Singh et al. (1995)
	Both components equally sensitive to environment	Singh et al. (1986)
	Fixable epistasis more sensitive to environment	Singh (1980); Singh and Dahiya (1984); Singh et al. (1986, 1989)
	Unfixable epistasis more sensitive to environment	Singh and Dahiya (1984); Singh et al. (1995)
Grain weight	Additive component more important	Singh and Singh (1978); Singh and Dahiya (1984); Singh et al. (1985, 1986, 1988, 1989, 1995); Pawar et al.

Contd.

Character	Condition	Author (s)
		(1988a, b); Nanda and Singh (1989); Singh (1990); Singh *et al.* (1992); Pawar *et al.* (1994); Amawate and Behl (1995); Sarmah and Pawar (2000); Yadav and Behl (2002)
	Dominance component more important	Singh and Singh (1978); Sharma and Ahmad (1980); Singh (1980, 1990); Singh *et al.* (1982); Singh and Dahiya (1984); Walia *et al.* (1994)
	Both components equally important	Singh (1981); Singh *et al.* (1984); Acharya and Singh (1986); Singh *et al.* (1995)
	Epistasis present	Singh and Singh (1978); Singh (1981, 1990); Singh *et al.* (1985); Singh *et al.* (1992); Pawar *et al.* (1994); Singh *et al.* (1995); Sarmah *et al.* (1997); Dhiman *et al.* (1999); Singh and Pawar (2000)
	Fixable epistasis more important	Singh (1980); Singh and Dahiya (1984); Pawar *et al.* (1994)
	Unfixable epistasis more important	Singh *et al.* (1986, 1988, 1989, 1991, 1995); Sarmah *et al.* (1997); Dhiman *et al.* (1999); Sarmah and Pawar (2000)
	Epistasis absent	Singh and Singh (1978); Singh *et al.* (1988); Singh (1990); Singh *et al.* (1991)
	Additive component more sensitive to environment	Singh (1980, 1990); Singh *et al.* (1989); Singh *et al.* (1992); Sarmah *et al.* (1997)
	Dominance component more sensitive to environment	Singh and Dahiya (1984); Singh *et al.* (1995)
	Both components equally sensitive to environment	Singh *et al.* (1986)

Contd.

Character	Condition	Author(s)
	Interaction of additive and dominance components with environment absent	Singh (1990)
	Fixable epistasis more sensitive to environment	Singh and Dahiya (1984)
	Unfixable epistasis more sensitive to environment	Singh *et al.* (1986, 1989, 1995); Pawar *et al.* (1994)
Grains per spike	Additive component more important	Singh and Singh (1976); Singh and Dahiya (1984); Singh *et al.* (1985, 1986, 1988); Pawar *et al.* (1988a); Nanda and Singh (1989); Nanda *et al.* (1990); Singh (1990); Singh *et al.* (1992); Srivastava *et al.* (1992); Pawar *et al.* (1994); Amawate and Behl (1995); Yadav and Behl (2002)
	Dominance component more important	Singh and Singh (1976); Sharma and Ahmad (1980); Nanda *et al.* (1983); Singh *et al.* (1995); Prakash and Joshi (2003)
	Both components equally important	Khurana *et al.* (1983); Singh and Dahiya (1984); Singh *et al.* (1984); Singh *et al.* (1989)
	Epistasis present	Singh (1990); Nanda *et al.* (1990); Singh *et al.* (1992); Sarmah *et al.* (1997); Dhiman *et al.* (1999); Sarmah and Pawar (2000)
	Fixable epistasis more important	Singh and Singh (1976); Singh and Dahiya (1984); Singh *et al.* (1986, 1988, 1995); Nanda *et al.* (1990); Sarmah *et al.* (1997); Dhiman *et al.* (1999)
	Unfixable epistasis more important	Singh and Singh (1976); Singh *et al.* (1988, 1989); Dhiman *et al.* (1999); Sarmah and Pawar (2000)
	Epistasis absent	Singh *et al.* (1985); Singh *et al.* (1991); Pawar *et al.* (1994); Amawate and Behl (1995); Singh *et al.* (1995)

Contd.

Character	Condition	Author(s)
	Additive component more sensitive to environment	Singh and Dahiya (1984); Singh et al. (1989); Singh (1990); Sarmah et al. (1997)
	Dominance component more sensitive to environment	Singh et al. (1986, 1995); Singh (1990); Singh et al. (1992)
	Fixable epistasis more sensitive to environment	Singh and Dahiya (1984); Singh et al. (1986); Sarmah et al. (1997)
	Unfixable epistasis more sensitive to environment	Singh and Dahiya (1984); Singh et al. (1989)
	Epistasis × environment interaction absent	Singh et al. (1995)
Spike length	Additive component more important	Singh and Singh (1976); Singh (1980, 1981); Khurana et al. (1983); Singh and Dahiya (1984); Singh et al. (1984); Dasgupta and Mondal (1988); Nanda et al. (1990); Singh et al. (1995)
	Dominance component more important	Walia et al. (1994); Amawate and Behl (1995)
	Both components equally important	Nanda et al. (1982); Acharya and Singh (1986)
	Epistasis present	Singh et al. (1995); Dhiman et al. (1999)
	Fixable epistasis more important	Singh and Singh (1976); Singh and Dahiya (1984); Dhiman et al. (1999).
	Unfixable epistasis more important	Singh and Singh (1976); Singh et al. (1995)
	Epistasis absent	Singh (1980, 1981); Amawate and Behl (1995)

Contd.

Character	Condition	Author(s)
	Additive component more sensitive to environment	Singh and Dahiya (1984); Singh *et al.* (1995)
	Dominance component more sensitive to environment	Singh and Dahiya (1984)
	Interaction of additive and dominance components with environment absent	Singh (1980)
	Fixable epistasis more sensitive to environment	Singh and Dahiya (1984)
	Unfixable epistasis more sensitive to environment	Singh and Dahiya (1984); Singh *et al.* (1995)
	Epistasis × environment interaction absent	Singh (1980)
Spikelets per spike	Additive component more important	Singh and Singh (1976, 1978); Singh (1979, 1980, 1981); Singh and Dahiya (1984); Dasgupta and Mondal (1988); Walia *et al.* (1994); Amawate and Behl (1995)
	Dominance component more important	Singh (1979)
	Both components equally important	Singh and Singh (1976); Singh (1979); Acharya and Singh (1986)
	Epistasis present	Singh and Singh (1978); Dhiman *et al.* (1999)
	Fixable epistasis more important	Singh and Dahiya (1984)
	Unfixable epistasis more important	Singh and Singh (1976)

Contd.

Character	Condition	Author(s)
	Epistasis absent	Singh and Singh (1978); Singh (1980, 1981)
	Additive component more sensitive to environment	Singh (1980)
	Dominance component more sensitive to environment	Singh and Dahiya (1984)
	Interaction of additive and dominance components with environment absent	Singh and Dahiya (1984)
	Fixable epistasis more sensitive to environment	Singh and Dahiya (1984)
	Epistasis × environment interaction absent	Singh (1980)
Tiller number	Additive component more important	Singh and Dahiya (1984); Singh *et al.* (1985, 1986, 1988, 1989, 1995); Nanda *et al.* (1990); Singh (1990); Pawar *et al.* (1994); Sarmah *et al.* (2000); Yadav and Behl (2002)
	Dominance component more important	Singh and Dahiya (1984); Singh *et al.* (1986); Verma and Yunus (1986); Dasgupta and Mondal (1988); Pawar *et al.* (1988a); Singh *et al.* (1992); Singh *et al.* (1995); Shekhawat *et al.* (2000)
	Both components equally important	Singh *et al.* (1984); Acharya and Singh (1986); Yadav and Singh (1988)
	Epistasis present	Singh *et al.* (1985); Singh (1990); Singh *et al.* (1992, 1995); Pawar *et al.* (1994); Sarmah and Pawar (2000); Singh and Pawar (2000); Sharma and Sain (2002)
	Fixable epistasis more important	Singh and Dahiya (1984); Pawar *et al.* (1994)

Contd.

Character	Condition	Author(s)
	Unfixable epistasis more important	Singh et al. (1986, 1988, 1989, 1995); Pawar et al. (1996); Shekhawat et al. (2000)
	Both epistases equally important	Sarmah et al. (1997)
	Epistasis absent	Singh (1990); Pawar et al. (1994); Dhiman et al. (1999)
	Additive component more sensitive to environment	Singh and Dahiya (1984); Singh et al. (1986); Singh (1990); Singh et al. (1992)
	Dominance component more sensitive to environment	Singh and Dahiya (1984); Singh et al. (1989, 1995); Singh (1990)
	Interaction of additive and dominance components with environment absent	Singh and Dahiya (1984); Singh (1990); Sarmah et al. (2000)
	Fixable epistasis more sensitive to environment	Singh and Dahiya (1984)
	Unfixable epistasis more sensitive to environment	Singh and Dahiya (1984); Singh et al. (1986, 1989, 1995)
Plant height	Additive component more important	Singh and Singh (1978); Singh 1979, 1980, 1981, 1990); Singh and Dahiya (1984); Singh et al. (1985, 1986, 1988, 1989, 1995); Singh et al. (1992); Pawar et al. (1994); Amawate and Behl (1995)
	Dominance component more important	Singh and Dahiya (1976); Sharma and Ahmad (1980); Nanda et al. (1982); Singh et al. (1982); Pawar et al. (1988a); Prakash and Joshi (2003)
	Both components equally important	Singh (1980); Singh and Dahiya (1984); Acharya and Singh (1986); Virk et al. (1989)

Contd.

Character	Condition	Author(s)
	Epistasis present	Singh and Singh (1978); Singh (1981, 1990); Singh et al. (1985); Singh et al. (1992), 1995); Singh and Pawar (2000)
	Fixable epistasis more important	Singh and Singh (1976); Singh (1980); Singh and Dahiya (1984); Singh et al. (1986, 1988, 1989); Pawar et al. (1994)
	Unfixable epistasis more important	Singh and Singh (1976); Singh et al. (1995)
	Epistasis absent	Singh and Singh (1978); Singh (1980, 1981, 1990); Nanda et al. (1982)
	Additive component more sensitive to environment	Singh (1980, 1990); Singh and Dahiya (1984); Singh et al. (1989); Singh et al. (1992)
	Dominance component more sensitive to environment	Singh et al. (1986, 1995)
	Both components equally sensitive	Singh and Dahiya (1984)
	Interaction of additive and dominance components with environment absent	Singh and Dahiya (1984)
	Fixable epistasis more sensitive to environment	Singh (1980); Singh and Dahiya (1984); Singh et al. (1986, 1995)
	Unfixable epistasis more sensitive to environment	Singh and Dahiya (1984); Singh et al. (1989)
	Both epistases equally sensitive to environment	Singh and Dahiya (1984)

Contd.

Character	Condition	Author(s)
Days to heading	Additive component more important	Joarder *et al.* (1982); Singh and Dahiya (1984); Singh *et al.* (1984, 1986, 1988, 1989); Dhindsa and Bains (1986); Yadav and Singh (1988); Pawar *et al.* (1988a, 1994); Singh *et al.* (1995); Singh and Pawar (2000); Yadav and Behl (2002)
	Dominance component more important	Sharma and Ahmad (1980); Singh *et al.* (1992); Prakash and Joshi (2003), Parkash (2005)
	Both components equally important	Khurana *et al.* (1983); Virk *et al.* (1989); Singh *et al.* (1995)
	Epistasis present	Singh and Dahiya (1984); Singh *et al.* (1985, 1986, 1988, 1989, 1995); Singh *et al.* (1992); Pawar *et al.* (1994), Pawar *et al.* (1996)
	Fixable epistasis more important	Singh and Dahiya (1984); Singh *et al.* (1988, 1995); Pawar *et al.* (1996)
	Unfixable epistasis more important	Singh *et al.* (1986, 1989)
	Epistasis absent	Pawar *et al.* (1994)
	Additive component more sensitive to environment	Singh and Dahiya (1984); Singh *et al.* (1986, 1989); Pawar *et al.* (1996); Singh and Pawar (2000)
	Dominance component more sensitive to environment	Singh *et al.* (1992); Singh *et al.* (1995)
	Fixable epistasis more sensitive to environment	Pawar *et al.* (1996); Singh and Pawar (2000)
	Unfixable epistasis more sensitive to environment	Singh and Dahiya (1984); Singh *et al.* (1989); Singh *et al.* (1995)

Contd.

Character	Condition	Author(s)
Harvest index	Additive component more important	Nanda *et al.* (1982, 1990); Singh and Dahiya (1984); Yadav and Singh (1988); Nanda and Singh (1989); Srivastava *et al.* (1992); Yadav and Behl (2002)
	Dominance component more important	Singh *et al.* (1984, 1986);
	Both components equally important	Gill *et al.* (1980)
	Epistasis present	Singh and Dahiya (1984); Nanda *et al.* (1990)
	Fixable epistasis more important	Singh and Dahiya (1984); Nanda *et al.* (1990)
	Epistasis absent	Nanda *et al.* (1982)
	Additive component more sensitive to environment	Singh and Dahiya (1984)
	Fixable epistasis more sensitive to environment	Singh and Dahiya (1984)

CHAPTER 3

Breeding Objectives

There are three major objectives in wheat breeding : (1) *Increasing yield potential*; (2) *stabilizing yield levels* through minimization of losses caused by biotic and abiotic stresses; and (3) *improving product quality*.

Increasing Yield Potential

Like in other important cereal crops, yield potential is a primary factor among the objectives of wheat breeding. Since the amount of product harvested is affected by yield potential, this character is the most important property of a variety. Further, yield potential is a very complex quantitative character and is dependent upon its component characters like *grain weight*, number of *grains per spike*, number of *productive spikes per plant* and number of *productive plants per unit area*. Each component character shows positive correlation with yield potential, but the association between different component characters is not always positive. Some component characsters show a negative correlation between them. For example, if the breeder tries to increase grain weight, there is a reduction in the number of grains per spike, that is, if the breeder wants to increase the value of one character, the value of other character is automatically reduced.

Because of its complex nature, yield potential has a low narrow sense heritability and, therefore, it is difficult to achieve considerable improvement in this character by using simple selection procedures. Some breeders feel that efforts should be made to improve yield potential by improving its component characters rather than using selection procedures directly for the improvement in yield. But, a negative correlation between some component characters creates difficulty in such approach. However, this problem can be overcome, at least to some extent, by making improvement in one component character while keeping the value of the other character almost constant. This approach has been followed in India and other countries and a considerable progress has been achieved in some cases. Not only a negative correlation but also a positive association between some characters may creat problem in improving yield potential in wheat. For example, a positive correlation between plant height and spike length is not in the favour of wheat breeders as the tall wheats are susceptible to lodging. However, this association has been broken in some cases and some semi-dwarf wheat varieties have long ears like those of tall wheats. Furthermore, the ultimate aim of wheat breeder is to harvest more yield per unit area and not more yield per plant. Therefore, number of productive plants per unit area or number of productive spikes per unit area is more important than single plant yield.

One point which signifies the importance of component characters of yield is the high *heritability* of some of these characters as compared to that of yield itself. As we know heritability is a measure of the heritable part of the phenotypic variation and helps in choosing the selection procedure for better improvement. Higher is the heritability of a character, more are the chances of improving that character through simple selection procedures. The level of heritability for grain yield in wheat is low and is around 15 per cent (Weibel, 1958), 24% (Fida *et al.*, 2001), 22% (Omara *et al.*, 2004). The heritability for productive tillering (number of productive ears per plant) is still low. According to Karain (1958), Pollmer (1957), Weibel (1958) and Pawar *et al.* (1989) the heritability of this component character was 4.6%, 5.3%, 7%, and 31.6%, respectively. The reason of low heritability of productive tillering is the predominant role played by ecological effects in the control of this character. On the contrary, the heritability of grains per spike is 24 per cent (Pollmer, 1957), 30.3 per cent (Karain, 1958) and 35.4 per cent (Weibel, 1958) and thus the degree of heritability ranges from 24-35.4 per cent. This indicates that the character grains per spike is more important than productive tillering for achieving improvement through selection. However, the component character 1000-grain weight shows maximum heritability among the components characters of grain yield in wheat. According to Póllmer (1957), Karain (1958) and Fida *et al.* (2001), the heritability of this character is 52 per cent 81.7 and 74 per cent, respectively. Further studies on heritability in wheat by Sharma and Knott (1964), Reddi *et al.* (1969), Khadr (1971), Rachinski (1971) and Sun *et al.* (1972) indicated that heritability for grain weight ranged from 45-85 per cent. Therefore, 1000-grain weight is the most reliable component character for breeding work. Thousand-grain weight has two additional advantages : (1) The selection for this character is easy as the determination of the character is easy and quick; and (2) large embryos contained by larger grains have a positive correlation with plant density (productive plants per unit area).

However, on the basis of cultivation criterion the character number of productive ears per plant (productive tillering) is more important than the number of grains per spike and 1000-grain weight (Sikka and Maini, 1962; Mijo, 1962; Prikryl, 1962). This view was also supported by Damisch (1970). Therefore, in the growing practice, the relative importance of the component characters is reversed.

It is clear from the above discussion that the genetic stabilization of yield potential is affected by the different component characters differently and, therefore, coordinated and proportionate improvement of yield components is necessary for exercising genetic influence on the yield potential (Grafius, 1964; Johnson *et al.*, 1966; Langer, 1967; Jha and Ram, 1968; and others).

In addition to the component characters of yield mentioned earlier, some other characters are also related to yield potential. Lupton and Pinthus (1969) have emphasized the role of *sterile tillers* in increasing yield potential. The assimilates of these tillers are transferred to productive tillers through remobilization and thus increasing the nutrient supply of the latter. However, the extent to which the sterile tillers influence the yield potential is not sufficiently known. The *leaves* constitute the major part of foliage and thus are an important site of assimilation influencing yield potential. Although the number, size, and shape of leaves and the position of leaf blades all form important criteria for selection, the role of leaf mainly depends on its place (lower or upper leaf) on the plant. The positive correlation between leaf surface area and dry matter accumulation indicates a physiological relationship between leaf surface area and yield potential in wheat. It is an established fact that the *flag leaf* plays an important role in influencing yield in wheat. The share of flag leaf, its sheath and upper part of the stem in determining grain weight in wheat is 75 per cent, whereas the share of the spike is only 25 per cent (Lupton, 1966b,c). However, the extent of role played by flag leaf in influencing yield potential depends on the size, shape, position of leaf blade and the lifetime of the flag leaf (Simpson, 1968; Hsu and Walton, 1971; and others). An errect flag leaf generally plays a greater role (especially in a thick stand) than a horizontal or droopy flag leaf. The role of *spike* in determining yield potential is undeniable since spike is an important organ of wheat plant which has a role in the assimilation and respiration. However, the morphological characters on which selection should be based have not yet been identified, nor the importance of awns in determining yield potential could be decisively known.

Not only the above ground parts of wheat plant are important in determining yield potential, but the underground parts also contribute towards yielding ability. According to Troughton (1962), Dobrinin (1969), Whittington (1970) and others, *root system* plays a decisive role in determining yield potential in wheat. The parameters of both the *seminal roots* and *adventitious roots* should be compared and used as a method of selection for increasing yield. However, the direct relation of root system with 1000-grain weight and grains per ear could not be proved so far. Unfortunately, the genes determining the properties of root system have not been studied in detail and the effect of the loss of any chromosome(s) on root characteristics could not be ascertained so far.

Although, sometimes, the quantity and quality of wheat straw is important for the farmers, the term yield potential is mostly defined as the ability of the wheat plant to synthesize (manufacture), translocate the manufactured food materials from the source to the sink, and store these food materials in the sink (wheat grain). The grain yield potential, therefore, depends on three physiological processes (1) The availability of solar energy and its conversion into chemical energy by the photosynthetic apparatus of the plant; (2) the efficiency of the translocating tissues; and (3) the capacity of the sink. A well-balanced *sink-source relationship* may be a great help to the wheat breeders. Each of three physiological processes mentioned above is complex and is affected by three factors : (1) The plant genotype; (2) the environment in which the genotype has been grown; and (3) the interaction between genotype and environment. It is not practically possible to measure the expression of the three physiological process separately, rather a combined effect of all the three processes is measured in terms of grain yield. For achieving improvement in yield potential, crosses are made between desirable parents and transgressive segregants for more yield are selected in the segregating generations of crosses. However, this approach has no physiological basis.

Till date, there is no method available to precisely know the *optimum ecological requirements* neither the *maximum hereditary yielding ability* of any variety since the yield potential has a complex dependence on genetic, ecological and pathological factors. Nevertheless, the development of high yielding, photo-insensitive, fertilizer responsive, disease resistant and physiologically more efficient semi-dwarf wheat varieties has made a significant contribution towards *green revolution*. This could be possible because of the use of dwarfing genes in wheat. The large scale exploitation of these genes took about 50 years from the beginning of the development of semi-dwarf wheat varieties in the early years of twentieth century in Japan and Korea to their introduction into Mexico (the international breeding programme of CIMMYT) in 1953. Before their introduction into Mexico, these semi-dwarf wheats were introduced into Italy and United States of America in the years 1911 and 1946, respectively. However, to achieve further heights in wheat yield potential, some new approach has to be used as the effect of dwarfing genes is now levelling off.

As discussed earlier, high single plant yield may not be an important criterion for harvesting high grain yield per unit area, but plants having low yields and poor competitive ability may give the most productive crop. This signifies the importance of the concept of *ideotype* given by Donald (1968). The development of an improved plant type and its use in the evolution of a new variety help in explaining the scientific basis of the superiority of the new variety.

The results of many studies have shown that the level of yield heterosis in wheat is low. The reasons of this low heterosis in wheat are :

1. Presence of homozygous genomic heterosis due to the homeologous nature of the chromosomes of the three genomes (A, B and D);
2. predominance of additive and additive × additive variation for important component characters of yield;
3. widespread absence of unfixable epistasis (additive × dominance and dominance × dominance interactions) and overdominance for component characters;
4. the major cause of heterosis in wheat is the dispersion of favourable dominant alleles in the parents used in hybridization programmes.

Therefore, the scope of improvement in yield potential in wheat through the exploitation of heterosis in the old germplasm appears to be limited. Perhaps spring × winter wheat crosses may help the wheat breeders in overcoming this problem.

As discussed in Chapter 2, the genes influencing yield potential in wheat are found on almost all the 21 chromosomes. But, so far, the action mechanism of these genes is not clearly known. However, the results of gene mapping and several other studies clearly indicate that there is exceedingly high possibility of recombination and transgression may also occur in case of individual component characters as well as in case of yield potential itself. Transgression has played an important role in the development of several outstanding wheat varieties.

The introgression of individual alien genes or group of genes into wheat provides new opportunities for breaking yield barriers in wheat. Now, with the availability of sophisticated biotechnology techniques, genes can be transferred from any organism to any other organism and *transgenic* plants can be produced. The breeding techniques like mutation breeding and haploidy breeding may also be used in some cases to incease or stabilize the yield potential in wheat.

For increasing yield potential in wheat, the breeder should have a clear understanding of the following :

1. The breeder should be able to identify the most effective way of increasing yield potential, that is, whether he should go for selection empirically for yield itself or should use a more challenging and intellectually satisfying approach by identifying the physiological processes limiting grain yield potential. Perhaps it will be more appropriate to use the above mentioned approaches at different stages of the breeding programme. The use of physiological criteria in the early stages of the breeding programme might permit more discriminating selection. On the other hand, selection empirically for yield itself is likely to be most effective at the later stages of the breeding programme when selection for yield potential is done on plot yield basis.

2. The breeder should have the knowledge about the most important characters contributing towards yield potential and the stage of the breeding programme at which these component characters should be considered. It can be said on the basis of long experience of wheat breeders that 1000-grain weight, number of grains per spike and productive tillering are the most important components characters of yield potential in wheat and these characters should be considered at the time of the selection of parents for hybridization since the assessment and composition of these characters are easier and, based on heritability estimates, selection may be started at the earliest stage of the breeding programme.

3. The breeder should know the extent and the type of correlation among different component characters of yield. Unfortunately, the three most important component characters mentioned in point (2) are inversely correlated and, therefore, a co-ordinated and proportionate approach is necessary for improving these characters rather than improving them individually.

4. The breeder should be able to decide about the relative values of single plant yield and collective yield based on yield potential per unit area. The relative contributions of component characsters may be different in these two kinds of criteria. If the ideotype concept of Donald is accepted then individual plant yield becomes less important.

5. The breeder should know the importance of *early testing*. Many breeders feel that testing of the plant material at an early stage of the breeding programme may help in cutting short the time period of the programme. The use of an appropriate biometrical genetic procedure which can precisely estimate general combining ability of parents and the specific combining ability of hybrids, may greatly help the breeder in this respect.

Stabilizing Yield Levels

Yield stability means the ability of a plant genotype to give uniformly high yield over a wide range of environmental conditions, that is, a plant genotype showing broad adaptation. Several factors (maturity, diseases and insect pests, drought, lodging, soil factors, etc.) affect the stability of a plant genotype. A genotype showing optimum maturity and possessing resistance to diseases and insect pests, drought, lodging and adverse soil factors, is expected to express its yield potential over a wide range of environments. Therefore, for evaluating the yield stability of genotypes, they are grown on different sites (representing different environments) over several years or seasons and the genotypes showing high yield potential and least genotype × environment interaction are selected. Several biometrical genetic procedures (simple analysis of variance, regression approach and multivariate approach) are available to test and measure the yield stability of genotypes (For details, see Singh and Pawar, 2005). A variety should be released only after its testing for yield stability under varying environmental conditions,

Nevertheless, to capitalize maximum advantage from plant genotypes, two types of genotypes—those which perform best over all environments and those which perform best under specific environments—are identified. The first type of genotypes are recommended for release for cultivation in the whole country and the second type of genotypes are recommended for specific regions of the country. This type of approach is now not restrsicted to a particular country but such testing of genotypes is being done at international level. CIMMYT is following a *shuttle breeding* programme for this purpose where the material at some specific stages is grown in rich environment and at some other stages in poor environment.

Yield stability is very important in a country like India where wheat crop is grown under extremely diverse soil and climatic conditions ranging from plains to high altitude hills, rainfed to irrigated areas, low to high fertility conditions, mild to severe winters, light to heavy and deep to shallow soils, short (3.5 to 4 months) to lengthy (5 to 7 months) crop seasons, etc. The country has been divided into different wheat zones. Since it is very difficult for a genotype to perform uniformly under such a great diversity of conditions, the zonal performance of genotypes is also given due weightage.

A brief description of the factors affecting yield stability is given hereafter.

Maturity period : Although, manytimes, it is difficult to prove correlation between maturity period of a wheat variety and its yield potential, we cannot expect high yields from extremely early maturing varieties. In fact, many important economic properties of varieties are largely affected by the length of the vegetative period. According to Kis (1963) and Keim *et al.* (1973), earliness is generally dominant over late maturity and transgressive segregants for earliness have also been observed in some cases.

Early maturity of wheat varieties protects them from various types of losses caused by diseases and adverse climatic factors like heat and drought and facilitates desired crop rotation. However, early maturity has some disadvantages too as very early maturing varieties are generally low yielding because of poor tillering, poor blooming and poor storage of nutrients in the grain due to shorter growth period. But, extra-ordinary performance of some early maturing Mexican spring wheat varieties in terms of yield potential indicates that late maturity is not necessarily correlated with high yielding ability, that is, a long vegetative period is not a precondition for high yield potential. However, a too much decrease in maturity period may cause a considerable reduction in hereditary yielding ability.

According to Borlaug (1968), the cultivation of day-length insensitive varieties of spring wheats has considerably promoted the geographical adaptation of these wheats. However, such insensitivity may become dangerous in case of winter wheat.

Drought tolerance : The primitive forms of the genus *Triticum* possessed enough tolerance to drought probably because the evolution of this genus took place under arid conditions. But, after domestication of common wheat and development of high yielding varieties of this cereal, we cannot expect a similar water requirement by the new wheat varieties. In fact, two preconditions for harvesting high wheat yields are : (1)The required amount of moisture; and (2) a balanced nutrient supply. Of course, durum wheats possess a high degree of resistance to drought and this is the reason why these wheats are principally grown in dry areas of Middle East and North Africa.

Insufficient availability of water to plant or drought causes a decrease in the water content of cytoplasm and increase in the concentration of cell-sap until it becomes toxic followed by a permanent change in mitochondria and chloroplasts and ultimately the cell dies (Santarius and Heber, 1972). Nevertheless, death of cells is an extreme situation which may occur only rarely when drought continues for a long period of time. Under medium drought conditions, only the metabolism of the plant is adversely affected followed by a reduction in grain weight, grains per spike and the number of spikes per plant.

The consequence of drought can be measured by calculating the values of *drought-tolerance coefficient* (difference in yield between plants having an optimum availability of water and those facing a drought condition) for different varieties at different phases of plant development. However, Chinoy (1962) though could understand the effect of drought in a better way, but his trials did not indicate varietal differences due to drought, neither these trials could prove genetic relations of drought.

But, the studies carried out by Lelley (1964) in large culture pots for determining interrelations of drought, development phase of the plant, changes of yield components and cultivars, decisively proved a genetic basis for drought tolerance as different cultivars gave different responses to the same type of drought. Grebner (1964) performed *transpiration coefficient* tests and noted a reduced hereditary resistance to drought in some wheat varieties as these varieties showed increased water consumption during drought period. Several other investigators pointed out varietal differences for drought tolerance (Milica and Juncu, 1968; Kaul, 1969; Jakubziner, 1970; Vlasyuk *et al.*, 1970; Kozhusko and Volkova, 1971). According to Jakubziner, the hexaploid group, among all spring wheats of the world showed highest tolerance to drought. All these studies proved beyond doubt that drought tolerance is a genetically established hereditary property of wheat genotypes. However, these investigators could not identify physiological or morphological parameters to assess drought tolerance.

A number of investigators came to a general conclusion that wheat plant responds to drought differently at different phases of its development. According to Farsky (1961), the most sensitive stage of the wheat plant to the adverse effect of drought is the appearance of the third leaf, whereas Joffe and Small (1964) noted a considerable reduction in yield due to drought at the time of tillering and heading. Milica and Juncu (1968) also found that the most sensitive stage of the plant to drought effect was the beginning of shooting. According to El Nadi (1969), flowering time and seed setting are the most sensitive stages to drought effect. However, it appears that the beginning of heading is the most critical phase of wheat plant for drought effect. According to Vlasyuk *et al.* (1971), a self-controlled protective mechanism operates in drought tolerant varieties to reduce the adverse effects of drought.

The adverse effect of drought on various characteristics of wheat plant would depend on the stage of development at which the drought has the most drastic effect. If the drought effect occurs at the time of tillering, it may reduce the size of the spike, whereas the occurrence of drought during spike differentiation may cause sterility in basal or apical spikelets. Similarly, the occurrence of drought during flowering time and after fertilization generally causes reduction in the number of grains per spike and in 1000-grain weight, respectively.

Till date, no relationship between reactions to drought in different phases of plant development and the genotype could be established. However, it appears that due to some mosphological and physiological changes in the plant, there is a gradual development of a protective mechanism against drought. But, these changes have no correlation with varietal differences. As a result, no reliable explanation is available on the basis of morphological, physical or biochemical properties of genotypes. Of course, during reactions to drought, the plants undergo a process of *hardening* which may be different in the different phases of development. The hardening of plants for drought in wheat has been found related to the acceleration of root growth (Shu-Wen and Tsing-Tsi, 1964; Belyakov, 1968), increase in chlorophyll content, higher capacity of drymatter accumulation of plants, increase in protein content (Tyamkova, 1966) and accumulation of free amino acids (alanin, asparagin, glutamic acid and prolin) in the leaf, stem and ear (Protsenko *et al.*, 1968). The relation of increased osmotic pressure with drought tolerance observed by Ilyin (1929), could not be confirmed. Smaller cell size of leaves has been found directly correlated with drought tolerance (Levitt, 1956). However, cell size cannot be used as a selection criterion in plant breeding programmes. According to Uglou and Volkova (1970), the occurrence of drought causes contraction of openings on the plasma membrane which brings about changes in the permeability of the protoplasm and ultimately there is a gradual increase in the water retention capacity of cells.

Unfortunately, the plant characteristics (smaller cells, narrower leaves, thinner stems and light green colour of foliage) which are generally found correlated with drought tolerance, may show a negative correlation with productivity. Of course, earliness is a worth considering quality of a genotype.

Drought resistance, like grain yield, is a polygenically controlled complex character and thus improvement in this character is not easy. Of course, identification of transgressive segregants and their use in breeding programmes may help the wheat breeders to some extent.

Lodging resistance : The bending or breaking-over of the wheat culm due to some climatic factors (excess of rain and strong wind), diseases or insect pests, is called as lodging. Excess of precipitation and fast wind are the major factors causing lodging in wheat. Depending upon the stage at which the lodging occurs and its duration, the grain losses in wheat generally range between 9.9-31.0 per cent. The adverse effects of lodging are as follows :

1. Lodging creates a favourable environment for the development of diseases.
2. It causes a reduction in the quantity of the photosynthate produced because of shading.
3. Causes obstruction in the translocation of photosynthate.
4. Causes reduction in the number of grains per spike due to poor seed-setting.
5. Causes reduction in 1000-grain weight as a result of reduced filling of the endosperm.
6. It causes difficulty in the mechanical harvesting of the crop.
7. Despite somewhat increase in protein and wet gluten content, lodging causes deterioration in milling and baking qualities and a decrease in flour production.

Depending upon the length and stiffness of wheat culm, the stalk may bend irreversibly at the lower internodes or the plant may fall down due to loosened adventitious roots without bending of the stalk. The long and flexible wheat culms bend more easily than short and stiff culms. Therefore, the first type of lodging (bending of stalk at lower internodes) occurs in tall wheats with flexible stalk, whereas the second type of lodging (plant falling without bending of culm) takes place in dwarf wheats with stiff stalk. However, the major causes of both types of lodging are excessive rain and the pressure of wind. In fact, precipitation causes increase in shoot weight (increase in the weight of stalk, leaf and spike) and ultimately the plant becomes imbalanced.

In addition to the stiffness and flexibility of the culm and the size and toughness of the roots which play an important role in lodging, some other characteristics of wheat plant like tillering intensity, length of culm at flowering time, flag leaf length-width index, number and spread of adventitious roots, and relative length of the lower internode, have also been found correlated with development of this property. The presence of thick-walled cells of mechanical tissue between phloem and metaxylem and more number of vascular bundles are also found correlated with lodging resistance. However, thickness of the culm and the diameter of internodes cannot be considered as reliable parameters to measure lodging resistance.

Although the hereditary nature of lodging resistance is undeniable since substantial differences in the level of lodging resistance are found in wheat varieties having same height and phenotypic appearance, the property is also influenced by environmental conditions. Gulkayan *et al.* (1971) concluded that lodging resistance is a complex quantitative character and it not only depends on several complex morphological, anatomical and physiological properties of wheat plant, but environmental factors also play a role in the gradual development of this property. The character, however, can be improved by interspecific hybridization followed by selection of transgressive segregants and through mutation breeding. The main objective in developing lodging resistance wheat varieties is to reduce the length of culm. For this, the use of Rht dwarfing genes has played an important role.

Cold hardiness : A certain range of temperature during different stages of plant development is indispensable to realize the hereditary yield potential of a wheat cultivar. Exceptionally low temperatures can cause serious injury to wheat plant either through freezing of plant tissues or may cause death of the plant, that is, unrecoverable injury. Such temperatures exert a hereditarily determined adverse influence on the development of various components of yield. Resistance to extremely low temperatures is referred to as *cold hardiness, winter-hardiness* or *resistance to winter injury*.

The effects of winter stress may be summarized as follows :

1. Reduction in temperature;
2. change in temperature;
3. mechanical effects on plants due to frost-bite;
4. creation of special microclimate due to a permanent cover of snow; and
5. water deficiency caused by frozen soils or oversaturation of soils due to melting of ice.

The occurrence of these effects may be individual or simultaneous and depending upon the region and season there may be a change in their order of succession as well as in their duration. Winter stress, therefore, consists of manifold effects varying from season to season and region to region with changing intensity.

The plant density (number of plants per unit area) and the vigour of the surviving plants may be adversely affected by winter stress. It can also have an unfavourable temporary or permanent effect on productive tillering.

Frost is the most significant factor which has an adverse effect on the survival of winter wheats. Frost induced cytological changes are : (1) Detachment of the living matter of the cell (plasm) from the cell wall; (2) ice crystal formation in extra-cellular (intercellular) spaces causing interruption in normal physiological processes; (3) destruction of cell organelles due to the rapid growth of ice crystals; (4) maximum formation of harmful ice occurs between minus 21 and minus 22°C; and (5) discolouration and swelling of chloroplasts. Some other effects of freezing are : (1) The process of cell division is slowed down; (2) physiological activity of nuclei is reduced and, as a consequence, there is occurrence of gradual plasmolysis; (3) reduction in the size of vacuoles; (4) appearance of a dense reticular structure in the cytoplasm; (5) change in the morphology of mitochondria of coleoptile cells; (6) change in the fractional composition of protein content; (7) frost induced dehydration shows positive correlation with the enzymatic activity and sulphydryl quantity; and (8) ribose nucleic acid (RNA) shows higher sensitivity to freezing than deoxy-ribose nucleic acid (DNA). Except the changes in chloroplasts which occur only in the above-ground parts of the plant, all the above mentioned changes occur in above-ground parts as well as in roots. Further, since roots are relatively more sensitive to frost, these changes start occurring earlier in roots than in the above-ground parts of the plant.

The wheat plant has an inherent capability to face the consequences of winter stress. For this, the plant has to undergo the process of *hardening* which can be attained through gradual cooling and medium low temperatures. Hardening is positively correlated with cold resistance. It has been found that there is substantial sugar accumulation in the tissues during the process of hardening (Valeev, 1967). According to Trunova (1970), the increase in sugar content is more than two times and a substantial portion of this sugar is stored in chloroplasts and cell-sap. A considerable accumulation of monosaccharides, disaccharides and oligo-saccharides in tillering nodes has been noted by Zlobina (1970). According to her, saccharose is mainly responsible for providing protection under the snow cover. Some other compounds like arabinose, galactose, mannose, ramnose and xylose, can also affect cold tolerance in plants by increasing the concentration of the cell-sap. The role of sugar accumulation in the process of hardening and in the development of cold resistance can be further emphasized on the basis of the remarkable difference between winter and spring wheats in terms of sugar concentrtion of the cell-sap. According to Salcheva *et al.* (1964), long-wave light plays an important role in the hardening of plants as it enhances both the synthesis and accumulation of sugars. Nevertheless, a change of carbohydrate concentration is not entirely responsible for inducing hardening in plants, but a decrease in nitrate reductase activity (Toman and Pauli, 1964), change in the fractional composition of the protein (Vasileva *et al.*, 1964) and an increased content of free amino acids like asparagin, glutamine and protein (Babenko and Gevorkyan, 1967) also contribute towards hardening.

There are two stages of the occurrence of the process of hardening (Trunova, 1965; Salcheva and Gramatikova, 1965) : (1) Accumulation of glucose and oligosaccharides; and (2) mobilization of fructose and saccharose followed by an increase in the quantity of amino acids. The process of hardening has also been found associated with a reduction in the activity of iron-containing oxydases and a decrease in the biological effect of respiration. Further, although the principle involved in the hardening process is the same both in the above ground parts of plants and in the roots, sugar accumulation occurs at a much faster rate in the above-ground parts than in the roots.

Varietal differences for cold hardiness have been observed in a number of cases. It has been concluded that cold hardiness is a polygenically controlled complex character and can be improved through transgression.

Diseases : Resistance to diseases has increasingly become as one of the major objectives of wheat breeding. A large number of disease pathogens (air-borne fungi, soil-borne fungi, bacteria and viruses) attack the wheat plant and cause considerable yield losses. The major diseases of wheat are the rusts, smuts and powdery mildew.

The **rusts** (leaf rust, stem rust and stripe rust caused by *Puccinia recondita*, *P. graminis* and *P. striiformis*, respectively) probably cause maximum damage in wheat yields. Therefore, maximum importance should be attached to the breeding of rust resistant varieties. The pathogens causing leaf and stem rusts may spend part of their life cycle in either of the two ways : (a) On wheat plants of other area; (b) on alternate host plants. New physiological races of each rust species have come up and have created problems for wheat breeders. About 34 races of *P. recondita*, 37 races of *P. graminis* and about 16 races of *P.striiformis* have so far been identified. Therefore, an integrated approach which can ensure resistance to all important races of different rust species may perhaps help the wheat breeders to a great extent. Such an approach is being followed by the CIMMYT scientists in Mexico.

Among the smuts, **loose smut** caused by *Ustilago tritici*, is responsible for maximum destruction. Four races of *U.tritici* have so far been identified. The pathogen destroys the spike completely.

Powdery mildew is caused by *Erysiphe graminis*. Cool temperatures and high humidity provide the most favourable environment for the rapid spread of the pathogen. Under favourable environmental conditions, a white coloured mycelium rapidly grows on the surface of the leaves. So far, 30 physiological races of *E. graminis* have been identified.

Leaf blight, caused by a complex of three pathogens, namely, *Bipolaris sorokiniana, Alternaria triticina* and *Pyrenophora tritici repentis*, occurs in all major wheat growing zones in India and affects yield and quality of wheat in warm and humid regions.

There are some region specific diseases of wheat which may cause minor damage to the crop and thus much attention has not been paid to the resistance of these diseases. These diseases include **head scab** caused by *Fusarium graminearum*, **flag smut** caused by *Urocystis agropyri*, **foot rot** caused by *Sclerotium roefsii* and **hill bunt** caused by *Tilletica foetida, T. caries*.

However, **Karnal bunt** disease is causing considerable damage to wheat quality in India and has considerably threatened wheat consumption. Another problem faced by wheat breeders about this disease is the presence of low variability for the disease. Mutation breeding is perhaps an appropriate approach to increase variability for the control of Karnal bunt and overcome this problem.

Insect pests : Although a number of insect pests (Hessian fly, greenbug, cereal leaf beetle, termites, etc.) attack the wheat crop, but fortunately none of these pests could pose a serious problem before wheat breeders. As a result, resistance to insect pests is not considered as an important objective of wheat breeding.

Hessian fly may cause serious injury to wheat plant. The infested plants show reduction in height and tillering capacity, higher sensitivity to winter stress and straw breaking after ripening. So far, 8 biotypes of the fly are known.

Cereal leaf beetle may cause considerable yield loss. Large portions of the leaves are eaten up by both the adult and the larvae which have preference for non-pubescent leaves.

So far, eight biotypes (A-G and I) of **green bug** have been identified. The bug multiplies rapidly with a rise in temperature. The damage is mostly done by the adult.

Termites, foliar aphids, root aphids, shoot fly, brown wheat mite army worm, pink stem borer cause minor damage to wheat crop in India.

Further, among the insect pests, cereal cyst nematode disease (molya) caused by *Heterodera avenae* is also a major problem in sandy loam soils of some areas of Haryana, Rajasthan, U.P. and J&K.

Miscellaneous : A number of environmental stresses and weather induced losses influene the yield potential in wheat. Important abiotic factors affecting grain yield in wheat (drought, lodging and winter stress) have already been discussed in detail. Some other factors like presence/absence of awns, grain shattering, preharvest sprouting and nutrient imbalance caused by aluminium, manganese and sodium toxicity, may also have more or less effect on grain yield.

The presence of **awn** in wheat (bearded wheat) may be advantageous as well as disadvantageous for the wheat breeder. The main advantages of bearded wheats are : (1) Awns contribute towards spike photosynthesis and ultimately towards yield potential; and (2) the presence of awns helps in considerably reducing the damage caused by birds and other animals. The disadvantages of the presence of awns are : (1) Bearded wheats are relatively more sensitive since presence of awns causes increase in spike weight and hence increases wind stress (though it has not been experimetnally proved as yet that awns cause a significant increase in the wind stress); and (2) awnless wheats are easier to thresh than awned wheats.

Grain shattering generally occurs when threshing of wheat is too easy. On the other hand, difficult threshability causes problem in separating grains from the ear particularly in those areas where there is high atmospheric humidity at the time of harvesting. Therefore, a wheat cultivar should have a balanced threshability.

Preharvest sprouting may sometimes create a serious problem for the wheat breeder particularly under prolonged periods of rain. Resistance to preharvest sprouting is though genetically controlled, but is also sensitive to environmental conditions. Selection criteria for this property are generally based on certain plant morphological characters, reduced rate of water uptake by spikes and high seed dormancy. However, no genotype has yet been identified which possesses complete resistance to preharvest sprouting under extreme unfavourable environmental conditions.

Aluminium toxicity has an adverse effect on the development of roots and the above-ground parts of the plant and ultimately causes reduction in yield. The property is controlled by both the major and minor genes and thus shows quasi-continuous variation. The tolerance to aluminium toxicity and acid soils has been studied in more detail than the tolerance to alkaline soils.

Improving Product Quality

Although the quality of straw produced by a wheat variety is also important at least in some parts of the world, product quality in wheat refers mainly to the grain quality. Therefore, our discussion on product quality will be restricted to grain quality only.

In botanical language, the grain of wheat (sometimes also termed as seed) is a nut-like fruit and is called as *caryopsis*. A caryopsis contains a single *seed* surrounded by a thin *shell* or *pericarp*. The two parts of caryopsia are not easily separable. Wheat grain has a furrow or crease on the ventral side but the dorsal surface of the pericarp of the grain is rounded and smooth. The pericarp is composed of a layer of an outer epidermis, a layer of inner epidermis, and 2-3 layers of parenchymatous tissue in between these two epidermal layers.

The seed, in turn, is consisted of four parts : (1) *Testa* or *seed-coat* which acts as a cover for the embryo and endosperm and determines the colour of the grain; (2) a bright colourless *layer of nucellus* or *hyaline layer*; (3) the *endosperm* or *floury part* which is composed of thin-walled parenchymatous cells and acts as a store-house of food for nourishing the embryo during germination and is further divisible into two parts, *aleurone layer* and *starch- and gluten-parenchyma*; and (4) *embryo* which is situated on the dorsal side at the base of the grain with one side very close to the endosperm and is a highly differentiated body capable of producing a full plant. Embryo is a very small part of the grain and constitutes only about 3 per cent of the total weight of the grain. On the other hand, encosperm parenchyma which contains starch and gluten, is the largest part and constitutes about 88 per cent of the total weight of the grain. The four remaining parts of the grain, namely, aleurone layer, nucellar layer, seed-coat and pericarp, like embryo, make a minor contribution (about 8.25 per cent) towards the total weight of the grain.

Since wheat grain is utilized in many ways (leavened bread making, unleavened bread or chapati making, buiscuit making, cake making, noodles making, etc.), grain quality in wheat generally means different things to different persons. For example, for a miller, milling quality of the wheat grain is more important and, similarly, for others, other qualities are more important. The chemical composition of the wheat grain is not always considered as a basis for deciding the wheat grain quality, but some other characteristics like colour and texture of the grain and taste of people, become more important than chemial composition of the grain. For example, wheats with white and amber grains are preferred over red grained wheats in India and, because of this preference, the former type of wheats fetch a premium in the market. Further, according to some people, the wheat crop raised under no-manure conditions or under organic-manure conditions produces a better quality grain than the crop raised using artificial manure. However, the fact remains that the quality of the grain should be decided on the basis of its chemical composition. Of course, as mentioned earlier, the quality of the wheat grain would differ according to its use. Therefore, though improvement in grain quality is one of the most important objectives of wheat breeding, the breeding for numerous quality characteristics is not an easy task. The inheritance of the quality characterstics is complex since not only varietal differences are found for these characteristics but also the same are considerably influenced by environmental conditions.

Based on the utilization and market value, mainly two types of hexaploid wheats, namely, hard bread wheat and soft wheat, of *Triticum aestivum* group and one type of tetraploid wheats, namely, durum wheat, of *T, durum* group, are under commercial cultivation. These three types of wheats have their own specific properties which determine the suitability of these wheats for different purposes. Hard endosperm and strong gluten stands are the main characteristics of hard bread wheat. The hard-textured endosperm found in this type of wheat has high water absorption capacity. Further, the endosperm and bran of this wheat are easily separable with a high recovery of good quality white flour. This wheat is suitable for bread making. On the other hand, weak gluten and soft endosperm are the main characteristics of a soft hexaploid wheat. Here, the endosperm cannot be readily separated from the bran. The recovery of good quality flour is low since bran particles get mixed with the flour. Soft hexaploid wheat is mostly used for making flat-bread, cakes, pastries, cookies, etc. and thus has special importance in confectionery industry. Durum wheat has its unique characteristics. It has extremely hard endosperm and its flour is mainly used for making noodles.

All kinds of tests which are used to measure the grain quality in wheat may be classified into following four types :

(1) **Grain texture or grain hardness :** Two parameters, namely, percentage of flour and its extraction rate (recovery), are used to measure grain hardness. More are the values of these two parameters, more economical it will be to the miller. Therefore, grain hardness is directly related to the milling quality and ultimately to miller's economy. Grain hardness characters have high heritability and thus can be improved by using simple selection procedures.

(2) **Flour strength :** Protein percentage (content) and dough strength (extensibility) are the two charateristics which are mainly associated with this type of flour test. Flour strength has a low heritability and is thus highly influenced by environmental conditions.

(3) **Flour stability :** It is an aspect of protein quality, especially gluten percentage. This characsteristic has high heritability and thus genetic improvement in this trait is easy.

(4) **Flour stiffness :** Like flour stability, it is also an aspect of protein quality, especially gluten percentage. To some extent, this characteristic is influenced by flour stability.

Gluten protein is composed of two components (a) Gliadin and (b) glutenin. The baking differences among different varieties are generally due to gliadin proteins. The gliadin composition is highly heritable and is thus almost uninfluenced by environmental conditions.

Aneuploid studies carried out on the inheritance of quality characters have indicated that many of the baking quality characteristics of bread wheat are governed by genes located on the chromosomes of D genome. The baking quality characteristics have complex inheritance as these are governed by genes present on several chromosomes.

One more point about the grain quality in wheat needs discussion. The point is related to the relative amounts of total protein and lysine in the wheat grain. The improvement in these two quality attributes is too difficult because of the following reasons :

1. Both the total protein content and lysine content are highly influenced by environmental factors.
2. There is a strong negative correlation between protein content and grain yield.
3. The two protein attributes (protein content and lysine content) are also negatively correlated.
4. The differences among most of the modern wheat varieties for total protein produced per unit area, are statistically non-significant.

As a result, a limited progress has been achieved in improving both the total protein content and lysine content simultaneously.

Mutual Exclusiveness of the Three Major Objectives

The three major objectives of wheat breeding, namely, increasing yield potential, stabilizing yield levels and improving grain quality, are not mutually exclusive. As discussed above, protein content has a negative correlation with grain yield. Therefore, simultaneous improvement for grain yield and grain quality is a difficult task. Only minor adjustments can be made. Similarly, it is not necessary that a high yielding cultivar will also show high degree of resistance to all major diseases of wheat. The wheat breeder, therefore, has to do some sacrifice for one objective or the other. Nevertheless, an integrated research approach considering all the three objectives together may help the wheat breeders in achieving their goal. Such integrated research activities are also necessary to achieve success within an objective. For example, breeding for disease resistance in wheat involves control of several diseases and of several races of the same pathogen.

CHAPTER 4

Breeding Methods

Before we discuss various plant breeding methods being applied in wheat, let us give a brief description of different parts (both under-ground and above-ground) of the wheat plant and flowering, pollination, crossing technique, etc.

The Wheat Plant

As discussed in Chpater 1, the wheat plant comes under the tribe *Triticeae* of the grass family *Poaceae* (*Gramineae*) and possesses all important features of this tribe.

Roots : Root system in wheat is bit complex and may differ according to the environmental conditions under which the wheat crop has been raised and according to wheat type. For example, winter wheats mostly have a better root system than spring wheats.

There are two types of roots in wheat :

1. Primary roots or seminal roots : The number of primary roots generally varies from 5-8. Primary radicle is the first seminal root. The first pair of lateral roots originates from the hypocotyl soon after the germination of the seed. Immediately after the emergence of the first pair, the second pair of lateral roots originates. If necessary, the sixth root originates after considerable time when the first primary root and the two pairs of lateral roots have attained a good length. The third pair of seminal roots emerges just above the second pair. In some cases, there is no emergence of the third pair and in some others even the sixth root does not appear at all. The presence of extremely delicate root pairs can be seen on the surface of these roots.

Although the primary roots generally remain functional throughout the life of plant, the main function of these roots is to absorb water from the soil during the early stages of the development of the plant and thus these roots constitute a small part of the total root system. However, two factors, the soil texture and the depth at which the grain is sown, mainly determine the degree of development of these thin roots and their depth in the soil.

2. Secondary roots or adventitious roots or nodal roots : These roots originate from the nodes (and thus also called as nodal roots) of the main axis and its branches under the soil or just above the soil. The first pair of these roots originates from the tillering node of the main axis, one on the right side and the other on the left side of the first bud. Similarly, pairs of these roots appear at the second and succeeding nodes. At the position of the straw where the internodes are bit longer, 2-3 symmetrically arranged pairs of roots develop at each node. The development of these roots begins only after the appearance of leaves of the first or second buds and continues for months together. The position of these roots has a correlation with the arrangement of the buds and leaves. In addition to the absorption of water and nutrients from the soil, these roots also help the plant in maintaining its balance.

As discussed in Chapter 3, a better root system helps in increasing lodging resistance and thus stabilizing yield levels in wheat.

Stem : The wheat plant has a typical, mostly cylindrical, erect and elastic stem which is solid at nodes and hollow at internodes and is termed as culm. The culms of wheat remain green (particularly their upper part) for a long time and do the process of photosynthesis to a considerable extent. At maturity, the colour of culms become pale yellow and ultimately change to brown colour when the straw has completely dried.

Although the length of straw in wheat is dependent on both the genetic factors and environmental factors and has great influence on lodging resistance, the number of nodes in culms of bread wheat is not highly variable. This number generally varies from 5-7, with six nodes in majority of the culms. As the plant grows, the length of the internode also increases so that the basal internode is mostly shortest and the uppermost internode, bearing flag leaf, is the longest. Most part of the internodes, particularly at lower and middle portions of the culm, is covered with leafsheaths.

A single grain of wheat when sown in the soil, is capable of producing several shoots. This ability of producing shoots near the surface of the soil is called as **tillering capacity** or **stooling capacity** of a genotype. The number of productive tillers is an important component character of grain yield in wheat and thus plays a considerable role in stabilizing yield potential in this imortant creal crop. Tillering capacity is not only under the control of genetic factors and the internal physiological peculiarities of plants, but some exteral climatic factors (amount and distribution of rainfall, light intensity, plant density, type of soil, etc.) also play an important role in governing this character.

However, three important points arise about stem characteristics from the standpoint of their significance in increasing and stabilizing yield potential in wheat : (1) The area of green portion of the stem which contributes towards photosynthesis (2) The length and stiffness of culm; and (3) the capacity to produce ear-bearing tillers.

Leaves : Although several forms of leaves are found in wheat (foliage leaves, scutellum, coleoptile, prophylls of lateral axes and glumes), our discussion will be restricted to the foliage leaves only. Foliage leaves have an alternate arrangement on the culm. There are two opposite vertical rows of these leaves on the stem and each leaf shows a 180° divergence from its lower and upper leaf.

A foliage leaf consists of four parts, leaf sheath, leaf blade and ligule and a pair of auricles at the base of leaf blade. The leaf sheath surrounds most part of the internode except the uppermost internode bearing flag leaf and protects the culm from unfavourable weather conditions (frost, drought, etc.) and from insect pests. It also provides support to the young growing internode.

Leaf blade is the largest part of the foliage leaf and grows faster than the leaf sheath. The leaf blade has a linear shape with a parallel veination and is mainly responsible for the occurrence of photosynthesis and transpiration.

A thin memberanous colourless structure, called ligule, is found at the base of the upper surface of leaf blade. It closely surrounds the culm and checks the entry of dust, rain water, aphids, etc. between the stem and the leaf sheath. The ligules of upper leaves are larger than those of the lower leaves.

Attached to the base of the leaf blade and loosely encircling the leaf sheath and the culm, there is a pair of pale-green or pinkish clow-like structures, called auricles. Although the size of the auricle is a characteristic of the genotype, the upper leaves possess larger auricles than the lower leaves.

Like the number of internodes, the number of leaves on a culm is generally six (in 70 per cent cases), but five (in about 20 per cent cases) or seven (in about 10 per cent cases) leaves are also found. The leaves perform two main functions : (1) They transpire the excess water present in the plant; and (2) the process of photosynthesis takes place in the leaves.

Inflorescence : After the completion of vegetative phase, the apex of each productive tiller, instead of producing new leaves, becomes greatly elongated and turns into an *ear*, the inflorescence of wheat. The wheat inflorescence is a compound distichous raceme called *spike*. The main axis of inflorescence, called *rachis*, is a zigzag structure on which sessile spikelets are alternately arranged in two opposite rows. In addition to lateral spikelets, there is a single terminal spikelet. All the spikelets including the terminal one are fertile except in *Triticum monococcum* where the terminal spikelet is absent.

Like spike, each spikelet also has an axis called *rachilla* on which sessile florets are alternately arranged. The number of florets in each spikelet ranges from 2-5 but out of these only 2-3 are mostly fertile. At the base of each spikelet, there are two boot-shaped sterile outer bracts called *glumes* which are placed opposite to each other.

Each floret is enclosed by two bracts. The outer one is called as *lemma* and the inner one as *palea*. The tip of lemma turns into a thin long structure called awn. In between lemma and palea, there are three stamens possessing large anthers and an ovary with two feathery stigma branches. In addition, each floret possesses two ovate *lodicules*, the modified perianth structures which help in opening of florets at anthesis.

Anthesis and pollination : Opening of the flower (anthesis) in wheat begins mostly 5 or 6 days after the emergence of spike from the upper leaf sheath. The development of androecium and gynaeceum in the same flower shows a very high degree of synchronization. The initiation of anthesis occurs with the swelling of lodicules followed by separation of lemma and palea. Flowering in wheat starts in the early hours of morning and goes on occurring almost throughout the day. A spike generally takes 2-3 days to complete flowering. The flowering starts from about one-third portion from the tip of the spike and proceeds upwards as well as downwards. In a spikelet, the flowering begins from the basal floret and proceeds upwards. As regards the flowering of different spikes of a plant, the ear of the primary culm flowers first and then the process of flowering occurs in other tillers of the plant according to the order of their origin. A plant takes about one week to complete flowering in all the tillers.

The separation of lemma and palea is followed by a rapid growth in the filaments of anthers and the spreading out of the two feathery stigmas. At the same time, the dehiscence of pollen sacs occurs and it is followed by spreading of pollen on the stigmas. The maximum receptivity of the stigmas is between 0-3 days. However, they may remain receptive even upto 13 days after anthesis (de Vries, 1971). It is the natural way of pollination in wheat. Ultimately, the anthers protrude from the glumes resulting in the shedding of large amount of pollen in the air. During flower opening, some amount of foreign pollen may go inside the floret and can cause cross pollination. The degree of cross pollination in wheat may vary from 1-2 per cent.

However, to make crosses between two parents to combine their desirable characteristics in a single genotype, it is necessary to do artificial pollination. For this, the florets of the parent plant to be used as female are emasculated at an appropriate age of the floret (that is, 1-3 days before anthesis). Before emasculation is done, a few basal and upper spikelets of the ear are removed. Then, middle florets of each spikelet leaving only two outer florets, are removed. After this, about one-third upper part of these florets is cut off with the help of scissors. The stamens are then removed with the help of a pair of forceps. When emasculation is complete in the whole ear, the ear is covered with a paper bag to protect it from undesired pollen. One-two days after emasculation, pollination is done by putting a ripe anther on the stigma or by some other method. One such method is *twirl pollination method*. This method is used when large number of crosses are to be attempted and the pollen is available in large quantity (CIMMYT, 1976). The method is simple and fast. In this method, spike of suitable age (having a few freshly extruded yellow coloured anthers) is taken from the male parent. About one-third upper part of each floret (primary and secondary) is removed with the help of scissors for facilitating the extension of anthers and release of pollen. The peduncle is inserted in the soil for some time to keep the spike erect in the natural sunlight so that the filaments elongate and the anthers come out of the floret and dehisce. As soon as there is dehiscence of anthers, the top of the paper bag covering the emasculated ear is cut off with the help of scissors. The spike with dehisced anthers is inverted into the paper bag and vigourously rotated around the emasculated ear by twirling its peduncle with the help of thumb and forefinger. The paper bag is then stappled to prevent the entry of undesired pollen. The male spike may be left inside the bag for sometime to allow additional pollination.

Another pollination method is the *approach method*. This method was suggested by Rosenquist (1927). Here, the spike of the male and female parents are positioned in such a way that the emasculated ear remains slightly below the male ear. Both the spikes are covered with a single paper bag. Occasionally, the bag is shaken to facilitate dissemination of pollen inside the bag. This method is more appropriate for movable greenhouse plants. In field, it may be used by detaching the male spike from the plant and covering in the same bag with the emasculated ear or by growing male and female parents in closely sown rows. At maturity time, the crossed seed is collected from the plants.

Fertilization and grain development : As in other angiosperms, there is occurrence of double fertilization in wheat. However, before describing the process of double fertilization, it is perhaps important to know in brief about microsporogenesis, megasporogenesis, microgametogenesis, megagametogenesis and the germination of pollen.

Microsporogenesis is the development of microspores or pollen grains. In the beginning, there is formation of an archesporial cell in each of four corners of the anther. The archesporial cell undergoes mitotic division to give rise to parietal and sporogenous cells. Due to the occurrence of radial divisions in the parietal cell, four cells are formed and these with other cells form a layer around the sporogenous cell. Further successive mitotic divisions in the parietal layer give rise to three concentric layers of cells, the outer one is called as endothecium and the inner one as tapetum. There is a single layer of pollen mother cells in the anther chamber. Each pollen mother cell undergoes meiotic division and produces a microspore tetrad. Since chromosome number is reduced to half during meiosis, each microspore or pollen grain contains only n number of chromosomes.

During **microgametogenesis** (the development of male gametes or male gametophyte), each microspore generally undergoes two successive mitotic divisions. After first division, it gives rise to a generative nucleus and a vegetative nucleus. The generative nucleus again divides and produces two male gametes.

Megasporogenesis is the development of megaspores. During megasporogenesis, a hypodermal archesporial cell undergoes meiotic division and a linear tetread of megaspores (each with n number of chromosomes) is formed. Only the innermost megaspore (chalazal) acts as a functional megaspore and the other three disintegrate.

The functional megaspore shows tremendous enlargement and undergoes three successive mitotic divisions to form an embryosac containing eight cells. These eight cells are then organized in a specific way. Three of them occupy a place near micropylar end (the egg cell and two synergids, one on each side of the egg cell), three near the chalazal end (three antipodal cells) and two of them come in the centre of the embryo sac and are called polar nuclei. This whole process of the development of the functional megaspore into an embryo sac (the female gametophyte) is known as **megagametogenesis**.

When pollen grains come in contact of stigma, a tube like structure (pollen tube) emerges from each pollen grain. The pollen tube travels through the stigmatic and stylar tissues, reaches the micropylar end of the ovule, enters the ovule through micropyle and ultimately discharges the two generative nuclei in the embryo sac. One of these nuclei, unites with the egg cell (called **syngamy**) and other unites with the two polar nuclei (called **triple fusion**). This process of syngamy and triple fusion is called as **double fertilization**.

The fertilized egg cell undergoes mitotic divisions and develops into a diploid embryo. The triple fusion nucleus undergoes numerous mitotic divisions to produce triploid endosperm. Ultimately, there is formation of a full-fledged wheat grain with its all essential parts, pericarp, seed coat, nucellus, embryo and endosperm. In botanical terms the fruit of wheat is a nut-like complex structure and is termed as caryopsis (Chapter 3).

Breeding Procedures

Wheat is one of the oldest cereals and thus it is not possible to tell the exact time of the beginning of wheat breeding. Since ancient times, farmers/breeders have been making efforts to select better types of plants, collect seed from these plants and sowing this seed for the next crop. However, with the beginning of the twentieth century when Mendel's laws of inheritance came into light, wheat breeding was put on a scientific basis. In fact, the year 1900 was also the year of beginning of scientific plant breeding.

Since wheat is a highly self-fertilizing species, all breeding procedures recommended for improving self-fertilized crops, are also used in wheat. Singh and Pawar (1998) presented a summary of breeding plans and procedures to be used in self-pollinated crops and emphasized that to bring another breakthrough in the production and productivity of these crops, the genetic base of the varieties of self-pollinators must be expanded. They suggested several ways (use of most appropriate breeding method, widening the limits of hybridization, utilization of folk knowledge, enhancing input use efficiency, use of novel techniques, etc.) to accomplish this goal.

Before we go into details of the breeding procedures being used in wheat, it is perhaps necessary to discuss two other aspects of breeding programme : (1) Choice of most appropriate parents for hybridization; and (2) the aids to selection. Like the breeding procedure used, these aspects can also influence the success of the breeding programme.

Choice of parents : Before starting a breeding programme, the wheat breeder should have clearly defined the objectives of his programme. In most of the cases, increase in yield level is not the sole objective of the breeder. Other factors like level of disease resistance, quality and adaptation should also be taken into consideration while selecting parents for hybridization. Generally, one parent is selected on the basis of its proven performance in the area for which the breeder is trying to evolve a new variety. Since the main objective of hybridization is to combine together the characteristics of two or more parents, the other parent should complement the weaknesses of the first parent. The intensity of the specific characters for which the other parent is chosen should be very high (more than desired in new variety) since some degree of intensity of these characters may be lost during the breeding programme due to a different genetic environment of the new variety. In case all the desirable characters do not occur in two parents, a third or fourth parent may be included in the hybridization programme.

Since the success of every breeding programme mainly depends on the types of the parents involved in hybriudization. Utmost care should be taken at the time of the selection of parents. Some crosses produce wonderful progeny. A faulty selection of parents cannot be compensated at any stage of the breeding programme.

Aids to selection : The plant breeder's skill will always play an important role in the success of a breeding programme. Therefore, despite all scientific and technological advancements in breeding methodology, the discipline of plant breeding will always remain more or less of an art. The job of a wheat breeder becomes easier if he is very well acquainted with the different characteristics of the wheat plant like floral morphology, time of anthesis and pollination, crossing technique and several physiological, biochemical and disease characteristics. For example, artificial inoculation may help the breeder in identifying resistant plants even under unfavourable conditions for disease spread. Similarly, taking off-season crop at a relatively humid location helps the breeder in cutting short the time period of breeding programme and in identifying the plants with real resistance to a disease. Many plants which show resistance to a wheat rust in plains, show a high degree of susceptibility to the same rust in hilly regions. Taking too much time for the release of the new variety, sometimes may create a serious problem for the wheat breeder.

The testing of lodging reistance is not possible in a season when there are no too much rains and fast winds. Under such condition, laboratory test may help the breeder in determining the physical worth of the wheat culm. Similarly, the breeder may face problems in identifying plant materials resistant to drought and post-harvest sprouting. Further, reliable information about the grain quality may increase the success of the wheat breeding programme.

Nevertheless, it is not necessary that the good looking parents will always produce desirable progeny. This is possible because manytimes the *per se* performance of the parents is not indicative of their combining ability. Therefore, to have a manageable size of the breeding material, it is necessary to reject undesirable crosses at an early stage of the breeding programme. Such an **early generation testing** can be carried out by testing the combining ability of plant material using some appropriate biometrical technique.

Selective intermating within a cross or between crosses may sometimes help the breeder in producing desirable transgressive segregants.

These aids to selection may enhance the efficiency of wheat breeders in selecting better type of plants and thus may considerably influence the success of the breeding programme.

Making crosses : After the choice of suitable parents for hybridization, the next step of the breeding programme is to make crosses between the selected parents. Depending upon the availability of desirable genes in the parents, *single crosses* (involving two parents), *three-way crosses* (involving three parents), *four-way crosses* (involving four parents) or *composite crosses* (involving generally 6-8 parents) may be made. However, single crosses and three-way crosses are most frequently made.

As regards the case of breeding procedures in wheat, let us begin with the three basic methods of plant breeding, introduction, selection and hybridization followed by selection in segregating generations. The introductin of new germplasm from different sources increases the spectrum of genetic variability and provides opportunity to the breeder in making use of new gene combinations. However, we will not discuss plant introduction as a breeding procedure.

Among selection methods, pure line selection was used in many crop species to evolve new cultivars in early years of plant breeding. However, with the advancement in some related disciplines (genetics, plant pathology, entomology, biochemistry, etc.), plant breeding has been put on a very sound scientific basis. As a result, pure line selection is no more used as a breeding method to develop new varieties in almost all the self-fertilizing crops. Now-a-days, this method is only used to purify the already existing varieties. Hence, this method also needs no further discussion.

Nevertheless, several hybridization methods (pedigree method, bulk method, single seed descent method, backcross method, diallel selective mating system, multiline breeding, etc.) are being applied to wheat materials. All the three types of hybridizations, namely, *intervarietal, interspecific* and *intergeneric*, are being applied in wheat. Of course, intervarietal hybridization is most frequently applied followed by interspecific hybridization and intergeneric hybridization. Interspecific hybridization is used only for specific objectives, whereas intergeneric hybridization is applied only in exceptional cases.

The choice of breeding method depends on several factors like objective of the breeder based on specific problem, facilities available in terms of funds, labour, etc, and scientific help available to the breeder. In fact, no breeding procedure has outright superiority over any other method, rather it depends on the situation that which particular method will prove best under that situation. For example, if the objective of the breeder is to improve several characters simultaneously, pedigree method will be superior to backcross method. On the contrary, if the objective is to remove some specific defect (controlled by one or a few major genes) of an otherwise outstanding cultivar, backcross method will be superior to pedigree method.

Pedigree method : Because of some important advantages (the method provides opportunity to the breeder to use his full skill, inheritance studies can be carried out as the pedigree records of all selected plants are maintained and the method helps in exploiting transgressive segregation), this method has been most frequently and extensively used for brining improvement in wheat. Pedigree method has some disadvantages too. Its main disadvantages are : (i) Since large segregating generations are raised and pedigree records of all selected plants are maintained in this method, it requires lot of man-power, time and land and thus the method is very costly; (ii) the method puts a limit on the amount of material to be handled by the breeder; (iii) the importance of natural selection is totally ignored in this method; and (iv) early fixation of genotypes creates problem in the selection for complex quantitative characters.

Various steps of pedigree method are :

1. Crosses between widely distant parents are made to produce F_1 generation heterozygous for maximum number of loci.
2. Sufficient quantity of the F_1 seed is produced to grow a large F_2 population to exploit the genetic variability to the maximum possible extent.
3. Since F_2 generation shows maximum variability, large number of single plant selections are made in space-planted rows of this generation considering all important characters.
4. Progeny rows of F_2 selected plants are raised in F_3 and both the between families and within family selections are made in F_3 generation.
5. Same process is repeated in F_4 and F_5 generations. However, after F_5 generation, more emphasis is given on selection between families/lines than on selection within family.
6. By F_6 generation, the families/lines become homozygous for most of the loci and thus within family selection is ineffective at this stage. Promising F_5 rows may be harvested in bulk for yield and quality tests.
7. When all the important charactrs have stopped segregating (at F_7 or F_8 stage), a few most promising lines in terms of yielding ability, disease resistance, adaptation, grain quality, etc. are selected and harvested as bulk for yield and quality testing. Pedigree records are maintained throughout the programme. Several systems are used for maintaining pedigree records : The maintenance of these records is made so that each progeny in each generation can be traced back to F_2 plant. It should be ensured that the selected lines are from different lines of descent.
8. These selected lines are grown in preliminary yield trials at multilocations with check varieties and only 3-4 best performing lines from yield, disease and quality point of view, are retained for final evaluation in *National Varietal Trials*.
9. A more vigorous test for yield, disease and quality is applied at the time of final evaluation at state or national level and after a testing of 3 years, one best performing line which shows statistically significant superiority over the best check variety is recommended for release (For more details, see Singh and Pawar, 2006).

However, random crossing among selections in early generations or one or more cycles of selective intermating in between the selfing series can minimize the adverse effects of successing selfing (restricting appearance of new recombinants and fixation of linkage blocks in early generations) in pedigree method after hybridization. Random mating among selections in early generations helps in preventing early fixation of genotypes and breaking linkage blocks. Selective intermating in between selfing series ensures appearance of hidden variability by fostering gene recombinations, accumulates desirable genes in experimental material, shifts genetic correlations in desired direction and increases population mean, genetic variability and the degree of heritability. Selective intermating has been found to be effective for increasing the mean yield and its components in wheat (Pawar *et al.*, 1990, 2000).

A number of modifications and refinements have been suggested from time to time to make this method more purposeful. These modifications have been made to combine the merits of two methods, to obtain quantitative estimates of yield and product quality at an early stage of the programme or according to the prevailing climatic conditions. Some variants of pedigree method are *mass pedigree method* of Harrington (1937), *modified pedigree method* of Breakwell and Hutton (1939), *pedigree trial method* of Lupton and Whitehouse (1957), *bulk pedigree selection* of Weiss (1949), F_2 *progeny method* of Lupton and Whitehouse (1957), *modified F_2 progeny method* of Smith (1987), *accelerated pedigree selection* of Valentine (1984), *simplified method of bulk and pedigree selection* of Sneep *et al.* (1979), *shuttle breeding system* discussed by Osmanzai *et al.* (1987) and *backcross pedigree method* suggested by Allard (1960). Singh and Pawar (2006) have described these methods in detail.

The applications of pedigree method to wheat materials are numerous. In fact, most of the improved varieties of wheat have been developed using this method. It is still the most frequently used breeding method in wheat.

Bulk method : This method is called by several other names like population breeding, bulk population breeding, bulk population method, mass method and evolutionary method of breeding. The method is easiest and cheapest as no artificial selection is done from F_2 to F_6 generation. Therefore, no science is involved during this period of the breeding programme. The method is largely based on natural selection. The improvement achieved by using this method is though slow but longer lasting. Another advantage of this method is that the breeder can handle large amount of plant material. The method is also a good source of information regarding the survival of genotypes and genes in populations. The bulk method is an easy way of detecting and exploiting transgressive segregants. Further, since natural selection acts during almost all segregating generations (from F_2 to F_6) of the breeding programme, no testing of the variety evolved through this method is required at farmer's field. However, in this method, the breeder does not get the chance of using his skill and experience in full, the improvement attained is slow, and inheritance studies are not possible.

Bulk method was firstly used by Nilsson-Ehle (1908) to combine resistance to winter stress with high yield potential in winter wheat by crossing high yielding cultivar Stand-up with variety Squarhead possessing winter-hardiness. This method has also been suggested to select lines resistant to wheat stem rust (Knott, 1989).

The main steps of the bulk method are :

1. By making crosses between carefully chosen parents, large quantity of F_1 seed is produced so that a very large F_2 population may be raised.
2. The large F_2 population raised is bulk harvested and the bulked seed is used to raise the F_3 generation. This process of growing large plant populations and bulking of seed is continued for several generations till the progeny lines become almost completely homozygous (may be F_5, F_6, F_7 or F_8 stage).
3. The next step of this breeding method is the evaluation of homozygous or nearly homozygous lines obtained after F_5 or F_6 (or in some cases, after F_7 or F_8). At this stage, like in pedigree method, single plants with desired characteristics are selected and their progeny rows are raised. Drastic rejection of undesirable lines is made and ultimately a few promising lines are retained for final evaluation.
4. A vigorous testing of these lines is done to select a best performing line. This line if shows significant superiority over the best check variety, is recomended for release as a new variety.

Some variants of bulk method are *modified bulk method* (will be discussed separately), *composite crosses* described by Harlan and Martini (1929), Harlan *et al.* (1940) and Suneson (1956), *backcross bulk method* (Florell, 1929), *mass pedigree method* of Harrington (1937), *single seed descent (SSD) method* (will be discussed separately), *modified mass method* used by Atkins (1953) and *pedigree bulk method* proposed by Allard (1960). All those methods which have been proposed to combine merits of pedigree method and of bulk method (like mass pedigree method of Harrington and pedigree bulk method of Allard) may be considered as variants of pedigree method as well as variants of bulk method.

Since every newly evolved plant variety, sooner or later, has to face the consequences of natural selection, it is always better to have some element of natural selection in a crop improvement programme. Growing of plant materials under natural conditions without doing artificial selection, helps in determining correlation between the competitive ability of a type to survive and its agricultural worth. However, nature may or may not favour those plant characteristics in which plant breeder is interested.

Two main factors, namely, the number of seeds produced by a genotype and the potential of these seeds to produce surviving progeny, determine the survival of a genotype in competition. These two factors, in turn, are influenced by several genetic, environmental and genotype × environmental factors.

Modified bulk method : This variant of bulk method or of pedigree method has been proposed and is being used to take advantage of the merits of both the bulk method and the pedigree method. In this method, instead of bulking seed of unselected plants, the selected spikes of promising plants are bulked during F_2 and F_3 space-planted generations. After F_3 generation, the method is exactly similar to pedigree method. A similar bulking of selects is followed in shuttle breeding system (to be discussed later) during F_3 and F_4 generations. Modified bulk method is being followed at some research centres in India and abroad, particularly by CIMMYT scientists. The simplified method of bulk and pedigree selection described by Sneep *et al.* (1979) also involves bulking of F_3 selected rows in F_4 generation in the pedigree programme. Pawar *et al.* (1990) found simplified pedigree selection (bulking at F_3 stage) better than or equal to traditional pedigree method in terms of mean performance, coefficient of variation and number of high yielding lines retained.

Single seed descent method or SSD method : For the first time, Goulden (1941) proposed this method to overcome limitations of bulk method and pedigree method. This method is also known as *complete bulk* or *random method* and has several other advantages : (i) The method is less expensive; (ii) allows rapid advancement of generations; (iii) allows to obtain the F_2 genetic spectrum in homozygous condition in the shortest possible time; (iv) helps in minimizing the effect of natural selection on the genetic structure of the original population; (v) the efficiency of this method is uninfluenced by the degree of heritability; (vi) allows better exploitation of transgressive segregation; (vii) the method proves better than bulk breeding when competitive effects are important; and (viii) allows best use of green houses, off-season nurseries, etc. since the material can be grown at high plant densities at each stage of the breeding programme. The main disadvantages of this method are: (1) Taking only one seed from a plant is a too small sample, (ii) the method is inferior to pedigree method in terms of disease resistance; and (iii) there are chances of loosing many genotypes through genetic drift.

Different steps of the SSD method are :

1. After making crosses between the chosen parents, the F_1 generation is space-planted to

produce sufficient quantity of seed. About half of the F_1 seed is saved and the remaining half is sown to grow a large F_2 population.

2. The second step relates to the generations of single seed harvesting. A single seed is randomly harvested from each F_2 plant. All such seeds are bulked and are used to grow a high density F_3 generation. This process of single seed harvesting, bulking all the seeds together and growing next generation is continued upto F_6 generation. The seed of F_6 generation is space-planted.

3. The third step relates to large single plant selections. The selections are made considering all important characters (yield potential, general vigour, disease resistance, etc.), as is done in pedigree method. The seed of selected plants is raised in individual plant progeny rows. All undesirable plants are rejected at this stage to save a few promising lines. The seed of these promising lines is bulked and raised in preliminary yield trials. After this, the method is just like bulk population breeding. In case any outstanding transgressive segregant appears at this stage, it is handled through pedigree selection.

The SSD method does not have many variants except one major variant of this method. This variant is known as *multiple seed descent method* or *MSD method* and will be discussed separately. A few variants like *one-plant-one-line method* of Yonezawa and Yamagata (1981) *one-spikelet-one-plant method*, *single spike selection* of Qualset (1977) and *single head descent* of Jensen (1988) have also been suggested to overcome the problem of small sample.

Multiple seed descent method or MSD : This method was suggested by Ndondi in the year 1987. The method has three main advantages over the SSD method : (i) The genetic variability of a cross is maximized; (ii) the risk of loosing genetic variability is minimized; and (iii) the method allows selection between families as well as within families.

In this method, a random sample of 100 promising plants was taken from space-planted F_2 generation and 12 seeds from each plant were separately grown in green house to produce F_3. The F_4 generation was raised in green house by taking a single seed from each F_3 plant. Three-meter head rows were raised in the field from the seeds of F_4 plants and ultimately 360 lines were retained for further testing.

A comparison made by Ndondi among SSD method, MSD method and bulk method for yield potential and protein content in wheat indicated superiority of MSD method over other two methods for yield potential and extent of phenotypic variance in the lines obtained. However, MSD and SSD methods exhibited equal effectiveness for improving protein content. On the contrary, bulk method was better than SSD method for producing high yielding lines. But, for phenotypic variance among line means, SSD method proved better than bulk method.

Backcross method : Backcross method is one of the important conventional breeding methods used in self-fertilizing crop species. The basis of choosing parents in this method is different from that used in other breeding methods. Here, one parent, called as recurrent or recepient, is the most outstanding variety of the area but with a single specific defect. The other parent, termed as non-recurrent or donor parent, possesses that desirable characters for which the recurrent parent is deficient. The purpose behind the use of backcross method is to remove the defect of the recurrent parent. For this, it is necessary to smoothly transfer the character from the donor parent to the recurrent parent, reconstitute the genotype of the recurrent parent and to maintain high intensity of the character under transfer throughout the breeding programme.

The requirements of the backcross method are : (1) A suitable recurrent parent must be available; (2) it should be possible to reconstitute the genotype of the recurrent parent fully; and (3) the character under transfer should have high heritability and it should be possible to maintain a worthwhile intensity of this character throughout the breeding programme. Nonfulfilment of these requirements may severely affect the success of the breeding programme.

The genetic basis of backcross method is not much different from that of pedigree method. The percentage of homozygosity and the percentage of homozygous individuals in the two methods are the same except that the percentage of desired homozygotes is more in backcross method than in pedigree method. Further, if no selection is done against an undesirable allele, the elimination of the undesirable allele is easier through backcrossing than through selfing series.

The advantages of backcross method are : (i) The results of the method are predictable and repeatable; (ii) allows easier elimination of an undesirable allele if no selection is done against that allele; (iii) facilitates introgression of germplasm from wild species into cultivated species; (iv) can be used to transfer disease resistance from different sources to the same recurrent parent; (v) requires small amount of material; (vi) the method is unaffected by environmental conditions; (vii) no publicity and no extensive testing of the new variety are needed; and (viii) the method can be applied in self- as well as cross-fertilizing crop species. This method has some disadvantages too which are: (i) The upper limit of the improvement is fixed; (ii) a tight linkage between an undesirable character and the character under transfer may create a serious problem; (iii) method has a restricted applicability since it cannot be used successfully in those crop species where emasculation and crossing are difficult; and (iv) there is no easy transfer of characters with low heritability.

The main steps of backcross method are :

1. The first step of the breeding programme consists of choosing a suitable recurrent parent and a donor parent. Then the crosses are made between the two parents, using recurrent parent as female and the F_1 is produced. The F_1 plants will contain equal proportions of germplasms of the two parents.

2. The second step relates to the backcrossing phase. Several backcrosses are made to reconstitute the genotype of the recurrent parent. However, the time required for this phase would depend on whether the allele under transfer is dominant or it is recessive. It is much easy to transfer a dominant allele than a recessive one. For the transfer of a dominant allele, generally, 5-6 successive backcrosses are sufficient. However, for transferring a recessive allele, selfing is necessary after every backcross or after two backcrosses to identify the plants with recessive phenotype. The selection during this phase is restricted to the character under transfer except in selfed generations when selection is done for all the important characters.

3. When the genotype of the recurrent parent is fully reconstituted, the plants possessing the character under transfer are selfed to bring the allele in homozygous condition. Progeny rows of these selfed plants are raised for exercising intensive selection for the character under transfer. This process of selfing may involve 2-3 generations for obtaining homozygous lines exactly similar to the recurrent parent plus the presence of character under transfer with worthwhile intensity. These homozygous lines are bulk harvested and their seed is increased for distribution among farmers for commercial cultivation.

Backcross method is now being used at IARI Regional Station, Wellington to develop HW-series backcross derivative lines (near isogenic lines) of earlier wheat varieties (C 306, Kalyansona, Sonalika, WL 711, HD 2009, WH 147, HD 2329, WH 542, VL 421, etc.) by incorporating different Lr and Sr genes for rust resistance. One such variety is HW 2004 (a backcross derivative line of C 306) which carries Lr 24 and Sr 24 genes from TR 380-14#7/3AG14 and was released in 1997 for timely sown, rainfed conditions of Central Zone (Madhya Pradesh, Gujarat and small parts of Uttar Pradesh and Rajasthan) of the country. Another variety is Sonak (a backcross derivative line of Sonalika) which carries Lr 24 gene and was released in 1998 for late sown conditions of Haryana state.

Some variants of backcross method are **convergent improvement method** of Richey (1927), **modified backcross method** of Mac Key (1954) or **multiple non-recurrent parent backcrossing, multiple recurrent parent backcrossing** and **intermittent backcrossing** described by Allard (1960). In convergent improvement method, two backcross programmes are run parallelly to improve two inbreds simultaneously. Modified backcross method or multiple non-recurrent parent backcrossing involves several non-recurrent parents (unadapted strains) which are crossed to the same recurrent parent (a well adapted variety) followed by a few backcrosses of the progenies of crosses to the recurrent parent. This is done to prepare optimum parental material for a multiple cross. When desirable characters are scattered in several varieties or strains, it is advisable to use two or more varieties as recurrent parents and to cross all these parents to the same donor parent. Involving two or more recurrent parents in a backcross programme is termed as multiple recurrent parent backcrossing. Intermittent backcrossing allows exploitation of transgressive segregation. Thus this method helps in overcoming the major weakness of the successive backcrossing.

Diallel selective mating system : In mid- and late 1960s, many plant breeders working with self-fertilizing crop species felt that the use of conventional breeding procedures in this group of crops was not making much headway. In fact, the main reasons of a slow improvement in these crops are some inherent limitations (early fixation of genotypes due to successive selfing after hybridization, narrow genetic base of the initial material and lack of intermating) associated with the conventional breeding methods. According to Joshi and Dhawan (1966), the breeding methodology being used in self-fertilizing crops, should be reoriented. They suggested some ways (use of germplasm having broad genetic base, scientifically based choice of parents, selective intermating in segregating generations and making best use of component breeding) to overcome the limitations of conventional breeding approach.

However, Jensen (1970) proposed a complex but an ingenious approach (a new method) for enhancing the speed of improvement in self-fertilizing crops and named it *diallel selective mating system* (DSMS). The method allows simultaneous utilization of several genotypes into a small group of central populations, inclusion of new germplasm and extraction of experimental varieties at any stage of the procedure and ensures additional recombination between genotypes. According to Jensen, DSMS overcomes the drawbacks of the conventional breeding system without sacrificing its advantages. However, DSMS should be considered as a supplement to the conventional breeding methodology and not as an alternative approach of this methodology. Further, it is difficult to use this method in those crop species where emasculation and crossing are difficult. This problem, however, can be overcome by using genetic or cytoplasmic male sterility if usable male sterility exists in the crop species under investigation. Jensen (1978) tried to remove all confusions and reservations of many plant breeders about the application of DSMS in self-fertilizing crops. But despite all assurances given by Jensen, the practical application of DSMS has so far been very limited.

Jensen (1970) divided his method into two parts, *planning phase* and *implementation phase*. The planning phase includes : (i) Making decision about the project objectives to be accomplished, (ii) identification of desirable genes in the germplasm based on the objectives of the project; and (iii) choice of suitable parents and their number to be incorporated in the beginning of the project. The number of parents to be incorporated at the initial stage of the programme would, however, vary according to the type of crop, the availability of desirable genes in the germplasm and the facilities available to the breeder. The implementation phase was further divided into four steps : (i) Production of single cross hybrids called as F_1 diallel series or P_2; (iii) application of mass and recurrent selection methods termed as selective mating series or P_3–P_5; and (iv) standard line selection. In fact, DSMS is a combination of mass selection, bulk method and recurrent selection and involves simultaneous input of several parents. Therefore, it is better to call it as a variant of composite breeding.

Multiline breeding : The objective to develop a multiline variety (a mixture of near-isogenic lines) is to incorporate disease resistance from different sources into a single agronomically superior variety so that the new variety shows uniformity for agronomical characters but is genetically heterogeneous for disease resistance. This approach helps in preventing spread of air-borne diseases in an epidemic form. Rusts of wheat are the most serious air-borne diseases. The development of a multiline using backcross method to incorporate disease resistance from various sources is perhaps the best method to incorporate multiple disease resistance into one genetic background. Some other advantages of multiline breeding are : (i) The approach helps in stabilizing the pathogen's race structure; (ii) helps in extending the life of resistance genes; (iii) tightly linked genes in repulsion phase can be exploited; (iv) replacement of component line(s) is possible at any stage; (v) allows exploitation of multiple alleles; and (vi) puts a check on yield losses. However, the method is expensive and helps in the development of new complex races.

There are three main requirements of the multiline approach : (i) A recurrent parent with proven yielding ability must be available; (ii) availability of good resistance donors; and (iii) complete information about the race flora of the pathogen must be available.

The development of multiline cultivars helps in combining together the characteristics of both the vertical resistance and horizontal resistance. Browning and Frey (1969) demonstrated that multiline cultivars possess a reduced initial amount of the disease (a characteristic of vertical resistance) as well as a reduced rate of disease development (a characteristic of horizontal resistance) for oat stem rust. A similar situation was observed by Gill *et al.* (1979) for brown and yellow rusts in wheat.

Although the importance of the concept of diversification was, for the first time, realized by Rosen (1949), it was Jensen (1952) who firstly proposed the concept of multiline in its true sense and emphasized the importance of both the agronomic uniformity of a cultivar and its heterogeneity for resistance to disease. A similar breeding approach for combining stem rust resistance in wheat was suggested in 1959 by Borlaug.

The whole procedure of the development of a multiline variety may be divided into three main steps : (1) Develoment of component lines; (2) screening of component lines; and (3) composition of multiline. For developing component lines, a well proven commercial variety is used as recurrent parent. Any one of the four methods, namely, backcrossing, multiple crossing, mutation and heterozygote selfing, can be used to develop component lines.

In *backcross method*, the progeny of each cross (between recurrent parent and one of the donor parents) is backcrossed to the recurrent parent. Generally, 3-4 backcrosses are made and selection is practiced for disease resistance in each backcross generation. In *multiple crossing*, a composite cross is made by crossing the same recurrent parent with different donor parents possessing disease resistance from various sources. With one recurrent parent (R) and four donor parents (D_1, D_2, D_3 and D_4), the composite cross will take the farm $[(R \times D_1)(R \times D_2)][(R \times D_3)(R \times D_4)]$. This method has two advantages : (a) It is relatively rapid; and (b) like limited backcrossing, provides scope for alround improvement including disease resistance. *Mutation method* includes treatment of the parental pure line with a suitable mutagen and identification of homozygous mutant lines in M_3 or later generations. The purpose behind *heterozygote selfing* is to develop a number of line pairs homozygous for two alternate alleles in different genetic backgrounds. For this, after the initial cross, heterozygotes for a particular locus are selected and selfed for a number of generations to derive pairs of homozygotes with alternate alleles at the locus. However, backcross method has been more frequently used for developing component lines than the other three methods.

In the **second step**, the component lines are screened for their reaction to individual races of the pathogen. Identification of resistance genes carried by component lines is done followed by their assessment under field conditions. It should be ensured that these lines are superior to the recurrent parent in respect of all important agronomical characters.

The **third step** relates to the selection of superior component lines in terms of disease resistance and other agronomical characters for the formation of a multiline variety. Generally, 8-16 component lines are mixed for this purpose. The component lines may be mixed in equal proportions or in different proportions depending upon the type of genes (for resistance and for agronomic performance) carried by the component lines and the reaction of the adult plant towards specific races of the pathogen under field conditions.

The general observation of the breeders is that a multiline variety is superior to its individual component lines in terms of yielding ability, adaptability and disease resistance.

Nevertheless, there are different views regarding the proportion of resistant population in a multiline variety. According to the supporters of *clean crop approach* (Borlaug, 1959; and others), the proportion of the resistant host population in a multiline variety should be very high (87.5–94 per cent). According to this view, each component line should have a high level of resistance. On the other hand, according to the supporters of *dirty crop approach* (Leonard, 1969; Frey et al., 1975; and others), the stabilization of rust population in a multiline variety is in no way less important than stabilizing the level of resistance and 60-65 per cent proportion of resistant host population in a multiline is sufficient.

The credit of releasing the first multiline variety of wheat at commercial scale goes to Columbia. This variety was developed against stripe rust in the background of the wheat variety Frecor in 1963 and was named as *Miramar 63*. In India, three multiline varieties (*KSML 3, MLKS 11* and *UPKML 7406*) were released for commercial cultivation.

Shuttle breeding method : This method is a combination of pedigree method and modified bulk method and is thus similar to the simplified method of bulk and pedigree selection proposed by Sneep *et al.* (1979). The method has been discussed in detail by Osmanzai *et al.* (1987). As the name indicates, the method involves growing of material under investigation at different sites with different fertility and moisture conditions. The method is being used by CIMMYT scientists to evaluate their germplasm for adaptability, yield potential and phenotypic stability at alternate sites of contrasting fertility and moisture conditions.

The main steps of the method are :

1. Space-planted F_2 generation is raised under optimal conditions of fertility and moisture and

single plants are selected (as in pedigree method) considering productive tillering, disease resistance, ear development, leaf retention capacity and grain plumpness.

2. The selected F_2 plants are bulk harvested and grown in F_3 and F_4 under stress environment (reduced moisture and low fertility conditions) following modified bulk method.
3. F_5 and F_6 generations are again raised under high moisture and high fertility conditions following pedigree method. The selection at this stage is done based on the characters discussed in step 1.
4. The lines which perform best under both the optimal and stress environmental conditions are selected and assessed in international trials for yielding ability and drought tolerance.

The main objectives of the CIMMYT scientists to use this method are to combine input efficiency and input responsiveness of wheat germplasm using alternate sites of contrasting environmental conditions and to breed wheat for drought tolerance for semi-arid regions of the world.

The shuttle breeding approach was started in 1945 by N.E. Borlaug with the sole objective of speeding up breeding for stem rust resistance. The shuttle breeding at CIMMYT is a part of conventional breeding. Thousands of crosses are made every year and the progenies of these crosses are screened and evaluated under different environmental conditions. According to Ceccarelli (1989), the widespread cultivation of wheat genotypes should not be taken as a criterion of wide adaptation as many of the sites are similar or made similar by providing irrigation and/or fertilizer. It is, therefore, better to use the term wide adaptation on the basis of geographical rather than environmental differences. However, this logic was not accepted by Braun *et al.* (1992) as they found G × E interaction greater than genotypic variance in most of the cases, indicating that sites chosen for growing material were considerably different from each other. Their view was also supported by the farmers growing CIMMYT material.

As regards shuttle breeding programme within Mexico, segregating wheat populations are shuttled between the two environmentally contrasting locations *Ciudad Obregon* (dry, sunny, fertile and irrigated site situated at sea level in north west Mexico) and *Toluca* (a cool high land environment with high humidity, situated near Mexico city). The yield potential of Ciudad Obregon is high (about 10 tonnes/ha) and only a few wheat diseases (leaf rust, Karnal bunt and black point) are prevalent in the area. At this location, planting of wheat is done in November (low temperature period) and harvesting is done in April/May (high temperature period). On the contrary, at Toluca location, planting is done in May/June and the material is harvested in October. Since this location is characterized by high humidity, there is incidence of many wheat diseases.

According to Singh *et al.* (2004), a shuttle breeding programme at CIMMYT's pattern was initiated in 1995-96 at the Directorate of Wheat Research (DWR), Karnal, India. The main objective to start this breeding programme was to support the wheat research activities of research centres in North Eastern Plains Zone (NEPZ) of the country. NEPZ represents one of the two mega environments of India (the other mega environment is North Western Plains Zone or NWPZ) and includes Eastern part of U.P., Bihar, Jharkand, West Bengal, Assam and Orissa. In the beginning of the programme, Varanasi and Faizabad, were as two shuttle breeding stations. After some time, two more stations, namely, Shillongani and Cooch Behar, were added. The breeding materials developed at DWR, Karnal, are shuttled between all the five stations (Karnal, Varanasi, Faizabad, Shillongani and Cooch Behar) for evaluating important characteristics (adaptability, disease resistance, etc.). DWR scientists feel that this approach would help in minimizing the gap between potential yields and the yields harvested at farmers' fields in eastern India. As a result of the concerted efforts made by the DWR scientists, a wheat variety, namely DBW 14 has been released for the late sown irrigated conditions of eastern India. Some other promising matrerials are at the various stages of testing.

Comparison Between Breeding Procedures

A number of investigators have compared the efficiency and effectiveness of different breeding procedures applied for bringing improvement in wheat. As has been discussed earlier, no breeding method has absolute superiority over any other method but the situation may vary from character to character for the same material and also from material to material for the same character. For example, Ndondi (1987) found that multiple seed descent (MSD) method was superior to single seed descent (SSD) method for yielding ability but the two methods showed equal effectiveness for improving protein content. Further, bulk method was more effective than SSD method for producing high yielding lines. On the other hand, SSD method showed its superiority over bulk method for phenotypic variance among lines. Similar results have been found by other investigators also. In fact, the suitability of a breeding procedure depends on several factors like the objective of the investigator, the material selected for study, environmental conditions prevailing in the region where the investigation has been carried out and the facilities available to the investigator. A comparison of some breeding methods applied to different wheat materials by various investigators is presented in Table 4.1.

Table 4.1. Comparison between different breeding procedures for grain yield in wheat

Procedures	Situation	Author(s)
Pedigree method *versus* bulk method	Pedigree method better	Pawar (1985a, 1985b, 1986); Pawar *et al.* (1987); Singh *et al.* (1987); Srivastava *et al.* (1989); Pawar and Singh (1991); Deghais and Aurian (1993)
Modified pedigree method *versus* Selected bulk selection method	Selected bulk method better	Wang *et al.* (2003)
Selected bulk selection method *versus* Bulk selection method	Selected bulk method better	Wang *et al.* (2003)
Pedigree method *versus* SSD method	Pedigree method better	Pawar *et al.* (1985a, 1985b, 1986, 1987, 1994, 1997, 2001); Pawar and Singh (1991)
	SSD method better	Kumar (1973); Knott (1979); Pande *et al.* (1998)

Contd.

Procedures	Situation	Author(s)
	Both equally effective	Kumar (1973); Wright and Thomas (1976); Knott (1979); Singh *et al.* (1987); Srivastava *et al.* (1989); Pawar and Singh (1991)
SSD method *versus* Bulk method	SSD method better	Tee (1971); Knott and Kumar (1975); Pawar *et al.* (1985a, 1985b, 1986, 1987); Singh *et al.* (1987); Srivastava *et al.* (1989); Pawar and Singh (1991); Deghais and Aurian (1993).
	Bulk method better	Tee and Qualset (1975) for competitive effects; Ndondi (1987) for yield
	Both equally effective	Tee (1971); Tee and Qualset (1975)
SSD method *versus* MSD method	MSD method better	Ndondi (1987)
	Both equally effective	Ndondi (1987) for protein content

CHAPTER 5

Mutation Breeding

Both the natural evolution and plant breeding (man-directed evolution) greatly depend on the basic genetic changes called mutations. Artificial induction of mutations in plants using some mutagenic agents (X-rays, gamma rays, EMS, etc.) has become an important breeding technique for creating new genes and new gene combinations, utilizing them in the improvement of crops and thus widening the genetic base of crop species. According to Mac Key (1956) and many others, the importance of the concept of mutation breeding was realized since the technique facilitates induction of a single, simply inherited character into a genotype without disturbing the delicate balance of other characters. Coincidently, in the same year, Sears utilized a radiation-induced gene substitution procedure for transferring a leaf rust resistant gene from *Triticum umbellulatum* (a wild diploid grass species) to the *Chinese Spring* variety of *T. aestivum* (hexaploid bread wheat). In this classical procedure, *T. umbellulatum* was first crossed with *T. turgidum* (tetraploid emmer wheat) and the chromosome number of the F_1 hybrid was doubled. Then, this hybrid with 42 chromosomes was crossed to Chinese Spring variety. After repeated backcrossing to Chinese Spring, plants possessing one extra chromosome and leaf rust resistance were identified. These plants, before flowering, were treated with X-rays and subsequently their pollen was used to pollinate Chinese Spring variety. Fortunately, one of these Chinese Spring plants possessed resistance to leaf rust without undesirable characteristics of *T. umbellulatum*. Therefore, Sears was able to prove beyond doubt that the technique of mutation breeding can be used to transfer alien genes to cultivated varieties.

Mutant Varieties Produced

There are a number of examples where wheat cultivars have been improved throught direct induction of mutations (Konzak, 1987). For example, in India, the variety NP 799 (an awnless wheat variety) was treated with X-rays and a new mutant variety *NP 836* (with presence of awns and higher yield) was released in 1961. Similarly, *Sharbati Sonora* is a mutant version of Sonora 64A. The variety Sharbati Sonora which has amber grain colour and was released in 1967, was developed by irradiating

Sonora 64A with gamma rays. A third variety *Pusa Lerma* is a mutant form of Lerma Rojo. This variety was approved for release in 1971 and has amber grain colour (an improved characteristic).

There are many examples of wheat cultivars developed through direct mutation breeding in other countries. In Germany, hexaploid wheat (*T. aestivum*) materials were treated with X-rays in 1950s and were subsequently screened for reduced height and lodging resistance. Two mutant varieties, namely, *Els* (approved in 1960) and *Sirius* (approved in 1968-1974), possessing desirable characters, were released. Many other successful attempts were made in other countries in 1950s, 1960s and early 1970s for bringing improvement in hexaploid and tetraploid wheats for these two characters (plant height and lodging). In USA, two varieties, *Lewis* and *Stadler* (both approved in 1964) were developed using thermal neutrons; in Japan, the variety *Zenkouzi-komugi* (approved in 1969) was developed through gamma rays treatment; in USSR, the variety *Novosibirskaja* 67 (approved in 1970), was evolved after giving gamma rays treatment; and in Finland, the variety *Hankkijas Taava* (approved in 1970) was developed using gamma rays. All these mutant varieties belong to *T. aestivum* and possessed both the desired characters mentioned above.

Six varieties of tetraploid wheat (*T. turgidum durum*) which had reduced height and lodging resistance were developed. Of these, four varieties, *Castelporziano* and *Castelfusano*, developed using thermal neutrons and approved in 1968, *Castel del Monte*, developed using fast neutrons and approved in 1969, and *Castelnuovo* developed using X-rays and approved in 1971, were evolved in Italy. One variety, G-0367 developed using thermal neutrons and approved in 1970, was evolved in Greece. The sixth variety, *Durox* (approved in 1981) was evolved in USA using EMS.

Some other mutant varieties of hexaploid wheat were developed with different objectives in mind. For example, variety *Sinvalocho Gamma* (approved in 1962) was evolved in Argentina for stem and leaf rust resistance by giving gamma treatment; the variety *Shirowase-Komugi* (approved in 1977) was developed in Japan for closed canopy phenotype using gamma radiation; and the variety *Jauhar* (approved in 1979) was evolved in Pakistan for amber grain colour using fast neutrons.

In addition to the development of wheat varieties by direct mutations breeding, several varieties of *T. turgidum* (*Augusto, Tito, Creso, Mida, Attila, Miradur, Lozen 76*, etc.) and *T. aestivum* (IAS 63, *Martonvasar 8, Odesskaja 75*, etc.) were evolved in Italy (4), Austria (3), Bulgaria (1), Brazil (1), Hungary (2) and USSR (1) by applying *mutation cross-breeding* or *mutation recombination-breeding*.

Mutation cross-breeding is an indirect method of evolving mutant varieties. In this procedure, characters from two or more mutants are combined in the same background to allow recombination between mutant characters and the characters from other germplasm. However, mutation cross-breeding is a lengthy procedure of developing mutant varieties and takes about double time than is normally required by direct mutation breeding method in diploid cereals (Yamagata, 1981). Sigurbjornsson (1972) and Micke and Donini (1982) also emphasized the importance of direct mutation breeding as it cuts short the time taken to develop a mutant cultivar. Nevertheless, in cases where selected mutant alleles are uniquely valuable (e.g. semidwarf mutants), mutation cross-breeding may be preferred over direct mutation breeding (Yamagata, 1981; Konzak et al. 1984). Therefore, the special importance of some specific mutant alleles, sometimes, becomes more important than the time required by a particular method.

When to Use Mutation Breeding

Despite the fact that mutation breeding has some important advantages (The technique excels other breeding procedures in its potential for creating new genes and gene combinations in a species; the technique facilitates induction of any kind of heritable change right from point mutation to the loss or addition of entire genome; and new advancements and refinements in this technique allow induction of new genes at specific loci), the technique has some serious drawbacks too. The main drawbacks of mutation breeding technique are : (i) The proportion of desirable mutations in the total number of mutations produced is very low as most of the mutations are recessive and harmful; (ii) the success of this technique greatly depends on the availability of a suitable screening technique; (iii) in some cases, association of harmful side effects with useful mutations, makes the job of the plant breeder more difficult; (iv) the technique is relatively more costly; (v) manytimes, minor improvement brought by this technique fails to bring an identifiable change in the phenotype of the new variety which may create problem in the registration of the variety; and (vi) the technique is not very successful in improving agronomically important quantitative characters. Therefore, the use of mutation breeding technique in improving crop species should not be overrated and this technique should be applied only under specific situations :

1. When natural variability of any species is insufficient or lacks gene(s) for desired characteristics;
2. if the desired gene is tightly linked with some undesirable gene(s);
3. when some sort of compensating mechanism (strong negative correlation between component characters of grain yield, etc.) imposes a ceiling on the yield level and the biological system becomes helpless in further increasing the productivity through conventional recombination breeding;
4. if an outstanding cultivar sucumbs to a new race of a pathogen and the breeder is interested to remove the defect of the cultivar without disturbing its superior genetic background;
5. when a negative correlation exists between a quality trait and disease resistance; or
6. when the objective of the breeder is to change or modify some biochemical pathway in a crop species.

Fortunately or unfortunately, some of the specific situations mentioned above, are very well found in wheat. For example, genetic variability for *Karnal bunt* (KB) or *partial bunt* (a smut disease caused by *Tilletia indica* fungus) is low. The disease has considerably threatened wheat consumption in several parts of the world (India, Pakistan, Nepal, etc.). Therefore, mutation breeding has a good scope for widening the spectrum of genetic variability for controlling this serious disease. Similarly, there is a strong negative correlation between two most important component characters of yield, namely, grain weight and grain number per ear. If the wheat breeder tries to increase the value of one component character, the value of the other character is automatically reduced. Some attempts have been made to increase variability of one component trait through artificial mutagenesis while keeping the value of the other component character constant. It is claimed that the approach has given some positive results. Furthermore, there is a strong negative correlation between lysine content and total protein content in wheat. A change in biochemical pathway may probably help in increasing the lysine percentage while keeping the total protein content constant.

However, it should be kept in mind while using mutation technique in any plant breeding programme that this technique is considered as complementary to other procedures rather than as an alternate method to conventional breeding methods (Brock, 1977).

Selection and Use of Mutagens

There is a long list of physical (ionizing and non-ionizing radiations) and chemical (alkylating agents, base analogues, etc.) mutagenic agents which can be used to induce mutations in plants. However, the selection of an appropriate mutagen to be used in a research programme depends on several factors : (1) Objective of the investigator; (2) effectiveness and usefulness of the mutagen; (3) the nature of the material to be treated; (4) laboratory facilities available to the researcher; (5) cost and availability of the mutagen; (6) reproducibility; (7) persistence of the mutagen and its derivatives in tissues of the material treated; and (8) risk involved in handling of the mutagenic agent and the information available regarding the specific safety practices to be employed.

In general, the use of chemical mutagens is preferred over that of physical mutagens because of the following reasons :

1. The application of chemical mutagens is relatively simple than that of physical mutagens.
2. Costly equipments are not needed for their use.
3. Chemical mutagens produce higher rate of point mutations and thus have less damaging effect on the material than some of the physical mutagens which cause chromosomal disruptions.

However, the handling of chemical mutagens is more risky, these mutagens and their derivatives remain in the tissues for longer time, and the reproducibility of these mutagens is poor.

Among physical mutagens, X-rays and gamma rays (more sparsely ionizing radiations) are most widely used because of their higher penetrating ability. On the contrary, UV light has a poor penetrating ability and, therefore, its use is restricted to the tender plant material only like pollen and thin layer of cultured cells. Similarly, densely ionizing radiations (L-rays, thermal and fast neutrons, etc.) which cause more chromosomal disruptions, are also less preferred by researchers.

Among the chemical mutagens, *ethyl-methane-sulphonate* (EMS), an alkylating agent, has been used most widely for treating plant materials. However, since EMS is a powerful carcinogen, it should be used with utmost care. Swaminathan et al. (1962) soaked the seeds of all three types of wheats (diploid, tetraploid and hexaploid) in EMS solution with four concentrations (180, 220, 280 and 400 ppm) for 18 hours and found that EMS was more effective than α-ray treatment for inducing chlorophyll mutations and chromosome breakage. It was also observed that the loci close to centromere responded more in terms of the occurrence of mutations than the loci situation away from the centromere. Rao (1969) also observed frequent occurrence of mutations in wheat after treating it with EMS. Similar effectiveness of this mutagen for producing mutations in wheat has been found by many others (Kaul, 1969; Edwards et al., 1969; Upadhya and Swaminathan, 1969; Khadr, 1970; Pinthus et al., 1972; and others). According to Kaul, EMS causes high degree of lethality if old wheat seeds are treated with this mutagen. Edwards et al. used three concentrations (0.5%, 0.6% and 0.65%) of EMS to treat wheat variety Little Club and isolated a stem rust resistant mutant. Different types of mutants (speltoid, turgidum, durum and vaviloid) were obtained by Upadhya and Swaminathan after treating *T. piramidale* with EMS. Similarly, Khadr obtained mutants for grain weight and size. Pinthus et al. were able to isolate herbicide resistant mutants after EMS treatment. A variety of *T. turgidum durum* namely, Durox I, was developed in USA using EMS.

According to several investigators (Chopra and Swaminathan, 1966; Edwards and Williams, 1966; Goud, 1967a, b), the effectiveness of EMS increases considerably when it is used in combination with some other mutagen. Chopra and Swaminathan compared the mutagenic efficiency of individual and combined treatments of EMS and hydroxylamine in emmer wheat. They observed that the combined use of the two mutagens was more efficient than their individual use. Similarly, according to Edwards and Williams, combined mutagenic effect of EMS and X-rays proved to be several times more effective than the individual effect of EMS for inducing chlorophyll mutants in *T.durum*. Goud also noted a similar increase in the frequency of morphological mutants in *T. aestivum* after using EMS and gamma rays together. However, his studies indicated that EMS treatment was more efficient than gamma rays and fast neutrons in producing mutations which influence yielding ability. Rao and Swaminathan (1963) found that joint application of EMS and X-rays resulted in the production of *vavilovoid* mutants in *T. aestivum*.

In addition to the use of EMS, several attempts have been made to use other chemicals as mutagenic agents. For example, diethyl sulphate (DES), N-methyl nitrosourea (MNUA), N-ethyl nitrosourea (ENUA), N-methyl urethane (MNU) and N-ethyl urethane have been very effectively used for inducing mutations in wheat (Konzak, 1981). Earlier also, a number of investigators (Haarring, 1962; Gilbert, 1963; Zoz, 1965; Zoz and Makarova, 1964, 1965; Eiges *et al.* 1971; Skvarniko *et al.* 1971; and others) had used various chemical mutagens to obtain different kinds of mutations in wheat.

Among the physical mutagens, *X-rays* and *gamma rays* have been used at large scale for inducing mutations in many plant species. Scossiroli (1962) treated dry wheat seeds with 10000r dose of X-rays and noted an extreme variability for several characters (plant height, number of internodes, tillering capacity, time of flowering, number of grains per ear and grain weight per plant). A large number of positive mutants were produced by Borojevic (1963b) in durum as well as aestivum wheats by treating dry seeds with 15000r and 25000r doses of this mutagen. Galachlova and Skurina (1963) found that the water content of the grain is directly related to the number of mutations produced. More the water content, more are the mutations produced. If the germinating seeds are treated with X-rays, even a lower dose of 5000r proves lethal (Ostrowska, 1964). According to Babayan *et al.* (1965), X-rays treatment was more effective in producing mutations in wheat when physiologically young embryos (6-10 days after fertilization) were treated than when mature grains were treated. Dubinin (1969) opined that when dry wheat seeds of F_1 and F_2 generations were treated with 10000-15000r or when repeated treatment was given to these seeds, both the treatments were very effective in inducing mutations. However, in some cases, the parents responded more to the type of treatment than to the generation. According to Vozvozov (1969), even lower doses of X-rays (250-2000r) can be used to treat germinating seeds for inducing large number of mutations in wheat.

According to some investigators, X-ray treatment is variety specific as the same dose proves lethal in case of some varieties but not for others.

X-rays have been used to produce a large number of mutant varieties in plant species. The variety NP 836 of hexaploid wheat (in India) was developed using X-rays as a mutagen. Also, the varieties Els and Sirius of *T. aestivum* (in Germany) and the variety Castelnuovo of *T. turgidum durum* (in Italy) were developed using X-rays.

Like EMS, X-rays are more effective when used in combination with other physical mutagens. According to Bhatia and Swaminathan (1963b), the joint treatment of X-rays and beta-particles proved more efficient in inducing mutations than the individual treatments of the two mutagens.

Like X-rays, *gamma rays* have been used by a large number of investigators to artificially induce mutations in tetraploid and hexaploid wheats. Many researchers have used gamma rays produced by cobalt gun for inducing mutations., Tavcar (1962) treated dry wheat seeds with three doses (5000r, 7500r and 10000r) of gamma rays and obtained useful mutations for plant height, vegetative period, ear length, awn length, quality traits, rust resistance and cold stress resistance. According to Fonstein (1963), if the dry wheat seeds are treated with a lower dose and then those of the next generation (M_1) with higher dose of this radiation, the progeny shows increased resistance to the radiation.

However, Savin (1963) and Yoshizo (1968) found that a lower dose of gamma rays stimulates plant growth in wheat, but a higher dose of the radiation causes an increase in the genetic variability. Tavcar (1965) noted that a lower dose of gamma radiation causes less chromosomal disruptions and enhances formation of useful mutants. The critical dose of this radiation, according to Novy and Urban (1965), is 12500r. A repeated application of this radiation results in a considerable increase in the frequency of mutations (Volodin, 1966). If the radiation is applied after crossing, there is a significant increase in the number of mutations (Savov, 1969). Similar results were found by Eiges et al. (1971) who recorded maximum number of useful mutants when 10000r dose of this radiation was applied. Siddiqui and Haahr (1971), Korotkova (1972) and Mujica et al. (1972) observed different reactions of wheat mutants to a systemic fungicide, higher yielding mutants, and stem rust resistant mutants in wheat, respectively.

The use of permanent gamma radiation during vegetative period caused reduction in plant height and spike length and an increase in the sterility (Kozhusko, 1961). According to Donini et al. (1964), a dose higher than 72r of this radiation causes total sterility. Donini et al. (1968) observed that for producing useful mutants in durum wheat, the doses higher than 10r should be avoided. However, the maximum number of desirable mutants can be produced by treating the plants during embryogenesis.

Many wheat varieties have been developed using gamma radiation. For example, Pusa Lerma and Sharbati Sonora in India, Sinvalocho Gamma in Argentina, Zenkouzi-komugi and Sohirowase-komugi in Japan, Hankkijas Taava in Finland and Carolina in Chile have been produced using this radiation.

As mentioned earlier, the joint use of gamma radiation and EMS increases the frequency of morphological mutants.

Fast neutrons have also been used to induce mutations in wheat. These neutrons generally cause frequent chromosomal disruptions. Fast neutrons show some degree of specificity to variety and prove better than X-rays (D'Amato and Scarascia, 1962). According to Borojevic (1965), fast neutrons are capable of producing speltoid, sphaerococcoid and awned mutants and causing chromosome breakage and bridge formation in wheat. Fast neutron treatment helps in selecting stem solidity (Bozzini, 1965). According to Martini and Bozzini (1965), recessive sterile mutants can be obtained through the use of fast neutrons and these neutrons are more efficient than gamma rays and X-rays. Hassan-Khan (1973) was able to obtain early dwarf mutants of wheat with high protein content through the use of these neutrons.

Although a joint treatment of fast neutrons and EMS produced a number of dwarf mutants in durum wheat, but also caused reduction in fertility.

The variety Jauhar-78 in Pakistan and the variety Castel del Monte in Italy were developed through the use of fast neutrons.

Thermal neutrons have also been used to develop mutant varieties of wheat in USA (varieties Lewis and Stadler), Italy (varieties Castelporziano and Castelfusano) and in Greece (variety G-0367) (Konzak, 1987).

Some *isotopes*, namely, P^{32}, S^{35}, K^{32}, B^{10} and Cs^{137} have also been used as mutagens. The treatment with P^{32} causes reduction in DNA content in plants (Klechovskii et al., 1962). After treating the seeds of *T. turgidum* × *T. aestivum* hybrids with S^{35}, Swaminathan et al. (1966) observed pollen sterility and abnormal spike due to meiotic irregularities.

As discussed earlier, radiation treatment can cause a variety of mutations in wheat. In addition, several other types of mutations affecting grain weight, tillering capacity, earliness, lodging resistance and pollen sterility have been observed (Konzak, 1966; Grinvald *et al.*, 1967); Savchenko *et al.*, 1971). According to Konzak (1973), even isogenic lines can be produced through the use of suitable mutagen.

Irrespective of the type of mutagen (chemical or physical) used, the type of mutation produced is mostly a matter of chance. Of course, the type of mutagen, its dose and duration of treatment and its repeated application may considerably affect the frequency of mutation. However, in some cases, mutagen-specific and locus-specific occurrence of mutations has been indicated. For example, Rana and Swaminathan (1967) noted some correlation between frequency of mutation at certain loci and the mutagen used. This suggests that a more systematic use of mutagens can be made. Similar observations were made earlier also. Matsumura (1966) had noted that the occurrence of certain mutations can be controlled by making some appropriate modifications in the dose of the mutagen. Similarly, a change in temperature may modify the effect of irradiation (Skvarnikov, 1963). The view of Rana and Swaminathan has also been supported by Singh (1969) based on the activity of Q suppressor locus.

It is now generally agreed by most of the investigators working an mutation breeding that smaller doses of mutagens are more favourable for inducing useful mutations. Higher doses of mutagens and their repeated use generally cause chromosomal disruptions and abnormalities in plant characteristics.

Let us discuss in brief the effect of mutagens at molecular level. Mutagens cause a change in DNA structure. In fact, the point mutation is the consequence of an intra-genic change in the hereditary material. There may be a change in the number or sequence of nitrogenous bases in a DNA molecule or a base is replaced by some other base. However, orgaisms have an apposing natural force for correcting such minor changes in the hereditary material through enzymatic activity. If the disorder is corrected, then there will be no apparent mutation in the phenotype of the individual. Such correction of disorders may be seen in two opposite ways : (1) In one way, it is advantageous since it helps in maintaining the gene structure and thus making the gene more stable; (2) in other way, it may be considered as a disadvantage from the point of view of breeding since it restricts the increase in genetic variability. This fault-correction is again a matter of chance. According to Hanawalt (1972), no relationship between correction tendency and the frequency of mutations, mutagen type or genotype is yet known.

Mutagenic Effect and Ploidy Level

Wheats are found in three forms, diploid wheats, tetraploid wheats and hexaploid wheats. Since the chromosomes of the three genomes involved in the evolution of polyploid wheats are homeologous, the stock of the genes is two-fold in tetraploid wheats and three-fold in hexaploid wheats. The genes found in homeologous chromosomes are able to compensate for one another. Therefore, it is difficult to identify gene mutations in polyploid wheats. This difficulty is of more intensity in hexaploids than in tetraploids. This situation of identifying mutations is also seen in two opposite ways : (1) Polyploid wheats create difficulty in the identification of gene mutations, especially the defective mutation, and thus the situation is not favourable; (2) in other way, polyploid wheats show higher resistance against mutagens and thus the situation is favourable in terms of the stability of the genotype.

Tetraploid wheats have been found more reactive to X-ray treatments (Palenzoni, 1961). According to Scossiroli *et al.* (1961), *T. durum* was more sensitive to higher dose of X-rays than *T.aestivum*. Similar situation has been observed when repeated X-ray treatment was given. According to Kao (1965), the mutation frequency due to X-ray treatment was four times high in tetraploid wheats than in hexaploid wheats.

Ploidy level increases resistance against fast neutrons also. Matsumura (1964) found that hexaploid wheats are least reactive to fast neutron treatment, while tetraploids and diploids show intermediate and maximum sensitivity, respectively, to this treatment.

Similarly, hexaploid wheats have been found less sensitive to gamma rays than tetraploid wheats. According to Donini *et al.* (1964), *T.aestivum* showed better response against gamma rays in terms of seed setting than *T. durum* which had higher rate of mutation frequency.

According to a number of investigators, the results of the EMS treatment in wheat are also influenced by ploidy level. Ploidy level shows its effect on both the mutation rate and the degree of sterility.

Ploidy level considerably influences the relative proportion of mutant types induced in wheat (Mac Key, 1967). Diploid wheats show a high tendency of producing chlorophyll-deficient mutants. On the contrary, the fraction of such mutants in polyploid wheats (both tetraploid and hexaploid wheats) is small and that too of only a few types of mutants. Nevertheless, according to Mac Key (1981a) and Konjak (1981), polyploid wheats produce significantly large number of viable mutants than are generally produced by diploid wheats. This clearly indicates that the total number of mutations produced is higher in polyploids than in diploids.

Sponaneous Mutations in Wheat

A large number of investigators (Schmalz, 1962a; Urich and Heyne, 1968; Gustafsson *et al.*, 1970; Zoz, 1971; and others) have emphasized the importance of natural mutations occuring in wheat. In fact, a major mutation which occurred in 5B chromosome has played a key role in the evolution of polyploid wheats. This mutation which does not allow pairing between homeologous chromosomes (so that there is pairing between homologous chromosomes only), is responsible for the diploidization of polyploid wheats. Similarly, mutation at Q locus in wheat has considerably affected threshibility. In fact, when we are measuring the rate of mutation due to some mutagenic treatment, the possibility of the occurrence of spontaneous mutations cannot be ruled out.

Induction of Desired Mutants

Production of desired mutants has a unique importance in practical wheat breeding. A number of mutants of specific interest in wheat breeding have been developed and are being successfully used by wheat breeders. Some of them will be discussed here.

Dwarf mutants : The genes responsible for reduced height (Rht) in wheat have played a key role in increasing yield levels of this important cereal. The most important point which goes in favour of Rht genes is that Rht mutants can be easily induced in almost all genetic backgrounds (Gaul and Aastviet, 1966; Konzak, 1981). Many Rht genes (Rht 1 to Rht 20) have been produced and thus relative merits and demerits have been discussed (Konzak, 1987). Semi-dwarf wheats carrying Rht genes are now being grown worldwide.

Of the 20 Rht genes, Rht 1 and Rht 2 which are located on the 4A and 4D chromosomes, respectively, have been most widely used in wheat breeding. The sources of these two genes are the old Japanese cultivars Shirodaruma and Akadaruma through Norin 10 (Konzak, 1987). However, the main drawback associated with Rht 1 and Rht 2 mutants is that they have short coleoptile which may create serious problem during seedling emergence and may adversely affect stand establishment under low moisture conditions (Allan, 1980).

The Rht 8 and Rht 9 genes located on 2D and 7B chromosomes, respectively, have been moderately used in wheat breeding programmes. However, no confirmed report is yet available about the effect of these two mutants on seedling emergence. The source of these two mutant alleles is an old Japanese land variety, Akakomugi.

The gene Rht 13 carried by Magnif 41 is though different from Rht 1 and Rht 2 but is not different in respect of dominance behaviour. However, the new gene Rht 20 carried by Burt, seems to be a useful mutant allele (Konzak, 1986).

The gene Rht 12 carried by Karcagi 522 mutant, is an important mutant allele showing almost complete dominance (Konzak, 1984). According to Sutka and Kovac (1987), this mutant has a considerable agronomic value because of its strong dominant characteristic, stiff culms and large fertile ears. However, before this mutant is accepted as an agronomically superior genotype, it is necessary to remove its undesirable characteristics (thick and wide leaves, spreading habit and late maturity). The gene Rht 12 is located on 5A chromosome.

All the five Rht mutants induced in durum wheat, namely, Capelli (containing semidominant Rht 14 gene), Durox (containing partially recessive gene Rht 15), Edmore SD1, Anhinga and Vic SD 1 (all three containing partially dominant genes, Rht 16, Rht 18 and Rht 19, respectively), have sufficiently long coleoptiles.

Mutagen-induced disease resistance : Although breeding for resistance to biotic stresses (diseases and insect pests) is always one of the main objectives of wheat breeding programmes, there are not many examples of mutagen-induced disease resistance in wheat. Of course, the cultivars *IAS 63* (developed by crossing two M_2 mutants of IAS 20 and released in Brazil in 1974) and *Sinvalocho Gamma* (developed using gamma irradiation and approved in Argentina in 1962), are two striking examples of mutation-induced disease resistant varieties. IAS 63 possesses greater resistance to more rust races and has higher yield potential than IAS 20. Similarly, Sinvalocho Gamma has increased resistance to stem and leaf rusts.

However, there are several reports that there is a common occurrence of disease resistance suppressor genes in wheat (Law *et al.*, 1978; Pink *et al.*, 1983; and others). The occurrence of such genes in wheat germplasm offers an excellent opportunity for the development of mutagen-induced disease resistance genotypes. Production of such isogenic lines may help in understanding the types of host-pathogen interactions in a better way.

Development of male-sterile facilitated recurrent selection (MSFRS) populations : Recessive as well as dominant male sterility mutants have been induced in wheat. Two mutants, namely, recessive mutant ms 1C called as Cornerstone and dominant genetic male sterility mutant Ms 3, are being widely used to develop male-sterile facilitated recurrent selection populations in *T. aestivum* (Ramage, 1977; Driscoll, 1984; Konzak, 1984; Konzak *et al.*, 1984a). Both these mutants are artificially induced mutants. The mutant Ms 3 was initially induced in *T. aestivum* stock carrying *T. tauschii* cytoplasm and then was transferred to stocks carrying *T. aestivum* cytoplasm. This dominant allele (Ms 3), is found on the short arm of 5A chromosome and may help in developing hybrid wheat if a suitable restorer gene for this gene is found. However, it is easy to induce recessive male sterility mutants in tetraploid as well as hexaploid wheats.

Earliness : According to Solari and Favret (1968), both the induction and detection of mutants for earliness are easy in wheat. However, the frequency of mutants for lateness is higher than that of the mutants for earliness (Konzak, 1981; Larik et al., 1984). Zenkouzi-komugi and Shan Nong or Radio 63 are two early maturing varieties of *T. aestivum* and have been evolved in Japan and PRC-Shanolong, respectively, using gamma irradiation.

Kar et al. (1978), in India, developed a physiologically potential mutant from the famous wheat variety Kalyansona. The mutant HD 2237 has several desirable characteristics. It is superior to Kalyansona in terms of yielding ability, earliness (matures 25 days earlier), grain weight (15 per cent more), height (10 cm shorter) and synchronous tillering. In addition, the mutant has a reduced vegetative phase and an extended reproductive phase (Konzak, 1987).

Plant canopy : Mutants for better plant stature have been induced both in hexaploid and tetraploid wheats (de Kock, 1972; Konzak, 1981). The mutant variety Shirowase-Komugi directly developed from Shirogane-Kamugi in Japan using gamma rays is one of the best examples of such mutants. This mutant cultivar has a better plant canopy than that of Shirogane-Komugi.

Awned mutants : Development of awned mutants has a special importance in some environments where awns may make a considerable contribution towards yield. Further, according to Konzak (1981), awned mutants may play an important role in developing more truly isogenic lines. The development of awned mutants is easy in wheat. One useful awned mutant (NP 836) was developed in India by treating the awnless variety NP 799 with X-rays. The variety NP 836 was also higher yielder than NP 799.

Grain colour : Mutation breeding may prove to be an efficient means to convert undesirable grain colour to a desirable one. The mutants Sharbati Sonora (from Sonora 64A) and Pusa Lerma (from Lerma Rojo) developed in India, are some good examples of grain colour mutants.

Protein quantity and quality : The research on the development of mutants with improved protein has been limited due to the non-availability of standard procedures of analysis and those of efficient screening techniques to detect such mutants. However, despite these difficulties, some promising protein mutants have been developed without any reduction in yield. The development of Carolina in Chile (Parodi and Nebreda, 1982a, 1982b), of TW-1 in Pakistan (Bhagwat et al., 1979), and production of several mutants at FAO/IAEA, Vienna (Hermelin, 1984) are some examples of such promising protein mutants.

There are several reports that mutants with improved lysine content have been developed in Argentina, USA and Russia.

Concluding Remarks

1. It has become an established fact now that mutation breeding can greatly help the wheat breeders in increasing genetic variability, especially in case of characters for which genetic variability is limited.
2. The success of mutation breeding programme is determined by several factors like the mutagen used, material used and duration of treatment, genotype and the screening technique available to detect mutants.
3. Mutation breeding offers better opportunity for developing more truly isogenic lines than conventional breeding methods.
4. Mutation breeding should be used as a complementary rather than an alternate method to conventional breeding methodology.

CHAPTER 6

Alien Gene Transfers

Wheat has been and will be playing a major role in feeding the ever increasing human population. However, for the well-being of our people in future, it should be ensured that crop production increases stay abreast of population growth, that is, food production should go on increasing in proportion to the increasing human population. But there are certain hard facts before us :

1. According to the experts' prediction, in the year 2020, world's human population is expected to be around 8 billion and to feed this population, our wheat requirement would be about one billion metric tonnes, that is, we should harvest 4 tonnes of wheat per hectare. Further, if the human population grows with the same speed, around 12 billion human beings would be walking on the earth in the year 2050 and we can estimate the quantity of wheat, the world would require in that year.
2. The modern wheat varieties which have almost completely replaced the old wheats, have generated about 1 per cent average increase in wheat productivity each year (Sayre *et al.*, 1997), but this annual rate of increase in wheat productivity is now steadily declining because the gains from dwarfing genes are now gradually levelling off.
3. Since the developing countries would be the principal contributors towards population growth (approximately 90 per cent), the people of these nations would be affected most by the food scarcity, if any, in future.
4. The genetic improvement of crop plants is the most critical requirement for maximizing their yield potential. However, the desirable genetic variability in cultivated wheat is limited. Therefore, for increasing appropriate genetic variability in this cereal it becomes necessary to incorporate useful genes from wild species into the cultivated wheats. In fact, inter-varietal hybridization has a very limited scope for bringing further jump in the yield levels of wheat and wide hybridization is not only a matter of academic interest but now it has become a need of the day for breaking yield barriers in wheat.

The ominous circumstances mentioned above have placed a formidable task before the wheat breeders of the world since, on one front, they are busy in getting a worthwhile increase in wheat production but, on the other front they are facing problem of insufficient desirable genetic variability present in the germplasm of cultivated wheats.

Our discussion in this chapter will be restricted to the point (4) mentioned above.

An alien gene transfer in wheat means when one or a group of genes is transferred to wheat from some other species. This transfer of genes, chromosome segments or of whole chromosomes may be from a closely related or a distantly related species. The success of transferring alien genetic material to wheat is generally determined by the degree of pairing between the chromosomes of alien species and those of wheat. However, by producing amphidiploids (hybridization between two species followed by doubling of chromosomes), we not only can add or substitute whole chromosome or chromosome pair (production of addition and substitution lines), but also the whole genome of a species can be transferred to wheat (production of a new species). *Triticale* or *Triticosecale* is the only one example of such man-made crop species, where whole genome of rye (*Secale cereale*) has been transferred to wheat. Nevertheless, rye has some undesirable genes too which have come in triticale along with its desirable characteristics. This is the biggest disadvantage of whole genome transfers and this is also the biggest reason that triticale till today could not take the form of a completely successful crop species. Of course, in some countries of the world, triticale is being grown on commercial scale.

Hexaploid wheat ($2n=6x=42$) is different from other cereal crops in three main respects in terms of the possibilities for incorporation of alien genetic material.

1. Since there are three sets of genomes in this wheat, the species is able to tolerate the addition or loss of whole chromosomes without significantly influencing the viability of the plant.
2. The deleterious effect of the alien genes of the added or substituted chromosome is generally marked by the duplicate genes present in the chromosomes of the other two genomes.
3. A variety of efficient aneuploid cytogenetic techniques have been developed in this crop species.

Let us first discuss the production of synthetic amphidiploids, wheat-alien addition lines and wheat-alien substitution lines in bit detail. The production of these three types of genotypes may not have any significant economic value, but their production can greatly help in pin-pointing the chromosomal location of desirable genes and in transferring useful genes to cultivated wheats since the production of an amphidiploid is mandatory to restore fertility of a sterile F_1 hybrid.

Production of Amphidiploids

An amphidiploid generally means the hybridization between two distantly related species followed by spontaneous or artificially induced doubling of chromosomes of the sterile F_1 hybrid. Both the processes (distant hybridization and chromosome doubling) may occur in nature or may be carried out by man. Although the evolution of polyploid wheats must have occurred through natural hybridization between two species of the tribe *Triticeae* followed by spontaneous doubling of the chromosomes of the sterile F_1 hybrid or through natural hybridization between two species having unreduced gametes, the credit for producing first synthetic amphidiploid between *T. aestivum* and *Secale cereale* with spontaneously doubled chromosomes, goes to Rimpau (1891). Tschermak and Bleier (1926) and Kihara and Katayama (1953) made similar efforts for producing spontaneous amphidiploids from the hybrids between tetraploid wheat and *Aegilops* species.

However, the credit of the induction of first deliberately produced amphidiploids involving wheat goes to Dorsey (1936). Here, the hybrid zygotes of *T. aestivum* × *S. cereale* were given heat treatment. But at about the same time, Blakeslee and Avery (1937) discovered that the alkaloid *colchicine* (extracted from the plant *Colchicum autumnale*) can be used as an efficient agent for doubling the chromosomes. Colchicine prevents spindle fibre formation and, as a result, all the longitudinally divided chromosomes are again enclosed by the same nuclear membrane. This discovery of Blakeslee and Avery provided a big stimulus to the scientists working in this field and, as a result, many synthetic amphidiploids were produced (Sears, 1941; Kihara and Kondo; and others). In addition to colchicine, some other chemicals like *nitrous oxide* (Kihara and Tsunewaki, 1960) and halothane (Nunn, Louis and Kimball, 1971) have also been used for doubling the chromosomes of sterile F_1 hybrids.

Nevertheless, Tsuchiya and Larter (1968) have used a more relevant method (especially in case of spontaneous amphidiploids) called as *direct amphidiploid synthesis*, for the production of amphidiploids. In this method, instead of doubling the chromosomes of the sterile F_1 hybrid, the chromosomes of parents are doubled before hybridization to produce a fertile amphidiploid with already doubled chromosomes. The main advantage of the method is that doubling of chromosomes of the parents is easier than that of the sterile F_1 hybrid. However, the use of the method has so far been very limited.

Production of amphidiploids facilitates development of alien addition lines and alien gene transfers. In addition, it provides opportunity for creating new commercial synthetic crops. Development of hexaploid triticale has proved that new crop species with desirable stability can be produced. However, it appears that hexaploidy is the optimum ploidy level in case of triticales. Of course, according to Feldman and Sears (1981), the scope of producing agronomically superior new crop species has not completely exhausted.

The CIMMYT scientists have been doing a commendable job for the last 25 years by conducting a vigorous gene transfer programme involving perennial and annual wheat relatives. According to Mujeeb-Kazi (1995), *T. tauschii* [(an annual wild relative of wheat and, according to Kimber and Feldman (1987), an unequinocally accepted D genome donor to bread wheat)] has a wide range of useful characteristics. These characteristics include resistance or tolerance to biotic and abiotic stresses (Valkoun *et al.*, 1990) and the species is a potent source of new variability for grain weight, bread making quality and photosynthetic efficiency. As regards the biotic and abiotic stresses, *T. tauschii* is resistant to leaf rust (*Puccinia recondita*), stripe rust (*P. striiformis*), Karnal bunt (*Tilletia indica*), scab (*Fusarium graminearum*), spot blotch (*Helminthosporium sativum* syn. *Bipolaris sorokiniana*),etc. and tolerant to drought and salinity. Since the D genome of *T. tauschii* is also present in *T. aestivum*, the crosses between bread wheat and *T. tauschii*, are considered as interspecific and not as intergeneric by the CIMMYT scientists.

At CIMMYT, *T. tauschii* accessions are being utilized in three ways : (1) Making crosses between *T. turgidum* varieties and desired *T. tauschii* accessions for producing synthetic hexaploids; (2) making direct crosses between elite but susceptible *T. aestivum* varieties and *T. tauschii* accessions and backcrossing the F_1 hybrids with *T. aestivum* variety used in the initial cross; and (3) extracting AABB genomes from commercial varieties of *T. aestivum* and then producing hexaploids by crossing with appropriate *T. tauschii* accessions.

Producing synthetic hexaploids : To develpe amphidiploids, *T turgidum durum* is crossed as female with *T. tauschii* as male parent. Hybrid embryos with 21 chromosomes are rescued by growing them in embryo cultures and then the plantlets are transplanted to a potted soil mix and maintained in greenhouse.

Spontaneous or induced (with colchicine treatment) chromosome doubling is done for producing amphidiploid with 42 chromosomes. Resistant/tolerant plants are selected after thorough screening. The selected plants with useful characteristics are then crossed to *T. aestivum* varieties and ultimately resistant/tolerant plants are selected from the progeny.

Numerous synthetic hexaploids have been produced at CIMMYT. The hexaploids resistant to Karnal bunt, spot blotch and scab have been identified. Those showing tolerance to salt stress have also been identified. Some characters of agronomic and taxonomic importance (grain yield, total biomass, harvest index, maturity period, days to anthesis, plant growth, pubescence, pigmentation, etc.) have been studied by Villareal *et al.* (1990).

According to molecular biologists working in collaboration of CIMMYT, some of the synthetic hexaploids developed at CIMMYT are highly polymorphic. Some of the synthetic hexaploids produced by the CIMMYT/Cornell University collaboration have facilitated the development of doubled polyhaploid plants.

Making direct crosses between *T. aestivum* and *T. tauschii*: The purpose of making such direct crosses with bread wheat is to achieve direct transfers of resistance or tolerance from *T. tauschii* to *T. aestivum*. The procedure is simple and straightforward. The elite *T. aestivum* cultivar is crossed as female parent with desired *T. tanschii* accession as male parent. The F_1 plants having 28 chromosomes (ABD-D) are backcrossed as female parents with the *T. aestivum* cultivar used in the initial cross. During backcrossing, selection is done for the desirable characters of *T. tauschii*. In such backcrossing, the reconstitution of the genotype of the recurrent parent is very fast. According to Alonso and Kimber (1984), there was 92 per cent reconstitution of the genotype of the recurrent parent after one backcross.

Using this procedure, Karnal bunt resistant genotypes (with 0.0 per cent infection) have been developed by crossing Karnal bunt susceptible *T. aestivum* varieties with appropriate *T. tauschii* accessions.

Extracting AABB genomes from *T. aestivum*: In this method, the old DD genome of bread wheat is replaced by the DD genome of *T. tauschii* to incorporate characters of *T. tauschii* into *T. aestivum*. The method involves crossing of elite *T. aestivum* cultivar with a tetraploid to develop pentaploid progeny; development and identification of plants with AABB genomes but phenotypically similar to the *T. aestivum* variety used in the beginning of the programme through backcrossing; crossing AABB type plants with desired *T. tauschii* accession to obtain triploid F_1 (ABD); chromosome doubling of F_1 hybrid by colchicine treatment; and screening for desirable characteristics (resistance to diseases, tolerance to salinity, etc.) of *T. tauschii*. These useful characteristics then can be transferred to other *T. aestivum* cultivars.

Production of Alien Chromosome Addition Lines

The addition of a single pair of homologous chromosomes from a related species to the wheat chromosome complement is known as wheat alien disomic addition and the line possessing such addition is called as wheat-alien disomic addition line. The development of alien chromosome addition lines helps in identifying useful genes present on the alien chromosomes and cytogenetically transferring alien genetic material to wheat. However, these lines are associated with three main drawbacks :

1. In most of the cases, wheat-alien addition lines are agronomically inferior to wheat with normal chromosome complement (Sears, 1954).
2. These lines have a lower cytological stability and thus it is necessary to ensure their cytological maintenance at each generation of selfing (Miller, 1984).
3. Since the male gametes carrying alien chromosome have a lower competitive ability than normal wheat gametes, there is danger of quick degeneration of stocks.

Although Leighty and Taylor (1924) had observed wheat-like plants with *hairy neck* characteristic of rye which indicated presence of alien addition line, it was Florell (1931) who, for the first time, provided undisputed proof of wheat-rye disomic addition lines. These lines were isolated from backcross progenies of an F_1 of hexaploid wheat × rye cross. O'Mara (1940) described a standard procedure for producing such lines by crossing an amphidiploid with wheat and then making backcrosses. Driscoll (1983) presented a list of many other wheat-alien disomic additions produced by using different procedures. The methods are :

1. **Through amphidiploids or standard method :** In this method, first an amphidiploid is produced by doubling the chromosomes of the F_1 hybrid of hexaploid wheat × diploid alien species. The amphidiploid ($21^{II}+7^{II}$) is crossed with hexaploid wheat to produce 49 chromosome hybrid ($21^{II}+7^{I}$). This hybrid is again crossed to hexaploid wheat followed by selection for monosomic additions and disomic additions. Three types of amphidiploids, namely, *Triticum-Secale* (O'Mara, 1940; Riley and Chapman, 1958a), *Triticum-Agropyron* (Dvorak and Knott, 1974), and *Triticum-Aegilops* (Kimber, 1967), have been used to produe wheat-alien addition lines.

2. **Through F_1 hybrids :** Here, the F_1 hybrid ($21^{I}+7^{I}$) produced by crossing hexaploid wheat with alien diploid species, is backcrossed to hexaploid wheat. The backcross progeny is subjected to selection for monosomic and disomic additions. This method has been followed in *Triticum × Secale* (Florell, 1931) and *Triticum–Hordeum* (Islam et al., 1975) F_1 hybrids.

3. **Through bridging species :** This method is used when the alien species cannot be directly crossed with hexaploid wheat. Here, the diploid alien species is first crossed with tetraploid wheat (a bridging species). An amphidiploid is produced by doubling the chromosomes of the F_1 hybrid. The amphidiploid thus produced is then crossed with hexaploid wheat to obtain a 42-chromosome hybrid ($14^{II}+7^{I}+7^{I}$). This hybrid is again crossed to hexaploid wheat followed by selection for monosomic and disomic additions. The method has been followed in *Triticum × Haynaldia* hybrids (Hyde, 1953).

The whole scheme of producing monosomic additions and disomic additions by the three methods given above has been diagrammatically described by Gale and Miller (1987).

4. ***Hordeum bulbosum* method :** This method has been used in *Triticum × Hordeum* hybrids where it is difficult to produce disomic addition lines from the monosomic addition lines. The method is based on the progressive elimination of chromosomes and is called as *Hordeum bulbosm* induced chromosome elimination (Islam et al., 1975). The *bulsosum* method is being used as a routine method for developing doubled haploids in *Hordeum vulgare*.

Cuckoo quality of chromosomes : The production of wheat-alien monosomic and disomic addition lines, in several cases, are influenced by the differential rates of transmission shown by different chromosomes during backcrossing with wheat. Some alien chromosomes have a tendency of preferential transmission during backcrosses to wheat (Miller *et al.*, 1982; Miller, 1983). Such propensity of preferential transmission (*Cuckoo quality*) of certain alien chromosomes is found in *T. caudatum, T. cylindricum, T. longissimum, T. triunciale*, etc. (Endo and Tsunewaki, 1975; Maan, 1975; Endo and Katayama, 1978; Endo, 1979). According to Miller (1984), different *Secale cereale* chromosomes also show different rates of transmission. It means that the genes conferring this quality to chromosomes are of widespread occurrence.

Identification of the added alien chromosome : Two methods have been suggested to identify the added chromosome : (1) *On the basis of karyotype*; and (2) *on the basis of phenotype*. A chromosome can be easily identified if it is morphologically distinct from wheat chromosomes in respect of size and/or the location of the centromere (median, submedian or terminal). The presence of secondary constriction or satellite in the alien chromosome makes the job of the investigator more easy provided the satellite is clearly visible. Inconspicuous satellite may create problem in the identification of the alien chromosome. For example, the satellite of 1R chromosome (rye chromosome 1) is so inconspicuous that it is very difficult to identify this chromosome (Lucadena *et al.*, 1984). On the contrary, the satellite of 1U chromosome (*T. umbellulatum* chromosome 1) is quite conspicuous. But, according to Martini *et al.* (1982), it has suppressing effect on the satellites of both the wheat chromosomes 1B and 6B (first and sixth chromosomes of B genome). However, silver satellite staining technique may facilitate identification of active nucleolus organizer regions (Lacadena *et al.*, 1984) which is turn may become a criterion for identifying an alien chromosome. Nevertheless, in this age of biotechnology, the problem of the identification of an alien chromosome cannot frustrate the investigator since several sophisticated chromosome banding techniques are now available which can provide undisputed identification of such chromosomes.

As regards the identification of an alien chromosome on the basis of phenotype, it is easy in some cases where distinct phenotypic effects are found associated with specific chromosomes. For example, 'hairy neck' characteristic of rye is associated with a specific single chromosome of this species and when this chromosome is added to wheat, it can be easily identified. Phenotypic identification of alien chromosomes also helps the investigator in determining the degree of homeology between wheat and alien chromosomes.

Production of Alien Chromosome Substitution Lines

Producing alien chromosome substitution lines in wheat means replacement of a pair of chromosomes of wheat by a pair of chromosomes of an alien species. The main purpose of producing these lines is to know the ability of a pair of alien chromosomes to compensate for the loss of a pair of wheat chromosomes. The advantages of these lines over addition lines are :

1. Substitution lines are relatively more stable than addition lines and, therefore, large scale multiplication of substitution lines is more easy.
2. Production of substitution lines helps in ascertaining the extent of homeology between an alien chromosome and a wheat chromosome.
3. Production of substitution lines permits the evaluation of genes carried by the alien chromosome against each of the three possible alleles carried by the three homeologous chromosomes of wheat. Such evaluation of lines would help in determining the advantageous effect of an alien chromosome as well as in knowing its best position in the wheat genotype.

Of course, the production of substitution lines is bit difficult. For producing these lines, a wheat monosomic ($20^{II}+1^{I}$) is crossed as female parent with a disomic addition line having a pair of alien chromosomes ($21^{II}+1^{II}A$). The chromosome for which the female parent is monosomic should be homeologous to the alien pair in the male parent. In this way, a genotype is produced which has meiotic configuration $20^{II}+1^{I}+1^{I}A$, that is, monosomic wheat + monosomic alien. This genotype is backcrossed as female to the disomic alien addition line and selection is done for monosomic wheat-disomic alien genotype ($20^{II}+1^{I}+1^{II}A$). Selection is again made to obtain a disomic alien substitution genotype ($20^{II}+1^{II}A$).

Incomplete homeology between the wheat chromosome and the alien chromosome can create difficulty in the production of disomic alien substitution lines. The cause of incomplete homeology may be the occurrence of chromosome translocations. The 4R/7R translocation in *Secale cereale* is an example of such translocations.

Kota and Dvorak (1985) suggested an alternative method for producing alien substitution lines. Here, the first step is to produce a separate amphidiploid nullisomic for each substituted chromosome. The amphidiploid nullisomic is then backcrossed to a monotelocentric line of the substituted chromosome and selection is done in backcross progeny for disomic substitution.

Law *et al.* (1977) studied the relative effects of wheat chromosomes 2A, 2B and 2D and *T. comosum* chromosome 2M on grain protein. For this, the chromosome 2M was substituted in the three available homeologous sites (2A, 2B and 2D) in the variety Chinese Spring of *T. aestivum* and the four genotypes, Chinese Spring (2A, 2B, 2D), 2M for 2A (2M, 2B, 2D), 2M for 2B (2A, 2M, 2D) and 2M for 2D (2A, 2B, 2M), were compared to know the effect of the four chromosomes on grain protein. The absence of 2A chromosome (second genotype) was associated with lowest protein content. On the contrary, absence of 2D chromosome (fourth genotype) was associated with highest protein content followed by the absence of 2M and 2B. This indicates that the chromosome 2A has maximum effect and the chromosome 2D the minimum effect on protein content. The chromosomes 2B and 2M have intermediate effect, in order. Therefore, only the substitution of 2M for 2D showed improvement in the protein content, whereas the two other substitutions proved ineffective.

In most of the cases, wheat alien substitution lines are poor yielder than the recipient wheat cultivar. However, because of the presence of specific useful genes (e.g. controlling resistance/tolerance to biotic and abiotic stresses) in the substituted chromosome, some alien substitutions have been released as commercial varieties.

Nevertheless, although a number of advancements and refinements have been made in techniques used to develop three types of genotypes, namely, wheat synthetic amphidiploids, wheat-alien addition lines and wheat-alien substitution lines, this approach could not make a worthwhile contribution towards wheat improvement except where the development of any of these genotypes has been used as an initial or intermediary step in the programme meant for transferring specific useful alien gene(s) to wheat. There are rare cases, where these genotypes have been directly used as commercial varieties. The main reason of this insignificant contribution of these genotypes is that during the transfer of whole chromosomes, along with useful genes, many undesirable genes are also transferred to wheat, that is, the benefits of desirable genes are outweighed by the undesirable genes.

Classification of Wild Relatives of Bread Wheat

Based on the genomic constitutions, the wild relatives of bread wheat have been classified into three gene pools :

Primary gene pool : This gene pool includes hexaploid land races (AABBDD), wild tetraploid *T. dicoccoides* (AABB), cultivated tetraploid *T. turgidum durum* (AABB), wild diploid *T. urartu* (AA), cultivated diploid *T. monococcum* (AA), wild diploid *T. tauschii* (DD), etc. All these relatives have chromosomes homologous to the chromosomes of bread wheat. Therefore, the transfer of genes from this gene pool to bread wheat does not require any special cytogenetic manipulation since such genetic transfers can be carried out by direct crossing followed by normal recombination between homologous chromosomes, backcrossing and selection (Gill and Raupp, 1987; Cox, 1991). Of course, in certain cases (e.g., bread wheat × *T. tauschii* F_1 hybrids), embryo rescue is required for the production of F_1 hybrids.

Secondary gene pool : This gene pool includes polyploid *Triticum* species like wild tetraploid *T. araraticum* (AAGG), cultivated tetraploid *T. timopheevii* (AAGG), wild tetraploids *T. cylindricum* (CCDD), *T. crassum* (DDMM), *T. ventricosum* (DDM^vM^v) and wild hexaploids *T. syriacum* sp. vavilovii (DDMMSS) and *T. juvenale* (DDMMUU). These relatives share at least one genome in common with wheat. Since the contributor of B genome to wheat is not yet fully known, the diploid species falling under Sitopsis section, namely, *T. speltoides* (SS), *T. bicorne* (S^bS^b), *T. longissimum* (S^lS^l) and *T. searsii* (S^sS^s), are also included in the secondary gene pool (Jiang *et al.*, 1994). These species are supposed to be related to B genome of wheat but their chromosomes do not normally pair with the chromosomes of B genome probably because of the occurrence of large chromosomal differentiations. As a result, the transfer of genes from these diploid species to wheat is not easy. The type of technique to be used for the transfer of genes from secondary gene pool to wheat would depend upon the location of gene(s) to be transferred. If the genes are located on the chromosomes homologous to wheat chromosomes, such genes can be easily transferred using direct hybridization and selection. However, if the genes to be transferred are present on the non-homologous chromosomes, some special cytogenetic technique is to be used for transferring such genes.

Tertiary gene pool : This gene pool consists of diploid and polyploid species whose chromosomes are not homologous to the chromosomes of any genome of wheat. These species may belong to *Triticum* genus (e.g., *T. umbellulatum* containing UU genome, *T. caudatum* containing CC genome, *T. comosum* having MM genome, *T. triunciale* containing UUCC genomes, *T. triaristatum* containing UU M^tM^t genomes and *T. ovatum* having UUM^oM^o genomes) or to some other genus. Due to non-homology of chromosomes, genetic transfers from tertiary gene pool to wheat cannot be made through direct hybridization and selection. For such genetic transfers, any especial cytogenetic technique or some other method (tissue culture, use of ionizing radiation, chromosome translocations, etc.) is to be used.

It is an established fact that the wild relatives of wheat carry genes controlling many desirable characters including wide adaptation (Zohary *et al.*, 1969; Brezhnev, 1977; Feldman and Sears, 1981; Sharma *et al.*, 1981; McGuire and Dvorak, 1981; and others). In addition to the adaptation over a broad range of environmental conditions, these relatives of wheat possess useful genes for resistance/tolerance to biotic and abiotic stresses (diseases, drought, lodging, cold, and salinity), high yield, early maturity and high protein. Therefore, to take maximum benefit from these relatives, a thorough screening must be done before their use in the wheat breeding programme. In fact, the identification of an appropriate alien genotype to be used in any wheat improvement programme, is one of the most difficult tasks before the wheat breeder, especially in case of complexly inherited characters.

After the identification of an appropriate alien species, the next essential step is to transfer the alien gene(s) to wheat and reconstitute the wheat genotype with minimum undesirable characteristics. However, the success of transfer is determined mainly by three factors : (1) The type of character, that is, whether the character to be transferred is simply inherited or complexly inherited; (2) the easiness/difficulty in making crosses between alien species and wheat; and (3) the extent of pairing between the chromosomes of alien species and those of wheat, that is, whether the chromosomes of the two species are homologous, homeologous or non-homologous. The factors (2) and (3) mentioned above are not independent of each other. Kimber (1984) emphasized the importance of the thorough knowledge about genome relationships between the two species involved in the transfer before any technique is selected and applied to transfer the genetic material from alien species to recepient wheat genotype.

Transfers from Primary Gene Pool

Transfers from primary gene pool means transfers between homologous chromosomes and are the easiest possible genetic transfers from alien species to bread wheat. As discussed earlier, homolgous transfers can be made by direct hybridization and selection. These transfers may be from tetraploid wheats to bread wheat, from einkorn wheats to bread wheat and from *T. tauschii* to bread wheat.

Transfers from tetraploid wheats to common wheat : Here, both the genomes (AABB) of tetraploid wheat are in common with two genomes of bread wheat (AABBDD). Some important examples of such transfers are the transfer of rust resistance from Iumillo (durum wheat) to Marquillo by Hayes *et al.* (1920), transfer of rust resistance from Yaroslav (emmer wheat) to Hope and H44 (bread wheats) and transfer of stripe rust (*Puccinia striiformis*) resistance from *T. dicoccoides* to common wheat by Grama and Gerechter-Amitai (1974). In general, hexaploid wheat is used as female parent in such crosses, but Grama and Gerechter-Amitai had a different experience in this regard. They found that there was no seed set when *T. aestivum* was used as a female parent.

However, transfers between tetraploid and bread wheats are not problem-free. Sometimes, tight linkage between useful and deleterious genes creates serious problem. According to Loegering and Sears (1963), the transfer of stem rust resistance from Gaza (durum wheat) to Bobbin (bread wheat) was associated with the transfer of a pollen-killer gene. Another problem is about the expression of the transferred gene(s). Some genes when transferred from tetraploid wheat to bread wheat fail to express in hexaploid genetic background. For example, Kerber (1983) could not transfer leaf rust (*Puccinia recondita*) resistance from Stewart 63 (durum wheat) to Canthatch and Marquis (bread wheats) even after making repeated attempts. According to Kerber and Green (1980), a suppressor of resistance to stem rust (*P. graminis*) is found in 7DL chromosome of Canthatch. In a test of 6 bread wheat varieties and 6 synthetic hexaploids, Kerber (1983) noted the presence of the same suppressor of resistance.

Nevertheless, according to Avivi (1979), the transfer of genes from *T. dicoccoides* to bread wheat has a good scope in future as some accessions of *T. dicoccoides* have very high levels of grain storage protein.

Though very rare, but there is possibility of transferring genes from bread wheat to durum wheat if the genes belong to A or B genome. The transfer of the gene Sr 7a (for stem rust resistance) from bread wheat to durum wheat by Kerber (1984), is an example of the reverse transfer (Knott, 1987).

Transfers from einkorn wheats to common wheat : Einkorn wheats, namely, *T. urartu* and *T. boeoticum* (both diploid wild species) and *T. monococcum* (diploid cultivated species), have AA genome in common with bread wheat. Einkorn wheats are, in general, easily crossable to bread wheat. But, the hybrid embryos obtained from such crosses show great variation for their culturability. However, hybridization between these two types of wheats can be made easier by crossing the einkorn species first with *T. durum* and then crossing the F_1 hybrid with bread wheat. Two types of approaches have been suggested : (1) Einkorn wheat is crossed with durum wheat and the F_1 thus obtained is crossed with bread what: and (2) the F_1 of einkorn and durum wheats is backcrossed to durum wheat (1-2 backcrosses) and then hybridized with bread wheat. Either of these two approaches can be followed. According to Kerber and Dyck (1973), all crosses between einkorn and durum wheats are not compatible. Kerber and Dyck (1973) and Knott (1979) were able to transfer stem rust resistance from *T. monococcum* to bread wheat. However, they observed a progressive loss of resistance during these transfers. According to Austin *et al.* (1984), the use of *T. urartu* and *T. boeoticum* ssp. *thaoudar* in future wheat breeding programmes can help in developing genotypes with high rate of photosynthesis.

Transfers from *T. tauschii* to common wheat : The D genome of *T. tauschii* (a wild diploid species) has various genes responsible for bread making quality. As discussed earlier, a lot of work is being done at CIMMYT for transferring desired genes (for biotic and abiotic stresses and some other important characteristics) from *T. tauschii* to common wheat. To transfer genes from *T. tauschii* to bread wheat, this wild diploid is either directly crossed to bread wheat (Merkle and Starks, 1985; Mujeeb Kazi, 1995) or AABB genomes are extracted from bread wheat and then crossed to *T. tauschii* (Mujeeb Kazi, 1995). A more common and successful approach is to cross *T. tauschii* first with *T. turgidum* (used as a bridging species) followed by chromosome doubling by colchicine treatment. The synthetic hexaploid thus produced is then crossed with common wheat (Mujeeb Kazi, 1995).

T. tauschii is a potential source of resistance to leaf rust of wheat. Two genes for seedling resistance and one gene for adult plant resistance were transferred to bread wheat by Kerber and Dyck (1969) and Dyck and Kerber (1970). However, the adult plant resistance to leaf rust was found linked with tenacious glumes (an undesirable characteristic preventing free threshbility). A synthetic hexaploid having a single dominant gene for resistance to greenbug (*Schizaphis graminum*) was developed by crossing *T. turgidum* with *T. tauschii* (Joppa *et al.*, 1980). A similar approach was used to develop wheats possessing resistance for greenbug as well as for Hessian fly (*Mayetiola destructor*) by Martin *et al.* (1982) by using synthetic hexaploids developed by Tanaka. However, an amphidiploid developed by Kerber (1983) by crossing Stewart 63 (durum wheat) with *T. tauschii* showed susceptibility to leaf rust. This indicated that a suppressor of resistance was present in the D genome of *T. tauschii*. Cox *et al.* (1993) also used *T. tauschii* for transferring leaf rust resistance to common wheat.

Transfers from Secondary Gene Pool

As discussed earlier, the transfer of genes from secondary gene pool is easier if the genes are present on the homologous chromosomes but it is difficult when genes to be transferred are found on non-homologous chromosomes. Two tetraploid species, *T. timopheevii* (AAGG) and *T. ventricosum* ($DD M^v M^v$) have been most extensively used for transferring useful genes to bread wheat. Although

T. timopheevii which is a potential source of disease resistance, is readily crossoable to bread wheat, but the *T. aestivum* × *T. timopheevii* hybrids are much less fertile than *T. aestivum* × *T. turgidum* hybrids. Further, former type of hybrids are found associated with male sterility even in early backcross generations. However, the crosses between *T. aestivum* and *T. timopheevii* are more successful when *T. timopheevii* is used as male than when it is used as female. One important example of the transfer of useful genes from *T. timopheevii* to bread wheat is the transfer of resistance to leaf rust (*Puccinia recondita*), stem rust (*P. graminis*) and powdery mildew (*Erysiphe graminis*) by Allard and Shands (1954). According to them, two linked genes governed the resistance to stem rust and that there was a close association between rust resistance and mildew resistance. But, Nyquist (1962) found involvement of only one stem rust resistant gene (Sr 3b). However, according McIntosh and Gyarfas (1971), *T. timopheevii* carries more than three genes for stem rust resistance. Maan and McCracken (1968) noted meiotic irregularities in the lines derived from bread wheat × *T. timopheevii* crosses. According to Deodikar *et al.* (1979), disease resistance from *T. timopheevii* can also be transferred to durum wheat.

Like *T. timopheevii*, *T. ventricosum* also has one genome in common with bread wheat. Whereas AA genome of *T. timopheevii* will pair with AA genome of bread wheat, it is the DD genome of *T. ventricosum* which will pair with DD genome of bread wheat. In both the cases, one genome (GG of *timopheevii* and M^vM^v of *ventricosum*) will remain unpaired.

Several investigators (Sprague, 1936; Maia, 1967; Dosba and Doussinault, 1977; and others) have reported the presence of resistance to eyespot (*Cercosporella herpotrichoides*) in *T. ventricosum*. Maia transferred eyespot resistance from *T. ventricosum* to bread wheat.

According to Delibes *et al.* (1977), three types of approaches have been used to transfer resistance from *T. ventricosum* :

1. **Direct crossing of *T. ventricosum* with bread wheat :** This approach has not been used successfully.

2. **Crossing *T. ventricosum* first with tetraploid wheat (*T. turgidum*) and then crossing their F_1 (ABDM^v) with bread wheat :** This method has been successfully used by Dosba and Doussinault (1977) to transfer resistance from *T. ventricosum*. According to them, not only the D genome of *T. ventricosum* was responsible for transferring resistance but at least one chromosome of the other genome (M^vM^v) of this species and its cytoplasm were also involved in such transfers. Using biochemical markers, Doussinault *et al.* (1983) showed that the D genome of *T. ventricosum* played major role in transferring resistance to bread wheat. However, according to them, the genome contains other useful genes.

3. **An amphidiploid produced by crossing *T. ventricosum* with *T. turgidum* (AABBDDM^{v}M^v) is crossed to bread wheat :** This method has also been used quite successfully.

Transfers from Tertiary Gene Pool

Tertiary gene pool includes many of the more distant relatives of wheat which have no genome homologous to any of the three genomes (A, B or D) of bread wheat but contain many useful genes, especially the genes conferring resistance against biotic and abiotic stresses. Non-homology of genomes hinders direct hybridization between bread wheat and its distant relatives and thus makes transfer of genes more difficult. Such gene transfers require use of some special techniques. Several techniques, from time to time, have been developed to transfer targeted genes from these distant relatives to wheat.

The first pre-requisite for transferring an alien gene into wheat is the development of an F_1 hybrid between wheat and the alien species. The crossability between two species would largely depend on the wheat genotype used in hybridization programme. However, the use of an appropriate embryo rescue rechnique may greatly help in making wide hybridizations successful.

Fortunately, a lot of variability is present in wheat germplasm for crossability of wheat genotypes with wild relatives (Mujeeb-Kazi *et al.*, 1987, 1989; Zeven, 1987; Farooq *et al.*, 1990; Luo *et al.*, 1992). Some crossability (kr) genes have been identified in wheat varieties. For example, the Chinese Spring variety (the best crossable genotype) contains three crossability genes (kr 1, kr 2 and kr 3) which are found on the group 5 chromosomes (Riley and Chapman, 1967; Snape *et al.*, 1979; Falk and Kasha, 1983). However, some new highly crossable genotypes (local landraces) have been identified by Yen *et al.* (1986) and Luo *et al.* (1992) in Sichuan (China). According to Zheng *et al.* (1992), these genotypes contain an additional crossable gene (kr 4) on chromosome 1A and possess higher crossability with rye than Chinese Spring.

Wheat germplasm has a very wide potential range of distant hybridization. Wheat genotypes have been crossed with several members of *Poaceae* family like maize, sorghum, pearl millet and barley (Laurie and Bennett, 1986c, 1987; Wang *et al.*, 1986; Laurie, 1989; and others). In most of the wheat × maize hybridizations there was elimination of the maize chromosomes in early cell division cycles. A similar situation was found in wheat × pearlmillet and wheat × sorghum hybridizations. Such chromosome elimination has helped in producing wheat haploids. However, if the goal of the breeding programme is to produce wheat haploids, this goal can be accomplished in a much better and easy way by crossing wheat with *Hordeum bulbosum*. But, elimination of the whole genome of a species after distant hybridization is a barrier to gene transfer from one species to another. However, there are reports that the use of some strains of *H. bulbosum* in wheat × *H. bulsosum* hybridization, sometimes, allows incomplete elimination of the *bulbosum* genome and thus helps in the production of wheat-*bulbosum* addition lines (Wang *et al.*, 1986). A similar chromosome retention of maize chromosomes has been observed by Comeau *et al.* (1988) in wheat × maize crosses.

Production of amphidiploids, alien addition and alien substitution lines : The production of these three types of genotypes has already been discussed earlier in this chapter. However, some specific points will be discussed here.

In most of the cases, the F_1 hybrids obtained from wide crosses are sterile and the best way of overcoming sterility of such hybrids, is the production of amphidiploids.

Although wheat alien addition lines are, in general, fairly vigourous but are, manytimes, associated with cytological instability due to alien-chromosomes-induced sterility (e.g., chromosome 5 of barley– Islam *et al.*, 1978), presence of gametocidal genes on the alien chromosome or some other abnormality associated with hybrid (Endo, 1990) and/or tendency of preferential transmission or elimination of certain chromosomes (Jiang, *et al.*, 1993b). Further, manytimes, there is formation of translocation chromosomes because of the misdivision of the univalent alien chromosomes and reunion of an arm of one chromosome with the arm of another chromosome (a centric breakage-fusion process). Also, the poor transmission of the alien chromosomes, sometimes, creates difficulty in the isolation of disomic addition lines.

Zhang *et al.* (1992) suggested a technique for producing alien substitution lines. In this technique, a wheat-alien amphidiploid is crossed with a fertile wheat nullisomic line and the hybrids thus produced are backcrossed to nullisomic line as male parent. However, for this, an amphidiploid and a fertile nullisomic line should be available.

Production of wheat-alien chromosome translocations : Wheat-alien chromosome translocations are generally generated by using wheat-alien addition lines or wheat-alien substitution lines as bridging materials. Several authors (Sears, 1972, 1981; Gale and Miller, 1987; Feldman, 1988) have reviewed strategies for generating wheat-alien chromosome translocations on the basis of wheat-alien additions and wheat-alien substitutions. Various methods used for inducing wheat-alien chromosome translocations can be classified into three main groups : (1) Inducing homeologous chromosome pairing; (2) exploiting spontaneous wheat-alien chromosome translocations; and (3) inducing random wheat-alien translocations.

1. Inducing homeologous pairing : The diploidization (that is, the genetic control of chromosome pairing or suppression of homeologous pairing) in polyploid wheats, on one hand, made these wheats to behave like diploids but, on the other hand, the discovery of this genetic control opened a new door for the possibilities of transferring genes from alien chromosomes to wheat. Although several genes present on different wheat chromosomes are responsible for the suppression of homeologous pairing, the Ph 1 gene located on the long arm of 5B chromosome plays the major role in this suppression. Induction of homeologous pairing not only helps in achieving homeologous pairing in wheat with appreciable frequency but it also facilitates hybridizations between wheat and other related species. There are three ways of achieving homeologous pairing : (i) By eliminating chromosome 5B (Sears, 1972); (ii) by using ph mutants (Sears, 1981; Koebner and Shepherd, 1985); and (iii) by suppressing the effect of Ph 1 gene (Riley *et al.*, 1968).

A simple way of *producing plants lacking Ph 1* is to pollinate wheat plants monosomic for 5B with pollen from an alien species carrying useful genes. The F_1 plants having absence of chromosome 5B but monosomic for the alien chromosome should show high frequency of homeologous pairing. This method was used by Riley (1966) for transferring genes from *T. bicorne* to wheat. A similar attempt was made by Joshi and Singh (1979) to transfer rust resistance from Russion rye to PbC 591 variety of wheat. A cross was made between a monosomic 5B of PbC 591 and Russian rye to obain F_1 plants with 27 chromosomes. However, though no 27-chromosome plant was present in the progeny, one plant with 28 chromosomes showed high level of homeologous pairing. This suggested that either this 28-chromosome plant was nullisomic for 5B and disomic for another wheat chromosome or it possessed a mutant ph 1. This plant was backcrossed to PbC 591 twice and plants with resistance to all three rusts of wheat were isolated. However, manytimes, the investigator has to face a lot of difficulty in producing backcrosses between F_1 plants and the wheat variety. A similar difficulty is often faced by the investigator in producing amphidiploid before backcrossing. A better method, free of these difficulites, was suggested by Sears (1972). In this method, monosomic 5B is crossed with an alien substituion line. Selected plants with $19^{II}+1^IW+I^IA+I^I$ 5B meiotic configuration (W stands for wheat and A for alien substituted chromosome carrying gene for rust resistance) are pollinated by nulli-5B tetra-5D. Plants showing resistance to rust and absence of 5B are selected from the progeny and are backcrossed to bread wheat to obtain rust resistant plants. The procedure was used by Sears (1973) for transferring leaf rust resistance from two wheat-*Agropyron* derivatives to wheat. The derivatives were TAP 67 (source of resistance in Agent) and Agrus (source of resistance in Agatha).

However, there were several cases of reduced transmission of resistance through the pollen. As observed by Sears (1973), in *Agropyron*–wheat transfers, substantial segments of the *Agropyron* chromosomes were involved.

Several *ph mutants for inducing homeologous pairing* have been reported by various investigators, e.g., ph 1b (a deletion of Ph 1 on chromosome 5B) and ph 2a mutants obtained by Sears (1977, 1982), Cappelli Des 35 mutant reported by Giorgi (1978) on short arm of chromosome 5B and 10/13 mutant reported by Wall *et al.* (1971). According to Sears (1984), the mutant 10/13 is located on the short arm of the chromosome 3D. The main advantage of using ph mutants to induce homeologous pairing is that no complex aneuploidy is required during their use. Further, the procedure allows transfers to 5B itself. As the ph mutants are recessive, they can be effectively used in homozygous or hemizygous condition only. The standard procedure to use these mutants is to cross a line in which the alien chromosome is substituted for a homeologous chromosome, as male, with a monosomic 5B. About 75 per cent progeny should have 41 chromosomes ($19^{II}+3^{I}$) with three univalents (alien chromosome, its wheat homeologue, and 5B chromosome). The plants thus obtained are crossed with the muant line (say ph 1b). Selection is done for plants which show homeologous pairing and possess the character carried by the alien chromosome. Selected plants may contain 42 chromosomes (with the alien chromosome and the 5B chromosome carrying mutant gene) or 43 chromosomes (with the alien chromosome, its wheat homeologue, and the 5B chromosome carrying mutant gene). The 43-chromosome plants are preferred as the alien chromosome and its wheat homeologue should pair with one another as they have no homeologues. This method was used by Liang *et al.* (1979) for transferring resistance to wheat streak mosaic from *Agropyron intermedium* to wheat. However, the use of both the methods (use of mutant as well as of nulli-5B tetra-5D) was made by Kibirige-Sebunya and Knott (1983) for transferring stem rust resistance from *A. elongatum* to wheat.

Homeologous pairing can also be induced by making crosses of wheat with some alien species possessing *suppressor genes*. It has been found that certain strains of *T. speltoides* and *T. tripsacoides* when crossed with wheat facilitate homeologous pairing by inhibiting the effect of Ph 1. This method was used by Dvorak (1977) for transferring leaf rust resistance from *T. speltoides* to wheat. These two species (*T. speltoides* and *T. tripsacoides*) have also been found helpful for transferring useful genes from other alien species to wheat. For example, Riley *et al.* (1968) were able to transfer stripe rust resistance from *T. comosum* to wheat by crossing a wheat-alien addition line (carrying *T. comosum* chromosome) with *T. speltoides*. However, the production of wheat lines possessing Ph^1 (called as *high pairing gene*) derived from *T. speltoides* (Chen *et al.*, 1994) may be considered as an important finding. This gene permits homeologous pairing by suppressing the effect of Ph 1. Further, since this gene is dominant, its single dose is sufficient to inhibit the effect of Ph 1. However, according to Chen *et al.*, the disadvantage of the method is that Ph^1 is less efficient in inducing homeologous pairing than other methods like using Ph 1b mutant or eliminating 5B chromosome.

2. Exploiting spontaneous wheat-alien chromosome translocations :
The second group of methods inducing wheat-alien chromosome translocations is by exploiting spontaneous wheat-alien chromosome translocations. There is frequent occurrence of spontaneous wheat-alien chromosome translocations in wide crosses (Jiang *et al.*, 1994). Although at a very low frequency, but there may be occurrence of wheat-alien chromosome recombination in the derivatives of wheat-alien hybrids. One important example of the consequence of such wheat-alien chromosome recombination is the origin of wheat-*Agropyron elongatum* translocation line *Agent*. This line carries Lr 24 (a leaf rust

resistance gene) from *A. elongatum* and might have arisen from a rare homeologous recombination between the two species since there is an exchange of similar-size fragments between homeologous chromosomes in this recombination (Smith *et al.*, 1968).

Centromeric-breakage and reunion of the wheat and alien telocentric chromosome arms at the centromeres gives rise to another class of spontaneous wheat-alien translocations. In this process, there is misdivision of univalent chromosome centromeres followed by reunion of the wheat and alien telocentric chromosome arms at the centromeres (Sears, 1972). The frequency of such translocations may be increased by creating specific univalent chromosomes. The wheat-rye translocation 1BL/1RS is the best example of this type of spontaneous translocations. This translocation has been most extensively used all over the world. Rabinovich (1998) discussed the importance of wheat-rye translocations for breeding modern cultivars of *T. aestivum* and emphasized that a great success has been achieved in obtaining wheat-rye chromosomal translocations 1BL/1RS and, rarely, 1B(R) substitutions and 1AL/1RS translocations. These translocations play an important role in determining several useful characteristics like high productivity, wide adaptation, increased regeneration capacity and resistance to diseases (resistance to Pm 8, Pm 17, Yr 9, Sr. 31, Lr 26) and insect pests. However, the positive effect of the translocatin may be increased with the help of the pedigree record of the genotypes since the effect of the translocation is determined by the genetic background in which the translocation is placed. Unfortunately, the presence of 1RS in wheat is associated with poor dough quality of the flour. However, certain recombinant lines isolated from 1DL/1RS translocation possess a better dough quality (Koebner and Shepherd, 1988).

The credit of the widespread use of cultivars with 1BL/1RS wheat-rye translocation in 1960-1990, basically goes to the sincere efforts made by two German scientists, Riebesel and Kattermann, during the period 1920-1930. Riebesel's first and second commercial wheat varieties, *Salzmunder Bartweizen* and *Weique* carrying 1BL/1RS translocation were released in Germany in the years 1957 and 1960, respectively. The line Riebesel 47-51 is the main source in many of the wheat varieties released in 1960-90 in the countries of western Europe. Rabinovich (1998) gave a long list of cultivars developed in many countries of the world with 1BL/1RS translocation and 1B (R) substitution. Some cultivars are *Warbler* and *Triller* released in 1993 and 1994, respectively, in Australia; *Almus, Apollo* and *Palur* released in 1976, 1984 and 1986, respectively, in Germany; *Beafort* and *Rialto* released in 1995 in Great Britain; HUW 206, *Aradhna* (HPW 42), WH 542, UP 2338 and PBW 343 released in 1985, 1991, 1992, 1993 and 1995, respectively, in India; *Salmon* released in 1960 in Japan; *Veery, Kauz* and *Cumpas 88* released in 1977, 1985 and 1988, respectively, in Mexico; *Faisalabad 85, Rawal 87* and *Sutlej 86* released in 1985, 1987 and 1988, respectively, in Pakistan; *Lanca* and *Koda* released in 1985 and 1986, respectively in Poland; *Aurora* and *Kavkaz* released in 1971 in Russia; *Gamtoos* released in 1983 in South Africa; *Viri* released in 1983 in Tanzania; *Freedom* and *TAM 301* released in 1992 and 1996, respectively, in USA; and *Iskra* released in 1984 in Yugoslavia. The cultivars *Amigo, Century* and *Niobrara* released in 1976, 1986 and 1994, respectively, in USA, carry 1AL/1RS translocation. The progenies of some of these cultivars are now being used for the development of new improved wheat varieties in some countries. The main source of 1BL/1RS translocation in Veery's wheat has been Kavkaz.

Occurrence of spontaneous wheat-alien translocations with non-centromeric breakpoints has also been reported. According to Jiang *et al.* (1994), spontaneous wheat–*Elymus* translocations with either centromeric or non-centromeric breakpoints were obtained in the alloplasmic derivatives of wheat × *E.trachycaulus* hybrids in USA. A specific characsteristic was associated with these translocations because of the involvement of *Elymus* chromosomes carrying fertility restoration (Rf) gene(s). A selective survival was shown by the plants having Rf carrier chromosomes or translocation chromosomes involving the fertility restoration gene(s). This can, therefore, facilitate transfer of a useful gene to wheat if it is present on the chromosome arm carrying Rf gene(s).

3. **Inducing random wheat–alien translocations :** Any one of the three techniques, *use of ionizing radiation* (Sears, 1956), *use of tissue culture* (Lapitan *et al.*, 1984), or *application of gametocidal genes* (Endo, 1988; Tsujimoto and Noda, 1988) can be used to induce random wheat–alien translocations. The classical method of Sears (1956) used for transferring leaf rust resistant gene from *T. umbellulatum* to Chinese Spring variety of *T. aestivum*, comes under this category of methods. *T. umbellulatum* is a diploid wild grass and is not easily crossable to *T. aestivum*. Therefore, it was first crossed with *T. turgidum* (a tetraploid emmer wheat and used here as a bridging species) to obtain an allotriploid F_1 hybrid. The chromosome number of the triploid hybrid thus produced was doubled by treating it with colchicine to obtain allohexaploid amphidoploid. Then, the allhexaploid was crossed with Chinese Spring variety of *T. aestivum*. The hexaploid hybrid thus produced was then repeatedly backcrossed to Chinese Spring variety. Selection was done in backcross progeny for 43-chromosome (wheat-*T. umbellulatum* monosomic addition) plants possessing resistance for leaf rust. The selected 43-chromosome plants were treated with X-rays before flowering. The pollen formed on these plants was used to pollinate the Chinese Spring variety and selection was made in the progeny for 42-chromosome plants showing resistance to leaf rust. Fortunately, one such plant was available in the progeny. This indicated that the leaf rust resistant gene was transferred from the *T. umbellulatum* chromosome to Chinese Spring chromosome. The whole procedure has been shown in the Figure 6.1.

Some species of *Aegilops* contain gametocidal genes which can induce random wheat-alien chromosome translocations in the selfed progenies of wheat–alien addition or substitution line if these genes are introduced into such an addition or substitution line (Endo, 1988). According to Endo (1990), gametocidal genes can cause chromosome breakage and then can induce chromosomal changes.

Friebe *et al.* (2001) gave a long list of wheat–alien translocations obtained through different methods (spontaneous, homeologous recombination, irradiation, tissue culture, etc.). However, only a few wheat–alien translocations have been successfully incorporated into wheat varieties because of the two main reasons: (i) In many cases, the lost wheat chromatin is not compensated well by the alien segments involved in translocations; and (ii) the alien segments often contain undesirable genes. As discussed earlier, even the wheat–rye translocations 1BL/1RS and 1AL/1RS which have been most extensively and successfully used all over the world are associated with the poor dough quality of the flour.

Characterization of wheat–alien translocations : Several techniques have been suggested and used for the characterization of wheat-alien chromosome translocations. The characterization of these translocations includes three important aspects : (1) To identify the translocated chromosome; (2) to localize the breakpoint; and (3) to estimate the amount of the transferred alien chromatin. However, no single technique has been found fully efficient to take care of all the three aspects of wheat–alien translocations. For example, the conventional technique, *chromosome pairing analysis*, may provide important information in some cases, but is inadequate to characterize some specific

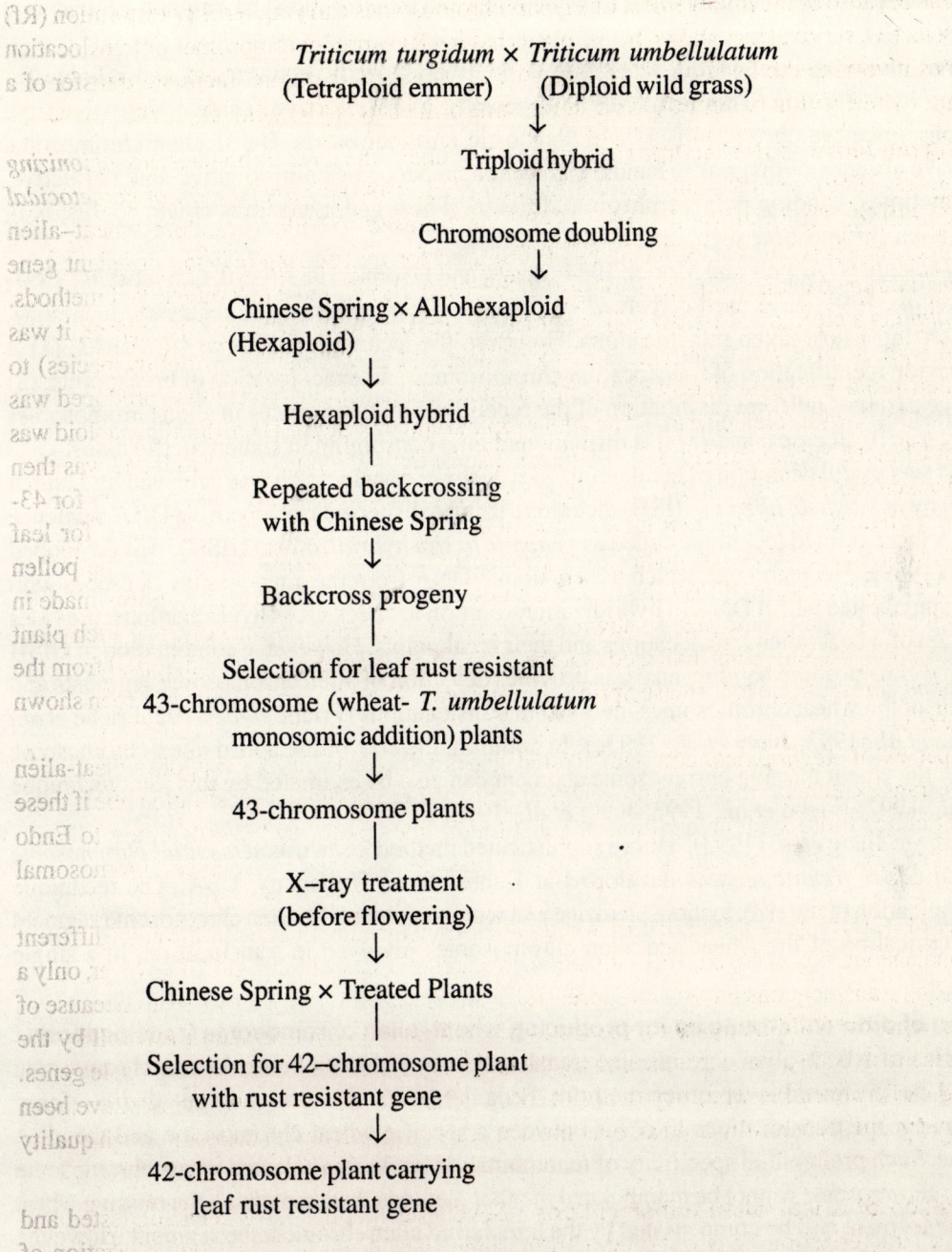

Figure 6.1. Sears' (1956) technique used for transferring leaf rust resistant gene from *Triticum umbellulatum* to Chinese Spring variety of *T. aestivum*

wheat alien translocations like interstitial translocations and translocations having non-centromeric breakpoints.

However, *chromosome banding* technique is relatively speedy, economical and reliable for chromosome identification. This technique is especially more effective for detecting wheat-rye translocations since rye chromosomes have diagnostic terminal bands. But if alien chromosome segments have absence of diagnostic bands, this technique becomes uninformative and ineffective. Further, sometimes, banding polymorphism in different wheat genotypes may create confusion in identifying alien chromosome segments.

Several scientists (Appels and Moran, 1984; Zhang and Dvorak, 1989, 1990; Guidet *et al.*, 1991; Rogowsky *et al.*, 1991) have used *dispersed species-specific repetitive DNA sequences* technique, for characterizing wheat–alien translocations. However, the technique has three drawbacks: (1) It does not provide identification of translocation chromosomes and exact location of breakpoints; (2) the technique assumes uniform distribution of the repetitive DNA sequences in alien chromosomes which is not true in all cases; and (3) it is difficult and time consuming in some specific cases.

The first successful detection of breakpoints of wheat-rye translocation was achieved by Lapitan *et al.* (1986) by *in situ hybridization* (ISH) technique using a dispersed rye repetitive DNA sequence as a probe. A more refined technique called as *genomic in situ hybridization* (GISH), was developed by Le *et al.* (1989). The technique which uses genomic DNA from the alien species as probes with an excess of unlabelled wheat DNA in hybridization solution to check cross hybridizations, provides clear detection of wheat–alien translocations and their breakpoints. However, a combination of GISH technique and chromosome banding analysis provides detection of alien chromosome segments and identification of the wheat chromosomes involved in translocations (Friebe *et al.*, 1992; Friebe *et al.*, 1993; Mukai *et al.*, 1993; Jiang *et al.*, 1993c). In addition, the size of the added alien chromosome segment and the wheat missing chromosome segment can also be estimated by this joint technique (Friebe *et al.*, 1992; Friebe *et al.*, 1993; Jiang *et al.*, 1993c).

According to Jiang *et al.* (1993), a more sophisticated method known as *sequential chromosome banding and GISH technique*, was developed at Kansas State University, USA. The technique allows determination of the size, loction, breakage and reunion point of the alien chromosome segment and the identification of the wheat and alien chromosomes involved in translocation, in a single experiment.

Comparison of different strategies for producing wheat–alien chromosome translocations : The production of wheat–alien chromosome translocation by inducing homeologous chromosome pairing may be preferred over other methods because of its main advantage of *directional manipulation* for the translocations to occur between a specific wheat chromosome and the alien chromosome. Such preferential specificity of recombination between a selected wheat chromosome and the alien chromosome cannot be manipulated in other methods. In this method, the missing wheat chromosome segment will be compensated by the transferred alien chromosome segment. However, the method has two limitations : (1) The potential of chromosome pairing and recombination between the alien chromosome and its wheat homeologue are, manytimes, low; and (2) the efficiency of inducing useful translocations will be determined by the location of the target alien gene. If the useful gene is located near the centromere or in subcentromeric region, the efficiency of inducing useful translocations will be low because of more frequent occurrence of genetic recombinations near the telomeric region than in the proximal half of a chromosome arm. Further, the structural modification of alien chromosomes (e.g., most rye chromosomes) greatly reduces the recombination between the alien chromosome and its wheat homeologue.

The induction of wheat-alien translocations by ionizing radiation has three main advantages: (1) Since ionizing radiation breaks chromosomes at random, the efficiency of inducing useful translocations will not be influenced by the position of the target gene on the alien chromosome; (2) the efficiency of inducing chromosome translocations will be independent of the potential of pairing between the wheat chromosome and the alien chromosome; and (3) the method has a theoretical superiority over other methods as the target gene (with minimum undesirable genes) could be inserted into the wheat chromosome without any loss of wheat chromatin. However, the technique has some drawbacks too. First, the biggest drawback of the method is that most of the translocations induced by ionizing radiation are associated with genetic imbalance. The genetic imbalance has, to a great extent, restricted the exploitation of translocations produced by using ionizing radiation. Secondly, the radiation treatment, in addition to the induction of wheat-alien translocations, also brings other chromosomal changes in the wheat genomes. As a result, several generations of backcrossing may be required for stabilizing a useful translocation. Thirdly, the chances of the recovery of theoretically assumed translocation by radiation treatment are very low since for inducing such a translocation, two chromosome breaks will be required near the target gene, one break in wheat chromosome and then the reunion of the chromosome segments.

The tissue culture technique, so far, could not be used as an efficient method for inducing useful wheat-alien translocations. The cytological analyses of tissue culture-derived plants indicated that most of the translocations involved non-homeologous chromosomes and thus these translocations were associated with genetic imbalance.

Nevertheless, during the last two decades, a considerable progress has been achieved in the field of wheat-alien gene transfers and with the significant improvement in crossing techniques, the range of distant hybridization of wheat has been considerably widened.

CHAPTER 7

Biotechnology and Wheat Breeding

Biotechnology has been and is being used in plant breeding in a number of ways like rescueing embryos obtained after distant hybridizations, producing doubled haploids in wheat, rice and several other crop species, isolating useful somaclonal variants, producing somatic cell hybrids and cybrids through genetic engineering, preparing chromosome maps using molecular markers (like RFLPs and RAPDs), identifying alien chromosome-segment and estimating size of the added alien chromosome segment and the missing chromosome segment of the recepient species, *in vitro* conservation of genetic stocks (cryopresevation) and producing transgenic plants/varieties (For details, see Singh and Pawar, 2006). Efforts are also being made to enhance photosynthetic activity of the plant and to fix atmospheric nitrogen by using novel biotechnological techniques. The use of modern biotechnological techniques in plant breeding is becoming increasingly relevant since, on one hand, human population (especially in developing countries) is alarmingly increasing and, on the other hand, resources are considerably depleting.

While discussing progress, problems and prospects of incorporating biotechnology tools into crop breeding programmes, Toenniessen (1993) emphasized that plant breeding has made a spectacular contribution in increasing food production and economic development. However, the use of novel biotechnology tools would enrich the knowledge of the plant breeders and enhance their efficiency in achieving their ultimate goal (further jump in the yield levels of important crops). Biotechnology tools can be used at both the stages of plant breeding, the *evolutionary phase* (production of variable plant populations) and the *evaluation phases* (selection of desirable genotypes). Biotechnology techniques like distant hybridization followed by embryo rescue somaclonal variation and genetic engineering can be used to considerably expand the range of variability available to the breeders. Similarly, use of techniques like anther culture, biochemical and molecular markers and nucleic acid probes can help the breeder for evaluating newly developed genotypes. Therefore, an active and positive collaboration between plant breeders and biochnologists is necessary for maximizing the yields of crops.

According to Snape (1996), new biotechnologies resulting from current advances in the fields of genetics, molecular biology and tissue culture can make a worthwhile contribution in increasing the efficiency of wheat breeding programmes through the production of doubled haploid varieties using most modern techniques (like use of maize and *Tripsacum* pollen for producing wheat haploids), preparation of comprehensive genetic maps based on molecular markers, identification, location and tagging of loci (major genes as well as quantitative trait loci or QTLs) governing all agronomic characters, improvements in post-pollination treatments and embryoculture techniques, new developments in tissue culture techniques, recent discoveries on the genetics of adaptation in wheat based on the identification of loci governing flowering time, techniques for introducing new and novel sources of genetic variation, etc. Although modern biotechnologies may help in reliably transform the wheat plant, efforts should be made for overcoming the problems relating to gene expression and gene stability. Also, it should be kept in mind that the produce is acceptable to the farmers and the consumers.

Despite the fact that bread wheat has a high ploidy level (6x) and repetitive DNA sequences and the regeneration of wheat plants from protoplasts is comparatively difficult, several innovative and unconventional techniques have been successfully used in this important cereal. The procedures used for alien gene transfers and the role of alien genes and gene combinations in wheat improvement have already been discussed in Chapter 6.

Production of Haploids

Despite the foreseeen possibility of directed genetic manipulation of the wheat genome through marker-mediated selection and genetic analysis, the development of a completely homozygous and genotypically stable wheat variety still requires many generations of selfing and selection of superior genotypes. However, this long process of selfing and selection has been short-circuited by developing wheat doubled haploids. Therefore, development of doubled haploid systems must be considered as a major contribution to wheat breeding, especially for speeding up the breeding cycle and increasing selection efficiency. However, a doubled haploid system will be successful only when it satisfies the three expected criteria :

1. The system should be efficient for producing large number of haploids;
2. it should be possible to produce genetically normal and phenotypically stable doubled haploids; and
3. the system should allow exploitation of the genetic variability present in the parents to the maximum possible extent.

Since the basic chromosome number (x number) in wheat is 7, there are seven types of chromosomes in a genome. Therefore, a haploid plant of any diploid wheat species will contain 7 chromosomes, a haploid plant of a tetraploid wheat will contain 14 (=2x) chromosomes and, similarly, a haploid plant of bread wheat will have 21 (=3x) chromosomes. It means, a haploid plant, irrespective of ploidy level, contains one chromosome of each type in each genome and the haploid plants of tetraploid and hexaploid wheats are in fact, polyhaploids.

Various *in vitro* techniques are used to produce haploids of bread wheat and durum wheat. Among these techniques, anther culture and genome elimination techniques, have been used most frequently. The application of these two types of techniques has substantially increased the efficiency of the production of haploids and has aroused considerable interest in the recent years.

Anther culture technique : The successful production of haploid plants from anthers proves the *totipotency* of microspores or pollen grains, that is, microspores are potentially capable of producing full-fledged plants. The first phase of the microspore totipotency is *androgenesis* (the development of embryo from microspore). The second phase of this totipotency is the regeneration of complete plant from this embryo.

Liang and McHughen (1987) have described the procedures of anther culture technique in wheat. The first step of the anther culture technique in wheat is the selection of spikes of suitable age. For this purpose, the most suitable age of a wheat spike is G_2 period (uninucleate stage of microspores), that is, the time when microspores in central florets have undivided nucleus. Then the surface sterilization of selected whole spikes is done with 1.7 per cent hypochlorite solution or 60 per cent ethanol in a laminar-flow hood. Anthers may be dissected out from the florets immediately after surface sterilization and placed in a suitable callus-induction nutrient medium or spikes may be wraped in aluminium foil and kept at a low temperature (4-6°C) for sometime (usually 1-7 days) before removing the anthers from the florets.

According to Liang and McHughen, nutrient media used for callus-induction in wheat may be put under two categories : (1) *Potato callus-induction nutrient medium*; and (2) *chemical or synthetic callus-induction nutrient medium*. The composition of the potato medium is boiled potato extract + sucrose + iron + hormones. This medium is cheap and can be prepared easily because of the use of natural extracts in it. High concentration of sucrose (about 10 per cent) in the medium increases the effectiveness of the medium. However, the use of this medium is disadvantageous on one front that the investigator has no knowledge about the substances and their proportion in the extracts, that is, problem of unknown concentration of unknown substances in the extracts.

Hu *et al.* (1978) and Liang *et al.* (1982) have described the composition of chemically defined or synthetic medium. The main advantage of the use of this medium is that there is scope of stepwise adjustment of individual components or groups of components in the medium for callus induction as well as for plantlet regeneration from microspore calli.

The anthers are placed on the medium and kept in dark for some days (generally from 5-7 days) at low temperature (about 5°C) before transferring to an incubation chamber where they are kept till calli formation. The process of calli formation takes about three weeks.

In general, the composition of the medium used for regeneration of plantlets from microspore calli is not different from that used for the induction of calli except that there is a change in the proportion of growth hormones. In some plant species like *Nicotiana tabacum*, there is no need of a separate regeneration medium since a direct regeneration of the haploid plantlets is possible. However, the situation in wheat is different where a separate medium is required for the regeneration of haploid seedlings from microspore calli (Hu *et al.*, 1978; Schaeffer *et al.*, 1979; Liang *et al.*, 1982). The regeneration requirements are a temperature of 24-29°C and a photoperiod of 10-14 hours. When the seedlings attain a 2-3 leaf stage, they are shifted to moist vermiculite in pots. To protect the seedlings from desiccation, the seedling pots are covered with a translucent plastic box. The low temperature and light intensity requirements of the seedlings are continued till they start showing vigorous growth. Colchicine (0.2 per cent solution for 5-8 hours) and dimethyl sulfoxide (1.5 per cent) at a pH of 5.5 can be used for doubling the chromosome number (Liang and McHughen, 1987).

However, several factors determine the success of producing haploid plants by anther culture method. These factors are :

1. **Experimenter's understanding about the suitable age of the spike :** The investigator must be able to precisely identify the most suitable age of the spike when the microspores are uninucleate.
2. **Experimenter's knowledge about the composition of media :** The experimenter must be well acquainted about the culture media currently being used.
3. **The care taken to handle the selected spikes and the dissected anthers :** The spikes of suitable age should be carefully selected and the anthers should be dissected out from the spike quite gently. No anther should be injured.
4. **Experimenter's knowledge about the pretreatment of spikes :** The investigator should clearly know about the pretreatment to be given to the spikes like surface sterilization and washing (if necessary).
5. **Experimenter's understanding about the variety to be used :** Since anther culture is genotype-dependent, the investigator should be well acquainted with the nutritional requirements of the variety to be used.

Although anther culture technique has been quite frequently used for producing haploids, the method has some serious drawbacks which are as follows :

1. **The method is genotype-dependent :** Different varieties of wheat generally respond differently to the same nutrient medium. In some cases, there is normal callus induction and normal regeneration of plantlets, whereas in some others, there is no callus induction at all. This genotype dependency of androgenesis indicates that callus formation is under genetic control. The F_1s mostly behave like their better parent with regard to androgenesis. Reciprocal crosses generally show same response in this respect. However, due to genotype dependency, the doubled haploids produced from a heterozygous plant may not completely represent the total number of gametes possibly produced by that plant.

As regards the effect of culture environment, light and humidity are not important factors. However, different wheats genotypes generally have differrent culture temperature requirements. Of course, in most cases, the optimal culture temperature varies from 24°C to 30°C.

Further, the inclusion of optimum levels of hormones like indole-3-acetic acid (IAA), α-naphthaleneacetic acid (NAA) or 2,4-D, in the culture medium, helps in initiating the growth of wheat microspores and keeping the somatic cells inert. However, the use of wrong amounts of these hormones may cause the occurrence of a reverse process, that is, callus formation from somatic tissues but keeping the microspores inert. Although plants can synthesize their own auxins, the endogenous levels of auxins and cytokinins in wheat microspores appear to be genotype-dependent. Nevertheless, the exogenous treatment with some hormones may increase the efficiency of the production of haploids.

Since different wheat genotypes have different nutritional requirements, a variety of nutrient media are being used by different investigators.

According to Sunderland and Roberts (1977), floating anther technique in which anthers are floated on shallow layers of liquid medium, is simple, produces calli at a much higher rate and is free from maternal anther tissue. The only drawback of this technique is the lower frequency of green plantlet regeneration. However, a combination of this technique with agar medium technique may enhance the frequency of regenerated green plantlets (Henry and de Buyser, 1981).

2. **Production of aneuploids alongwith the production of haploids :** Anther culture technique cannot be considered as a good method for producing haploids in terms of genetic purity since all the plants obtained after using this method are not haploids but some of them are aneuploids.

3. **Occurrence of somaclonal variation :** The occurrence of unwanted somaclonal variants along with haploids in plants produced using anther culture technique is another example of the genetic impurity of this technique.

Despite these all odds, the anther culture technique has been used by numerous investigators in different countries of the world and has been greatly helpful in making doubled haploid breeding a reality. This technique has been used at a large scale in China and many wheat and rice varieties/ strains have been developed (Hu, 1986; Loo and Xu, 1986). The winter wheat variety *Jinghua No. 1* was released in China in 1986 (Hu *et al.*, 1986). The popular wheat variety *Florin* which was released in France in 1987 (de Buyser *et al.*, 1987) was also developed through anther culture technique. Conventional breeding and *in vitro* androgenesis were used in combination to develop another wheat variety *GK Delibab* (Pauk *et al.*, 1995) which is superior to initial forms. According to Hu (1997), 21 wheat varieties and lines were developed using anther culture and registered in China till 1991. Recently, Milkova *et al.* (2003) made an attempt to combine the use of embryo culture and anther culture to develop new economically superior wheat lines and were successful in releasing a highly-productive line, 74/1-581 (from the cross Dobrotitsa × Flamura 85), as a candidate variety.

Ovule culture : Not only anthers but ovules or ovaries may also be cultured to produce haploids. The development of haploids from the culture of unfertilized ovules or ovaries is known as *gynogenesis*. If ovules or ovaries are cultured in an appropriate medium, any cell of the embryo sac (female gametophyte) like egg cell, any of the synergids or antiplodal cells may give rise to an embryo without fertilization. If the haploid egg cell develops into an embryo without fertilization, it is called as *haploid parthenogenesis*. But, if any other haploid cell of the embryo sac except the egg cell gives rise to embryo without fertilization, it is termed as *haploid apogamy*.

The basic medium for inducing callus in wheat is N_6+sucrose (8 per cent) + 2,4-D (Liang and McHughen, 1987). Unpollinated ovules or ovaries are cultured at an appropriate stage. Like anther culture, ovule culture is also genotype-dependent. Zhu *et al.* (1981) and Yang and Zhou (1982) have compared the percentage of ovaries giving rise to gynogenic calli in four wheat varieties. According to them, this percentage varied from 1.3 to 10.9.

Yang and Zhou (1990) have discussed applications and limitations of gynogenesis. However, ovule culture technique has been used much less frequently than anther culture method for producing haploids probably because of the unsuitability of ovule culture as a method for large-scale haploid production. The biggest drawback of this technique is the formation of callus or embryoid from somatic tissues. The proliferation of somatic tissues may produce subtances which may adversely affect the egg cell growth, prevent callus induction in these cells, or may create difficulty in the identification of true haploid calli. However, this problem may be overcome by maintaining a proper hormonal balance in the medium.

In fact, the use of ovule culture does not always result in the development of haploid plants only but, sometimes, polyploid plants are also obtained probably because of a spontaneous chromosome doubling at the time of callus proliferation. This technique can be used to regenerate green as well as albino plantlets. However, under special situations, this technique may be used as an alternative procedure to anther culture. For example, anther culture technique cannot be used in male sterile plants. In such plants, ovule culture proves to be the most useful *in vitro* method for the production of haploids. Further, culturing of immature ovules or ovaries may provide additional information about megasporogenesis (development of megaspores) and apomixis (development of embryo in the absence of fertilization). According to Costillo and Cistue (1993), the haploids produced by ovule culture may be qualitatively better than those produced using anther culture. Nevertheless, the scope of the use of ovule culture as a successful method for the production of haploid plants in wheat is yet to be seen.

Genome elimination technique : In view of the drawbacks associated with anther culture technique (genotype-dependency and occurrence of somaclonal variation and aneuploids). The genome elimination technique, at present, is receiving maximum attention of the wheat scientists throughout the world. Genome elimination technique is genotype-independent, relatively more efficient for producing haploids at large scale, and is superior to anther culture technique in terms of genetic purity since the plants produced by this procedure are all haploids.

The ingenious system of genome elimination for the artificial production of haploid plants was discovered by Kasha and Kao (1970) by making crosses between *Hordeum vulgare* (cultivated diploid barley) and *H. bulbosum* (wild diploid barley) used as pollinator. The technique was named as *bulbosum* method. Later on, this technique was used to develop haploids in other plant species and crosses were made accordingly. For example, to produce bread wheat polyhaploids, crosses were made between *Triticum aestivum* and *H. bulbosum*. This technique became very famous for eliminating the genome of the pollinator. However, in barley, the reciprocal cross of *H. vulgare* × *H. bulbosum* (that is, *H. bulbosum* × *H.vulgare*) is also successful.

Nevertheless, a search was on to find out a potentially promising alternative procedure. Fortunately, an important discovery was made by Laurie and Bennett in the year 1988 that wheat polyhaploids can be produced by making crosses between wheat and maize (as pollen parent). The technique of Laurie and Bennett proved so effective that now it is being used by most of the leading research centres of the world for producing wheat polyhaploids at large scale. The experience of the scientists shows that this method is superior to both the anther culture and *bulbosum* techniques (Mujeeb-Kazi *et al.,* 1995). We have already discussed the major limitations of anther culture technique. The major drawback of *bulbosum* technique is the genetically determined *low crossability* (governed by the homeologous group 5 crossability genes Kr 1, Kr 2 and Kr 3) in several varieties (Snape *et al.,* 1979; Falk and Kasha, 1981; Mujeeb-Kazi and Asiedu, 1990; and others). Wheat polyhaploids have also been produced by using pollen of *Tripsacum* (Riera-Lizarazu and Mujeeb-Kazi, 1993), teosinte (Ushiyana *et al.,* 1991), pearl millet (Ahmad and Comeau, 1990) and sorghum (Ohkawa *et al.,* 1992). In addition to the production of wheat polyhaploids, wheat × *Tripsacum* and wheat × maize hybridizations may also be made for producing wheat-alien addition lines by retaining one or a few chromosomes of *Tripsacum* or maize.

A vigorous wheat polyhaploid production programme by using pollen of maize or *Tripsacum* is going on at CIMMYT since 1991. This programme is helping the CIMMYT scientists in cutting short the number of generations for producing completely homozygous wheat lines (after doubling the chromosome number) which, in turn, are a great help in their basic research like preparation of RFLP maps of wheat.

Once the successful fertilization takes place in any of these hybridizations (wheat × maize, wheat × *Tripsacum dactyloides*, etc.), there is fast elimination of the chromosomes of the pollinator and only the chromosomes of the female parent remain. In wheat×maize hybridizations, there is a rapid elimination of maize chromosomes in the first few cycles of cell division since the centromeres of maize chromosomes fail to attach to the spindle of wheat origin (Laurie and Bennett, 1987). According to Laurie *et al.* (1990), the embryos formed after such integeneric hybridization would generally abort if they are not protected by giving an exogenous treatment with 2, 4-D. Later on, the embryos are excised and put in a suitable nutrient medium for the regeneration of plantlets. Mujeeb-Kazi *et al.* (1995) believe that this *sexual route* of producing polyhaploids in wheat is more successful than the tissue culture based approach. Snape (1996) has expressed a similar opinion about this method for producing wheat polyhaploids at commercial scale and developing populations of homozygous recombinant lines at large scale. This technique is now being followed by several private wheat breeding companies.

The wheat × maize hybridization technique allows production of wheat polyhaploids from any wheat genotype since maize pollen growth and fertilization activity do not show sensitivity to crossability alleles of wheat, However, exogenous 2, 4-D treatment can considerably promote seed setting and embryo development in wheat × maize crosses. Several 2, 4-D treatment techniques like tiller injection, floret culture, floret treatment and spike spraying, have been suggested for enhancing seed and embryo development. Nevertheless, use of detached spikelets or detached tillers facilitate haploid production under desired controlled conditions.

A lot of work is being done at CIMMY on the production of wheat haploids from wheat × maize and wheat × eastern gamma-grass (*Tripsacum dactyloides*) hybridizations. The selection of *Tripsacum dactyloides* was based on its taxonomic proximity to maize. It is believed that some portion of *Tripsacum* genome has spontaneously introgressed into maize genome during the course of evolution and has become an integral part of the latter genome. A reverse process might have also occurred in nature. In fact, *Tripsacum* and teosinte (*Zea mays* ssp. *maxicana*) are the two close relatives of maize and both of them might have involved in the introgression of genes or small chromosome segments into the maize genome.

At CIMMYT, two sets of field grown plants (at El Batan, CIMMYT, Mexico) were used (Mujeeb-Kazi *et al.*, 1995) :

Set 1 : The *Triticum aestivum* variety *Morocco* was crossed with Pool 9A (a *Zea mays* population).

Set II : Each of the four types of materials, namely, *T. aestivum, T. turgidum,* amphidiploids obtained from *T. turgidum* × *T. tauschii* hybridization, and rye (*Secale cereale*) was pollinated with bulk pollen from several cross-pollinating *Zea mays* populations.

For making wheat × maize crosses, wheat spikes of appropriate age (before anthesis) were hand-emasculated and then were covered with glassine bags to prevent undesired pollination. Fresh maize pollen was used to pollinate the emasculated spikes 3-4 days after emasculation. For obtaining better results, the tillers of the pollinated ears were detached from the plant and were then put in a beaker containing 2, 4-D aqueous solution. Surface sterilization of the basal halves of detached tillers was done with sodium hapochlorite for five minutes followed by six-time washing with sterile deionized water. After surface sterilization and washing, the detached tillers were shifted to Murashige and Skoog (1962) or MS nutrient medium containing 2, 4-D. The test tubes containing detached tillers were then placed in green house with appropriate light intensity, photoperiod and humidity. After keeping the tillers in the 2,4-D medium for 48 hours, they were shifted to a 2, 4-D free medium for about 12 days.

After excising the embryos, they were put in a sucrose medium. The germination starts after 10-12 days. The plantlets were shifted to peat pots and then to greenhouse. Based on cytological studies, polyhaploid plants were identified. The chromosome number of the polyhaploids was doubled by colchicine treatment.

Among the three techniques used, namely, detached tiller method, tiller injection method and floret spray method, the detatched tiller technique proved better than the other two techniques in terms of embryo recovery in wheat × maize crosses.

In wheat × *Tripsacum* crosses, almost similar techniques were used for making crosses, rescueing embryos, regenerating plantlets and transplanting plantlets to greenhouse except some changes made in the procedure to evaluate the effect of 2,4-D on embryo recovery. The 2,4-D treatment was also found important in wheat × *Tripscum* hybridization as it was in wheat × maize hybridization for the recovery of seeds and embryos (Mujeeb-Kazi *et al.*, 1995).

The use of maize and *Tripsacum* pollen has increased the range of pollen donors for the production of wheat polyhaploids. Further, efforts can be made for transferring desirable traits from maize to wheat like more efficient C-4 photosynthetic pathway (Laurie and Bennett, 1986) and from *Tripsacum* to wheat like insect resistance and drought tolerance by producing wheat-maize and wheat-*Tripsacum* alien chromosome addition lines.

In addition to the other uses of wheat doubled haploids [(instant production of completely homozygous lines, production of alien chromosome addition lines, transfer of alien gene(s) to wheat, etc.)], these haploids can be used for RFLP genome mapping in wheat.

The results obtained by several scientists (Oury *et al.*, 1993; Mujeeb-Kazi *et al.*, 1995; Sadasivaiah *et al.* 1999) have now conclusively proved that the use of maize pollen for producing wheat haploids has considerably reduced the influence of the wheat genotype, that is, the wheat × maize hybridization technique for producing wheat haploids is genotype-independent. This is the main reason that wheat × maize hybridization technique is now being used more frequently than the anther culture technique which is genotype-dependent.

Sharma *et al.* (2002) assessed the feasibility of wheat × maize hybridization to produce doubled haploids by pollinating seven intervarietal hybrids of soft red winter wheat (SRWW) with the same maize genotype (Seneca 60) in a greenhouse followed by postpollination application of 2, 4-D to rescue embryos. The 2, 4-D-facilitated fertilization showed high success in seed set (81-90 per cent). In fact, 2,4-D treatment was critical for seed development in early stages of embryo as there was no seed set without this treatment. Use of coin envelops proved better for haploid seed development than that of glassine bags.

To study the responsiveness and influence of wheat and maize genotypes on the induction of haploids in wheat, Singh *et al.* (2004) crossed six elite and diverse genotypes of winter wheat (Bounty, Envoy, Pnfjoumee, Saptdhara, Sentry and WW 24) with those of spring wheat (HPW 89, HPW 93, HPW 147, RL 10-22, VL 763 and VL 784) to produce six F_1 hybrids (Bounty × VL 784, Envoy × VL 763, Pnfjoumee × HPW 93, Saptdhara × HPW 147, Sentry × RL 10-22 and WW 24 × HPW 89). Two separate experiments were conducted. In experiment 1, all the twelve wheat genotypes were pollinated with Early Composite maize to study the responsiveness of wheat genotypes to wheat × maize system. In Experiment 2, the six F_1 hybrids of wheat were crossed with four diverse maize genotypes (Early composite, Sabet sweet corn, Palampur Popcorn and KH 517) in a line × tester fashion to investigate the effect of wheat and maize genotypes on maize-mediated production of wheat haploids.

The response of differents wheat × maize hybrids to four maize genotypes was different for haploid embryo formation as well as for regeneration. The maize genotypes played a major role for regeneration of haploid wheat embryos. Embryo formation was considerably influenced by wheat genotypes. Therefore, all the three factors, namely, wheat genotype, maize genotype and the interaction between wheat and maize genotypes, were important in one way or the other.

In an attempt to study the effect of colchicine enriched culture medium on embryo regeneration and the production of wheat doubled haploids, Danied et al. (2005) have obtained some interesting results. For their study, they selected four German winter wheat (*Triticum aestivum*) varieties, namely, *Certo*, *Petrus* (both possessing 1BL/1RS translocation), *Dream* and *History*, as female parents and two sweet corn hybrids, namely, *Tasty Sweet* and *Rival*, as pollinators. After vernalizing for about two months at 4°C, the wheat plants were cultured in greenhouse. The pollinators were also cultured in greenhouse. One-two days before anthesis, 115 spikes of each wheat variety were emasculated and bagged. Two days after, emasculated florets were pollinated with mixed fresh pollen of the two corn hybrids and were again bagged. Surface sterilization of the extracted caryopses (15-19 day after pollination) was done followed by washing with distilled sterile water. Then the embryos were placed in a basal nutrient medium. The whole study included three treatments : (1) *Treatment A* without colchicine treatment; (2) *Treatment B*, medium enriched with 300 mg/colchicine; and (3) *Treatment C*, medium enriched with 900 mg/colchicine. After distributing the excised embryos of each spike to three treatments, the petri dishes were placed in dark for incubation. After three day of incubation, the embryos of B and C treatments were shifted to colchicine-free medium used in treatment. After 2 weeks, petri dishes were shifted to a culture room at 22-24°C and, later on regenerated plantlets were shifted to semi-sterile lidded plastic boxes and ultimately well-develop plantlets were transplanted to peat soil. Eight-week old haploid plants of treatment A were treat with colchicine and were replanted in peat soil after washing with running water. Vernalization treatment of about 2 months was given to plants of B and C treatments after acclimatization. The results we as follows :

1. The embryo formation was independent of 1BL/1RS translocation.
2. Wheat genotypes influenced the embryo formation.
3. Interactions between wheat varieties and corn hybrids might have affected the results of study.
4. Regeneration rates were adversely affected by colchicine treatment.
5. The toxic effect of colchicine on embryo regeneration was directly proportional to concentration; higher the dose of colchicine, lower was the regeneration capacity.
6. The four wheat varieties responded differently to calchicine treatment.
7. Three factors, namely, wheat genotype, colchicine concentration and chromosome doubli technique, affected the percentage of doubled haploid plants.

However, the genome elimination technique has two limitations (Snape, 1996) :

1. The technique is costly as compared to conventional breeding; and
2. the technique puts a limit on the number of crosses that can be usually handled.

Perhaps some improved microspore culture technique which would ensure large scale production of wheat doubled haploids may help in overcoming the above mentioned limitations. According to Harwood *et al.* (1994), such a large scale production of doubled haploids is possible in barley. If so, efforts must be made to transfer that technology to wheat.

Alien cytoplasm technique : Kihara and Tsunewaki's (1962) discovery about the ability of *Triticum caudatum* cytoplasm to induce haploids in wheat opened a new door for the scientists working in this field. The wheat variety *Salmon* (a common wheat variety obtained by crossing two 8x triticales, contains normal wheat cytoplasm and possesses 1BL/1RS translocation and a modified chromosome 2B) was used for this purpose. Using repeated backcrossing, the nucleus of Salmon was transferred to *T. caudatum* cytoplasm. The progeny contained about 30 per cent haploids and 11 per cent twin seedlings.

When other cytoplasms were tested for inducing haploids in wheat, it was observed that all the species capable of inducing haploids were those which had genome C in common (Tsunewaki *et al.*, 1974; Tsunewaki *et al.*, 1976). However, according to Mukai (1981), the two factors determining the frequency of haploids were the type of cytoplasm and the pollen parent used. There was a clear indication that an interaction between the nuclear genes and cytoplasmic genes was responsible for the haploid production. According to Kobayashi and Tsunewaki (1980), the interaction between the gene(s) of rye chromosome 1R and certain types of cytoplasms apparently caused the induction of haploids.

Other techniques : Some other methods like the use of chemical agents (Lacadena, 1974) and physical agents such as irradiation (Pandey and Phung, 1982), have also been suggested for inducing haploids. Further, the occurrence of haploid initiator factors in some plant species (Hagberg and Hagberg, 1980; Hagberg and Hagberg, 1981) may be responsible for the production of haploids when these factors come in contact with certain cytoplasms. But there is no specific report about the use of these methods at large scale in wheat.

Combination of techniques : It has been observed that the joint use of some techniques may considerably enhance the frequency of haploid production. For example, according to Picard *et al.* (1987), there was considerable improvement in anther culture (in the production of haploids and dihaploid lines) in wheat when the plants were sprayed with *fenridazone-potassium*, a gametocide. They believe that the joint use of anther culture and the chemical hybridizaing agent should decrease the effect of the genotype which is the main drawback of the anther culture technique. Schmid and Keller (1986) had also found similar results in wheat by using androgenesis and the gametocide.

Not only the use of a chemical agent, but abrupt change in temperature may also enhance the efficiency of anther culture technique (Keller *et al.*, 1983; Bajaj and Mahapatra, 1990). According to Bajaj (1978), low temperature helps in increasing pollen viability, delaying senescence and in checking pollen abortion. Thermal shocks may have a similar effect in wheat.

Production of Somaclonal Variants

Larkin and Scowcroft (1981) defined somaclonal variation as the "spontaneous genetic change taking place in cells growing *in vitro*." Since this variation occurs in cells having somatic origin, it has been called as somaclonal variation (Poehlman and Sleper, 1995). Although somaclonal variation is a reality, but its mechanism of action is not yet known. Further, whole of the somaclonal variation is not genetic, but a part of it is epigenetic or transient and is thus unstable. The occurrence of somaclonal variation, however, indicates that :

1. The plants regenerated through cell culture are not always exact duplicate copies of the parent plant used for culture, but plants originating from the same parent may show heritable differences.
2. Genetic variation can take place without the presence of known mutagenic agents and thus somaclonal variants are different from the induced mutants.

Somaclonal variants are different from and superior to induced mutants in several ways (Singh and Pawar, 2006). The main difference between the two is that the frequency of useful somaclonal variants is significantly higher than that of the beneficial induced mutants. Somaclonal variation remained unknown for a long time mainly because of the presumption of many scientists that the plants regenerated through *in vitro* culture are the exact duplicate copies of the parent plant.

Somaclonal variation is also different from *gametoclonal variation*. Whereas somaclonal variants are somatic cell-derived plants, the gametoclonal variants are gamete-derived plants. According to Morrison and Evans (1987, 1988), who have thoroughly discussed gametoclonal variation, there are two main differences between *somaclones* and *gametoclones* :

1. Recessive alleles are readily expressed in gametoclones and in plants (doubled haploids) obtained after their chromosome dubling, whereas in case of somaclones selfing is necessary for the detection of recessive alleles.
2. Whereas no chromosome doubling is required for the fertility of somaclones, chromosome doubling is necessary to make the gametoclones fertile. Further, the process of chromosome doubling may itself be responsible for gametoclonal variation and if such is the case, there is possibility of heterozygosity in the doubled haploids.

However, somaclonal variations and gametoclonal variations have two similarities :

1. The mechanism of action of both types of variations is not yet fully known. Like in case of somaclonal variations (pre-existing genetic variation in the donor parent, dominant and recessive point mutations, structural and numerical changes of chromosomes, symmetric and asymmetric mitotic crossing over, gene amplification, activation of transposable elements, synthesis of intracellular mutagens during *in vitro* growth, etc.), a number of possibilities (point mutations of both dominant and recessive types, genetic recombination, residual heterozygosity, chromosomal changes, DNA amplification, culture conditions, type of origin of the haploid embryos, that is, whether from generative cell or from vegetative cell, 2n gametes, modification in the organelle genome, etc.) have been given for the origin of gametoclonal variations. According to San Noeum and Ahmadi (1983) and Kumashiro and Oinuma (1985), the variation among androgenetic haploids is much greater than the variation among gynogenetic haploids probably because of the use of different types of media in the development of two types of haploids.
2. Both the somaclonal and gametoclonal variations may play an imortant role in crop improvement as both the variations can influence qualitative as well as quantitative characters.

According to Bingham and Lupton (1987), somaclonal variation may be an attractive genetic tool for the breeders of vegetatively propagated crops like sugarcane, potato and many fruit species. For improvement of sexually reproduced crops like wheat, somaclonal variation has a limited scope. In wheat, two types of difficulties have to be faced :

1. It is not easy to differentiate somaclonal variation from other mutation procedures.
2. A great part of the somaclonal variation is generally found associated with aneuploidy (Karp et al., 1982). Such association may create difficulty for the wheat breeder.

Of course, the importance of somaclonal variation in alien genetic transfers cannot be denied. However, Liang and Mc Hughen (1987) feel that despite difficulty in regenerating wheat plants, it is feasible to take advantage of somaclonal variation in wheat improvement programmes.

Procedures for producing somaclonal variants in wheat : Two popular procedures are used for the production of somaclonal variants in wheat (Liang and Mc Hughen, 1987):

1. **Immature embryo culture or somatic embryogenesis from scutellar callus :** In this procedure, immature embryos are excised from the caryopses collected 14-16 days after fertilization. The excised embryos are placed on the surface of initial culture medium. The time of collection of caryopses in wheat is a critical factor since if the embryos are younger than 14 days after fertilization, they would not respond to culture environment and if the embryos are older than 16 days after fertilization, they will show normal germination. Such older embryos though may regenerate into plantlets but with a low frequency. However, generally, different media are used by different investigators for different genotypes. The embryos are placed on the surface of the medium in such a way that the scutellum is on the upper side. The culturing is done at room temperature. The material is transferred to fresh media after every month or so. For induction of shoot, the callus is shifted to a regenration medium. But, according to Ozias-Akins and Vasil (1982), Maddock et al. (1983) and Eapen and Rao (1984), there is no need to transfer the callus to a regenerating medium since there is spontaneous occurrence of the regnation. However, it is advisable to shift the young shoot arising from the scutellar callus to a hormone-free medium so that the plantlets are fully established with presence of both the shoot and roots. In short, the whole procedure of immature embryo culture is the culturing of immature embryo followed by regeneration of plantlets from the scutellar tissue through somatic embryogenesis.

2. **Shoot organogenesis from leaf or other callus :** Young leaves are the most suitable material for callus formation if placed in an appropriate basal medium. Shoot induction requires transfer of callus to another medium. However, the whole procedure (callus induction + plant regeneration) appears to be highly dependent on the wheat genotype used. So this procedure, in short, is the culturing of young leaves followed by regeneration of plantlets through shoot organogenesis.

Both the methods mentioned above (regeneration from immature somatic embryo callus and shoot organogenesis from leaf or other callus) are being used successfully in wheat for producing somaclonal variants. The first method (somatic embryogenesis from scutellar callus) is superior to the second method is terms of regeneration capacity, but the second method is better than the first in terms of the frequency of somaclonal variants. Therefore, the choice of the method would depend upon the objective of the investigator whether he is interested in higher regeneration of plants or he wants to produce more somaclonal variants. However, Mahalakshmi et al. (2003) have suggested a method for rapid induction of somatic embryogenesis in leaf based explants of wheat (*Triticum aestivum*).

Bozhanova and Dechev (2002) analyzed third selfed generation of *in vitro* culture-regenerated plants (R_3) of 8 durum wheat somaclonal lines from Bulgarian variety *Progress*. The performance of regenerated plants was compared to that of original genotype for seven agronomical traits (plant height, ears per plant, spike length, spikelet number, grains per spike, grain weight per spike and 1000-grain weight) and for cold and drought resistance. Two types of materials (mature embryos and immature inflorescences) were used for regeneration of plants. The R_3 plants differed significantly from the initial genotype for all the characters studied indicating that useful and stable somaclonal variants can be produced in durum wheat through *in vitro* culture. The regeneration of plants from immature inflorescences proved better than regeneration from mature embryos since the coefficient of variation for most of the characters was higher in first case than in second case.

Recently, Ahmed and Abdelkareem (2005) evaluated field performance of 31 spring bread wheat somaclones in sixth and seventh selfed generations of tissue culture-regenerated plants (R_6 and R_7, respectively) during two agronomic seasons for days to heading, days to maturity, plant height, number of spikes/m, number of kernels per spike, kernel weight and grain yield. These somaclones were regenerated *in vitro* from immature inflorescences or embryos of six *Triticum aestivum* varieties, namely, Sakha 8, Sakha 69, Giza 157 and Giza 160 (all Egyptian), Tobari 66 (Mexican) and Lerma Rojo 64 (Spanish). A comparison of somaclones with their donor parental lines indicated highly significant differences between the two groups (somaclones and their original varieties). The differences observed within and between somaclonal lines and their original parents for all the seven characters studied were mainly due to the four Egyptian varieties. Ten somaclones (5 derived from Sakha 8, 4 from Sakha 69 and 1 from Giza 157) out of total 26 somaclones (19 somaclones regenerated from Sakha 8, 5 from Sakha 69, 1 from Giza 157 and 1 from Giza 160) derived from these 4 Eghyptian cultivars showed superiority over their parental varieties. These results clearly indicate that tissue culture derived somaclones have a potential role in genetic manipulations and wheat breeding programmes. Similar results were obtained earlier also by Larkin *et al.* (1984), Chen *et al.* (1987), Quareshi *et al.* (1992), Villareal *et al.* (1999), Bozhanova and Dechev (2002) and several others.

Spectrum of somaclonal variants : It has now been experimentally proved that the somaclonal variants have a broad spectrum. Somaclonal variation can influence simply inherited qualitative characters like grain colour (white grain colour in a Yaqui 50E variant, Larkin and Scowcrcft, 1981) as well as highly complex quantitative charcters like grain yield in wheat (Ahmed and Abdelkareem, 2005; and several others). In Ahmed and Abdelkareem's study, all the seven agronomically important characters studied by them, namely, days to heading, days to maturity, plant height, number of spikes/m, kernel weight, number of kernels per spike and grain yield, were considerably affected by somaclonal variation and ten somaclones were found significantly better than their original parents. Similarly, influence of somaclonal variation on quantitative characters like grain weight and days to maturity, was observed by Larkin *et al.* (1984) and Woloschuk and McHughen (1984). However, according to Larkin *et al.* (1984), it is difficult to explain the genetic basis of some somactonal variants. Further, some somaclonal variants have no agronomic value at all. Nevertheless, one advantage of somaclonal variants over induced mutants is clear that there is no destruction of any part of the genome (as it occurs during induced mutagenesis) during the occurrence of somaclonal variation. Therefore, the pattern followed by somaclonal variation is different from that followed by induced mutation (Evans *et al.*,1984). Furthermore, the genetic instability of variant traits in some cases, clearly indicates that a part of the somaclonal variation is epigenetic. This shows that transposable elements may or may not be the cause of somaclonal variation.

Importance of somaclonal variation : As discussed above, somaclonal variation can affect both the qualitative and quantitative traits in wheat and thus can be used as a method in wheat breeding programmes for exploiting already existing variability in a desirable background. However, somaclonal variation should never be treated as a method for turning an extremely undesirable variety into a superb variety. What somaclonal variation does is that the method allows selection of additional desired traits (or for traits previously unknown) present in a well adapted desirable variety, at cellular level. It means superior lines are already present within a desirable variety but they are unable to express their superiority under field conditions. Somaclonal variation, therefore, can be used as a procedure for uncovering and exploiting such variability present in a desirable background.

As discussed earlier, during the occurrence of somaclonal variation, no part of the variety genome is at all destroyed but this advantage is, manytimes, nullified by the instability of the variant traits. Therefore, it is necessary to observe a somaclone for several generations for ensuring its stability. Although there are views in favour of and against somaclonal variation as a source of novel variation for wheat improvement, Lazzery and Shewry (1993) feel that breeders should be more cautious while using somaclonal variation for cereal improvement. According to them, instead of using somaclonal variation, some other procedure(s) may be preferred. Therefore, before applying any new procedure for wheat improvement, all merits and demerits of the method must be properly assessed.

Use of Biochemical Markers

The construction of genetic maps of individual chromosomes based on morphological markers started in the third decade of the 20th century soon after the discovery that genes are located on the chromosomes. Later on, biochemical markers (especially isozymes) were preferred over the morphological markers because of the superiority of the former over the latter in several ways (simple detection, low cost, speedy screening of material and independence from environmental effects). The use of biochemical markers expanded rapidly in 1970s and 1980s. Refinements were made in electrophoretic techniques. A large number of different proteins were recognized and their genetic control was determined using sophisticated electrophoretic techniques. These studies led to the identifications of hundreds of genes in different crop species and the location of these genes on different chromosomal segments.

Biochemical marker techniques utilizing seed storage proteins and isozymes can be used to distinguish alien chromosomes in wheat for distant hybridizations. These techniques facilitate speedy identification of genes and their location on different chromosomal segments. Their application in wheat has resulted in the identification of many structural genes and in determining their location on chromosomes. The techniques also help in ascertaining the homeology of the alien chromosomes in the addition lines. The development of efficient techniques which rapidly identify alien genetic material in wheat background can greatly help the incorporation of such genetic material into bread wheat. Two types of biochemical markers, namely, involving *seed storage proteins* and *isozymes*, are being used at CIMMYT for the characterization and identification of alien genetic material (William and Mujeeb-Kazi, 1995).

Seed storage proteins are composed of two components, namely, *glutenins* (largely responsible for gluten elasticity) and *gliadins* (responsible for viscosity), are the source of energy required for seed germination and can be used for the characterization and identification of alien genetic material. High molecular weight (HMW) glutenins are composed of a number of glutenin submits (constituent polypeptide chains).

According to Wrigley and Shepherd (1973) and Payne *et al.* (1982), the genes responsible for the coding of gliadins, are found on the short arms of chromosomes of homeologous group 1 and group 6.

In addition to the importance of seed storage proteins as biochemical markers for characterizing and identifying alien genetic material, these proteins can be used as effective cytogenetic markers for determining the presence or absence of particular chromosomes or arms of chromosomes. Further, their knowledge helps in establishing relationship between flour quality and allelic combinations.

Several different forms of an enzyme (protein) performing the same basic function involving plant metabolism, are called as *isozymes*. As discussed earlier, the main reason of using isozyme markers for the detection of alien chromatin is that they facilitate a speedy screening of the materials under investigation. According to Asiedu *et al.* (1989), a large number of structural genes (more than 100) have been identified for isozyme markers in wheat and the locations of these genes on the chromosomes have been known. The use of these markers also helps in ascertaining the homeology of the alien chromosomes in addition lines on the basis of the knowledge regarding the genes possessed by these chromosomes and the bread wheat genes with known chromosomal locations.

The basic principle involved in the identification of biochemical markers is the relative migration of charged molecules in an electric field. The identification of biochemical markers can be carried out using electrophoresis where an electric field is used to cause the migration of charged protein molecules. However, the main factors which determine the rate of migration of proteins are : (1) Electric field's strength; (2) shape and size of the protein molecules; (3) the net charge; and (4) the ionic strength and viscosity of the medium used for the movement of the molecules. Banding profiles for the different enzyme systems are developed using enzyme-specific stains (William and Mujeeb-Kazi, 1995).

Fortunately, compensating nullisomic-tetrasomic stocks are available in bread wheat. Using alien disomic addition lines and ditelosomic addition lines, the genes for isozymes have been located on the chromosomes and chromosome arms. Electrophoresis is an equally good technique for knowing the putative parents of polyploid wheats.

Efforts are also being made at CIMMYT for tracking chromosomes in intergeneric and interspecific hybrids. For example, eight geographically different accessions were used for developing isozyme markers to track *Psathyrostachys juncea* chromosomes in wheat background. *Ps. juncea* is a grass species possessing tolerance to salinity and drought and resistance to barley yellow dwarf virus (Plourde *et al.*, 1990). Similarly, for transferring salinity tolerance to wheat, the biochemical characterization of *Thinopyrum bessarabicum* (a self-fertilizing maritime grass with $2n=2x=14$, JJ) has been done.

It is felt that only a small number of *T. tauschii* genotypes of restricted geographic origin participated in the evolutionary origin of hexaploid wheat for contributing D genome (Lagudah *et al.*, 1991). There are many other diverse wild accessions of *T. tauschii* which can considerably contribute towards bread wheat improvement. For example, ecological adaptability of bread wheat may be widened by transferring genetic material from *T. tauschii*. Successful transfer of genetic material containing genes for wide adaptability would increase the scope of bread wheat cultivation in marginal areas. Therefore, interspecific hybridizations between wheat and some *T. tauschii* accessions may prove valuable for the wheat breaders.

Scientists at CIMMYT, evaluated variability present in some *T. tauschii* accessions for high molecular weight submits of glutenins and gliadins (seed storage proteins) and for the isoenzymes, seed esterase-5 (EST-5), β-amylase (β-AMY) and glucose phosphate isomerase (GPI). A large number of synthetic hexaploids were produced involving these accessions. The variability of *T. tauschii* accessions was compared with the variability of synthetic hexaploids. Polymorphisms for storage proteins and isozymes were observed for 60 accessions. The *T. tauschii* accessions exhibited comparatively more variability for high molecular weight submits of glutenin in Glu-D1 locus than the variability noted earlier. Further, it was observed that D genome of *T. tauschii* has more variability for the isozyme EST-5 than the variability possessed by the D genome of hexaploid wheat. However, no polymorphisms were shown by these accessions for glucose phosphate isomerage (GPI).

Because of the presence of resistance genes Lr 19, Sr 26, Yr 9 and Pm 8 on short arm of the chromosome 1 of rye, the wheats carrying 1BL/1RS translocation have high yield and high stability (Rajaram *et al.*, 1983). However, by growing seven pairs of isolines (seven CIMMYT bread wheats and their near-isogenic lines in which homozygous 1BL/1RS were substituted by 1B chromosomes) under drought conditions in 2000-01 and under drought and irrigated conditions in 2001-02, Monneveux *et al.* (2003) found that the effect of 1BL/1RS translocation depended on the environmental conditions and genetic background. According to Dhaliwal *et al.* (1987), the wheats carrying 1BL/1RS translocation have inferior dough quality. Of course, the findings of Pena *et al.* (1990) do not support the opinion that inferior dough quality in wheat is associated with 1BL/1RS translocation. To know precisely that whether or not 1BL/1RS translocation is the cause of low dough quality in wheat, efforts are being made at CIMMYT to produce and analyse substitution lines of such translocation stocks. Several *T. aestivum* varities homozygous for 1B (that is, 1B, 1B) or 1BL/1RS) (that is, 1BL/1RS, 1BL/1RS) and their heterozygote (1B, 1BL/1RS) F_1 progenies were included in the study. The varieties having 1B, 1B chromosomal constitution were crossed with varieties with 1BL/1RS, 1BL/1RS constitution to produce 1B, 1BL/1RS translocation heterozygotes. Five seeds were randomly selected from each parent and their F_1 hybrids. The analysis of these seeds was carried out for GPI and gladian electrophoretic patterns. For differentiating F_1 hybrid cross combinations (1B, 1BL/1RS) from their homozygous parents, a combination of protein separation techniques (GPI isoelectric focusing or GPI-IEF and polyacrylamide gel electrophoresis in acid medium or Acid-PAGE) was used. However, GPI banding profile alone was used to develop isozyme markers for the identification of translocation heterozygote in durum wheat substitution lines (William and Mujeeb-Kazi, 1995).

Use of Molecular Markers

Since both the biochemical and molecular markers are generally independent of environment and genotype, these markers have proved to be a powerful tool for studying genetic variability present within a species and tracing its evolutionary history (Grivet and Noyer, 1993). Whereas biochemical markers are used to determine the polymorphism of sequences of certain proteins, the polymorphism of DNA can be directly known through the use of molecular markers. However, since the nucleotide sequences of DNA can be known on the basis of amino acid sequences of proteins and *vice versa*, biochemical markers indirectly reveal the polymorphism of DNA sequences.

The use of molecular markers like RFLPs (restriction fragment length polymorphisms), RAPDs (random amplified polymorphic DNA) and AFLP (amplified fragment length polymorphism) is becoming increasingly important for constructing chromosome maps, identifying cultivars, detecting alien introgressions and chromosomal interchnages, evaluating germplasm and for indirect selection criteria in many crop species.

RFLPs : RFLPs are being used quite frequently in many crop species since they are available in abundance; are independent of environmental effects, gene function, developmental stage and tissue type; are relatively more rapid, convenient and expected to exhibit Mendelian codominant inheritance; have least pleiotropic effects; and can be used as indirect selection criteria, for strain identification, germplasm evaluation and classification and for genetic mapping; to assess genetic diversity and to determine phylogenetic relationship between different species.

However, because of the polyploid nature of wheat and presence of a large number of chromosomes in the nucleus, there has been a limited success in the use of RFLPs in this important cereal. Of course, the work done by Devos and Gale (1993), Xie et al. (1993), Nelson et al. (1995), Van Deynze et al. (1995), Marine et al. (1996) and others for preparing detailed RFLP maps for wheat homeologous groups deserves full appreciation. Sceintists at CIMMYT, also have a plan to explore RFLP techniques in collaboration with other molecular laboratories for their germplasm (William and Mujeeb-Kazi, 1995).

RAPDs : Welsh and McClelland (1990) and Williams et al. (1990) independently developed this molecular marker technique. It is a polymerase chain reaction (PCR) based technique and is considered better than RFLP analysis in some respects. The technique is relatively simpler, allows rapid detection of polymorphisms among individual genotypes and requires a very small amount of DNA. Furthermore, no radioactivity is involved in the technique. The technique is being used in crop species for several purposes like tagging major genes as well as quantitative trait loci (QTLs), identifying somatic hybrids, detecting alien introgressions and chromosomal interchanges and for cryopreservation of genetic stocks. A number of variants of PCR based molecular marker techniques are now available to the scientists. However, according to Paran and Michelmore (1993) and Nair et al. (1996), RAPDs can be made more reliable and reproducible markers by converting them to SCARs (sequence characterized amplified regions).

In view of the importance of molecular marker techniques in the detection of alien introgressions and chromosomal interchanges, some of these techniques are being used in wheat wide crosses by CIMMYT scientists (William and Mujeeb-Kazi, 1995). The relative proportions of repeated DNA sequences and non-repeated DNA sequences in three wheat genomes are 75-80 per cent and 20-25 per cent, respectively (Flavell and Smith, 1976). According to Moore et al. (1993), the non-repeated DNA sequences are found scattered between the repeated DNA sequences.

As mentioned earlier, RAPDs are based on PCR and can be used to diagnose the presence of alien chromatin in wheat background. At CIMMYT, bread wheat has been crossed with *Thinopyrum bessarabicum* (possessing salinity tolerance) to produce disomic addition lines in wheat background. The main objective of producing such lines is to track *Th. bessarabicum* chromatin in wheat backgrounds and to ultimately detect the presence of minute chromosomal alien introgressions. CIMMYT scientists feel that it is better to use relatively less costly, less complicated and more general cytological techniques or biochemical markers for the initial identification and characterization of addition lines. After the characterization of the material, RAPDs can be used to detect the small segments of alien chromatin (William and Mujeeb-Kazi, 1995).

AFLPs : AFLP is a general method for DNA fingerprints (Zabean and Voss, 1993) and a novel PCR-based technique for plant and bacterial DNA fingerprinting (Lin and Kuo, 1995). This technique has been found as most efficient and extremely powerful tool for detecting polymorphism in several plant species like lettuce (Hill et al., 1996), soybean (Lin et al., 1996), tea (Paul et al., 1997) and barley (Qi and Lindhout, 1997). But, there has been a limited use of of molecular markers in wheat mainly because of limited success with RFLPs in detecting polymorphism and the problem of reproducibility of RAPDs across the laboratories. However, Barrett and Kidwell (1998) and Grunberg et al. (2001) have found AFLP analysis as an efficient technology for assessing genetic diversity in wheat. AFLP can also be used as a successful technique for DNA fingerprinting in wheat (Ranjekar et al., 1998; Grunberg et al., 2001).

Grunberg et al. (2001) investigated AFLP markers for assessing diversity and fingerprinting of 15 elite soft red winter wheat (*Triticum aestivum*) genotypes differeing for pre-harvest sprouting resistance and for the presence of awns. Their results indicated that AFLP is a powerful molecular tool for determining genetic distances between wheat genotypes and for fingerprinting wheat genotypes for plant variety protection use. They also concluded that the results obtained were more consistent and that it is relatively easy to use AFLP analysis. Furthermore, AFLP gave relatively more information in wheat than other molecular markers as was indicated by the mean polymorphism information content and the average marker index. Despite a high genetic similarity (since the range of the mean genetic similarity values among wheat genotypes was from 0.83-0.94) among the 15 wheat genotypes, the level of differences was sufficient for the assessment of both the genetic diversity and the plant variety protection use. The number of polymorphic AFLP loci between the resistant and susceptible genotypes was high indicating possible use of AFLP markers for constructing genetic maps of pre-harvest sprouting resistance in crosses of these genotypes in future.

Application of Recombinant DNA Technology

Novel techniques of plant genetic engineering have opened new avenues for inserting desired genes into plant genome from diverse biological systems. It means that now genes can be transferred from one plant species to another plant species, from an animal to a plant or from a microorganism to a plant, that is, transfer of genes across sexual barriers has now become a reality. The feasibility of the transfer of genes across sexual barrier provides opportunity to modify and improve crop plants in a desired direction. Biotechnology may also be used for constructing a stable agroeco system.

Recombinant DNA technology is a promising technique which can be used to direct the movement of specific and desirable genes or small DNA segments between unrelated organisms and modify and improve the crop plants in a desired direction. The technique has been used to transfer useful foreign genes governing various plant traits (e.g., genes for disease and insect pest resistance, for tolerance to abiotic stresses, for weed control, for storage proteins, for male sterility and genes for quality) to produce transgenic plants/varieties. However, for the practical application of this technique in plant breeding, two conditions should be fulfilled : (1) The transgenic plants should exhibit a continued expression; and (2) the transgenes should show a stable inheritance.

The procedure of recombinant DNA technology involves five steps : (1) Gene identification; (2) gene isolation; (3) gene transfer; (4) gene integration; and (5) gene expression. The genes can be transferred either using a vector (that is, vector-mediated gene transfer) or directly by incubating in polyethylene glycol, electroporation, inserting DNA by particle gun or by microinjection.

The biotic and abiotic stresses cause a considerable loss in wheat. According to Oerke *et al.* (1994), fungal diseases cause about 20 per cent loss in wheat production. If the losses caused by all diseases and pests of wheat are put together, the value of losses will be much higher than given by Oerke *et al.* Therefore, genes governing resistance to biotic stresses have a special place in wheat breeding programmes. Similarly, genes responsible for tolerance to abiotic stresses have their own significance in these programmes. Genes for induction of male sterility may play an important role in developing hybrid wheat varieties and in population improvement programmes where male sterility may facilitate intercrossing without hand emasculation and crossing (that is, male sterility-facilitated recurrent selection). Furthermore, grain quality in wheat (mainly determined by the number and composition of the high molecular weight glutenin subunits present in grain) is now becoming increasingly important for the wheat breeders.

Bohorova (1998) emphasized the importance of genetic engineering in plant breeding and discussed the genetic engineering work being done at CIMMYT. In the beginning the results of the studies done on wheat transformation were not encouraging as most of the cells did not accept the integrate foreign DNA. But, after the production of first fertile transgenic wheat plant by Vasil *et al.* (1992), the situation drammatically changed and a remarkable success was achieved in producing wheat transformed plants. However, there is still scope for the optimization of conditions for the transformation process in wheat.

At CIMMYT, nine highly regenerable genotypes of wheat, five (Attila, Kauz, Luan, Baviacora and Bobwhite) of bread wheat and four (Altar, Ariza, Minimus and Bajio) of durum wheat were selected to produce transformed wheat plants. The optimal micro projectile bombardment technique using gene constructs was followed (Bohorova, 1998). However, the efficiency of producing wheat transgenics by this technique is not encouraging and efforts are being made for *Agrobacterium*-mediated transformation using Attila and Kauz genotypes of bread wheat.

According to Khurana *et al.* (2004), useful work regarding regeneration and transformation of wheat is being done at Delhi University, India. They have noted an unusually high morphogenetic potential of wheat leaf base segments. According to Mahalakshmi *et al.* (2003), the induction of somatic embyrogenesis in leaf base explants of wheat can be considerably enhanced by giving a short term treatment of 2, 4-D. Khurana *et al.* (2002) reported an efficient and reproducible procedure for *Agrobacterium*-mediatd transformation of mature embryos of emmer wheat (*Triticum dicoccum*). It has been found that calli can be successfully produced by using mature embryos (which are available throughout the year) as an explant and then these calli can be used for transformation studies (Khurana *et al.*, 2002; Patnaik and Khurana, 2003). According to Patnaik and Khurana (2001), particle bombardment is emerging as an important technique for introducing genes for quality in wheat. Furthermore, efforts are being made to develop simplistic and cost effective transformation strategies. For example, Mahalakshmi *et al.* (2000) have developed *cellular permeabilization* technique for *direct exogenous DNA uptake* in wheat zygotic embryos keeping the cell viability and proliferative ability as such. Similarly, Chugh *et al.* (2004) have developed a *non-tissue culture technique* for *germline transformation* of bread wheat employing *Agrobacterium* and mature seeds as the target tissues.

Sautter (2004) has discussed opportunities and challenges of wheat transformation with special reference to European countries. As regards the opportunities, transformation facilitates addition of new gene(s) without severely affecting the rest of the genotype of the plant. In addition to the special importance of transformation for vegetatively propagated plant species like sugarcane, potato, sweet potato, banana and many other fruit trees, it also facilitates development of isogenic wheat elite lines. Also, the approach has no sexual barriers. Further, the goal of defeating all parasitic fungi can be accomplished in one single step. Clausen *et al.* (2000) introduced the antifungal gene from *Ustilago maydis* virus K 4 into smut susceptible Swiss wheat lines and observed antifungal activity of transgenic lines under laboratory conditions. They hope that the plants resistant to smut would also show resistance against Karnal bunt.

The challenges in wheat transformation are mainly due to the inherent characteristics of the polyploid wheat plant. The challenges are:

1. Like other monocotyledons, wheat is recalcitrant to *Agrobacterium* strategy.
2. Presence of a large number of chromosomes in the wheat genome creates lot of difficulty in molecular work and genetic studies.

3. Like in other cereals, transgenes in wheat show a tendency of silencing and inactivation. This tendency shows a high correlation with specific methylation of DNA.
4. According to Sautter, a Europe-specific challenge in wheat transformation is the *risk perception* by the public in using transgenic wheat plants since European people are religiously associated with this cereal.

However, Cheng *et al.* (1997) and Khanna and Daggard (2003) have clearly demonstrated the possibility of *Agrobacterium*-mediated transformation in wheat.

A long term target for biotechnology may be to breed wheat varieties with increased photosynthetic efficiency and with ability to fix atmospheric nitrogen. However, the past experience indicates that varieties with more photosynthetic efficiency would require more fertilizer and, similarly, varieties with ability to fix nitrogen are expected to be lower yielder.

CHAPTER 8

Hybrid Wheat

The choice of the optimum variety (that is, whether to evolve a line variety, hybrid variety, population variety or a clone variety for obtaining maximum benefit) is, in general, determined by three interrelated factors : (1) The relative role of dominance and overdominance (the two major mechanisms suggested to explain the nature of heterosis) towards heterosis; (2) the system of mating naturally occurring in the species (whether the species is self-fertilized, cross-fertilized, often-cross-fertilized or is vegetatively propagated); and (3) the type of experiment (whether the experiment is on a short term or on a long term basis). There is no confusion regarding the development of optimum variety in vegetatively propagated crops like sugarcane, potato and sweet potato. In these crops, breeders have no option except to evolve clone varieties. The biggest advantage associated with clone varieties is that the same genotype, irrespective of its degree of heterozygosity, can be maintained for indefinite period, that is, heterosis can be fixed in heterozygous condition since there are no chances of genetic recombination. Occurrence of mutations is the only force which can bring changes in the genetic composition of a clone.

As regards the development of optimum varieties in cross-fertilizing crops like maize, sunflower and pearlmillet, the optimum variety may be a hybrid variety (single cross, three-way cross or a double cross variety) or a population variety (synthetic or a composite variety) depending upon the objective of the breeder, relative advantage of a particular type of the variety over the other type of variety in a particular crop and other considerations including economics of the variety development. For example, single cross hybrids are generally highest yielder but have relatively lower adaptability and higher cost of production of hybrid seed than the three-way cross hybrids, double cross hybrids and synthetic and composite varieties. Similarly, other types of varieties (three-way and double cross hybrids, synthetics and composites) have their own adantages and disadvantages (For details, see Singh and Pawar, 2006).

Since long back, breeders have been developing line varieties as well as hybrid varieties (rarely population varieties) of often-cross-fertilized crops like cotton, sorghum and pigeonpea. In this group of crop species, the breeder has to be bit careful while taking decision about the development of an optimum variety. However, now-a-days, the production of hybrid varieties is being preferred over the development of line varieties in these crops.

Nevertheless, the breeder has to be extremely careful while deciding about the development of optimum variety in highly self-fertilizing crops like wheat, barley and gram. All positive and negative points about the breeding methodology to be adopted must be very well considered. Since these crop species are highly self-fertilized, development of line varieties has been the routine breeding methodology in these crops. However, since hybrid rice has become a commercial proposition in China, it is quite natural that scientists all over the world are now thinking and trying to develop hybrid varieties of wheat, one of the most important food crops of the world. If they become successful in their efforts, it will be a big gain for them.

However, the most basic question arises that whether wheat scientists should develop a homozygous (a line) variety or a hybrid variety? This question, in fact, has no plain answer because the choice of the optimum type of variety greatly depends on the genetic basis of heterosis and, unfortunately, the current knowledge about the contribution of mechanisms involved in the phenomenon of heterosis is poor.

Some Important Considerations

Let us discuss some points for assessing the possibility and success of hybrid wheat.

Nature of heterosis : Although the mechanism involved in the phenomenon of heterosis is not yet fully known, the two major hypotheses putforward to explain the genetic basis of heterosis are: (1) *Dominant favourable genes hypothesis* of Davenport (1908), Keeble and Pellew (1910) and Bruce (1910); and (2) *overdominance hypothesis* of Shull (1908) and East (1908). If heterosis is solely due to dominance, it (heterosis) can be fixed and it is possible to develop homozygous varieties as good as (in case of full dominance) or better than (in case of partial dominance) hybrids. On the contrary, if overdominance is the main cause of heterosis, it is not possible to fix heterosis (except in vegetatively propagated crops) and the best variety will always be a single cross hybrid.

However, many modern plant breeders and geneticists are of the opinion that the role of overdominance towards heterosis would be minor as compared to that of dominance and thus attach a comparatively greater weightage to dominance as the cause of heterosis (Gallais, 1989). The proof in favour of this opinion comes mainly from the quantitative genetic studies carried out in *Nicotiana rustica* by Jayasekara and Jinks (1976), Pooni and Jinks (1981), Jinks (1983) and Jinks and Pooni (1986) at the Birmingham School (U.K.). They have experimentally demonstrated that the average degree of dominance for heterotic and non-heterotic crosses in *N. rustica* was never significantly greater than 1. They further demonstrated that the heterosis exhibited by the F_1 of a *N. rustica* cross for plant height was due to the accumulation of the dominant favourable genes in the parents and not due to overdominance. Furthermore, Sprague (1983) reviewed a large number of experiments carried out in maize and came almost to a similar conclusion. However, the value of average degree of dominance around 1, does not completely rule out the contribution of overdominance towards heterosis since different genes controlling the same quantitative character may exhibit different degrees of dominance–some no dominance, some incomplete dominance, some complete dominance, and some may exhibit overdominance.

Nevertheless, apparent overdominance may not always be true overdominance but the linkage between favourable and unfavourable genes may generate pseudo-overdominance. This type of over-dominance, manytimes, is a consequence of linkages which are loose enough and can be broken by intermating. But, if linkages are very tight, it becomes difficult to make distinction between pseudo-overdominance and true overdominance.

Importance of gene effects : Huge literature is available on the application of diallel mating design to wheat populations. Many of these studies have revealed that general combining ability (determined mostly by additive gene effects) played a major role in the control of grain yield in wheat (Kronstad and Foote, 1964; Brown *et al.,* 1966; Gyawali *et al.,* 1968; Walton, 1971; Bitzer and Fu, 1972; Widner and Lebsock, 1973; and many others), particularly under competitive growth conditions. There are reports (Widner and Lebsock, 1973; Chang *et al.,* 1973; Li, 1975; and others) which indicate that grain yield and its major component traits are governed mainly by additive gene effects. The application of triple test cross design to wheat populations has also given similar results (Singh and Pawar, 1998). All these results clearly indicate that there is great scope for developing high yielding line varieties in wheat.

Homozygous genomic heterosis : The presence of homeologous genomes in polyploid wheats has provided a unique opportunity of fixing heterosis in these wheats and consequently has decreased the importance of the hybrid varieties in this cereal. The fixed heterosis which arises due to the homozygosity within each genome and heterozygosity between genomes is known as *homozygous genomic heterosis*. This type of heterosis, therefore, provides advantage of heterozygosity in homozygous condition. After evaluating 40 years of wheat hybrid development, Pickett (1993) and Pickett and Galwey (1997) have expressed their reservations about the hybrid wheat production. According to them, a number of factors like the presence of homozygous genomic heterosis, higher cost of hybrid seed, low levels of heterosis and low superiority of hybrids over line varieties in terms of agronomic worth and disease resistance indicate that hybrid wheat production has no economical feasibility.

Effect of recurrent selection : The main aim of recurrent selection is to increase the frequency of desirable alleles in the population. This type of selection, therefore, facilitates development of outstanding lines. However, with an increase in the superiority of inbred parents, there is a decline in the relative hybrid advantage (Jinks, 1981; Morgan *et al.,* 1989). Though the second cycle inbreds are superior to first cycle inbreds but the hybrids produced from these two types of inbreds do not exhibit significant differences. It means that it is possible to develop outstanding inbreds but development of outstanding hybrids from these improved inbreds is not an easy task. Nevertheless, the use of high yielding inbreds in hybrid breeding programme would reduce the cost of production of hybrid seed.

Degree of inbreeding depression : The generalization that overdominance makes a minor contribution towards heterosis appears to be an oversimplification of the problem since the importance of heterosis is related to the system of mating occurring in a species and, therefore, the relative role of dominance and overdominance would largely depend on the extent of inbreeding depression shown by a plant species. Wheat is a highly self-fertilized crop species with about 99.0 per cent self fertilization and shows no conspicuous inbreeding depression. On the contrary, cross-fertilizing crop species like maize, sunflower and brown sarson deteriorate drastically upon inbreeding. There appears to be no possibility of developing line varieties as good as hybrids in these crop species.

Further, the basic difference between the self-fertilizing and cross-fertilizing species is that, in nature, autogams maintain a *homozygous balance* and allogams maintain a *heterozygous balance*. It means that cross-fertilizers possess a large number of undesirable genes in the heterozygous state, that is, allogamous plant species have a *genetic load* and a large part of the inbreeding depression shown by these species is explainable by the genetic load. On the other hand, in autogamous plant species, the natural selection goes on acting on the resulting plants after selfed generations and ultimately succeeds in eliminating the genetic load of these species. This is how the discontinuity occurs between the two groups of the plants (allogams and autogams) in nature. According to Ohno (1970), duplication of whole or a part of the genome is another way of fixing heterosis by autogams.

Type of experiment : In a short-term breeding programme since the type of variety (hybrid or a line) would largely depend on the importance of heterosis, the development of hybrid variety should be preferred over that of a line variety even though there is a minor contribution of overdominance (that is, in almost all situations). Hybrid varieties have two main advantages; (1) They permit use of overdominance; and (2) development of hybrid variety is the most rapid method of accumulating the maximum number of desirable dominant alleles in a single genotype. However, the situation may altogether change in a long term breeding programme where an outstanding line variety may be developed using an appropriate recurrent selection procedure. Gallais (1989) has discussed the issue of the choice of the optimum type of variety in detail.

Nevertheless, the theoretical considerations discussed above may not always prove correct. For example, hybrid rice has now become a commercial proposition in China even though rice, like other self-fertilizing crop species, is an autogam with moderate degree of heterosis and low inbreeding depression. Of course, in common wheat which is a hexaploid, with the advantage of heterozygosity in homozygous condition, hybrid breeding programme may not be as successful as it is in rice.

Pickett (1998) has further emphasized the importance of the type of heterosis for developing hybrid varieties in wheat. In Pickett's opinion, if overdominance is the major cause of heterosis in wheat, then hybrid wheat can be an economical proposition since, under such situation, it will not be possible to derive homozygous lines as good as F_1 hybrids. On the contrary, if dominance and epistatic effects are the main cause of heterosis, then it is advisable to give more weightage to the development of superior line varieties. Efforts should also be made to enhance the extent of homozygous genomic heterosis by increasing the interaction between the three homeologous genomes.

There are reports which indicate that dominance and epistatic interactions are the major cause of yield heterosis in wheat. In an attempt to study the genetical basis of heterosis for yield in wheat, Snape and Parker (1985) observed that dominance was the major cause of heterosis in their material. According to Singh and Singh (1971), epistasis also contributed towards heterosis in wheat.

A different type of the approach for evolving superior line varieties in wheat has also been suggested. According to some scientists (Wienhues, 1968; Busch *et al.*, 1971; Snape, 1982; Snape and Parker, 1985), it is possible to extract outstanding inbred lines from F_1 hybrids. However, Jost and Hayward (1980) could not confirm the success of this approach.

Efforts have also been made to prove correspondence between genetic diversity and heterosis in wheat. Martin *et al.* (1995) used molecular markers and coefficient of parentage to assess genetic diversity directly between parents and tried to establish relationship between genetic diversity of parents and yield hetrosis. Jatasra and Paroda (1983) had also found similar results, however, using a different methodology. On the other hand, many scientists (Arunachalam, 1977, 1981; Srivastava and Arunachalam, 1977; Arunachalam and Bandyopadhyay, 1984; and several others) have advocated that heterosis should not be considered as a function of genetic divergence between parents (For details, see Singh and Pawar, 2005). It is true that significant heterosis shown by the hybrids is mostly indicative of the genetic diversity between the parents but it is not necessary that genetically diverse parents would always produce heterotic hybrids. A number of scientists (Arunachalam and Bandyopathyay, 1984; and several others) have found that the parents with intermediate genetic divergence generally produce higher number of heterotic hybrids than are produced by extreme parents.

Jordaan (1996) has critically discussed the advances made in, the challenges to be faced by and the future prospects of hybrid wheat programme. According to Jordaan, many scientists, especially Picket (1993), are of the opinion that development of hybrid varieties in wheat is not a viable option. While discussing the results and problems of hybrid wheat in the year 1993, Pickett did not agree with the views of other researchers who were in favour of hybrid breeding in wheat, arguing that

1. dominance is the major cause of heterosis in wheat,
2. there are low levels of heterotic effect in wheat, especially when superiority of F_1 hybrids is measured over the modern high yielding, photoinsensitive, fertilizer responsive and disease resistant wheat cultivars,
3. wheat hybrids do not exhibit superiority over the best line varieties in terms of phenotypic stability, improved ideotype, disease resistance, breeding time scales and grain quality,
4. cytoplasmic male sterility suggested for use in wheat is slow and suffers from versality in procedures of fertility restoration,
5. toxicity and inadequate selectivity associated with chemical hybridizing agents (CHAs), create problems in hybrid seed production in wheat,
6. the use of nuclear male sterility in wheat has been least successful as the method is not cost effective.
7. the floral morphology of wheat (particularly the morphology and biophysics of pollen) which enforces a very high degree of self pollination in this cereal, is poorly adapted to outcrossing, and
8. the induction of male sterility in wheat is costly and thus increases the cost of hybrid seed.

Hybrid varieties are especially suited for dry areas where heat and moisture stresses are common. However, judicious use of chemical hybridizing agents and application of novel techniques of biotechnology may help in reversing decisions made on hybrid wheat in the past by many researchers. To make wheat hybrids more competitive with conventional varieties, heterotic groupings of germplasm should be identified, male and female pools should be developed and within and between pools selections should be made for the characteristics like disease resistance, phenotypic stability and suitability of ideotype for which hybrids do not generally show superiority over line varieties (Jordaan, 1996).

Apart from the problems discussed by Pickett (1993), the hybrid wheat programme got set back mainly because of the following three reasons :

1. **The realizaton of the importance of homozygous genomic heterosis :** This type of heterosis which arises because of the heterozygosity between genomes and homozygosity within each genome allows fixation of heterosis in the homozygous polyploid wheats, that is, fixation of heterozygosity in an autogamous species.

2. **Development of semi-dwarf wheat varieties :** The discoveries of Kihara (1951) and Fukasawa (1953)

about the identification of cytoplasmically induced male sterility in wheat, coincided with the development of semi-dwarf wheat varieties using Norin dwarfing genes in early 1950s in USA. These high yielding, fertilizer responsive and photoinsensitive varieties made a significant impact on world agriculture and thus attracted the attention of most of the wheat researchers.

3. **Effect of 1BL/1RS translocation :** The transfer of a segment from the short arm of the chromosome 1 of rye to the left arm of the chromosome 1B of wheat (the 1BL/1RS translocation) has considerably increased yield of wheat. The wheat varieties carrying 1BL/1RS translocation are now being grown all over the world.

On the contrary, the scientists have been unable to resolve some of the basic problems related to hybrid wheat.

Essential Pre-requisites for Hybrid Wheat

For successful adoption of hybrid breeding technology in wheat, the three main requirements are: (1) Existence of substantial yield heterosis to make hybrid wheat a commercially viable breeding procedure; (2) availability of effective pollination control system enabling production of hybrid seed at commercial scale; and (3) a balance between the degree of commercial heterosis and the cost-effectiveness of the pollination control system so that the two factors are complementary to each other.

Level of Heterosis in Wheat

Numerous investigators (Briggle, 1963; Kronstad and Foote, 1964; Brown *et al.*, 1966; Briggle *et al.*, 1967; Rodriguez *et al.*, 1967; Fonseca and Patterson, 1968; Livers and Heyne, 1968; Wells and Lay, 1970; Singh and Singh, 1971; Walton, 1971; Bitzer and Fu, 1972; Allan, 1973; Dhindsa and Anand, 1973; Widner and Lebsock, 1973; Varenitsa and Zimina, 1976; Yadav and Murty, 1976; Hughes and Bodden, 1978; Cregan and Busch, 1978; Pinthus and Miliet, 1978; Bailey *et al.*, 1980; Shaowen and Shan, 1980; Tsunewaki *et al.*, 1980; Wilson *et al.*, 1980; Li *et al.*, 1982; Pinthus, 1987; Lucken and Johnson, 1988; Morgan *et al.*, 1989; Slafer and Andrale, 1991; Ikeguchi *et al.*, 1994; Eavis *et al.*, 1996; El-Hennaury, 1996; Jordaan, 1996; Peterson *et al.* 1997; Bruns and Peterson, 1998; Prasad *et al.*, 1998; Ratnalikar and Singh, 1998; and many others) have tried to know the extent of heterosis in wheat. In addition, hybrid wheat has been reviewed by several scientists (Johnson and Schmidt, 1968; Virmani and Edwards, 1983; Wilson and Driscoll, 1983; Pickett, 1993). According to Briggle (1963), heterosis in wheat may vary from 0-100 per cent. However, Lucken and Johnson noted 116.0 per cent heterosis over the better parent. Yadav and Murty (91.8%), Walton (88.1%), Tsunewaki *et al.* (73%), El-Hennaury (61.3%) and Prasad *et. al.* (59.7%) also observed high heterosis over the better parent. Based on a comprehensive 4-year study, Livers and Heyne reported an average hybrid superiority of 32.0 per cent. According to Jordaan, results from South Africa indicated 15.0 per cent superiority of hybrids over inbred lines. Peterson *et al.* also observed significant superiority of hybrids over homozygous lines. According to Bruns and Peterson, the hybrid superiority over homozygous lines ranged from 10-13 per cent. On the contrary, according to Eavis *et al.*, the recent reports of hybrid performance in Europe indicated only 5-12 per cent superiority of hybrids over homozygous lines. Pickett (1998) also opined that wheat hybrids have lower yield benefits than were reported earlier. However, as Hewstone (1997) has said, the absolute superiority of hybrids over the homozygous varieties should by seen in the light of the present yield potential (about 17 tonnes per hectare) of the modern homozygous bread wheat cultivars. Rajaram and Braun (2001) have critically discussed the issue of hybrid wheat.

Further, according to Allan (1973), Hayward (1975), Johnson (1977, 1978) and Edwards *et al.* (1980), the hand-produced wheat-hybrids gave more favourable results than those produced using cytoplasmic male sterility-fertility restoration systems. Also, the three component traits, number of fertile tillers, number of grains per spike and 1000 grain weight which mainly determine grain yield potential in wheat (Pinthus and Miller, 1978; Pinthus, 1987; Slafer and Andrale, 1991), are highly influenced by plant density (Dhindsa and Anand, 1973). Pickett (1993) reviewed a large number of wheat trials and found that the principal component of heterosis was different in different hybrids.

Pawar (2000) critically discussed the present status and probable future of hybrid wheat.

Pawar *et al.* (2003) discussed the emerging trends in hybrid wheat breeding and concluded that the main reasons of low heterosis in wheat are :

1. Fixation of a part of heterosis due to intergenomic heterozygosity, that is, presence of homozygous genomic heterosis;
2. grain yield and its component characters are mostly governed by additive gene effects and there is widespread absence of overdominance and additive × dominance and dominance × dominance epistasis for these characters; and
3. accumulation of favourable dominant alleles dispersed in the parents is the major cause of heterosis.

Another reason of low heterosis for grain yield in wheat is the dramatic increase in the yield potential of line varieties after the exploitation of dwarfing genes and 1BL/1RS translocation. The increased yield potential of line varieties may have reduced the level of the superiority of hybrids over line varieties in this cereal.

Although many scientists have reported high levels of heterosis in wheat, but most of such reports suffer from one or more of the following drawbacks :

1. The results of the studies were highly site-specific (Allan, 1973) and thus should not be generalized;
2. experimental materials were not grown according to normal agricultural practice followed by farmers where there is strong interplant competition, rather results were from space-planted experiments;
3. results were based on small scale trials; and/or
4. unproductive and substandard wheat varieties/strains were used as parents for producing hybrids.

The points mentioned above indicate that the results of such experiments cannot give a clear picture of the true level of heterosis in wheat.

According to Virmani and Edwards (1983), the poor performance of wheat hybrids produced by using cytoplasmic male sterility-fertility restoration systems in early studies was possibly because of the

1. inadequacy of fertility restoration,
2. non-availability of a suitable alternative male sterile cytoplasm, that is, total dependence on *timopheevii* cytoplasm,
3. relatively more importance given for restoration ability than for agronomic worth during restorer development, and
4. limited testing of various hybrid combinations.

Nevertheless, the degree of success of hybrid wheat breeding may be enhanced by :

1. Searching and using most suitable pollination control system (the use of most appropriate male sterile cytoplasm or most effective chemical hybridizing agent);
2. developing agronomically better restorers;
3. using parents possessing high combining ability;
4. using genetically diverse parents to widen the genetic base of hybrids;
5. maintaining a complementary balance between sink and source;
6. searching and identifying lines with favourable floral morphology for hybrid seed production;
7. modifying or restructuring floral morphology of promising lines to be used as parents; and
8. maximizing and economizing hybrid seed production using better selection strategies and seed production techniques.

Of course, it is not easy to take full care of all the points mentioned above. For example, more than 20 different types of cytoplasms have so far been identified for the induction of male sterility in wheat but the scientists have not been able to search a better cytoplasm than the cytoplasm of *T. timopheevii*. Chemical hybridizing agents or gametocides are also not disadvantage-free. Their main disadvantages are high cost and environmental pollution. Similarly, fertility restoration in wheat is a complexly inherited characteristic and is probably governed by both the major and minor genes. Further, sink and source relationship is associated with several other physiological and genetical characteristics. Also, restructuring of floral parts in wheat is the most difficult task. However, all efforts should be made to make the hybrid wheat breeding a success. Of course, the target is distant but not unreachable. Some of these points will be discussed in detail.

Cytoplasmic Male Sterility (CMS)

The term cytoplasmic male sterility here has been used for cytoplasmic-genetic male sterility where male sterility is caused by two factors, a sterile cytoplasm and a gene present in the nucleus. For using this type of male sterility in hybrid seed production, we require a suitable sterile cytoplasm, an effective nuclear gene for male sterility and restorer gene(s) for fertility. Three types of lines are develped : (i) A line or male sterile line, carrying male sterile cytoplasm and nuclear gene for male sterility in homozygous condition; (ii) B line or maintainer line, carrying fertile or normal cytoplasm and nuclear gene for male sterility in homozygous condition; and (iii) R line or restorer line, carrying restorer gene(s) for fertility. A line and B line differ only for the type of cytoplasm. B line is developed just to maintain the A line. The hybrid seed is produced by crossing A line with R line.

As regards the beginning of the search for male sterility in hybrid wheat, Kihara (1951) must be credited for making the first major attempt in this direction. By transferring genome of *Triticum aestivum* into the cytoplasm of *T. caudatum* (or *Aegilops candata*), he confirmed the possibility of transferring male sterility from *T. caudatum* to *T. aestivum*. But, two drawbacks were associated with this male sterility system : (1) the *caudatum* cytoplasm had an adverse effect on plant development; and (2) there was no availability of restorer genes. A similar effort was made by Fukasava (1953) by transferring genome of *T. durum* to the cytoplasm of *T. ovatum* (or *Ae. ovata*). The synthesized species *Aegilotricum* (*T. ovatum* × *T. durum*) was successively backcrossed to *T. durum* and male sterile plants were obtained. However, *ovatum* cytoplasm caused reduction in plant height and increase in maturity period. Several other attempts (Fukasava, 1957, 1958, 1959; Kihara, 1959; Kihara and Tsunewaki, 1961) were made in Japan to obtain male sterile plants of wheat.

Nevertheless, Wilson and Ross (1962) were the first to report a usable system of cytoplasmic male sterility in wheat. The genome of hard red winter bread wheat variety Bison was transferred into the cytoplasm of *T. timophevii* using successive backcrossing. The system which is based on the interaction of *T. timopheevii* cytoplasm with genome of *T. aestivum* has four main advantages;

1. The male sterility induced is complete and constant;
2. plant growth and development, by and large, are not adversely affected by *timopheevii* cytoplasm;
3. this cytoplasm has a neutral effect on agronomic and quality traits;
4. the system is least influenced by environmental fluctuations; and
5. restorer genes are available.

Since 1962, scientists have identified many cytoplasms donors like *T. zhukovskyi* (Ingold, 1968), *T. araraticum* (Maan and Lucken, 1968), *Secale cereale* (Maan and Lucken, 1971), *T. dicoccoides* and *T. bicorne* or *Ae. bicornis* (Maan and Lucken, 1972), *T. boeoticum*, *T. longissimum* or *Ae. longissima* and *T. unbellulatum* or *Ae. umbellulata* (Maan, 1973), *T. triaristatum* or *Ae. triaristata* (Panayotov and Gostov, 1973), *T. triunciale* or *Ae. triuncialis* (Endo and Tsunewaki, 1975), *T. biunciale* or *Ae. biuncialis* (Tsunewaki et al., 1976), *T. kotschyi* or *Ae. kotschyi* (Mukai and Tsunewaki, 1979), *T. comosum* or *Ae. comosa* and *T. muticum* or *Ae. mutica* (Panayotov, 1980) and *T. speltoides* or *Ae. speltoides* (Ghiasi and Lucken, 1982), for the induction of cytoplasmic male sterility in wheat. Pickett (1998) has given a list of 22 cytoplasm donors with their male fertility expression. However, many of these cytoplasms have adverse effect on some wheat key characters (general vigour, plant morphology, maturity period, etc.). They may cause reduction in vigour, increase in maturity time, zygote elimination and change in plant morphology. Further, many of these male sterility systems lack availability of genes for fertility restoration.

Although some scientists have noted differences between male sterile lines and maintainer lines in *timopheevii* system, no male sterility system better than this system is so far available. Of course, Ghiasi and Lucken (1982) opined that *T. speltoides* male sterility system is in no way inferior to *timopheevii* system. It may be because *T. speltoides* is a probable contributor of G genome and cytoplasm to *T. timopheevi*. If *T. speltoides* has contributed G genome and cytoplasm to *T. timopheevii*, then there should be no major difference between these two cytoplasms (*speltoides* and *timopheevii*) except the changes which occurred after the evolution of *T. timopheevii*.

The mechanism of the action of male sterility is not yet fully known. There are different views about the prevention of the production of functional pollen by cytoplasmic male sterility. It appears that tapetal tissues are implicated in this process of prevention since tapetum is directly related to the nutrition of the anther (Chapman, 1987). However, it is not clearly known whether the involvement of tapetum in preventing the production of functional pollen is the cause or consequence of male sterility (Rai and Stoskopf, 1974; Mascarenhas, 1990). According to Leaver et al. (1988) and Leaver (1989) cytoplasmic sterility may have a mitochondrial origin. It has been observed that the pollen abortion generally takes place between tetrad formation and the maturity of the pollen grain. It means that the beginning of the pollen development occurs in an almost normal way. These facts again indicate that the occurrence of cytoplasmic sterility could be due to the shortage of energy at the time of pollen development.

Male Fertility Restoration

The restitution of normal anther and pollen development (that is, restoration of complete male fertility) to F_1 hybrids carrying male sterility inducing cytoplasm, is one of the major factors influencing the speed of hybrid wheat development. Therefore, it is important to known all details (number and nature of genes governing male fertility restoration, location of these genes on the chromosomes, etc.) about this key factor. According to Livers (1964), the crosses between *T. timopheevii* and *T. aestivum* indicated presence of two dominant fertility restoring genes Rf_1 and Rf_2. The secret of the success of *timopheevii* male sterility system was the successful transfer of Rf genes from *T. timopheevii* to *T. aestivum* by Wilson and Ross (1962). It has been suggested by Krupnov (1971) that all species which are used for transferring male sterile cytoplasm to bread wheat also contain corresponding restorer genes. However, Zeven (1968) and Lucken (1973) opined that though *T. timopheevii* was the source of most of the Rf genes, but some Rf genes also occur in *T. aestivum*. According to Johnson and Schmidt (1968), common wheat may have contributed at least one restorer gene. Therefore, the restorer genes not only occur in the genome of the cytoplasm donor but conventional bread wheat cultivars may also contain Rf genes. However, the basis of the occurrence of such genes in conventional wheat varieties is not yet fully known.

While reviewing the literature on the fertility restoration, Sage (1976) opined that the earlier explanation given about the genetic nature of restorer genes was overs implication of genetic mechanism involved in male fertility restoration. In fact, male fertility restoration in wheat is a complex phenomenon and, therefore, is not explainable by a simple genetic model. The complexity of this phenomenon is indicated by the fact that different researchers have given different explanations for the restoration of *timopheevii* cytoplasm by Primepi. Whereas according to Oehler and Ingold (1966) and Gonjon and Ingold (1967), this restoration is caused by a single dominant gene, in the opinion of Miller (1970), Schmidt *et al.* (1971) and Miller *et al.* (1974), two incompletely dominant genes with major and minor effect, respectively, control this restoration. Further, Nettevich and Naumov (1970) opined that this restoration is caused by two incompletely dominant genes with the epistatic action of a single recessive gene. But, according to Shebeski (1971), this restoration is under the control of two complementary genes (one major and one minor dominant gene) plus one modifier gene and one inhibitor gene.

According to Sage, three major genes causing male fertility restoration in wheat are located on chromosomes 1A, 6B and 1B, but the restorer genes and their modifiers are found on 17 out of 21 chromosomes. In addition, there are some inhibitor genes also. Therefore, in a breeding programme meant for the development of restorer lines, three points should taken into consideration : (1) Selection for complementary restorer gene combinations; (2) accumulation of favourable modifiers; and (3) elimination of inbibitory genes. However, the situation is further complicated by the heterozygosity of the restorer genes in the hybrids since the effectiveness of these genes is more in homozygous condition than in heterozygous condition. In heterozygous condition, they may cause partial fertility and thus may complicate the selection process. Ghiasi *et al.* (1982) suggested selection procedures for developing fertility restorer lines in wheat. According to them, anther extrusion (open flowering) is the most useful criterion for determining fertility restoration in wheat breeding experiments since this characteristic can be easily scored for thousands of plants on the basis of visual observation.

The genetic background of the female parent could also affect fertility restoration. Several researchers (Lucken and Maan, 1967; Trupp, 1976; Jost, 1979, 1980, 1981; and others) have observed variation for *ease of restoration* (EOR) among different wheat genotypes in *timopheevii* cytoplasm. It means fertility restoration also depends on the genotype used as female parent. According to Trupp (1976), EOR is genetically controlled and prediction about this characteristic can be made well in advance. Therefore, due importance should be given to EOR evaluation while carrying out a hybrid breeding programme. In addition, environmental factors (temperature, photoperiod, moisture availability, etc.) not only influence general growth and development of the plant but may also have effect on the penetrance and expressivity of restorer genes. It has been found that a proper balance between major restorer genes and useful modifiers is necessary for stability of restoration and consistency of seed setting under varying environmental conditions. According to Wilson and Driscoll (1983), environmental interactions may create serious complications in fertility restoration.

However, stable and efficient restorer lines can be developed using marker-assisted selection. Using RFLP, Ma and Sorrells (1995) were able to identify two loci which showed association with genes governing EOR in male sterile line. This signifies the importance of novel biotechnology techniques in restorer breeding programmes. Furthermore, the use of an autoplasmic cytoplasm may have a more favourable effect than that of an alloplasmic cytoplasm.

Photoperiod-sensitive cytoplasmic male sterility (PCMS)

According to Wang *et al.* (1998), this system of male sterility was first reported by Sasakuma and Ohtsuka (1979) who observed complete male sterility in an alloplasmic line of Norin 26 (a Japanese common wheat cultivar) possessing cytoplasm (D^2 type) of *T. crassum* or *Ae. crasa*, under Hokkaido (north Japan) environment. In 1993, Murai and Tsunewaki suggested a *two-line system* for producing hybrid seed using PCMS by demonstrating that the male sterility of alloplasm Norin 26 was induced by long-day treatment (15 hour or longer photoperiod). However, according to Murai (1998), PCMS system was first reported by Murai and Tsunemaki (1993). PCMS was also expressed by alloplasmic lines of Chinese common wheat having *crassum* cytoplasm, under north China conditions (Xu, 1995). These all observations indicate that PCMS is caused by the interaction between *crassum* cytoplasm and *T. aestivum* nucleus. But, no such interaction was observed between *crassum* cytoplasm and Chinese Spring nucleus due to the presence of restorer genes in this *aestivum* cultivar (Murari and Tsuneuraki, 1993). According to Murari and Tsunewaki (1994), a single dominant gene (Rfd 1) found on the long arm of chromosome 7B and a large number of modifiers are responsible for fertility restoration in Chinese Spring. However, fertility restoration in Japanese wheat cultivars is controlled by multiple genes found on at least 4A, 1D, 3D and 5D chromosomes (Murari, 1997a). Pistillody of stamens is the cause of PCMS. Pistillate stamens have pseudo-ovules.

In PCMS system, there is no need to develop a maintainer line. The line which is male sterile under long day conditions, is male fertile under short day conditions. Thus, PCMS system is a two-line system. Further, there is no adverse effect of *crassum* cytoplasm on agronomic traits and F_1 hybrids have a good level of fertility restoration (Murai, 1997b). However, temperature has no significant adverse effect on fertility restoration.

Genetic Male Sterility (GMS)

A number of attempts have been made to identify gentic or genic or nuclear male sterility in wheat. Pugsley and Oram (1959) were the first to report this type of male sterility in wheat. In 1962, Suneson found that genetic male sterility in wheat is under the control of a single recessive gene. A similar genetic control (monogenic recessive) of this type of male sterility was reported by Bozzini and Scarascia-Muguozza (1968), Driscoll (1977), Lupton *et al.* (1980) and Barlow and Driscoll (1981). However, Bing-Hua and Jing-Yang (1986) reported a monogenic dominant control of genetic male sterility. Athwal *et al.* (1967) and Jan and Qualset (1973) found that the genetic control of genetic male sterility in wheat is more complex. According to them, three recessive genes govern this type of male sterility. Pickett (1998) gave a list of sources of genetic male sterility in wheat.

Like cytoplasmic male sterility, genetic male sterility also has advantages and disadvantages. The biggest advantage of genetic male sterility is that any promising variety of wheat can be used as male parent, that is, fertility restoration of the F_1 hybrid is problem-free. But, the difficulty in maintaining the male sterile line is the biggest disadvantage of this male sterility system. In fact, the line used as female parent in this system has both male sterile and male fertile plants and for the production of pure hybrid seed, the male fertile plants are to be rogued out from the hybrid seed production field before flowering. Removal of male fertile plants before flowering is not an easy task unless some marker gene with conspicuous morphological phenotype is available.

XYZ system : Driscoll (1972, 1985) suggested a method for producing male sterile line where no roguing of plants is required. The method was named XYZ system where three types of lines are involved : (1) An alien disomic addition line (X line) having 21 pairs of wheat chromosomes plus a pair of rye chromosome 5R; (2) an alien monosomic addition line (Y line) having 21 pairs of wheat chromosomes and single 5R chromosome of rye; and (3) a wheat line (Z line) having 21 pairs of wheat chromosomes with a recessive male sterile gene in homozygous condition. Driscoll (1985), however, suggested use of the progeny of selfed Y line instead of using X line.

The rye chromosome carrying gene for fertility, does not pair with any of the wheat chromosomes. Therefore, Y line which is male fertile produces two types of pollen, having 21 chromosomes and 22 chromosomes. The pollen having extra chromosome is less competitive than the pollen having normal chromosome number. As a result, pollen from addition line produces male fertile plants under self pollination but helps in maintaining male sterility under cross pollination.

Some other ways of overcoming the problem of the maintenance of male sterile line have been suggested (Pickett, 1998). For example, tight linkage between the sterile allele and herbicide tolerance may greatly help in roguing the fertile plants. Similarly, phenotypic restoration of fertility by chemical agents may be another possibility for solving the maintenance problem.

Temperature-sensitive and/or photoperiod-sensitive genetic male sterility (TGMS and PGMS) : Like cytoplasmic male sterility, genetic male sterility may also be sensitive to temperature and/or photoperiod. Qian et al.(1986) studied the effects of low temperatures and genotypes on pollen development in wheat and found that certain varieties of wheat possess genes which render male fertility sensitive to low temperatures. Such sensitivity of male fertility to low temperatures provides opportunity for producing hybrid seed in areas having consistent climates and using the hybrid seed for different regions. However, this approach has not yet received much attention of the scientists.

Despite the availability of number of genes, the use of genetic male sterility for hybrid seed production in wheat has not been much successful.

Chemical Hybridizing Agents (CHAs)

As has been discussed earlier, genetic male sterility so far could not be used as a successful system for producing hybrid wheat. Further, the cytoplasmic male sterility on which breeders have mainly relied for producing large quantities of hybrid seed, requires a male sterile line, a maintainer line and an effective restorer parent and hence lengthens the process of hybrid seed production. On the contrary, chemical hybridizing agents (CHAs) or male sterilizing agents (MSAs) or chemical pollen suppressants (CPSs) or male gametocides (MGs) can be used immediately. The term male gametocides is being used less frequently. In chemical induced male sterility system, any cultivar can be treated with CHA and used as the female parent in the hybrid breeding programme. No maintenance of male sterile line or identification of a suitable restorer is required. Further, the F_2 population of the hybrid does not show segregation for male sterility. However, according to Colhaun and Steer (1982), a commercially acceptable CHA must fulfil some basic requirements like compound's ability to induce complete or near complete (95% or more) male sterility and its least or no adverse effect on seed set. Some other requirements of a good CHA are

1. the systemic nature of CHA for effective sterilization of both the early and late tillers,
2. its effectiveness over a sufficient range of plant developmental stages,
3. it should not influence female fertility,
4. it should be genotype-free and environment-free,
5. its application should be easy,
6. it should cause least environmental pollution, and
7. it should be cost-effective.

CHAs facilitate cross pollination in plants having hermaphrodite flowersd by sterilizing the male sex cells or by interrupting the development of pollen grains. Many chemical hybridizing agents like maleic hydrazide (MH), ethaphon or ethrel (2-chloroethyl phosphoric acid), RH 531, RH 532, RH 2956, RH 4667, RH 5148, WL 84811, LY 195259, Jin Ao Lin (SC 2053) and Genesis (Non 21250), have been and are being used in wheat. The last two chemicals (SC 2053 and Genesis) are producing good results. According to CIMMYT scientists (Cukadar *et al.*, 2001), Genesis has been found a very effective CHA for inducing male sterility in spring wheat lines. Similarly, SC 2053 has been found very effective in China. A new hybrid variety of wheat named *Jinhua1* has been produced using SC 2053. This hybrid was released in 1997 (Zhang and Huang, 1998; Zhang *et al.*, 2001). Scientists in China are also using Genesis for inducing male sterility in wheat (Zhang and Huang, 1998; Zhang *et al.*, 2001). According to Zhang *et al.* (2001), SC 2053 can induce male sterility upto 100 per cent, is simpler and cost-effective and has little limitation on wheat varieties used for hybridization.

However, several CHAs have been found associated with some serious side effects. For example, application of maleic hydrazide though induced high pollen sterility, but also caused considerable female sterility and plant damage (Chopra *et al.*, 1960; Porter and Weise, 1961). Foliar application of ethrel did not have a considerable effect on female fertility but has the limitation of a narrow target period of application and phytotoxicity (restricted spike emergence) (Law and Stoskopf, 1973; Hughes *et al.*, 1974; Rowell and Miller, 1974). Similarly, some other CHAs could induce only incomplete and transient male sterility. Of course, Tschabold *et al.* (1988) claimed that LY 195259 can induce over 95 per cent male sterility without causing any serious defect.

The use of CHAs for hybid seed production has been criticized in some quarters. The main disadvantages of using CHAs are :

1. It is, manytimes, difficult to decide the optimum dose of a CHA. The use of lower or higher dose may create difficulty in producing large quantities of hybrid seed.
2. Continuity of rainfall and fast winds may adversely influence the breeding programme. Such conditions may create difficulty in the application of CHA at the most appropriate time.
3. The hybrid seed produced through the use of CHAs sometimes does not fulfil required seed certification standards.

4. Chemical-environment interactions may have serious implications. Such interactions may drastically pollute the environment which may have adverse effect on the health of animals and human beings.

Apomixis

Apomixis is the development of embryo without involving fusion of male and female gametes. Apomixis offers an excellent opportunity of fixing heterosis irrespective of the degree of heterozygosity. Savidan (1992) reviewed the progress in research on apomixis and discussed the prospects of the transfer of this method of reproduction to major grain crops. Apomixis (if it can occur in a species) permits the maintenance of the same level of heterozygosity with each cycle of multiplication, that is, the genotype of a hybrid variety can be maintained for indefinite period.

However, the maintenance of heterozygote genotype for indefinite priod has two main requirements:

1. There should be no occurrence of reduction division in the megaspore mother cell so that each cell of the female gametophyte contains diploid chromosome number; and
2. there should be no fusion of male and female gametes (that is, failure of fertilization).

So far, there is no report of the occurrence of apomixis in wheat. But, this form of reproduction occurs in the wild relatives of wheat like *Agropyron scabrum* and *Elymus rectisetus*. According to den Nijis and van Dijik (1993), preliminary work done on the crossing of *Triticum aestivum* with these two apomictic species indicates that this hybridization is successful. Though the possibility of producing hybrid wheat through this approach is remote, the transfer of genes governing apomixis to wheat will be a big achievement.

Hybrid wheat research at CYMMYT : Useful work on hybrid wheat is being done at CIMMYT. There, the scientists are mainly concentrating on the use of Genesis, a hybridizing agent. According to Cukadar *et al.* (1998), preliminary experiments were conducted in the year 1996 for determining the usefulness and efficacy of Genesis for spring bread wheat. Numerous bread wheat lines were evaluated for use in hybrid wheat breeding programme. A large number of hybrids (about 260) were produced during 1996-97. The hybrids produced by crossing top yielding lines, exhibited 12-23 per cent superiority over Rayon, a leading cultivar. However, hybrid seed set depended on several genetic (lines used as male parents) and environmental factors like temperature, intensity and duration of rainfall, wind velocity and relative humidity. Genesis has been found as an effective hybridizing agent. But, there is still scope for improvement in seed production systems.

Cukadar *et al.* (2001) observed that :

1. top yielding wheat hybrids showed 13-17 per cent yield advantage over Rayon, the leading wheat cultivar,
2. additive gene effects played a major role in the control of grain yield in wheat than non-additive gene effects,
3. highest yielding advanced lines are expected to produce highest yielding hybrids, and
4. in general, hybrids were not inferior to their parents in terms of bread-making quality and grain quality.

Hybrid wheat breeding in China : A lot of work has been and is being done on hybrid wheat in China and a remarkable success has been achieved. According to He (1998), hybrid wheat breeding in China could be a good alternative approach for bringing improvement in the yield potential and stability of this important cereal. All the three important male sterility systems, cytoplasmic male sterility system, chemical hybridizing agent system and photo-thermo-sensitive cytoplasmic system (a two-line system) are being used by the scientists in China. In cytoplasmic male sterility system, different types of cytoplasms like *T. timopheevii* cytoplasm or T type cytoplasm, *T. kotschyi* (*Ae. kotschyi*) cytoplasm or K type cytoplasm, and *T.ventricosum* (*Ae. ventricosa*) cytoplasm or V type cytoplasm, are being used for developing male sterile lines. It has been observed that the two-line male sterility system may play a big role in developing hybrid varieties of wheat. However, He feels that, at present, there are two big challenges before the Chinese wheat breeders :

1. The yield advantage of hybrid varieties over the varieties produced through conventional breeding is not very attractive; and
2. the use of high seeding density (ranging from 100-300 kg/ha) by Chinese farmers makes the hybrid wheat breeding relatively costly.

Further, the conventional wheat breeding gets more support from the scientists of other disciplines like plant pathology, agronomy and seed technology. A high cooperation between the hybrid and conventional breeding programmes may probably help in enhancing the hybrid wheat breeding in China.

Zhang and Huang (1998) reviewed the hybrid wheat breeding and its progress in China. After the inception of hybrid wheat programme in China in 1965, many wheat hybrids were developed using three main breeding systems, namely, cytoplasmic male sterility, chemical hybridizing agents and the two-line male sterility system. These hybrids were evaluated in regional yield trials. Out of these hybrids, one spring hybrid wheat named *XN 901* with K cytoplasm (*T. kotschyi* cytoplasm) produced through cytoplasmic male sterility system, was released in 1996. Another hybrid named *Jinhua 1* produced using Jin Ao Lin (SC 2053) chemical hybridizing agent, was released in 1997.

Zhang and Huang discussed in detail the three male sterility breeding systems being used in China. First of all, *T. timopheevii* cytoplasm male sterility system was introduced to China in 1965. Then Murai and Tsunewaki (1979) discovered *T. kotschyi* and *T. ventricosum* cytoplasms for inducing male sterility in wheat. At present, more than five types of cytoplasms (*T. timopheevii, T. kotschyi, T. ventricosum, T. tauschii, Avena fatua*, etc.) are being used in hybrid wheat breeding programme in China. Similarly, ethrel and DPX 3778 were used as potential CHAs in China in 1970s. Then the CHA WL 84811 was introduced. In view of the side effects of WL 84811 and two home made CHAs, BAU 1 and XN 8611, the CHA SC 2053 was introduced in 1989. The CHA Genesis which was introduced in China in 1996, is also being used as a potential CHA for inducing male sterility in wheat. The two-line system is now being considered as a potential method of for inducing male sterility in wheat in China.

In addition, Huang *et al*. (1991) suggested a nuclear system similar to the XYZ method of Driscoll (1972). The alien addition line in this system has 4E chromosome from *Elytrigia elongata*. This chromosome carries a restorer gene for recessive male sterility. The 43-chromosome plants (male fertile) on selfing, produce two types of plants, 43-chromosome male fertile plants with light blue grain colour and 42-chromosome male sterile plants with white grain colour. Some 44-chromosome useless plants with dark blue grain colour are also produced.

According to Zhang and Huang, hybrid wheat has a good future in China. However, there is scope for making more efforts towards making hybrid wheat a cost-effective proposition.

Zhang *et al*. (2001) further reviewed the advances of hybrid wheat breeding in China and emphasized that hybrid wheat has a bright future and is expected to make a big contribution towards crop production in China. According to Jizhong *et al.* (2001), the chemical hybridizing agent SC 2053 has a promising future.

Hybrid wheat research in India : Efforts are also being made in India to produce hybrid wheat at a commercial scale. According to Mahajan and Nagarajan (1998), CMS system has not been a very successful method of producing hybrid wheat in India. However, an attempt was made to find out the possibility of using CHA route in developing wheat hybrids, by treating three wheat varieties, namely, HD 2329, WH 542 and PPW 343 with an amino acid analogue, CH 9701 and two growth retardents, CH 9706 and CH 9707 at Directorate of Wheat Research, Karnal and at Punjab Agricultural University, Ludhiana in rabi 1995-96 (Mahajan *et al.*, 1998). The results indicated that for inducing complete male sterility, the amino acid analogue proved better than the two growth retardents. Mahajan *et al.* (2000) screened a large number of CHAs and found that only five of them could induce acceptable level of male sterility. Mahajan *et al.* (2004) have further advocated the use of CHAs as a method of producing hybrid wheat in India.

Making Hybrid Wheat a Commercial Proposition

Despite a remarkable progress made in hybrid wheat research, particularly in increasing the efficiency of the three main hybrid breeding mechanisms (use of several sterile cytoplasms like *T. timopheevii*, *T. kotschyi*, *T. ventricosum*, *T. tauschii* and *Avena fatua* in cytoplasmic male sterility system; application of more effective chemical hybridizing agents like Jin Ao Lin and Genesis; and the use of effective two-line cytoplasmic male sterility), the current prospects for making hybrid wheat a commercial proposition are poor. Several genetic, physiological and environmental factors affect large scale production of hybrid seed in wheat. One basic factor which is greatly responsible for making wheat ill-adapted to the production of F_1 hybrid varieties, is the self-fertilizing nature of this crop species. Wheat, with approximately 99.0 per cent self pollination, is a highly self-fertilizing species. However, according to Wilson (1968), wheat might have adopted a self-pollinating nature because of its cultivation outside the centre of origin. But, it is difficult to justify this opinion as maize, a highly cross-fertilized crop, has been grown outside the centre of its origin since ancient times. Although wheat floret does not fall in the category of structural cleistogamy but it is certainly a case of behavioural cleistogamy since when anthers come out of the floret they have no pollen. The swinging of anthers out of floret is, in fact, a deceiving process since the anthers come out of floret after the pollination has already occurred. Some characteristics of wheat plant organs which discourage cross pollination in this crop are :

1. As compared to cross-fertilizing species, the pollen production capacity (the number of pollen grains produced) of wheat anthers is lower (Pickett, 1993).
2. Wheat has a short pollen longevity (Fritz and Lukaszewski, 1989).
3. The aerodynamic characteristics of wheat pollen are poor and thus only a limited number of pollen grains reach the female parent.
4. Wheat has a short duration of stigma receptivity.
5. The crossability period of both the male and female parents in wheat is short.
6. The levels of seed set in wheat are strongly influenced by environmental factors (temperature, moisture, etc.).

However, according to de Vies (1971, 1972, 1973, 1974a, 1974b), considerable variation exists in wheat germplasm for most of the characteristics mentioned above. For example, the wheat cultivar

Chinese Spring has considerably longer stigma receptivity. Further, in wheat male sterile lines, the lodicules collapse after the *first-opening* of the floret but the carpels still continue to grow forcing the floret for *second opening* after some time (two or more days after the first opening) (Hoshikawa, 1960). Whereas, during first opening the wheat florets remain open just for half an hour or less (Leighty and Sando, 1924), during second opening, they remain open for a period of several days (de Vries, 1971). Thus, second opening of the floret provides sufficient time for cross pollination. Also, there exists a wide variability for seed yield in wheat hybrids and it should be possible to obtain a seed yield advantage of 50-60 per cent from best compatible combinations. especially in warm climates (Pickett, 1993). But, Pickett (1998) opined that the level of variation in *Triticum aestivum* germplasm for these characteristics appears to be inadequate for large scale hybrid seed production, particularly in regions where temperatures are low, and suggested that the modification of the reproductive system of wheat by transferring cross-fertilizing characteristics from another speceis could be a possible solution to this problem. For example, *Secale cereale* is a cross-fertilized species and has been crossed with wheat manytimes in the past. Efforts may be made to transfer genes governing some important cross-fertilizing traits, especially the ability to produce large number of pollen grains, open flowering and longer stigma receptivity, from *S. cereale* to *T. aestivum*.

Seed quality is anothr important consideration in hybrid wheat breeding. Some wheat scientits are of the opinion that it is very difficult to maintain a high seed quality of F_1 hybrids in wheat as is maintained in case of line varieties. The three main factors which can cause impurity in the hybrid seed are :

1. Incomplete sterility : If the sterilization of the female line is incomplete, there is a significant risk of selfing resulting in a considerable increase in the content of the female parent. Therefore, to maintain varietal purity, the female line should be completely male sterile.

2. Availability of foreign pollen : If the female parent receives some pollen from a source other than the designated male parent, the hybrid seed will not be pure. Such outcrossing from foreign pollen more likely occurs when the male and female parents are asynchronous in flowering. However, synchrony in flowering is greatly influenced by environmental factors.

3. Seed mixed at harvest : Since the parents are grown in close proximity, there is always a risk of the seed mixing.

However, the use of electrophoretic techniques may help in testing the purity of the hybrid seed.

The adoption of hybrid breeding technology in a highly self-fertilizing crop like wheat should also be seen in **terms of the cost** paid by the farmers for buying the hybrid seed every crop season. It is very convenient for the farmers to maintain the seed of line varieties and grow the same in the next crop season. If the additional cost paid by the farmers for buying the hybrid seed is not fully compensated by the yield advantage of the hybrid variety, it will not be possible to convince the farmers for growing hybrid wheat varieties. In fact, the cost of seed production is the most critical factor in determining the success of hybrid wheat breeding. The cost of seed production, in turn, is influenced by several other factors (seed multiplication ratio, percentage of seed set in female line, seed production technique used, transportation cost involved, etc.). The seed multiplication ratio for wheat (around 25 as compared to 215 and 450 for maize and sunflower, respectively; Lucken, 1982) is considerably low. Further, this crop requires higher seeding rates.

Nevertheless, to make hybrid a commercial proposition, the following points are worth considering:

1. Best possible method should be used to induce male sterility so that the female line is 100 per cet male sterile. As discussed earlier, incomplete sterility may cause significant risk of selfing. Fortuately, several good male sterile cytoplasms are now available. Similarly, some newly introduced CHAs are highly effective in inducing male sterility in wheat. Also, there are reports that photosensitive cytoplasmic male sterility is proving a potential tool for male sterility induction.

2. Every effort should be made to improve and stabilize the cross pollination capacity of wheat by exploiting genetic diversity existing in wheat germplasm and by transferring genes from other species to wheat. Several lines of CIMMYT germplasm have comparatively higher cross pollination capacity. Allan (1980) has reported higher rate of anther extrusion in wheat. Genotypic differences can be seen for many flowering characteristics like anther size, width and length and anther extrusion, filament length, lodicule size, head compactness, number of pollen grains per anther, quantity of pollen shed outside the floret and pattern and duration of flowering in wheat germplasm (Lucken, 1987). According to Kofoid (1991), there are two ways of improving outcrossing ability of wheat : (a) By making direct selection in wheat germplasm; and (b) by attempting random mating among genotypes.

   Further, efforts may be made to transfer some useful genes (contributing towards cross-pollinating habit) from rye (*Secale cereale*) to wheat.

3. Utmost care should be taken while selecting parents for producing hybrids in wheat. Most promising parents in terms of grain yield potential, disease resistance and adaptability should be selected. It is always better to test the combining ability of the parents before their use in a hybrid breeding programme. The line used as pollinator should be able to restore complete fertility.

   The use of Veery lines carrying 1BL/1RS translocation may be helpful in producing promising wheat hybrids. Many of these lines possess desirable combination of high yield potential with high resistance/tolerance to biotic and abiotic stresses and wide adaptability.

4. All possible steps should be taken to maintain a high quality of the hybrid seed. Synchrony in flowering time of parents is an important condition for producing pure hybrid seed. Necessary adjustments in sowing dates and environmental sites may be made to ensure synchronous flowering of parents. Also, care should be taken to avoid seed mixing during harvesting.

5. It is necessary to examine the economic feasibility of the production of wheat hybrid varieties. For this, cost/benefit ratio should be calculated and try should be made to maintain a balance in this ratio.

6. Wherever necessary, help should be taken from biotechnologists. For example, biotechnologists may help in determining differences between different male sterility systems, identifying better fertility restorers and in knowing the chemical composition of hybrid seed.

In conclusion, it can be said that there is no scope for pessimism that hybrid wheat will never become a commercial proposition. In view of the expanding world population, hybrid wheat may significantly contribute towards solving food problem. The authors agree with those optimistic wheat breeders who think that the production of hybrid wheat varieties at commercial scale is an effort-oriented reality.

CHAPTER 9

Resistance Breeding

Wheat is the most widely adapted cereal and is grown under a wide range of soil and climatic conditions all over the world. However, considerable losses in wheat yields are caused every year by both the biotic and abiotic stresses.

Biotic stresses

Biotic stresses include all diseases (rusts, smuts, blights, etc.) and insect and mite pests (aphids, mites, sawflies, etc.) of wheat.

Breeding for Disease Resistance

Disease resistance is one of the most important objectives of modern wheat breeding programmes. But, unfortunately, the environmental conditions which are favourable for harvesting high yields (availability of sufficient moisture, nutrients, etc.), are also favourable for the survival of pathogens and rapid spread of diseases. Two factors which greatly influence the hereditary resistance are: (i) Nutrient level; and (ii) the general health or physiological condition of the plant. Temperature has also been found related with disease resistance. The abiotic stresses like drought tolerance and winter hardiness which are the causes of reduction in yield on one hand, restrict the growth of pathogens on the other, especially in winter wheats. Let us discuss the major diseases of wheat.

Rusts : Some important characteristics of wheat rusts are :
1. They had caused tremendous losses in wheat production in the past;
2. they have attracted maximum attention of the wheat scientists;
3. they are the best understood diseases of wheat;
4. it is easy to develop resistant varieties against them but frequent appearance of virulent pathotypes is the biggest problem before the wheat scientists; and
5. identification of new pathotypes and utilization of durable sources of resistance require lot of research efforts.

There are three types of wheat rusts: (i) Leaf rust or brown rust; (ii) stem rust or black rust; and (iii) stripe rust or yellow rust.

Leaf rust is caused by *Puccinia recondita* and is also known as brown rust (in Europe and many other countries of the world) or orange leaf rust (in USA). The disease is of wide spread occurrence and it occurs in all wheat growing areas having high rainfall or good irrigation facilities. However, the prevalence of the disease varies from region to region and its severity may differ from time to time. Although the fungus *P. recondita* is relatively less sensitive to fluctuations in temperature, leaf rust is less severe and is of sporadic occurrence in regions with a cooler climate. The actual place of attack of the pathogen is upper surface of the leaf blade where round, brownish, red spore pustules are formed. Small pustules are also formed on the inner surface of the glumes and rarely, on the inner surface of the leaf sheath. The infection occurs through open or closed stomata. Infection through other plant parts (spike, awn, glume, leaf sheath) is negligible probably because of some inhibitory effect. However, rainfall can considerably increase the course of infection of the disease. Further, air currents are able to carry infectious urediospores from long distances and thus are an important cause of the development of leaf rust epidemics.

In general, following biochemical changes take place in wheat plant after the attack of *P. recondita*:

1. Conspicuous alterations in the DNA, RNA and protein contents (Quick and Shaw, 1964; Bhattacharya *et al.*, 1965);
2. an increase in the amount of soluble nucleotides;
3. a change in the amount of amino acids (Bhattacharya *et al.*, 1965);
4. an increase in the activity of decarboxylase with the beginning of sporulation (Quick and Shaw, 1966; Johnson *et al.*, 1967);
5. an increase in the intensity of kinate and sikinate metabolism in the leaves (especially in susceptible plants) and an increase in the amount of soluble esterase (Rohringer *et al.*, 1967);
6. accumulation of glucose-6-phosphate dehydrogenase (Johnson *et al.*, 1968);
7. an increase in the amount of the 'A' coenzyme in attacked tissues (Krstev, 1964);
8. an increase in the intensity of photosynthesis in both the infected and unaffected parts of the diseased plant (Livne, 1964a,b) probably to compensate the loss caused by the disease;
9. an increase in the accumulation of nutrient at the site of infection (Johnson *et al.*, 1966);
10. increased carbon dioxide fixation in infected plants during dark period; and
11. a reduction in yield due to transpiration loss, nutrient deficiency and reduced root development.

The biological cause of resistance is not yet fully known. However, according to Kiraly (1968), there is some relationship between resistance for leaf rust and phenol accumulation and oxidation. As mentioned earlier, the experience of the scientists indicates that nutrient level and general physiological condition of the plant can influence the hereditary resistance. Further, drought tolerance and winter hardiness act as supplementary factors to leaf rust resistance in winter wheats. Extremely low temperatures also help in inhibiting the formation of urediospores. According to Donchev (1967), leaf rust resistance is related to the age of the plant. Therefore, the case of leaf rust seedling resistance and adult plant resistance should be considered as two separate characteristics. Similarly, specific resistance (resistance against one or two races) should be considered different from general resistance (resistance agaisnt all races of pathogen) in case of leaf rust.

The variability of *P. recondita* is very high and, therefore, breeding for resistance to leaf rust is not easy. Fifty-one genes for resistance to leaf rust have so far been identified. The protection against different races of the pathogen is provided by individual resistance genes. However, the action of a resistance gene greatly depends on the genetic background. A gene providing protection against a specific race in one genetic background may provide protection against another race or races in a different genetic background. Therefore, action of resistance genes is not genotype-independent in case of leaf rust.

The causal organism of **stem rust** is *Puccinia graminis*. Among the three rusts of wheat, stem rust has been the most dangerous disease in the past and caused significant losses of yield. According to Rao *et al.* (1962), this rust is the most widespread wheat disease in India and has, manytimes, caused serious damages to the crop.

Application of higher doses of nitrogenous fertilizers causes increase in stand density and vegetative period of the crop and thus creates a favourable environment for the spread of the this disease. Prolonged vegetative period provides more time to the pathogen for its establishment and spread. Similarly, the availability of sufficient moisture is a favourable condition for the pathogen. These two factors (prolonged vegetative period and the presence of sufficient amount of water in the soil) help in creating a microclimate favourable for the rapid spread of the disease.

However, despite the negative effect of the two factors mentioned above, some positive results about the control of this disease have been achieved :

1. Quite good information is available regarding the host-parasite relationship and the physiological and genetical causes of resistance to this disease.
2. Forty-five resistance genes have so far been identified for the control of this rust. These genes have been identified in many promising wheat varieties.
3. Using distant hybridization (interspecific and intergeneric crosses), large number of stem rust resistant varieties have been developed.
4. Although chemical control of the disease is also possible, but this type of control of stem rust is quite expensive and, therefore, this method is not generally recommended for the control of this disease.
5. Facilities to detect new races of *P. graminis* are now available in every major wheat producing country.
6. Development of resistant varieties is the best method to control this disease.

The infection takes place through stomata only. There is formation of a substomatal vesicle after penetration. From this vesicle, hyphae grow into intercellular space. The hypha comes in contact with the cell wall. The cell wall gets dissolved and a protuberance enters the cell. As a result, there is swelling of plasm, contraction of vacuoles and degeneration of plastids. Some other changes which take place after the penetration of protuberance are (Lelley, 1976);

1. After penetrating the epidermis, the haustoria enter the mesophyll cells (Chakravarti, 1968);
2. affected cells show a continued hexakinase activity (Einaghy and Shaw, 1966);
3. around the infection site, there is a general enzyme activation (Lunderstadt and Fuchs, 1968);
4. RNA content increases considerably (Manocha and Shaw, 1966);
5. intensity of protein synthesis increases (Bhattacharya and Shaw, 1967);
6. there is a tremendous increase (fifteen-fold) in the respiration rate in the centre of the developing uredio pustules, whereas intensity of respiration remains unchanged where hyphae are not

present indicating that the action of hyphae is restricted to the immediate surroundings only (Bushnell, 1964);
7. after infection, synthetizing processes are dominated by hydrolytic processes (Andreev, 1968);
8. there is extraction of glucose by the hyphae from the host cells (Pfeiffer et al., 1969);
9. there is accumulation of large amounts of carbohydrates around the spores (Semenko, 1968);
10. there is reduction in the rate of transpiration of leaves (Semenko, 1968);
11. after infection, amount of organic acids increases rapidly (Daly and Mrupka, 1962); and
12. there is reduction in the ADP content.

The stage of development of the host plant at which the pathogen attacks is the main determiner of the extent of actual damage caused by this disease. Depending on the stage of development, there may be reduction in the number of spikes, number of grains per spike or grain weight or grain quality may be adversely affected. There appears to be a direct relation between the nutrient supply to the developing grains and yield potential. Since a part of assimilates is consumed by the pathogen in the infected plants, there is a reduction in the nutrient supply to the developing grains and ultimately the yield decreases.

The causes of hereditary resistance to stem rust are not clearly known. However, resistance is related to certain changes:

1. Carbon dioxide (even in very low concentration) acts as an inhibitory factor for the penetration of the pathogen (Yirgoun and Caldwell, 1968);
2. resistance is related to the rapid accumulation and oxidation of phenolic compounds since oxidation products of phenols which are toxic, probably cause necrosis of tissues which, in turn, checks the spreading of the disease (Kiraly and Farkas, 1962);
3. resistance is also related to the quick decrease of reducing compounds (Kiraly and Farkas, 1962);
4. resistant wheat varieties contain considerably large amounts of oxazines than the susceptible varieties (Einaghy and Linko, 1962);
5. according to Heitefuss (1964), resistance is connected with RNA concentration;
6. glucoside content may also be a cause of resistance (Peruansky and Peruanskaya, 1965; Einaghy and Shaw, 1966);
7. according to Tsigrin and Rozum (1969), susceptible varieties show absence of β-glucosidase activity in the stem rust infected leaves;
8. Tsigrin and Alesin (1965) observed connection between resistance and intensity of floroglucin oxidation;
9. resistant varieties contain increased amount of the polymer forms of carbohydrates after infection than the susceptible varieties (Alesin and Tsigrin, 1966); and
10. Sr 6 resistance gene in Marquis wheat has been found sensitive to temperature (Fric and Fuchs, 1970).

However, except the phenol oxidation theory, none of the observations mentioned above prove connection with hereditary resistance. But, according to Brown et al. (1966), the hypersensitive necrosis is a result of resistance rather than its cause. As in case of leaf rust, here also the seedling resistance and adult plant resistance are two separate types of resistance. Also, the specific resistance, general resistance, slow rusting and tolerance should be considered as different types of resistance (Knott and Hughes, 1974).

Only **general resistance** (that is, resistance against all existing races of the pathogen) provides full protection against stem rust. This resistance does not put a pressure on the existence of the pathogen and thus chances of the arrival of new races are greatly reduced. Contrarily, specific resistance provides protection only against some specific races of the pathogen. Here, the pathogen comes under selection stress and thus new physiological races come into existence. In view of the dangerous nature of stem rust, it is necessary to keep complete record of all the races of the pathogen.

As mentioned earlier, 45 resistance genes for stem rust have so far been identified. These genes have been located on the chromosomes.

It is not possible to establish a general rule about the heredity and dominance of resistance to stem rust because of the following reasons :

1. In some cases, resistance genes are dominant, while in other cases they are recessive.
2. A single gene may be responsible for resistance to one, two or more than two races, while a single race may be controlled by a single, two or more than two genes.
3. The resistance genes may behave differently in different genetic backgrounds in terms of their dominance conditions and race specificity.
4. The resistance may be monogenically controlled or polygenically controlled or may be under the control of the combined effect of both the major genes and minor genes.
5. Environmental factors like temperature, light conditions and nutrient uptake, may influence the degree of resistance or virulence.

It means that resistance to stem rust is controlled by a complex genetic system. However, there is a positive point concerning the resistance to this rust that the resistance has high heritability and, therefore, selection is highly effective. This indicates that additive gene effects play an important role in the control of resistance against stem rust. Therefore, selection should be started at the earliest possible stage.

Stripe rust or yellow rust is caused by *Puccinia striiformis*. This rust is less important than the other two rusts (leaf rust and stem rust) of wheat. Maximum infection of stripe rust occurs at temperatures between 9° and 12°C. Warm climate (with temperature around 25°C or above) has an adverse effect on both the sporulation and the growth of the infecting mycelium of the fungus. Therefore, this disease is dangerous in cooler regions only.

Much is not known about the biology (especially sexual phase) of the fungus. During winter season when temperature is low, the fungus survives on many wild grass species. Although the infecting hypha has a symbiotic relation with the cells of the host plant, it adversely affects the water content of the tissues and increases respiration. It also creates disturbance in the equivilibrium of the processes of photosynthesis and oxidation. As a result, there is a reduction in the size of the vegetative parts of the plant and the roots remain shorter.

High air humidity and rainfalls are the favourable conditions for increasing the infection intensity of the pathogen and making sporulation faster. As the spores are heavy, their transmission through air is limited. Incubation period of the pathogen is determined by temperature. Low temperature increases the time of incubation. Though the mycelium may survive under low temperatures, the urediospores are highly sensitive to frost. Low light intensity has been found associated with high infection in some susceptible varieties.

Stripe rust causes considerable yield loss since not only the leaves (both the leaf blade and leaf sheath parts of each leaf) but the spikes are also infected. Experimental results indicate that the loss caused by this disease is greater than that caused by the artificial defoliation. The disease has a multidimentional effect and thus the infection has a complex physiological consequence. According to Doodson *et al.* (1964) following changes generally occur after infection:

1. Reduction in the size of leaves;
2. roots also become shorter;
3. reduction in the number of spikes;
4. decrease in the number of grains per spike;
5. 1000 grain weight decreases;
6. inhibition of growth vigour; and
7. an increase in the tendency to lodging.

The infection also causes decrease in the number of tillers and length of culms (Hendrix *et al.*, 1965b).

Puccinia striiformis rarely has a generative phase or the pathogen has no such phase at all. Therefore, the new races can come up only through mutation or somatic association. This is the reason that this pathogen has considerably lower variability and lower rate of transformation of races than the other two rust fungi. Thirty resistance genes have so far been identified. These genes are found in major wheat varieties.

Stripe rust appears in various forms and heredity of resistance is complex. The reasons for the complexity of the resistance transmission are :

1. Different races show different conditions of dominance (Lupton and Macer, 1962).
2. Different genetic systems have been found to operate for resistance to this disease. For example, resistance is governed by complementary epistasis (Allan *et al.*, 1963), by a single locus (Macer, 1963), by a major gene and several minor genes (Lewellen *et al.*, 1967), by polygenes (Allan and Purdy, 1970) and by both the dominant and recessive genes (Henriksen and Pope, 1971).
3. The resistance has been found dependent on environmental factors like temperature (Lewellen, 1967) and heat treatment (Brown and Sharp, 1969).

However, despite the complex nature of resistance transmission, intervarietal crosses have given good results. Since *Triticum dicoccoides* is highly resistant to the rust, crosses with this wild species may produce fruitful results (Gerechter-Amitai and Stubbs, 1970). A yellow rust resistant gene was incorporated into the wheat variety *Compair* (gene Yr 8 on chromosome 2D) from *T. comosum* (or *Ae. comosa*) by genetic interference through *T. speltoides* (Riley *et al.*, 1968a,b). Yellow rust resistance has also been transferred to wheat from *Secale* (Riley and Macer, 1966). Therefore, all three types of hybridization, namely, intervarietal, interspecific and intergeneric, have been successfully used for introducing yellow rust resistance into wheat. According to Hanis *et al.* (1969), mutation breeding too has a good scope for introducing resistance to this rust into wheat. In addition, yellow rust, like the other two rusts, can be controlled by chemical treatment. However, this method has its own disadvantages like high cost and environmental pollution.

Like in cases of leaf and stem rusts, seedling resistance and adult plant resistance should be considered as separate characteristics in case of yellow rust.

Slow rusting approach : According to Rajaram *et al.* (1995), *slow rusting* (or *partial resistance*) is a type of general resistance where the rate of progress of disease is low. This resistance is partially effective against all races of a pathogen. The basic principle involved in this type of resistance is the coexistence of the host and pathogen so that the variety is partially susceptible to the pathogen. On the contrary, *major gene-specific resistance* is governed by easily detectable major genes which confer resistance against specific races of the pathogen. In this type of resistance, the pathogen gets under the stress of selection. As a result, new physiological races come into existence. The resistance has a narrow genetic base and is short-lived. Of course, from the crop cleaniless point of view, this type of resistance was more attractive. However, this attraction got a setback after the early 1960s when many scientists realized that some alternative methods of gene deployment and management should be used to circunvent the problem of single gene erosion.

Numerous scientists (Jensen, 1952; Borlaug, 1953, 1958; Suneson, 1960; Jensen and Kent, 1963; Lewellen *et al.*, 1967; Leonard, 1969; Caldwell *et al.*, 1970; Sharp and Volin, 1970; Rajaram and Luig, 1972; Brennan, 1975; Frey *et al.*, 1975; Gavinlertvatana and Wilcoxson, 1978; Skoumand *et al.*, 1978; Southern, 1978; Martinez-Gonzalez, 1979; Parlevliet, 1979; 1988; Rees *et al.*, 1979; Ayers *et al.*, 1981; Wilcoxson, 1981; Martinez-Gonzalez *et al.*, 1983; Johnson, 1988; Knott, 1988; McIntosh, 1988; Rajaram *et al.*, 1988; Singh *et al.*, 1991; Das *et al.*, 1992; Roelfs *et al.*, 1992; Rajaram *et al.*, 1995; Rajgram and Braun, 2001; Tiwari, 2005; and many others) have realized the importance of broad-based resistance in crop plants. According to Leonard, stabilization of rust population is relatively more important than stabilizing the level of resistance. Frey *et al.* also pleaded for partial susceptibility in multilineal varieties. The dirty crop approach advocated by them was also based on the coexistence of the host and pathogen. Wilcoxson studied the genetics of slow rusting in cereals and came to the following conclusions :

1. Slow rusting is a more stable type of resistance than major gene-specific resistance;
2. slow rusting is related to resistance components like frequency of infection, quantity of spores produced, duration of sporulation and size of uredia;
3. slow rusting showed variation according to the planting dates of spring wheats at a particular site;
4. Thatcher spring wheat exhibited slow rusting with *P. graminis* but rapid rusting with *P. recondita*, whereas Lee wheat showed moderate rusting with both pathogens;
5. transgressive segregants were commonly found indicating that probably slow rusting is governed by many genes;
6. the genes had differential effect and in some cases, slow rusting may be governed by single genes; and
7. slow rusting is a heritable trait and the range of heritability was between 55% and 87% in Marquis, Thatcher and Lee wheats.

Martinez-Gonzalez *et al.* found that slow rusting in Era wheat is a quantitative charcter and is mostly governed by additive genetic effects. Genotype × environment interaction also plays an important role in control of this trait.

Das *et al.* studied inheritance of slow rusting resistance to leaf rust in wheat and had drawn following conclusions :

1. There was predominance of additive genetic variance for slow rusting since gca to sca ratio was high for this character;
2. additive × additive epistatic variance (fixable component of epistatic variance) was also important;
3. narrow sense heritability was mostly high and ranged from 45 to 92 per cent;
4. slow rusting exhibited negative and low correlation with plant maturity;

5. the correlation between slow rusting and plant height was positive and low; and
6. since fixable component of variance (additive and additive × additive) played a greater role than the unfixable component (dominance, additive × dominance and dominance × dominance) in the control of slow rusting, early generation selection should be effective for this charcter.

Rajaram *et al.* (1995) gave comprehensive information about CIMMYT's approach to breeding for durable disease resistance in bread wheat. According to them, the main objective of the CIMMYT breeding programme is the incorporation of durable resistance into wheat high yielding lines by utilizing the most diverse germplasm for resistance to rusts and other diseases. Some important points of their paper are :

1. A low *average coefficient of infection* (ACI) often indicates the presence of broad-based resistance.
2. Exceptionally, under some situations, a single gene (e.g., Lr 19 for leaf rust resistance) may give a low ACI if no virulent gene exists for that gene.
3. A genotype which exhibits resistance against a particular disease under different environmental conditions (sites), generally contains several resistance genes (Rajaram and Luig, 1972). Such genotypes often give a low ACI.
4. Lines containing several resistance genes often possess durable resistance against a changing pathogen than those lines which possess single gene resistance.
5. A further diversification of slow rusting can be done by combining this resistance with different specific genes.
6. Different component lines of a multilineal variety have uniformity in general resistance but they possess specific genes from different sources.
7. The effectiveness of the *backbone genes* (genes with potentially durable resistance) and the longevity of resistance may be enhanced and the genetic base of resistance may be broadened by combining the backbone genes with some other genes (or added genes).
8. The Sr 2 complex (the interaction of the Sr 2 gene with other Sr genes and derived from the variety Hope and the related line H44-24) probably has formed the basis of durable resistance to stem rust in CIMMYT germplasm. The gene Sr 2 (the backbone gene) alone can induce slow rusting but when it is present in combination with other Sr genes in a plant, the level of durable resistance is substantially enhanced.
9. Although both Lr 13 and Lr 34 genes are present in abundance in CIMMYT germplasm, only Lr 34 is effective in inducing slow rusting at adult plant stage against Mexican leaf rust races.
10. The variety Anza bred by CIMMYT possesses durable resistance to stripe or yellow rust.
11. Currently, efforts are being made to combine the high yield potential of CIMMYT wheats with disease resistance of Chinese wheats. Shuttle breeding is being followed to develop material for scab resistance and for *Helminthosporium* resistance.
12. Based on the stability assessment of CIMMYT germplasm for disease resistance, the wheat diseases may be classified into three groups : (a) Stem rust (mainly due to the presence of Sr 2 complex) – high stability of resistance; (b) leaf rust, yellow rust, septoria leaf blotch and powdery mildew – medium to high stability of resistance; and (c) other pathogens – low stability of resistance.

Rajaram and Braun (2001) discussed the situation of CIMMYT germplasm regarding resistance to major diseases of wheat. Following are the main points of their report.

1. Resistance to stem rust which is based on the gene complex Sr 2 (Sr 2 gene plus 8 to 10 minor genes pyramided into 3-4 gene combinations–Rajaram et al., 1988), appears to be durable.
2. Stabilization of resistance to leaf rust is mainly based on partial resistance genes (Lr 34 plus three other genes which give a slow rusting response). According to Singh (1992a, b), there is association between Lr 34 and leaf tip necrosis (a morphological marker). The gene Lr 34 is also associated with Yr 18.
3. Although identification of slow rusting genes (Yr 18 and other genes) for yellow rust is a positive point, there is still scope for understanding the status of durable resistance to this disease.
4. A combination of 2-3 genes provides acceptable resistance aginst *Septoria tritici*.
5. Genes for resistance to Karnal bunt (more than five partially dominant genes) have been identified and incorporated into promising lines.

The emergence of new races of rust pathogens may be checked by broadening the genetic base of resistance. To overcome the problem of narrow genetic base of leaf rust resistance in wheat, Roelfs (1988) suggested use of gene combinations irrespective of the type of genes (major genes or minor genes). Such use of several genes in a single variety can be achieved by pyramiding effective resistance genes (Rajaram et al., 1995; Tiwari, 2005). This approach is being successfully used by scientists all over the world to control all the three rusts of wheat. Tiwari emphasized the importance of molecular markers aided selection to tackle rust resistance in Indian wheat. According to him, marker assisted selection can enhance the efficiency and flexibility of a breeding programmes aimed to develop rust resistant varieties. He also suggested that the unexploited resistance genes (especially from alien sources) should be used in Indian wheat breeding programme since till now only a limited number of resistance genes have been used by the Indian wheat breeders. According to Sanchez et al. (2000), marker assisted selection has now taken the form of a practical breeding method.

Powdery mildew : Powdery mildew is a widely occurring disease and causes maximum damage in cooler moister regions. This disease is caused by the fungus *Erysiphe graminis*. Like rust pathogens, *E. graminis* is an obligate parasite on plant. Favourable conditions for the pathogen are increased use of nitrogenous fertilizers, microclimate of dense stands, high humidity and the elimination of crop rotation system, that is, growing wheat again and again in the same field (introduction of wheat mono-culture). The optimum temperature for disease infection is 20°C, but infection may take place from 6°C-27°C.

According to Schwinn and Dahmen (1973), the infecting powdery mycelium of the fungus spreads on the surface of the leaves without penetrating the plant tissues resulting in the removal of the waxy layer of leaf through an enzymatic reaction. Disease infection causes following physiological changes in affected plant :

1. Because of symbiosis between haustoria of the pathogen and the host cells, there is a change in the metabolism of the affected cells.
2. Rates of transpiration and respiration increrase.
3. Photosynthetic activity is reduced.
4. Early attack of the pathogen causes retardation in the development of the whole plant. As a consequence, there is shortening of roots and culms.
5. After infection, there is reduction in the amino acid content.
6. If infection occurs at a later stage of the plant development, it causes reduction in the number

of grains per spike and 1000 grain weight followed by a considerable yield loss. The quality of the grain may also be adversely affected.

Erysiphe graminis has relatively low variability than the rust pathogens. According to Poehlman and Sleper (1995), more than 30 physiological races of this pathogen are available and 24 resistance genes have been identified so far. Johnson and Lupton (1987) have given a list of 11 resistance genes, their chromosomal locations and sources. The source of the genes Pm 1 and Pm 9 is *Triticum aestivum*. Both these genes are located on the chromosome 7AL. The gene Pm 2 is found on 5DS chromosome and its source is probably *T. aestivum*. The gene Pm3 which is located on 1AS has three multiple alleles, Pm 3a (Japan), Pm 3b (Russia) and Pm 3 (Mexico). The source of this gene is also *T. aestivum*. Similarly, gene Pm 4 which is found on chromosome 2AL has two multiple allels, Pm 4a (*T. dicoccum*) and Pm 4b (*T. carthlicum*). The source of this gene is *T. turgidum*. The source of the gene Pm5 is *T. dicoccum* and it is found on the chromosome 7BL. The gene Pm6 is located on 2B and its source is *T. timopheevii*. The genes Pm 7 and Pm 8 are found on the chromosomes 4A and 1B, respectively. Both these genes are derived from *Secale cereale*. The gene Pm7 was transferred from rye to wheat through 2R/4A translocation. This gene is associated with two drawbacks: (1) The resistance due to this gene is detectable only at adult stage and not at seedling stage; and (2) the translocation 2R/4A is related with low yield potential. The gene Pm8 which was transferred from rye to wheat through 1R/1B translocation is being widely used in wheat breeding programmes. Johnson and Lupton used temporary symbols Mld and Mli for the remaining two genes. According to them, Mld is located on chromosome 4B and is derived from *T. durum*, whereas the source of Mli is *T. aestivum*.

The biological basis of the resistance to powdery mildew is not fully known. Bogdan (1968) found that the degree of resistance is determined by the difference between the pH value and the isoelectric zone of cell proteins since this difference is directly related to the degree of resistance. More the difference between pH value and the isoelectric zone, higher is the degree of resistance. Further, the amount of nitrogen originating from protein is more in the leaves of resistant varieties than in the leaves of susceptible varieties.

Like biological basis, the information about the genetic basis of resistance is still incomplete. The resistance has been found to be govenred by single major genes, polygenes or pleiotropic genes. The genes controlling resistance may be dominant, recessive or intermediate. In addition, the degree of resistance is also influenced by environmental factors. However, both the development of multilineal varieties and pyramiding of resistance genes may greatly help in inducing durable resistance against powdery mildew (McIntosh, 1978).

Karnal bunt : Karnal bunt or partial bunt or partial grain smut, a recently described smut disease of wheat, is caused by the fungus *Tilletia indica* (Mitra) syn. *Neovossia indica* (Mitra) Mundkur. Mitra (1931) was the first to report this disease at the Botanical Research Station, Karnal (India). The three main hosts of the pathogen are *Triticum aestivum, T. durum* and *Triticale*. The disease remained restricted to the plains of India and Pakistan for more than three decades. However, later on, the occurrence of the disease was reported from some other parts of the world (Nepal, Afghanistan, Iraq, Lebanon, Syria and Mexico). Even in India, Karnal bunt could not gain much importance till Kalyansona was a predominant variety of the country. Kalyansona was resistant to this disease. The varieties PVS 18 and Sonalika (a late sown variety) were also resistant to Karnal bunt. When other wheat varieties were introduced, the incidence of Karnal bunt increased considerably and the disease became of frequent occurrence in major wheat growing belt of the country.

Karnal bunt is a soil-borne disease. The pathogen attacks the plant at the time of anthesis. Both the plants and kernels are partially infected by the disease. Variable portion of the kernel is replaced by a cluster of fungal spores. The infection, in general, takes place along the longitudinal furrow of the kernel and into the scutellum and endosperm. As a result, the grain produces a foul smell. Even a minor destruction of grain by the fungus may make the grain unfit for human consumption. The colour, odour and palatability of whole meal and chaptis are adversely affected (Mehdi et al., 1973). Chemical quality of the flour becomes poor and its recovery is reduced (Gopal and Sekhon, 1988). Seed viability is also reduced.

The disease creates difficulty in the certification of seed. It is very difficult to maintain the minimum seed certification standards laid down for the national seed procurement. The standards are 0.05 and 0.25 per cent for foundation and certified seed, respectively. For export purposes, no Karnal bunt infection is allowed, that is, the grain should be completely Karnal bunt free.

Although an increase in disease severity is followed by a proportional reduction in seed weight (Singh, 1980; Bedi et al., 1981), Karnal bunt is a minor disease in terms of yield loss (Brennan et al., 1990). According to Joshi et al. (1983), even in the years of most severe epidemics (90 per cent infected grains in some fields) in India, the yield losses were less than 0.5 per cent.

Dhiman (1982) reported three races of *Tilletia indica* from Punjab state. The three pathotypes showed different degrees of virulence. However, according to Aujla et al. (1987), there were four pathotypes (K_1, K_2, K_3 and K_4) of the pathogen in Punjab and Himachal Pradesh. Mature teliospores are variable in size, shape (oval, spherical or subspherical) and colour (brown to dark brown). However, immature teliospores have spherical or angular shape, yellowish or sub-hyaline colour and are sterile.

Favourable conditions for Karnal bunt infection and disease development are high humidity, cloudy weather, rainfall during anthesis and heavy manuring. In India, late sown crop is relatively more prone to this disease than timely sown one.

As compared to rusts of wheat, Karnal bunt has considerably low variability and the development of resistant varieties is perhaps the best method to control this disease. According to Fuentes-Davila et al. (1995), Karnal bunt resistance in bread wheat is governed by two partially recessive and four partially dominant genes. However, some other scientists opine that partially dominant genes in combination with some polygenes are responsible for the control of this disease. According to Gill et al. (1993), the resistance genes are found on 2A, 7A, 3B, 1D, 3D and 5D chromosomes.

Results of some generation mean analyses indicated that additive gene effects played a major role in the control of this disease. Dominance gene effects were found relatively less important. The most suitable approach to control this disease would be to develop varieties with broad genetic base for resistance. For this, the first and the primary step is to screen diverse germplasm against the prevalent races of the pathogen. Some promising resistant lines are HD 29, HD 30, KBRL-10, KBRL-13, KBRL-22, K 9843 and WH 283. These lines are being used in national and international breeding programmes for developing Karnal bunt resistant varieties. Efforts are also being made to combine resistance for Karnal bunt and for rusts of wheat.

Common bunt : This soil and seed-borne disease is also known as *stinking smut* or *hill bunt* and is caused by two closely related fungal species *Tilletia caries* and *T. foetida* which readily hybridize in culture as well as in nature. The spores of *T. caries* are reticulate whereas those of *T. foetida* are smooth. It is a common disease in less humid regions of south Asia, west Asia and north Africa. First, the pathogen invades the floral initials and then the grains formed from these initials are filled with fungal spores. At the time of threshing, the fungal sori burst and spores spread on the soil and uninfected grains. The disease infection can be considerably reduced by fungicide treatment.

Breeding for resistance to common bunt is difficult since new physiological races of the pathogen arise very rapidly. Although many resistance genes are known, but due to pathogenic variability the resistance breeding programme is not much successful

Loose smut : This smut is caused by the fungus *Ustilago tritici*. Loose smut is a seed-borne disease and causes considerable damage to wheat crop in south Asia, west Asia and north Africa. According to Martens *et al.* (1984), this disease occurs in all the areas where wheat is grown but its incidence is more in humid regions. However, the losses due to this disease have been considerably reduced by using systemic fungicides. Of course, the diease has not completely disappeared.

The pathogen attacks the plant at the time of anthesis through the stigmas. The most striking symptom of the disease is that the floral parts of the plant are replaced by large numbers of fungal spores. In the beginning, these spores are enclosed in a fragile membrane but soon after the membrane ruptures and the spores are released. All the spores may be carried away by rain or wind leaving the bare rachis. In cases of extremely severe infection, the leaf tips are affected by the disease. In addition to the use of systemic fungicides, the disease can be controlled by producing uninfected foundation seed.

According to Oort (1944, 1963), certain wheat varieties showed hypersensitivity to loose smut (plants died at seedling stage in glasshouse environment) and that the genetic basis of this hypersensitivity can be explained through a gene-for-gene relationship between the host and the pathogen. Variety-dependent resistance to this disease has been emphasized by Swaminathan (1977). According to him, loose smut became an unimportant disease in the areas where the wheat varieties Kalyansona and PV 18 were grown. But when these varieties were replaced by other varieties, the disease again became important. Despite the availability of high levels of resistance, it is difficult to control this disease because of the pathogenic variability of the organism. Selection for resistance to this disease is not an easy task since for screening genotypes, the infection should be done at the time of anthesis and the degree of infection achieved is influenced by the extent of open flowering which is generally different in different varieties. Therefore, breeding for resistance to loose smut is bit difficult.

Flag smut : This disease is caused by *Urocystis agropyri*. The pathogen attacks several graminaceous plant species. According to Purdy (1965) and Wiese (1987), flag smut is a unique disease as it produces linear bunt balls or sori or clusters of fungal spores on the leaf blades, leaf sheaths and culms. When the pathogen attacks only wheat plants, it may also be called as *U. tritici* (Purdy, 1965). Since the pathogen attacks mainly the leaf blade and leaf sheath, this disease is also known as *leaf smut*. It is a seed and soil-borne disease.

Flag smut mainly occurs in dry wheat producing regions of the world (south Asia, Australia and Middle East). The losses due to this disease in USA are negligible. Many genes with additive effect are known to control this disease. However, no major genes are yet known for the control of the disease.

Helminthosporium leaf blight (HLB) : HLB occurs in south Asia and some sub-tropical areas where rice-wheat rotation is frequently followed. The disease is caused by *Bipolaris sorokiniana* syn. *Helminosporium sativum, Drechslera sativa* or *Cochliobolus sativus* and is generally less damaging than spot blotch caused by the same fungus in barley. *Cochliobolus sativus* attacks several plant species including a number of grasses. HLB in severe form causes widespread necrosis of the upper crop canopy and may ultimately spread to the spike and seed. Sources of resistance to HLB are available in CIMMYT germplasm.

Alternaria leaf blight : This disease is caused by *Alternaria triticina* and is restricted to India only. The symptoms are similar to those of leaf blight caused by *C. sativus*. The pathogen may attack the spikes and seeds. The disease is controllable by developing resistant varieties.

Septoria tritici blotch : This disease is found worldwide. According to Kema *et al.* (1996), the pathogen has high levels of variability and, therefore, break-down in resistance has been reported in some cases. They also found that differences between isolates were great from between species (*Triticum aestivum* and *T. durum*) than from within species. According to Gilchrist (1994), emmer wheats have high levels of resistance to this disease. However, the most important means of controlling this disease is to breed varieties for quantitative resistance and tolerance (Shaner, 1987).

Head scab or head blight : Head scab caused by *Fusarium graminearum* is a region-specific disease and occurs mainly in the Punjab state of India. The disease causes minor damage in the country.

Fusarium root rot : This disease is also region specific and occurs mainly in warmer environments of south India.

Bactrial and viral diseases and nematodes : In addition, there are some bacterial (bacterial stripe, bacterial leaf blight, basal glume rot and spike blight) and viral (soil-borne wheat mosaic virus, barley yellow dwarf virus or BYDV, wheat yellow mosaic virus, wheat spindle streak mosaic virus and wheat streak mosaic virus) diseases and nematodes (cereal cyst nematode and root lesion nematode) which cause damage to wheat crop. Bacterial stripe is an important disease in some regions of the world (north and south America, west Asia and north Africa). According to Tesemma and Mitiku (1992), wheat varieties of Mexican origin are relatively more susceptible to this disease. One the other hand, Ethiopian durum landraces show complete immunity against the disease. Five resistance genes are known to control the disease. Bacterial leaf blight occurs in northern USA and Canada, whereas basal glume rot is an important disease in eastern Europe and Ukraine. Spike blight is transmitted with gall nematode (*Anguina tritici*) and creates problem in India.

Soil-borne wheat mosaic virus is vectored by *Polymyxa graminis* fungus and attacks winter wheat in some parts of world (Japan, USA and Europe). BYDV is of wide occurence and causes considerable damage to wheat crop. The most important source of resistance to this disease is the gene Bdv1. This gene is closely associated with Lr 34/Yr 18 in chromosome 7D (Singh *et al.*, 1993). Several *Agropyron* species possess resistance to this disease. Development of partial amphidiploids, alien addition lines and alien translocation lines can greatly help in controlling this disease (Larkin *et al.*, 1995; Sharma *et al.*, 1995; Banks *et al.*, 1995). Wheat yellow mosaic virus disease is found in India, Japan, France, USA and Canada. The disease is vectored by *P. graminis* and may be controlled by developing resistant varieties.

In several countries of the world especially in developing countries, soils are nematode-infested. Cereal cyst nematode is of wide occurrence. The nematode creates problem in west Asia, north Africa, south Australia and parts of Europe. Resistance genes Cre 1 and Cre 2 have been identified. The nematode is associated with zinc deficiency (Braun, 1994). The sources of resistance to cereal cyst nematode (*Heterodera avenae*) which causes molya disease, are Aus.15854 and Raj MR-1. Root lesion nematode causes yellowing of plants but symptoms are not distinguishable from other diseases.

New strategy for disease control : While dealing with the control of wheat diseases, the ultimate aim of the breeder is to increase the effectiv life of a variety by avoiding frequent disease epidemics. Since the same approach cannot be used for controlling different diseases, all possible efforts should be made to control most of the prevalent diseases of a particular region. To prevent frequent epidemics of wheat rusts, for example, several approaches like development of multineal varieties, pyramiding of genes, cycling of genes and regional deployment of resistance genes, have been suggested by investigators. A multilineal variety mostly has durable resistance since its component lines have resistance genes from different sources. Similarly, in gene pyramiding, several (generally 3-5) resistance genes are incorporated in the same genetic background. The basic principle involved in this approach is that simultaneous breakdown of all the resistance genes has a very low probability. In gene cycling the use of resistance gene and that of the variety carrying the gene is discontinued temporarily as and when the variety becomes susceptible. The use of different resistance genes in different parts of a large area is termed as regional deployment of resistance genes. The purpose is to create genetic diversity in a large geographical area.

Seedling resistance and adult plant resistance are considered as two separate characteristics (especially in case of rust resistance) since some genes express themselves only at the adult plant stage. The plant may be susceptible at seedling stage but may show partial resistance at the adult plant stage. The simultaneous presence of both the major, specific resistance genes and adult plant resistance genes in the same variety would ensure increase in the effective life of the variety.

Alien gene transfers through translocations have played a significant role in overcoming the problem of different wheat diseases. Resistance genes have been transferred from *Agropyron elongatum, Secale cereale* and other plant species to wheat. So far, the translocation 1BL/1RS has proved to be most important and is being used by the wheat breeders all over the world. The rye chromasome segment 1RS not only contains resistance genes for all the three wheat rusts (Lr 26, Sr 31 and Yr 9) and powdery mildew (Pm 8) but also contributes towards increased yield potential and adaptation of wheat genotypes.

There are some wheat diseases, especially some smuts, which can be more easily controlled by using fungicides than developing resistant varietes.

Use of molecular markers can facilitate incorporation of multiple gene resistance in a wheat variety.

Breeding for Resistance to Insect Pests

As discussed in Chapter 3, insect pests are not a serious problem for wheat breeders. However, some insect pests have region-specific importance and cause considerable damage. Further, some of them are vectors of viruses and are indirectly responsible for widespread losses. Of course, most of them are only occasional pests and can cause only limited losses. Insect pest of wheat have great variations in their life cycles, reproductive rates, powers of dispersal, food habits, ecological requirements for survival and tolerance to adverse conditions. They have diverse food habits and their biological systems are mostly complex. Let us give a brief description of some insect pests of wheat.

Hessian fly (*Mayetiola destructure*) : This insect pest is found in almost all major wheat growing regions of the world and perhaps causes maximum damage to the wheat crop. The damage to the plant is done entirely by the larvae of the insect. They generally develop within the leaf sheath at the bases of young plants and suck sap from the stems and may ultimately cause lodging of the plant. Due to their attack, the plants remain stunted with smaller, more errect and dark green leaves and quantity and quality of the grain is adversely affected. Although this insect also infests rye and barley but the preferred host of the insect is wheat. Injury caused by the larvae substantially reduces the growth of internodes and stops transport of nutrients to developing ears. As a result, both the quantity and quality of the grain are reduced. In this way, the fly affects both the vegetative and reproductive phases of wheat plant.

Hessian fly can be easily controlled by evolving resistant varieties, but the main problem is the frequent emergence of new biotypes of the insect. According to Gallun and Khush (1980), there is a *gene-for-gene* relationship between resistance in wheat plant and avirulence in the fly, that is, the host and the insect have highly specific genetic interactions between them. More than 25 resistance genes for Hessian fly have so far been identified (Cox and Hatchett, 1994). According to Ohm *et al.* (1995), sveral of these resistance genes are present in chromosome 5A. Resistance genes may show dominance, partial dominance or recessiveness and resistance may be governed by single major genes, duplicate genes or polygenes.

Aphids : A large number of aphid species (more than 30) can cause damage to wheat crop. In addition, several of them are vectors of barley yellow dwarf virus (BYDV). Aphids are found all over the world. Some of them are widely distributed in some continents. Probably, the most widely distributed aphids are greenbug (*Schizaphis graminum*), English grain aphid (*Macrosiphum avanae* syn. *Sitobion avenae* and *Rhopalosiphum padi*) and corn leaf aphid (*R. maidis*). A few aphids are found in India also.

Aphids have a very high reproductive potential and within a few weeks, a single aphid may produce 20-100 young aphids. Their reproduction is mostly by apomictic parthenogenesis. As a result, the heterozygosity is maintained generation after generation which, in turn, becomes the basis for great adaptiveness and frequent emergence of new biotypes.

Greenbug : This aphid reproduces mainly by parthenogenesis. Although the insect can withstand relatively low temperatures, but its multiplication is rapid in the spring season with the rise in temperature. Greenbugs feed on mainly the wheat leaves and may cause death of young pants. Greenbug causes damage to wheat plant through phytotoxic effects by injecting its saliva into plant tissues. Several biotypes (A, B, C, D, E, F, G, etc.) of the insect have identified. According to Hatchett *et al.* (1987), several sources of resistance to greenbug have been used.

English grain aphid : This aphid is also reproduced mainly through parthenogenesis and causes yield losses mainly through spike infestation. However, if this aphid feeds on lower leaves of wheat plant, the yield losses are negligible. The insect may increase the spread of barley yellow dwarf virus (BYSV) by moving from plant to plant. According to Hatchett *et al.* (1987), varieties with hairy leaves are resistant to this insect.

Termites or white ants : Termites can cause damage to wheat plant at any stage of its development, that is, from young plant or seedling stage to a ripening crop stage. Dry areas with loose and sandy soils are the most suitable breeding grounds for termites and, therere, the incidence of the pest is restricted to certain well-defined regions. The wheat crops grown on light soils are more susceptible to termites' attack than those grown on heavier and compact soils. Infestation can be considerably reduced by giving one or more timely irrigations. Manytimes, the root system is not completely damaged by the pest and, therefore, timely irrigation may result in revival of plants which were heavily damaged.

Cereal leaf beetle (*Oulema melanopus*) : Cereal leaf beetle is an important insect pest and causes considerable losses to small grain crops. Although larvae cause maximum destruction, adult beetle also feeds on the leaves of the plant. The beetle has nonpreference for feeding on hairy leaves. Therefore, development of wheat varieties with pubescent leaves greatly helps in controlling this pest. chemical control has also been found effective. Further, biological control by parasitic wasps has also been recommended. However, according to Webster *et al.*(1982), the best and the most efficient method of cereal leaf beetle control is the development of resistant varieties.

Grasshoppers : A large number of grasshopper species occur in nature. The species which attack wheat, feed on a wide array of host plants. Some of the grasshopper species which attack the wheat crop are migratory grasshopper (*Melanoplus sanguinipes*), differential grasshopper (*M. differentialis*), red-legged grasshopper (*M. femurrubrum*) and two-stripped grasshopper (*M. bivittatus*). Migratory grasshopper perhaps causes maximum damage to wheat. This grasshopper mainly attacks the seedlings of winter wheat. The damage is more when this pest attacks spikes or the ripening grains. However, use of some chemicals is very effective in controlling this insect.

Integrated pest management approach : For an effective insect control, all possible methods (use of resistant varieties, use of chemicals, biological control and cultural practices) should be used. The use of resistant varieties is the most efficient method to control insect pests. However, for an effective insect control, two fundamental objectives should be kept in mind: (1) The pest population should be maintained below the economic injury level; and (2) the pest population should have minimal adverse effect on crop ecosystems (Hatchett *et al.*, 1987).

Weed Control

Weeds do enormous damage to wheat crop since they
1. reduce the amount of nutrients and moisture in the soil,
2. compete with crop plants for light and, therefore, cause reduction in wheat yields,
3. may harbour insect pests and diseases and thus may adversely affect both the quantity and quality of the produce,
4. make harvesting and threshing of the crop more laborious and costly, and
5. reduce the seelling price of the produce.

Competition with crop plants or **allelopathy** may be the main cause of yield losses by weeds. Competition is most effective when soil moisture, soil nutrients or light becomes a limiting factor. Therefore, weeds may cause considerable yield losses in wheat in arid and semi-arid areas. However, allelopathy (*where one plant inhibits another by releasing chemicals*) has not been extensively studied in wheat (Appleby, 1987).

Several weeds like *Phalaris minor, Chenopodium album,* (bathua), *Cyperus rotundus* (motha), *Convolvulus arvensis* (hiran khuri), *Asphodelus tenuifolius* (piazi) and *Melilotus alba* (senji), are found in wheat fields. However, *Phalaris minor* is the most dangerous weed of wheat since this weed not only competes with wheat plants for water, nutrients and light but it is very difficult to remove the weed from wheat fields because of its similarity with wheat plants.

Broadly, three types of methods, mechanical control, crop rotation and chemical control, are used to control weeds. Effective herbicides have been synthesized, but these chemicals are mostly costly and create environmental pollution.

Abiotic Stresses

Among the abiotic stresses determining the realization of genetic yield potential in wheat, drought, salinity and lodging are important factors. Tolerance to drought is now one of the main objectives of CIMMYT wheat breeding programme.

Breeding for Drought Tolerance

The application, dissemination and adoption of green revolution technology has been mainly restricted to the irrigated areas. In marginal environments, especially in semi-arid areas of the world, the speed of adoption of this technology has been quite slow. As a result, the annual gain in genetic yield potential in rich environments is about two times than that obtained in dry areas. However, certain CIMMYT wheat varieties are now successfully being grown in semi-arid environments (Rajaram and Braun, 2001). Several Veery lines not only perform excellently well in high yielding environments but these lines also give higher yields under drought conditions (Villareal *et al.*, 1995). Such a combination of two genetic systems (high yield performance in rich environments and adaptation to drought) in a single genotype could be possible mainly because of the presence of 1B/1R translocation in these lines.

Rajaram and Braun (2001) emphasized the importance of the line *Nesser* bred at CIMMYT (Mexico) and identified at ICARDA (Syria). The line was developed by crossing a high yielding CIMMYT variety *Jupataco* with a drought tolerant Australian variety *W 3918A* and carries a combination of input efficiency and high yield responsiveness. It is a uniquely drought tolerant genotype and, in the absence of rust, its performance is similar to that of Veery lines. They also described a breeding scheme to achieve the combination of the two genetic systems (input efficiency and input responsiveness). The methodology involves following steps :

1. F_1 generation is produced by crossing high yielding and widely adapted lines with proven drought tolerant lines.
2. Individual F_2 plants are grown under optimal environmental conditions. The plants are inoculated with a wide spectrum of rust virulence and vigorous plants with durable resistance are selected.
3. Modified pedigree/bulk breeding system suggested by Rajaram and van Ginkel (1995) is used to evaluate the selected F_2 plants under conditions of low water availability. In F_3 and F_4 generations, lines instead of single plants are selected on the basis of important characters like biomass/vigour, spike density and grains per unit area (van Ginkel *et al.*, 1995).
4. The F_4 selected lines are evaluated in F_5 and F_6 generations under optimal environmental conditions.
5. The F_6 selected lines are evaluated in F_7 and F_8 generations simultaneously under optimum and low water environments.
6. The lines exhibiting outstanding performance under both the environments are selected.
7. The selected lines are further evaluated in international environments to confirm their performance.

In this way, by alternating selection environments during breeding process, two genetic systems (input efficiency and input responsiveness) may be combined and improved environmental conditions can be translated into yield gains.

In India, wheat is exposed to damage from drought in parts of Haryana, Rajasthan and Punjab in the North Western Plains Zone. However, the greatest risk of damage from drought in India is in the Central Zone (Madhya Pradesh and surrounding areas) and Peninsular Zone (Maharastra, Karnataka, etc.) and other southern states. Some sources of tolerance to drought have been identified. These sources are Kharchia 65, C 306, Hindi 62, Hyb.65, HI 1011, HI 8351, Narbada 4, Bijaga Yellow and Pissi Local (Tandon, 1993).

It is natural that primitive forms of the genus *Triticum* were tolerant to drought since the site of origin of this genus has a dry climate. However, after the evolution of hexaploid wheat, its genomes have undergone considerable genetic changes. Now evolution of new wheat varieties according to man's will and needs has brought significant changes in the response of wheat genotypes to environmental conditions. Since human population is increasing in some parts of the world with an alarming rate, it is imperative to evolve such wheat varieties which have high input efficiency and high input responsiveness so that they are not only high yielding in optimum environments but their yields are also higher in marginal environments. Further, since many regions of the world have dry climate, development of such wheat varieties becomes more relevant in such areas. As has been discussed earlier, sincere efforts in this direction are being made by the CIMMYT scientists.

Results obtained by many scientists have clearly indicated that drought tolerance is a genetically governed characteristic of the plant. However, the different stages of plant development display different degrees of sensitivity to water deficiencies. Some scientists think that the third leaf stage is the most critical period for the adverse effect of drought, whereas some others are of the opinion that flowering and seed setting are the most critical stages for such effect of drought. Water deficiency may cause reduction in the size of the spike, the number of tillers per plant, fertility of spikelets, number of grains per spike and 1000-grain weight. However, it is not clearly known whether sensitivity to drought in the different stages of plant development is genotype-dependent or not. Of course, it is generally agreed by most of the scientists that the protective mechanism against water deficiency or resistance to drought develops gradually.

Tolerance to drought is a complexly inherited characteristic of the plant and is probably governed by polygenes. There is possibility of obtaining transgressive segregants during the breeding process. Hybridization between diverse genotypes is the best method to develop drought resistant varieties as varietal differences for this characteristic do occur in wheat.

Induced mutagenesis has not been attempted for this characteristic. However, mutation breeding has its own limitations to improve a quantiatively inherited character.

Breeding for Salinity Tolerance

Soil salinity creates **physiological water deficiency**, that is, non-availability of water to plants even when surface soil moisture is in abundance. This **physiological drought**, in turn, causes reduction in yield by adversely affecting plant growth. In addition to the detrimental effect of accumulated soluble salts in the soil profile on plant growth, soil salinity also adversely affects the availability of micronutrients to the plant.

Soil salinity is a major abiotic stress in irrigated semi-arid and arid regions of the world as it causes considerable reduction in crop yields in these areas. In India, about 3.0 million hectares of land in North Western Plains Zone and the irrigated regions of Peninsular Zone is saline (Rao, 2001).

However, different crops exhibit different degrees of response to salinity. Wheat has moderate to high tolerance to salinity. But, cotton, grain sorghum and barley are more tolerant to salinity than wheat. Further, sensitivity of a crop species to salinity may differ according to the growth stage of the plant. For example, wheat, rice and barley are more sensitive to salinity during early seedling growth than other stages of the plant growth (Singh and Tyagi, 1998). Furthermore, the effect of salinity is also determined by environmental conditions prevailing in the area and the soil type. Salinity causes more damage under hot and dry conditions than under cool and humid conditions. Singh and Tyagi (1998) have discussed different aspects of salinity tolerance in detail.

Significant differences for salinity tolerance have not only been observed between different crop species but different varieties and ecotypes of the same crop species may also differ considerably for this characteristic. In some cases, the differences between varieties of the same species are as large as differences between different species. These within species differences are, in some cases, attributable to single dominant genes governing tolerant adaptive characteristic. Such cases clearly indicate that there are immense possibilities of the success in this direction through tolerance breeding efforts. Ahsan *et al.* (1996) observed simple inheritance for ion uptake (Na, K and Cl contents in leaf sap), grain yield and its component traits (main tiller height, number of spikes per plant, number of fertile spikelets per spike, number of infertile spikelets per spike, number of grains per plant and average grain weight) in a spring wheat cross between the salt sensitive variety Alexandria and a salt tolerant variety KRL1-4. Their results indicated possibility of obtaining high yielding and salt tolerant recombinant lines using relatively simple breeding procedures. However, according to several other investigators (Ramage, 1980; Singh *et al.*, 1989; Yeo and Flowers, 1989), salt tolerance is a complex characteristic. However, the fact remains that multilocational and multiseasonal testing of wheat genotypes in replicated evaluation trials under salinity/alkalinity field conditions has been quite successful in developing a number of salt tolerant wheat genotypes like KRL 1-4, KRL 19, Job 666, WH 157.

In addition to the use of conventional breeding procedures, somatic variation may be exploited by cell culture (Larkin and Scowcroft, 1981). Further, heterozygosity of the materials in the early generations of breeding programme creates difficulty in the selection of desirable genotypes. Development of doubled haploids may help in overcoming this difficulty. Such effort has been made in India by developing doubled haploids by hybridizing wheat spikes of the crosses between Kharchia and some high yielding varieties (HD 2285, HD 2329 and WH 542) with maize pollen (Singh and Tyagi, 1998).

Some salt tolerant wheat varieties have been developed in India. These are Kharchia 65, KRL 3-4, KRL 7, KRL 8, KRL 9, etc. (tolerant), WH 157, KRL 104, Raj 3077, etc. (medium tolerant) and WH 542, HD 2329, HD 2009, WL 711, etc. (medium sensitive) (Singh and Tyagi, 1998).

Before using any method to reclaim and ameliorate salt-affected soils, it is extremely important to know the real problem. In case the soil has excess Na, use of organic matter and gypsum is beneficial to provide more porous surface. Leaching can decrease the amount of excessive salt. Improving drainage by installing tile drains can help in reducing the accumulation of salts. However, manytimes, it is not easy to reclaim a salt-affected soil rather reclamation is a very gradual process and may require several years.

Breeding for Lodging Resistance

Reduction in the length of culm in wheat has following types of effects :

1. Protection against lodging increases, that is, possibility of lodging decreases;
2. the ratio of grain yield to straw yield (that is, harvest index) increases;
3. possibility of sprinkling irrigation increases;
4. danger of the spread and multiplication of pathogens decreases; and
5. utilization of larger doses of fertilizers increases.

As a result, the use of dwarf-statured wheat varieties has spectaculary increased yields of this cereal. However, reduction in plant height cannot completely solve the problem of lodging. Short and stiff culms are usually resistant to irreversible bending or breaking-over of the stalk at the lower internodes at the time of heavy rains and/or fast winds. But short and firm straw is not helpful in preventing the other type of lodging where the culm does not bend or break but the plant falls down due to loosened adventitious roots. A positive relation has been found between the spread of roots and standing ability of the plant (Pinthus, 1967). Therefore, the number of adventitious roots plays an important role in preventing this type of lodging.

However, considerable differences for lodging resistance may be found among the varieties of the same height and phenotype. It means lodging resistance is a genotype-dependent characteristic. But, despite the fact that stiffness and flexibility of the culm and the size and the toughness of the roots play an important role in resistance to lodging, it is difficult to explain the anatomical cause of the differences between genotypes of the same height group for this genotype-dependent characteristic. Of course, the presence of a number of thick-walled cells of mechanical tissue between the phloem and metaxylan and an increased number of vascular bundles may be the probable anatomical causes of lodging resistance. But, it is very difficult to use these anatomical features of the genotype as selection criteria. As a result, scientists are mostly using visual assessment as the selection method for lodging resistance. According to Udagawa and Oda (1967a) and Pyatigin and Smihov (1967), the extent of lodging and the resulting yield reduction can be demonstrated by artificially producing a dense crop stand and then applying intensive sprinkling irrigation. Plant genotypes/varieties can be compared for lodging resistance under natural conditions if there are heavy and sudden rainfalls and strong winds during the time of experiment.

Lodging resistance is a gradually developing complex characteristic and is determined by several morphological, anatomical and physiological properties of the plant. In addition, the characteristic is considerably affected by environmental factors. It is presumed that lodging resistance is governed by both the major genes and polygenes. Dwarfing genes, especially Rht genes, have played the most significant role in reducing plant height in wheat. But, as discussed earlier, reduction in plant height does not help in preventing lodging when the plant falls down without bending of the culm at the lower internodes.

Although the identification of genes for lodging resistance and their locations on the chromosomes are not yet complete, some genes are known to control a few characteristics associated with lodging resistance. For example, a gene found on the chromosome 5A determines stiffness of the lower and upper internodes (Morris, 1962-1972). According to Larson and Mac Donald (1963), the gene for stem strength is located in chromosome 3B of durum what variety Golden Ball. However, due to the presence of a suppressor in chromosome 3D, stem stiffness of *aestivum* wheat could not be improved by crossing it with Golden Ball variety of durum wheat.

Polygenes play an important role in determining lodging resistance in wheat and there is a possibility of obtaining transgressive segregants. Therefore, hybridization between genetically diverse types is the best method for improving this characteristic. The parents for hybridization should be chosen in a way that their characteristics complement each other. The knowledge about the morphological and anatomical causes of culm strength may help in choosing the parents.

Mutation breeding may also help in improving lodging resistance in wheat. Some attempts made in this direction have produced good results.

Several wheat varieties (*Kavkaz, Aurora, Blue Boy, Parker, Capelle-Desprez, San Pastore, WH 711* etc.) are known to possess lodging resistance.

CHAPTER 10

Breeding for Quality

Improved grain quality is one of the major objectives in almost all modern wheat breeding programmes since wheat grain is not only processed into a number of manufactured products (leavened breads, unleavened breads, biscuits, cakes, etc.) and supplies the human population with more energy and nutrients than any other single food source, but it is also an important constituent of several animal feeds. It means that there are many different kinds of quality of wheat grain. Further, the criteria used in breeding for grain quality in different kinds of wheat (hard, soft and durum wheats) are usually different. Breeding for quality characters is complicated by large number of quality characteristics and their complex nature. Breeding for these characters is further complicated by different meanings of wheat quality to growers, processors and consumers. For a grower, wheat quality means proper maturity of the plant, high yield of clean wheat and high market value (good colur, appearance, weight, etc. of grain) of the produce. A processor wants that wheat produce should be physically pure with big and uniform size of grains and it should have standard moisture content (about 14 per cent) and protein content according to the particular end product. However, according to the consumer, a wheat product should be palatable with high nutritive value and should have good appearance and reasonable price.

Criteria for Assessing Wheat Quality

In general, three types of cirteria are used to assess the quality in wheat: (1) Botanical criteria; (2) subjective criteria; and (3) objective criteria.

Botanical Criteria

As discussed earlier, grain qualtiy in wheat is a combination of many complex characteristics. Further, not only different species of wheat and different varieties of the same wheat species differ in their quality characters, but different parts of the wheat grain also differ significantly in their quality characteristics. For example, three major parts of wheat grain, namely, endosperm, bran and germ, have different quality characteristics. As a result, the end uses of these three parts are also different.

Although there are many recognized species of the genus *Triticum*, three species of this genus, namely, *T. aestivum, T. compactum* and *T. durum*, make more than 90 per cent contribution to the world's total wheat production. Among these three species, *T. aestivum* is the most widely grown one. This species is most suitable for bread making and is grown in many parts of the world for this purpose. However, in India, this species is grown mainly for unleavened bread or chapati making. The species *T. compactum* is grown mainly for the preparation of cakes, pastry and cookies since this species contains relatively low protein content and has soft texture. However, *T. durum* contains high protein content and hard texture and is, therefore, used for preparing macaroni, semolina and pasta products.

Subjective Criteria

These criteria of quality evaluation are not based on scientific principles, but are based on the experience of the buyer and, therefore, are not very precise and generally differ from person to person. Of course, this method of evaluating quality is very quick and inexpensive. The method is used by the buyer at the time of initial purchase of wheat produce from the farmer or market and the quality is judged by considering several characters like colour, shape, size and vitreousness of grains, damage caused by diseases and insect pests to the produce and the occurrence of sprouting.

Objective Criteria

The objective criteria are based on scientific principles and the evaluation of grain quality involves measurement of specific physical, chemical and nutritional properties of the kernel. Although the method is more time taking and laborious, both the precision and reliability of the method are high. Objective criteria are of special significance since these criteria are the basis of the classification of wheat into different standards or grades in many countries of the world. Objective criteria include physical properties, chemical properties and nutritional qualities of wheat.

1. Physical properties : Grain weight, weight per unit volume, grain hardness and presence of impurities in wheat grains come under this category.

Grain weight : This characteristic is measured mostly in terms of 1000 grain weight. The characteristic is determined by grain size and grain density.

Weight per unit volume : This characteristic is usually measured in terms of kilograms per 100 litre and is the oldest and simplest method of evaluating wheat quality. The characteristic is directly related with plumpness, maturity of the grain (particularly the moisture content in the grain) and uniformity in grain shape. Grains having uniform shape, low moisture content and more plumpness usually have higher weight per unit value and produce more yield of flour.

Grain hardness : Milling quality of wheat is mainly determined by the hardness of the grain. According to Simmonds *et al.* (1973), hard wheats have high milling quality since these wheats yield more flour with minimum damage of bran. Also, these wheats have higher specific gravity than the soft wheats as hard wheats have larger and heavier grains.

Presence of impurities : Several kinds of impurities (grains of other crop(s), grains of other variety of the same crop, weed seeds, straw, dust, mites, insects, etc.) may be present in wheat grains and may adversely affect wheat quality.

2. Chemical properties : Chemical properties of wheat include protein content, carbohydrate content, lipid content, mineral matter content, enzymes, vitamins, pigments and moisture content.

Proteins : Since wheat is an important source of protein, protein content in wheat grain is considered to be one of the most important quality factors. The suitability of wheat for a particular type of product is usually determined by the percentage of protein. For example, for chapati making, presence of 10-12 per cent protein is desirable. Similarly, for bread making, wheat with higher protein per cent (>12%) is preferred, whereas for manufacturing cakes cookies and biscuits, wheat with low protein per cent (<10%) is more desirable. According to Mattern *et al.* (1970), the range of protein content in wheat grain is from 5.6 to 21.0 per cent. However, according to Johnson *et al.* (1973), the protein content in wheat ranges from 6-22 per cent with most of the values falling between 10-16 per cent in World Wheat collection maintained by the Agricultural Research Service, USDA. The range of lysine values (expressed as per cent of protein) has been reported from 2.2-4.2 per cent with an average value of 3.2 per cent. But, most of the values ranged between 2.8-3.6 per cent. However, wheat proteins are found unevenly distributed throughout the wheat grain. Wheat bran and germ contain relatively higher concentration of protein than endosperm. Even in different parts of endosperm, the protein is not evenly distributed. The outer portion of the endosperm is richer in protein than the central portion.

On the basis of solubility in different solvents, wheat proteins can be divided into four fractions: (1) *Albumin* (water soluble); (2) *globulin* (salt soluble); (3) *gliadin* (ethanol soluble); and (4) *glutenin* (acid soluble). Albumins and globulins constitute a small portion (10-15 per cent) of the total wheat proteins, whereas the major part (85-90 per cent) of wheat proteins in composed of gliadins and glutenins. As regards the occurrence of these four types of proteins in different parts of wheat grain, the presence of albumins and globulins is mainly restricted to embryo and aleurone layer. However, according to Dell' Aquila *et al.* (1983), these two components of protein (albumin and globulin) are needed for the proper growth and development of the wheat seedlings. On the contrary, gliadins and glutenins are found in endosperm. Albumin and globulin are low molecular weight proteins, have faster electrophoretic mobilities and are often put under the category of soluble proteins. On the contrary, gliadin and glutenin are high moleclar weight proteins, have relatively slower electrophoretic mobilities and are often called as insoluble proteins. Both the gliadin and glutenin are mixtures of high molecular proteins. Although different components of gliadin proteins vary greatly for their molecular weights, these components do not differ for amino acid composition and amino acid sequence (Bietz and Rothfus, 1971).

Gluten is a complex substance composed of gliadin and glutenin (two major components) and minor amounts of other proteins, lipids and starch together with water. Gluten provides possibility of preparing leavened products since it has the characteristic of retaining gases. Whereas glutenin imparts solidity to the gluten, gliadin (soft and sticky) is responsible for binding. The baking quality of flour is mainly determined by the ratio of gliadin and glutenin. Therefore, the ratio of these two types of proteins is of great significance. A gluten may be *strong* if it is elastic but still fairly tough or may be *weak* if it is sticky, less elastic and spreads if a dough ball is put on a plate.

As regards the amino acid composition of wheat proteins, the whole grain proteins contain highest content of glutamic acid followed by proline, leucine, aspartic acid and phenylalaline. However, different tissues of the grain usually have different amino acid compositions. For example, wheat germ and aleurone layer proteins have high content of arginine and lysine. But, since these tissues (germ and aleurone layer) are removed during milling process, the contents of arginine and lysine are relatively lower in wheat flour proteins than in whole grain proteins. Among different types of proteins, globulins contain highest amount of lysine and arginine followed by albumins. The contents of amino acids glutamine and proline are generally positively correlated with total protein content in wheat grain. On the contrary, there is a highly negative correlation between total protein content and the lysine content.

Carbohydrates : The most abundant constituents of wheat grain are the carbohydrates and they form about 83 per cent of the total dry matter. The carbohydrates of wheat grain include *starch* (the major constituent of wheat endosperm and is composed of amylose and amylopectin), *soluble sugars* (only 2.0 per cent, having glucofructosans and sucrose and traces of glucose, fructose, raffinose, galactose and maltose), *cellulose* or *crude fibre* (about 2.3 per cent, mainly in wheat bran and goes along with bran during milling) and *hemicellulose* (concentrated in bran portion of wheat grain).

Lipids : Lipids constitute a very small portion of the wheat flour (about 2 per cent by weight of the flour). They are concentrated in wheat germ. Wheat germ oil is mainly composed of triglycerides. But a higher proportion of phospholipids and glycolipids is found in endosperm and wheat bran lipids. Unsaturated and nutritionally important essential fatty acids are found present in wheat lipids. According to Mac Ritchie (1981), wheat lipids play an important role in determining dough properties and baking behaviour and in preventing bread staling.

Mineral matter : Ash or mineral matter constitutes about 1.8 per cent portion of the wheat grain. Its presence is mainly restricted to wheat bran and its content in endosperm is very low. As a result, high grade wheat flours contain only 0.42 to 0.48 per cent mineral matter. The main constituents of wheat ash are phosphorus and potassium. Since major portion (about 70 per cent) of wheat phosphorus is found in the form of phytic acid which interfers with the absorption of dietary calcium and iron, the presence of phosphorus in foodstuffs is considered undesirable. However, since the presence of phytic acid is mainly restricted to wheat bran and germ, the major portion of this acid goes with bran during the milling process. In addition to the major mineral elements, some minor mineral elements are also found in wheat in very small amounts. However, great variations for both the major and minor mineral elements are found in wheat grain. For example, according to Lorenz and Loewe (1977), soft wheat contains less iron and zinc than hard wheats. Similarly, durum wheat contains more copper and lead than soft wheat (Barbero and Cavalli, 1977). However, large genotypic differences occur in wheat for mineral elements like iron, zinc, manganese and copper.

Enzymes : Two types of enzymes, namely, *amylases* (which hydrolyse the starch into sugars) and *protease* (which is produced by insects and injected into the grain), influence the wheat quality. Amylases are more active during seed germination and their high activity indicates the sprout damaged grains. High activity of protease indicates that the damage to wheat grain has been caused by insects.

Vitamins : Wheat is not only an important and cheap source of proteins, carbohydrates and minerals but it is also an important source of certain vitamins (vitamins B_1 or thiamin, riboflavin, niacin, pyridoxin, etc.). Wheat does not contain vitamin A. The amount of ribolfavin is also low in wheat than in other cereals. In general, vitamins are unevenly distributed in the different tissues of the wheat grain. However, riboflavin is more evenly distributed throughout the whole grain than thiamin. The major portion (about 60 per cent) of pyridoxin is restricted to the aleurone layer alone.

Pigments : The pigments found in wheat include carotene, xanthophylls, favones and degradation products of chlorophyll. For milling purpose, colour of flour plays an important role. The colour of the flour should be uniform and acceptable to the consumer. However, liking of the flour colour also depends on the end product manufactured. For example, for the preparation of bread and cake, a flour of minimum yellowness and maximum brightness is preferred, whereas for preparing macaroni and similar products, the presence of natural yellow pigments is considered better. Carotene is mainly responsible for the yellow colour of the flour.

Moisture content : A certain level of moisture content in wheat is most desirable since wheat quality is greatly determined by the water content present in the wheat grain. Depending upon several facstors (harvesting stage and storage, processing and environmental conditions), wide variations in moisture content of the grain can be seen. Fourteen per cent moisture content in wheat is most favourable. Both the above and below 14 per cent moisture contents are undesirable. If the moisture level is above 14 per cent, there are more chances of damage to the grain due to microorganisms and insects. If the moisture level is below 14 per cent, the grains have a higher degree of brittleness. As a result, there is more breakage of grains during commercial handling operations and thus a reduction in wheat quality. Therefore, a desirable level of moisture content is most necessary to maintain the wheat quality.

3. Nutritional properties : Nutritive value is the potential ability of a foodstuff to make available the nutrients required by the body (Chavan and Adsule, 1985). Wheat, like several other foodstuffs, contains proteins, carbohydrates, minerals, vitamines and some other constituents and is a major source of protein for the population in many parts of the world. Further, since wheat is a staple food for a large portion of the human population, understanding the quality and nutritive value of wheat is extremely important.

However, both the producers and consumers generally give least consideration to the nutritional aspects of wheat quality. Of course, nutritional quality of wheat proteins is not high especially because of the low amounts of essential amino acids lysine and threonine in these proteins. Further, there is an inverse correlation between lysine content and total grain protein content in wheat. Nevertheless, if wheat is used in combination with some quantities of legumes, vegetables, fruits and/or some foods of animal origin, this cereal can play an important role in providing a cheap and nutritionally adequate diet to a large part of the human population. Furthermore, there is enough scope for improving nutritional quality by breeding for both the quantity and quality of proteins.

Different classes of wheat (hard, soft and durum wheats) generally differ strikingly in terms of physical and chemical properties and, therefore, quality of different types of wheat is also defined differently.

Quality of Hard Wheats

The maximum utilizatin of hard or common or bread wheats (*Triticum aestivum*) is done for bread making. However, in some south-east Asian countries (India, Pakistan, Bangladesh and parts of Tibet and China), chapatis (a type of unleavened bread) are the major form of consumption of these wheats. Spring bread wheat, in general, is richer in protein content (about 2-3 per cent) than the winter bread wheat. However, according to Finney (1978), the protein level of hard winter wheat has been raised (about 1 per cent) through development of high protein genotypes in recent years.

The main characteristics of hard wheats are that they have hard endosperm texture and strong gluten strands. Hard wheats have high extraction rates (that is, high recoveries) of white flour as the separation of endosperm from the bran is easy in these wheats. Madan *et al.* (2004) found that varieties WH 283 and WH 542 have higher flour recovery than other wheat varieties. Further, since only a few bran particles enter the flour, the quality of the flour is high especially in terms of the colour of the flour. The ash content is also low. In hard wheats, starch grains are firmly embedded in protein matrix and, therefore, a large number of these grains are damaged during milling. As a result, a gritty flour is produced. Since damaged starch grains have the ability of absorbing twice their weight of water during dough formation, the gritty flours of hard wheats have higher water absorption capacity than the fine flours of soft wheats. When yeast is used as leavening agent, carbondioxide is released because of the chemical action of yeast with large quantity of water aborbed by the gluten during dough formation. During solidification of the gluten strands, the carbon dioxide is trapped in the cellular structure of gluten. As a result, a large well-piled loaf of bread is formed.

However, significant variations among different cultivars of hard wheats have been observed for several characteristics like flour yield, water absorption capacity, dough mixing time and loaf size. High water absorption capacity, medium to medijm-long mixing requirement, good loaf-volume potential, satisfactory mixing tolerance and dough handling properties, small to medium oxidation requirement and a loaf of good quality and colour, are the desirable characteristics of a flour to be used for bread-making. Protein content of the grain has a direct and positive correlation with water absorption capacity and the loaf volume. The important characteristics and requirements of the three quality parameters (protein content, sedimentation value and hectolitre weight) for preparing various end products of bread wheat are:

Protein content : The amount of protein in wheat grain is an important parameter for the preparation of different products of common wheat. The protein requirements for preparing good quality bread, chapati and biscuits are >12 per cent, 10-12 per cent and <10 per cent, respectively.

Sedimentation value : This parameter indicates the strength of gluten. The required sedimentation values for preparing good quality bread, chapati and biscuits are, respectively, >60 ml, 30-60 ml and 30 ml.

Hectolitre weight : This parameter is found positively correlated with flour recovery and is thus important for millers. The parameter is of great significance for bread wheat trading in international market. According to US system of grain trading, the grade I bread wheat should have 76.4 kg/hl and above hectolitre weight. However, according to Canadian system, the threshold value is 78 kg/hl.

Quality of Soft Wheat

Soft hexaploid wheat is mainly used for preparing confectionary products like cookies, cakes, crackers, flatbread and pastries. The main characteristics of soft wheat are: (1) Soft wheat gives a lower extraction rate than hard wheats; (2) the protein content of soft wheat is lower as compared to that of hard wheats; (3) there is a greater contamination from bran since the soft endosperm is not readily separated from the bran and, as a result, the flour has poor colour quality; and (4) the soft wheat flour has a low water absorption capacity. A soft wheat produces a fine, silky flour with weak gluten strands. The endosperm texture (hard and soft) is a genetically controlled characteristic.

In soft wheat also, there are considerable differences among different cultivars especially for flour quality. However, these differences have a genetic basis and, therefore, improvement in flour quality, etc. can by made by using appropriate breeding procedures. In soft wheat, the quality would generally differ with the intended use. In this wheat, baking quality is assessed through a cookie test where instead of considering dough volume, the spread of the dough is measured. The appearance of the grain in this wheat is generally determined by the protein content. The grains of the low protein soft wheat are opague or mealy, whereas those of high protein wheat are translucent or vitreous. However, a change in appearance of the grain within a cultivar is not considerably related to the endosperm texture, that is, there is no considerable change in the milling quality due to a change in grain appearacne. For making measurement of flour yield potential of different varieties/lines more efficient, micromilling procedures can be used.

Quality of Durum Wheat

Durum wheat (*Triticum durum*) is a tetraploid species and is grown throughout the world. Of course, hard wheats are grown more extensively than durum wheat. Durum wheat has hardest endosperm and is generally milled to prepare a granular and coarse product called semolina which, in turn, is used to make pasta and durum flour. The flour is then used to prepare noodles. Therefore, the commercial milling process in durum wheat for preparing semolina is different from the milling process in hard and soft wheats where fine flour instead of granular product is manufactured.

Durum wheat grains are larger (both in size and weight), amber in colour and have vitreous appearance. Significant varietal differences are found in durum wheat for grain size and grain weight and for milling and baking properties. However, all these characteristics, as in other wheats, are governed both by genetic and environmental factors and thus may be improved using suitable breeding procedures. For good milling quality, larger size and weight of grain and greater hardness of the endosperm are desirable. Wheat with greater size and weight of grain gives more semolina yield and more hardness of endosperm ensures the proper particle size of semolina.

The whole grain protein content in durum wheat is mostly above 13 per cent. However, semolina generally contains about one percentage point less than the whole grain protein content. A lower protein per cent than this in semolina is undesirable. The ash content in both the durum wheat and semolina is higher than that in hard red spring wheat.

The gluten strength and water absorption capacity of semolina are generally lower than those of the flour milled from hard red spring wheats. However, durum wheats with greater gluten strength have been developed.

Colour of semolina has a special significance. Bright yellow colour of semolina and pasta products is most desirable. Xanthophylls (especially lutein) are the main source of colour in durum semolina. According to Johnston *et al.* (1983), semolina colour is governed by additive gene effets and is a highly heritable characteristic. Because of the high heritability of semolina colour, the breeders have been successful in maintaining a desired semolina colour in durum wheat.

The requirement of protein for preparing good quality pasta products is more than 12 per cent. According to US grading system, grade I durum wheat should have 78 kg/hl or above hectolitre weight. However, majority of the Indian durums have more than 78 kg/hl hectolitre weight.

For preparing good quality pasta products, the sedimentation value should be 40 ml and above. As regards the *yellow berry incidence*, its accepted value in durum wheat is less than 10 per cent. Yellow berry incidence is a physiological disorder caused by protein imbalance. In durum wheat, it lowers the cooking quality of pasta products.

β-carotene content is considered to be an important quality character of durum wheat in many countries of the world as it imparts attractive colour to pasta products. Being a vitamin A precursor, β-carotene has immense nutritional importance. In international market, durum wheat with >7 ppm content of β-carotene is preferred. The check durum wheat variety PDW 233 contains highest (7.95 ppm) β-carotene content. However, genetic stock DBP 01-16 developed by DWR contains 10 ppm β-carotene content.

Breeding for Quality Traits

As discussed earlier, wheat quality characteristics are many and complex and, therefore, there are many different kinds of wheat quality.

Milling properties : Milling properties of wheat grains generally differ according to different wheat products to be prepared. Milling is a complex characteristic and based on breeding objectives, may be divided into three important components: (1) Endosperm texture; (2) extraction rate or percentage of white flour; and (3) water absorption capacity. According to Lelley (1976), milling characters are controlled by genes located on the chromosomes 3 and 6 of B genome and 3,4,5 and 7 of D genome.

It is manytimes difficult to judge the milling textrue on the basis of the appearance of the grain since grains appearing hard may be soft textured. However, *endosperm texture* is a simply inherited characteristic. A number of tests can be used to measure this characteristic. One simple test is to measure the amount of endosperm adhering to bran after milling. Since, in a hard textured wheat, it is easy to separate endosperm from the bran, negligible portion of the endosperm remains attached to the bran. On the contrary, a considerable portion of the endosperm remains attached to the bran in a soft textured wheat. Therefore, endosperm texture may be used as a selection criterion in wheat breeding programmes. Grain texture can be measured by Near-infrared Reflectance Analysis (NIR). The milling of hard wheats is easy and rapid with higher recovery of white flour.

Higher **extraction rate** of white flour is a desirable characteristic for the wheat breeders and thus this characteristic is used as an important selection criterion in wheat breeding programmes. However, extraction rate of white flour may or may not be related to grain size. In general, large, plump grains are expected to give higher extraction rate, but it is not always true. For example, North American spring wheats though have small kernels but give high extraction rates. Similarly, the wheat variety WH 542 has low 1000-grain weight but has high flour recovery. The variety WH 283 also has high flour recovery but it has bold grains. The contamination of white flour with fine bran particles is generally measured on the basis of flour colour and ash content. A bright white colour of the flour indicates presence of less bran particles and a higher recovery. Flour colour may also be measured by NIR. Flour characters are governed by genes found on the chromosome 1D (Lelley, 1976). However, dough characsters are controlled by genes present on several chromosomes (2,3,4 and 5 of A genome; 2,3,4,5 and 6 of B genome; and 1,2,3 and 4 of D genome). The genes governing dough mixing time are located on the chromosomes 7B and 5D (Lelley, 1976).

High **water absorption capacity** of the wheat flour is considered to be an important breeding objective especially for bread making purpose. Wheat flours with higher water absorption capacity generally produce larger loaves of bread. Water absorption capacity of flour is directly related to starch damage. More the starch damage, higher is the water absorption. Stach damage in hard wheats is relatively more than in soft wheats. Therefore, flours of hard wheats have higher water absorption than those of soft wheats. According to Starr *et al.* (1983), starch damage can also be measured by NIR. Although starch damage is affected by the protein content and is genetically determined, but is also influenced by environmental factors, especially by growing conditions. Therefore, water absorption is a complex character and improvement in this character is not easy.

Protein content: Breeding for high protein content is one of the most important objectives of wheat breeding programmes. Genetics of proteins has been studied in detail. According to Lelley (1976), protein content in wheat is controlled by many genes locted on 19 chromosomes of the total 21 hexaploid wheat chromosomes (except the chromosomes 2D and 4D). The storage proteins (gliadins and glutenins which are deposited and stored in protein bodies during endosperm development) constitute the major part (more than 80 per cent) of the total protein in the grain.

According to Pogna et al. (1994), gliadins (Tω- and γ-gliadins) are controlled by genes mainly present on three loci, Gli-A1, Gli-B1 and Gli-D1 found in short arm of the chromosomes 1A, 1B and 1D, respectively. As indicated by quantitative Southern hybridization technique, there is presence of 3-5 γ-gliadin genes and a similar number of w-gliadin genes on each Gli-1 locus. However, there are only rare chances of intralocus recombination. The genes governing α- and β-gliadins are present on three loci, namely, Gli-A2, Gli-B2 and Gli-D2. The three loci are found in the short arm of the chromosomes 6A, 6B and 6D, respectively.

The genes responsible for high molecular weight glutenin (HMWG) subunits (the proteins determining the elasticity of gluten) are found on the long arm of chromosomes 1A, 1B and 1D (Payne, 1987). There are two genes, Glu-1-1 and Glu-1-2, on each of the three loci which code for x-type and y-type subunits, respectively. However, the occurrence of recombination between genes at each locus is very rare. According to the genetic evidence available, the low molecular weight glutenin subunits (LMWG) are governed by genes present at three loci, Glu-A3, Glu-B3 and Glu-D3, found in short arm of the chromosomes 1A, 1B and 1D, respectively.

In addition, there are some gliadins, called as D-zone omega gliadin, which have strong association with glutenins without covalent linkage (Bietz and Wall, 1975). These gliadins are under the control of genes present on the three loci, Gli-A3, Gli-B3 and Gli-D3, found on the short arm of chromosomes 1A, 1B and 1D, respectively. These loci are probably closely linked to the gliadin coding loci Gli-1.

The soluble proteins (the albumin-globulin fraction) represent a minor part of endosperm proteins and include several kinds of proteins like chloroform-methanol-soluble proteins (CM proteins), triticins or triplet proteins, high molecular weight albumins and α-amylase/trypsin inhibitors. There are three main components of CM proteins, namely, CM 1, CM 2 and CM 3, which are coded by genes located in chromosomes 7DS, 7BS and 4A, respectively. An unknown chromosome of D genome is also said to play role in the control of CM 3 component. The triticin proteins are governed by two loci, Tri-A1 and Tri-D1, located in chromosomes 1AS and 1DS, respectively.

In wheat, lysine is the first limiting amino acid. Lysine content is directly related to the content of gliadins. Since gliadins contain very low amount of lysine, low content of lysine is a direct consequence of high gliadin content in the grain. Lysine content is said to be controlled by a gene located in the chromosome 1D.

Screening for α-amylase activity is another important objective in many wheat breeding programmes as this enzyme adversely affects many wheat products. This enzyme causes degradation of starch into a mixture of glucose and maltose. The liberation of free sugars by this enzyme during the early stages of baking causes undesirable stickiness in products like bread, cakes and pastries. The propertry is, however, genetically controlled and significant variations in the amount of this enzyme are found in different flours.

However, breeding for protein content in wheat, especially for nutritional value, is difficult because of the following reasons :

1. Protein content of the grain is mostly negatively correlated with grain yield.
2. Lysine content is inversely correlated to total grain protein. Lysine content is low because:
   a) Gliadins which constitute a major portion (by weight) of grain protein are very poor in lysine; and
   b) lysine is found in higher percentage in wheat germ and aleurone layer which are removed during milling.
3. Both the quality and quantity of protein are influenced by environmental factors, especially by growing conditions.

But, following two points go in favour of breeding for protein content:

1. Additive gene effects play an important role in the genetic control of protein content in wheat.
2. Growing conditions do not cause large fluctuations in protein content.

Results of many studies support the first point mentioned above. Mandloi *et al.* (1974b) and Bhullar *et al.* (1978) found that additive genetic variance and partial dominance played a major role in governing protein content. For gluten strength (in terms of Pelshenke value), both additive and non-additive components of variance were important. According to Jatasra *et al.* (1978), additive gene effects were significant for grain protein percentage in a generation means analysis. Similar results were found by Gill *et al.* (1979), Lonts (1983), Bajwa *et al.* (1985), Thakral *et al.* (1986) and Sarrafi *et al.* (1989). According to Krishnawat and Sharma (1998), phenotypic coefficient of variation was high for grain protein content. These all results indicate that selection should be effective for improving protein content in wheat.

The results of a combining ability analysis carried out by Srivastava and Ram (1974) indicated that additive genetic variance played a major role in the control of grain protein content, gluten content, grain hardness and sedimentation value (used to predict the loaf volume and thus is a measure of bread-making quality). They found fairly high estimates of heritability for grain hardness and sedimentation value, but comparatively low estimates of this genetic parameter for grain protein and gluten content. Raine *et al.* (1979) concluded that Norteno M 67 for protein content, Norteno M 67 and S 331 for lysine content, Kalyansona for tryptophan content and Norteno M 67 and NP 876 for Pelshenke value proved to the best general combiners and both the additive and non-additive components of genetic variation played important role in the control of these four characteristics.

The results of the studies carried out by Halloran (1981) and Lapoujade *et al.* (1991) indicated low to moderately high estimates of heritability for protein content. McClung and Cantrell (1986) also found moderately high heritability for gluten strength. According to Bebyakin and Ishima (1983), selection was most effective for dough colour, gluten quality and content of carotenoid pigments in grain, but selection for grain protein content and flour gluten content was not effective. According to Dwivedi *et al.* (2002) who obtained estimates of variability parameters for quality traits in 72 bread wheat genotypes maintained at CCS HAU, Hisar, the values of phenotypic and genotypic coefficients of variation were high for sedimentation parameter but low for protein percentage and hectolitre weight. Heritability was high for sedimentation value and hectolitre weight but it was low for protein content.

Madan *et al.* (2004) observed regional variations in average protein content in wheat. The wheat grown in south Karnataka had maximum average protein content (more than 13 per cent) followed by wheats grown in Gujarat and Maharastra (12-13 per cent). Haryana, Punjab, Rajasthan, Madhya Pradesh, Uttar Pradesh and Bihar wheats had percentages between 11 and 12, whereas the lowest average protein content was found in Uttaranchal wheat (about 10.5 per cent). The whole country could be divided into three categories on the basis of average sedimentation values : (1) Areas having more than 45 cc value (Bihar and Madhya Pradesh); (2) areas having values between 40-45 cc (Uttar Pradesh, Haryana, Rajasthan, Gujarat and Maharastra; and (3) areas having less than 40 cc value (Uttaranchal, Punjab and Karnataka). Almost all the wheats were good in chapati making. However, partly because of an inverse correlation between grain protein content and grain yield and partly because of more emphasis on grain production by Indian what breeders, India wheat varieties, in general, are relatively poor in grain protein and end product quality.

Nevertheless, all efforts should be made to improve the wheat quality. The techniques like alien gene transfer, use of somaclonal variation and development of doubled haploids and hybrid varieties may be used for this purpose (Pogna *et al.*, 1994).

Combining high yield potential and grain quality : Efforts should be made to combine high yield potential and grain quality in wheat. To achieve this goal, following steps may be taken (Pena, 1996):

1. Cultural practices (like growing crop in rows) which increase nitrogen–use efficiency, should be used.
2. Rates and applications of nitrogenous fertilizer should be such that there is not only increase in grain yield but the translocation of nigrogen to the grain is also enhanced.
3. Since sulfur-containing amino acids and sulfur-rich glutenins are the determinants of wheat's nutritional and processing qualities, respectively, appropriate amounts of sulfur fertilizer should be applied at appropriate times for ensuring adequate synthesis of sulfur-rich proteins.

For improving nitrogen-translocation efficiency in wheat, it is necessary to identify characters associated with genotypic variations in grain protein content. Efforts are being made at CIMMYT to identify and manipulate such characters.

Making planned crosses between high protein wheat varieties (Atlas 66, Lan Cota, Nap Hal, WH 283, HI 977, HI 1077, UP 2338, WH423, WH 595, WH 711, WH 712, Pusa 5-3, etc.) and high yielding, disease resistant and well-adapted varieties (PBW 343, WH 542, HD 2687, PB 502, etc.) and searching for transgressive segregants, can be an effective approach for improving both the yield and the quality in wheat. Various steps of such breeding programme may be as follows :

1. Hybridization between high protein lines and high yielding and disease resistant varieties;
2. Visual single plant selection in segregating generations for yield components and disease resistance (i.e. pedigree selection);
3. Evaluation of advanced lines harvested as bulk in F_5 or F_6 generations for quality; and further testing for yield and disease resistance in replicated station yield trials;
4. Evaluation of superior lines in National Initial Varietal Trials (NIVTs) for judging their yield potential, disease resistance (rusts, Karnal bunt, etc.) and quality traits (protein content, sedimentation value, hectolitre weight, etc.).

CHAPTER 11

Biometrical Genetics and Wheat Breeding

Common wheat (*Triticum aestivum*) is a segmental hexaploid species possessing three genomes, A, B and D, but it behaves like a diploid species since chromosome pairing during meiosis is restricted to the homologus chromosomes only, that is, there is no intergenome chromosome pairing. The chromosomes of the three genomes are homeologous (that is, partly homologous and partly non-homologous) and thus have some corresponding genetic regions or loci. This situation provides a unique opportunity that there is homozygosity within genome but heterozygosity between genomes if different types of alleles are present on the corresponding loci of the different genomes, that is, heterozygosity between genomes is fixed. Such heterosis which occurs due to the interaction between genomes has been named as *homozygous genomic heterosis*, that is, heterozygosity in homozygous condition and allows exploitation of non-additive component of genetic variation by homozygous varieties of a highly self-fertilizing crop species. The occurrence of homogygous genomic heterosis helps in increasing and stabilizing yield potential in wheat. Therefore, one way of increasing and stabilizing yield potential in wheat is to increase the extent of homozygous genomic heterosis. This can be achieved by transferring alien genes to wheat from its wild relatives, especially from *Triticum tauschii*, and thus the magnitude of non-additive genetic variance can be increased. The D genome of *T. tauschii* contains several desirable genes which govern the resistance/tolerance against biotic and abiotic stresses and is thus different from the D genome of wheat in several respects. The change in the magnitude of non-additive genetic variance can be determined by using biometrical genetic methods.

Biometrical Genetic Techniques in Wheat

The use of biometrical genetic procedures may help the wheat breeders in many ways.

Detection and estimation of gene effects: Following two types of biometrical procedures are used to study genetic architecture of plant populations:

1. Methods based on generation means, that is, first degree statistics; and
2. methods based on variances and covariances, that is, second degree statistics.

Both types of methods have been used quite frequently in wheat. Among the procedures based on generation means, scaling tests of Mather (1949), joint scaling test of Cavalli (1952), digenic interaction models of Hayman (1958) and Jinks and Jones (1958) have been mostly used. Whereas scaling tests of Mather simply test the adequacy of additive-dominance model (that is, whether epistasis is present or not), the joint scaling test of Cavalli provides the estimates of gene effects and tests the adequacy of the model if the number of generation means is greater than the number of parameters estimated. The weighted analysis of Cavalli can be extended to consider any number of generation means. The six-parameter models of Hayman and Jinks and Jones are, in fact, perfect fit solution methods and provide estimates of all the six parameters [m, (d), (h), (i), (j) and (l)]. If any of these parameters is non-significant, the weighted analysis can be used to test the adequacy of the degenic interaction model and to obtain relatively more precise estimates of the remaining parameters.

The application of generation means analyses in wheat has indicated that the component characters of yield are governed by both additive and dominance genes. In many cases, there has been predominance of additive gene effects, whereas in several other cases, dominance gene effects have been found to play a greater role in the control of these characters. However, presence of significant epistatic effects has been quite frequently found for grain yield.

Detection and estimation of components of variance : The methods like diallel, line × tester and triple test cross (based on second degree statistics) are used to detect and estimate different components of variance. Huge literature is available on the application of diallel method in wheat populations. The component analysis of Hayman (1954b) and combining ability analysis of Griffing (1956) have been most frequently and extensively used to investigate wheat research materials. The results obtained through the use of component analysis indicate that in a large number of cases, additive genetic variance was more important than dominance variance and, similarly, in many other cases dominance component was relatively more important. There are also reports where both these components were qually important. The use of combining ability analysis, however, has provided very useful information about the combining ability of parents and potential hybrids. But, the results of the diallel analysis will be reliable only when the material under investigation satisfies the two most critical and unrealistic assumptions of diallel analysis, the absence of epistasis and absence of gene correlation. Methods (consistency of Wr-Vr over arrays and joint regression analysis) are available in the literature (Mather and Jinks, 1982; Singh and Pawar, 2005) to test these assumptions.

Another important method which is now being used quite frequently to investigate wheat populations is triple test cross method. This method has several advantages (provides unambiguous detection of epistasis, partitioning of epistasis and its interaction with environment, gives unbiased estimates of additive and dominance component of variance if epistasis is absent, provides detection and estimation of genotype × environment interaction and the method is independent of gene frequency, gene correlation and the mating system) over other multiple mating designs. Many investigators (Ketata *et al.*, 1976; Singh and Singh, 1976, 1978; Singh, 1980, 1990; Singh and Dahiya, 1984; Singh *et al.*, 1993; and many others) have applied triple test cross analysis in wheat. According to Singh and Pawar (1998), the results obtained through the use of this analysis in wheat may be generalized as follows:

1. Additive genetic variance plays a predominant role in the control of quantitative characters in wheat.

2. Additive component shows greater sensitivity to fluctuations in environment than dominance component.
3. Presence of epistasis for grain yield has been indicated by almost all studies.

Choice of parents : Choice of parents for hybridization is the most important and fundamental step of any breeding programme since the success or failure of a breeding programme would depend upon the type of parents selected for hybridization. Selection of parents on the basis of their *per se* performance may not give a correct picture of the real worth of the lines in hybrid combinations. This problem can be solved by testing the combining ability of parents before their use in the crossing programme. Biometrical methods like diallel and line × tester may be used for testing the combining ability of parents and their hybrids at an early stage of the programme. There are numerous reports where significant differences have been found between the *per se* performance and combining ability of parents. Manytimes, apparently good varieties/ lines do not click well in hybrid combinations. For example, Indian tall wheat variety C 306, well known for its superior grain characteristics, is not a good general combiner. In the same way, sometimes, poor looking parents produce highly desirable hybrids.

Improving genetic pattern of wheat populations : Biometrical genetics may greatly help in fulfilling the basic objective of wheat breeding programmes, that is, the genetic pattern of wheat populations may be improved by identifying and using best possible parents during crossing programme and exploiting different components of variance to the maximum possible extent.

Determining character association : The study of correlations between different characters is very important for the wheat breeders. Like in many other crops, grain yield in wheat is a complex character and is determined by several component traits like tiller number, spike length, number of spikelets per spike, number of grains per spike and 1000-grain weight. Each component trait is usually directly and positively correlated with grain yield. But, some component traits are found negatively correlated. For example, number of grains per spike and 1000 grain weight are mostly negatively correlated, that is, there is no possibility for simultaneous improvement for both the traits.

Whereas positive correlation between two desirable characters is favourable for the plant breeder, a negative correlation between two desirable attributes creates problems for the breeder. However, breaking of undesirable correlations may help in improving grain yield potential in wheat.

Further, through the use of path coefficient analysis, it is possible to know whether a correlation between two characters explains the true relationship between the characters or not. For example, a component trait may be significantly correlated with yield but it may not have a high direct effect on grain yield. It means the correlation between grain yield and the component trait does not explain the true relationship between the two characters and, in such situation, a direct selection through that component trait will not be effective.

Nevertheless, correlation based on breeding values is more reliable and thus more important for the plant breeder. Breeding values are determined by additive gene effects which are fixable and thus can be easily exploited. Fortunately, additive gene effects play an important role in the control of quantitative characters of wheat, especially the component traits of grain yield.

Quantifying genetic parameters : Heritability and genetic advance are two important genetic parameters in the hands of the plant breeder. These parameters help in deciding selection procedures to be followed to improve plant characteristics. However, heritability in narrow sense which is the proportion of additive genetic variance to the phenotypic variance is more important for the plant breeder than heritability in broad sense (the ratio of total genetic variance to phenotypic variance). Higher the percentage of narrow sense heritability, more are the chances of improvement in that character since additive gene effects are fixable and thus can be exploited more easily in self-fertilizing crop species like wheat. In wheat, grain yield usually has low to medium heritability, whereas most of its component traits have medium to high heritabilities. Therefore, many wheat breeders are of the opinion that to improve grain yield potential in this crop, no direct selection for yield should be made rather grain yield should be improved by making indirect selection for this complex trait (grain yield) through its component characters. Of course, some wheat breeders still feel that direct selection for grain yield in wheat is effective. However, it is now unequivocally accepted by the wheat breeders all over the world that additive gene effects play a major role in governing the component characters of grain yield in wheat.

The role of non-additive genetic variance in the control of quantitative characters in wheat cannot be denied. The inter-genome heterozygosity (that is, homozygous genomic heterosis) in common wheat contributes towards non-additive genetic variance but this non-additive component is fixable. The presence of homogyzous genomic heterosis in wheat is one of the main reasons of low heterosis in this cereal.

Sometimes, there is absence of a high correspondence between the values of heritability and those of genetic advance because of the difference in the magnitude of phenotypic standard deviation. As a result, a character having high heritability may not show high genetic gain under selection if the value of phenotypic standard deviation is low. Similarly, there is possibility of high genetic gain even if the character is associated with moderate heritability. Therefore, genetic advance is considered as a more important parameter than heritability.

Enhacing efficiency of selection procedures : The use of biometrical procedures may help the wheat breders in their decision making regarding the choice of an efficient selection procedure which can capitalize on all kinds of gene effects. The application of a superior selection method would help in exploring the limits of selection to a greater extent, minimizing the risk of loosing desirable genotypes during the breeding programme and deciding the dimensions of the different steps of a breeding method.

Knowing the cause of heterosis : In addition to the contribution of homozygous genomic heterosis in wheat, it is important to know that which one of the two major mechanisms (dominance and overdominance) is making relatively higher contribution towards heterosis in this crop species. Such an effort has been successfully made in *Nicotiana rustica* by the scientists (Jayasekara and Jinks, 1976; Pooni and Jinks, 1981; Jinks, 1983; Jinks and Pooni, 1986) at Birmingham School (U.K.) who came to the conclusion that the accumulation of favourable dominant genes dispersed in the two parents rather than overdominance, was the major cause of positive heterosis for plant height in this species. A similar situation has been found in maize (Sprague, 1983). Similar efforts can be made in wheat. There are numerous reports (Singh and Singh, 1976, 1978; Singh 1980, 1990; Singh *et al.*, 1992; and many others) that additive gene effects play a major role in governing quantitative characters in wheat. It means overdominance and unfixable epistasis (additive × dominance and dominance × dominance interactions) have only a minor role in the control of quantitative characters in wheat.

Predicting effect of environment on the magnitude of heterosis : Change in environmental conditions not only affects grain yield and other plant characters, but it also influences the extent of heterosis.

The effect of environmental change on the extent of heterosis can be predicted on the basis of the relative magnitudes of the interaction of additive gene effects with environment and of dominance gene effects with environment (Bucio-Alanis et al., 1969; Mather and Jinks, 1982; Singh and Pawar, 2005). If the magnitude of the interaction between dominance gene effects and environments is greater than the value of the interaction between additive gene effects and environments, the extent of heterosis is expected to increase with an improvement in the environment, that is, the heterosis should be maximum in the best environment. But, if the situation is reverse (the magnitude of additive gene effects × environments interaction is greater than that of the interaction between dominance gene effects and environments), the degree of heterosis is expected to decrease with an improvement in the environment, that is, the heterosis should be maximum in the poorest environment. However, if the linear sensitivity of the two types of gene effects to environments is equal, the magnitude of heterosis should remain constant over environments. The results of several studies carried out in wheat clearly indicate that the dominance gene effects are less sensitive to environmental change than the additive gene effects (Singh, 1980, 1990; Singh and Dahiya, 1984; Dhindsa and Bains, 1986; Pawar et al., 1994, 1996 and others).

Evaluating phenotypic stability of genotypes : In general, genotype × environment interaction has a considerable effect on the performance of genotypes. However, some genotypes show a significantly higher phenotypic stability over a range of environmental conditions than other genotypes. But, according to the plant breeder, an ideal genotype should possess three characteristics: (1) High mean value for the character; (2) good response to improved environment (that is, unit regression) and (3) least deviation from regression. Several genetical and statistical procedures have been suggested and described by different investigators (Mather and Jones, 1958; Jones and Mather, 1958; Bucio-Alanis, 1966; Bucio-Alanis and Hill, 1966; Bucio-Alanis et al., 1969; Finlay and Wilkinson, 1963; Eberhart and Russell, 1966; Perkins and Jinks, 1968; Freeman and Perkins, 1971; and others) to study genotype × environment interaction and identify stable genotypes. In addition to parameteric methods, non-parameteric methods to measure phenotypic stability have also been suggested (Huhn, 1979; Nassar and Huhn, 1987).

Huge literature is available on the application of stability analyses in wheat materials. However, to identify genotypes stable over a range of environments is not the sole objective of the breeder, but identification of genotypes performing extremely well in a particular area is also important. Identification of such genotypes would help in encouraging area-specific research and maintaining more genetic variability.

Measuring genetic divergence : It is not possible for the plant breeder to include all the potential genotypes in the hybridization programme. The extent of genetic diversity among the available parents is one of the important criteria for selecting genotypes for hybridization since genetically diverse parents are expected to produce promising progeny. Therefore, before finalizing the inclusion of genotypes in the crossing programme, it is imperative to have complete information about the genetic diversity among the available genotypes.

Several analyses (D^2 analysis, canonical analysis, metroglyph analysis, etc.) have been suggested to measure the spectrum of genetic divergence in plant populations. However, D^2 analysis has been and is being used most frequently for this purpose. This analysis allows categorization of genotypes into different clusters. Crosses between genotypes belonging to diverse clusters are expected to produce desirable progeny.

Categorizing environments according to regional and temporal variations : Sometimes, the number of relationships among different variables becomes unmanageably large and the systematic summarization, description and interpretation of the results become extremely difficult. Principal component analysis (PCA) which is a data reduction technique and facilititates transformation of multicorrelated variables into another set of uncorrelated variables and selection of a few of them according to the interest of the investigator, can be used to reduce the number of variables for exploring variance or to detect or describe redundancy in the data. This analysis can also be used to obtain detailed information about the data.

Application of principal component analysis to the data of ten wheat varieties for four quantitative traits (spike length, tiller number, grain number and grain yield) indicated that the first principal component accounted for about 85 per cent of the total variance in the four measurements. The character grain yield was the most important among the four characters followed by grain number (Singh and Pawar, 2005).

The application of principal component analysis in wheat has helped the wheat scientists to assess regional and temporal variation in yield in different parts of western Australia and identify areas for growing bulk of wheat crop for maximizing yield of this important cereal in that country (Goodchild and Boyd, 1975). Therefore, the use of principal component analysis is not restricted to the identification of the principal components which take care of the maximum variance present in the data to be analysed, but this analysis also helps in categorizing the environments to carry out area-specific research.

Role of Additive Genetic Variation

Additive genetic variation is the main and basic type of variation and reflects differences among different true-breeding lines. It is a fixable part of the genetic variation and thus has a special significance in plant breeding programmes. This type of variation is fixable since the coefficient of additive genetic component (D) remains constant from generation to generation (F_2, F_3, F_4 etc.) and, therefore, can be easily exploited. The relative magnitude of D component in plant populations helps in choosing a suitable selection procedure. Since heritability in narrow sense is the proportion of additive genetic variance to the phenotypic variance, higher the relative magnitude of D component, higher would be narrow sense heritability and more would be the chances of improvement. If the relative amount of additive genetic variance is high, simple selection procedures can be used to improve the character.

As mentioned earlier, additive gene effects play a major role in controlling quantitative characters in wheat, especially the component characters of grain yield. However, because of the presence of inter-genome heterozygosity, non-additive component of genetic variation also plays an important role in governing quantitative characters in wheat.

Role of Dominance Variation

Dominance is also known as intra-allelic interaction, that is, the interaction between the alleles of the same locus. The variation arising due to such interaction is unfixable since the coefficient of the dominance component (H) of genetic variation is quartered after every selfed generation.

In wheat, dominance variation is of two types : (1) Inter-genome dominance variation; and (2) intra-genome dominance variation. Inter-genome dominance component is exploitable by developing homozygous varieties and is as good as the additive genetic component. However, intra-genome dominance component can be exploited only by developing heterozygous or hybrid varieties of wheat.

Since the development of hybrid wheat varieties has not so far been successful at commercial scale, the best way to increase the magnitude of dominance variation in this cereal is to increase the magnitude of homozygous genomic heterosis.

Role of Epistatic Variation

Epistasis is the interaction between the alleles of two or more different loci and is also known as *non-allelic* or *interallelic interaction*. Epistasis can be divided into three components: (1) Additive × additive or homozygote × homozygote interaction; (2) additive × dominance or homozygote × heterozygote interaction; and (3) dominance × dominance or heterozygote × heterozygote interaction. The first component (additive × additive epistasis) is fixable since its coefficient, like that of additive genetic component, remains constant from generation to generation. But the two other components (additive×dominance and dominance × dominance types of epistasis) are unfixable since dominacne is involved in both these components.

However, the maximum advantage of all three types of gene effects (additive, dominance and epistatic) should be taken in wheat by evolving heterozygous (hybrid) varieties.

CHAPTER 12

Wheat Breeding in India

India is one of the major wheat growing countries and is second largest producer of wheat, after China, in the world. Wheat has a glorious history in India, especially after 1965. The success achieved towards increase in wheat production and productivity during the last about four decades in India is unprecedented and unparalleled in the history of any country of the world. The cultivation of semi-dwarf wheat varieties made a significant contribution towards *green revolution* (the term given by William Gaud in 1968) and, as a result, wheat production in India increased more than six fold after 1965 (from 12.3 million tonnes in 1965 to 76.4 million tonnes in the year 1999-2000) due to the increase in productivity (over three times) as well as in area (about two times). This spectacular increase in wheat production is the result of collaborative efforts made by the scientists belonging to different disciplines.

In India, three types of wheats, namely, *Triticum aestivum* (common wheat or bread wheat), *T. durum* (durum wheat or macaroni wheat) and *T. dicoccum* (dicoccum wheat or emmer wheat), are grown. Of these three types, *T. aestivum* occupies largest area (about 90 per cent). Second in order is *T. durum* which occupies about 8 per cent area and is mainly grown in central and peninsular India. *T. dicoccum* occupies only about 2 per cent of wheat area and its cultivation is restricted to Maharastra and Karnataka only. Except some small isolated pockets in northern hills of the country where some winter wheat is grown, only spring wheat is grown in India. Durum wheat is mainly grown in rainfed areas with moisture stress since this wheat is relatively more drought tolerant.

In India, wheat is grown on about 27.4 million hectares under diverse agroclimatic conditions (in plains, river valleys and hills; on different types of soils ranging from shallow to deep, light to heavy, etc.; in well irrigated to rainfed areas; under low input to high input levels; under varying temperature condtions; etc.). Howard had rightly said that "wheat production in India is a gamble with temperature" (Rao, 2001). The major wheat growing states of the country are Uttar Pradesh, Madhya Pradesh, Punjab, Rajasthan, Haryana and Bihar.

Introduction of Wheat in India

According to Vavilov (1926), the fold between Himalaya and Hindu Kush mountains (the north-western corner of the Indian subcontinent) is the secondary centre of origin of bread wheat (*T. aestivum*). From this place and from Afghanistan, wheat migrated towards east. From Afghanistan, it might have migrated to the plains of Punjab and the basin of Ganga and Yamuna through Khyber pass and gradually became human staple food. Around 2500 B.C., *T. sphaerococcum* (dwarf wheat) might have originated as a spontaneous mutant in the north-western region of the Indian subcontinent or in Afghanistan (Zevan, 1978, 1980).

During archaeological excavations in many parts of India (Harappa in Punjab, Mohanja-daro and Chanhu-daro in the Sindh Valley, Sonegaon, Inamgaon and Ter in Maharastra, Chalcolithic sites and Kayatha culture in Madhya Pradesh and Atranjikhera site in Uttar Pradesh), carbonized wheat grains were recovered (Rao, 2001). The period of these excavations ranged from 3500-50 B.C. According to Vishnu-Mittre (1974), such grains from some sites had resemblance to the grains of *T. sphaerococcum*. This resemblance between grains indicated that *T. sphaerococcum* was probably the wheat of ancient India. This wheat was under cultivation in a large part of northern India and its cultivation continued in some parts of Punjab till early 1940s. However, according to Kulshrestha (1985), *T. sphacrococcum* is no more under cultivation in India.

Archaeological excavations clearly indicated that wheat was probably the major food of the inhabitants of these areas. But there is no mention of wheat in *Rigved* which means that wheat was not the staple food of *Aryans*. Therefore, it seems logical that the art of wheat cultivation and the taste of this cereal perished with old cultures but once again wheat became a part of the human diet after about 1500 years when *Yajurved* was being compiled (1500-800 B.C.). However, wheat probably could not become a major part of human diet until about twelfth century A.D. since this cereal till the end of eleventh century A.D. was considered as an inferior food grain used by condemned people. However, according to Randhawa (1980), there is mention of wheat in Vishnudharmottara (9-11 century A.D.) as one of the five common grains. But in Kulshrestha's (1985) opinion, wheat became a major food grain in the 12th century A.D. only.

Scientific Wheat Breeding in India

Although there are some sporadic reports that wheat breeding work was being done in some parts of the country (Kanpur, Nagpur, etc.) during the last quarter of the nineteenth century (Howard and Howard, 1910), but the foundation of scientific wheat breeding in India was laid by Albert Howard and Gabriella Howard in 1906 at the Imperial Agricultural Research Institute, Pusa (Bihar). This institute is now known as Indian Agricultural Research Institute and is located at New Delhi.

Prior to the beginning of systematic wheat breeding work in the country, the wheat crop, in general, consisted of a mixture of different varieties. These mixtures of varieties were called as *sorts* and were classified on the basis of grain colour (amber or red) and grain texture (soft or hard). Some prominent sorts were known as *Sharbati* (with uniform amber grains, hard grain texture and with high chapati making quality; was also known as choice wheat), *Chandausi* (from Uttar Pradesh), *Saphed pissi* (with soft white grains and was under cultivation in Madhya Pradesh and eastern Uttar Pradesh), *Lal pissi* (prominantly grown in Uttar Pradesh), *Lal kanak* (with hard red grains and was grown in Punjab) and *Dara* (with un-uniform, small and low quality grains and used by poor people).

Rao (2001) divided the period of wheat improvement work done in India between 1905-1962 into three distinct phases:

Phase I : During this period, Howard and Howard did some very useful work at Pusa (Bihar) and produced several wheat varieties like Pusa 4 or P.4 or I.P.4 or N.P.4, Pusa 6 or P.6 or I.P. 6 or N.P. 6 and Pusa 12 or P.12 or I.P. 12 or N.P. 12 (*The prefix Pusa or P stands for Pusa, Bihar; prefix I.P. stands for Imperial Pusa which was used after the shifting of the institute to New Delhi in 1936 due to the devastating earthquake in 1930; and the prefix N.P. stands for New Pusa used after 1947*) through single plant selections. According to Haward and Howard (1910, 1928), some of the varieties developed by them became so popular that their cultivation was not restricted to India only but they were also grown in other countries like South Africa, Rhodesia and Hungary. For example, the variety Pusa 4 (developed through selection from a local awnless sort, Mundia) was so promising that it won the first prize successively from 1916-1920 in international grain exhibitions as one of the best quality wheats. According to Wenholz *et al.* (1940), its adaptability was so high that, in addition to India, it occupied considerable area in New South Wales, Queensland and Western Australia even until as late as 1939. Around the same time, some good wheat varieties were produced at Kanpur (C 13 or K 13, K 53, etc.), Nagpur (Ao 13, Ao 68, Ao 85, etc.) and at Lyallpur (Type 8, Type 9, Type 11, etc.). Lyallpur is now in Pakistan.

Phase II : This phase consisted of the production of wheat varieties (NP 100, NP 120, NP 165, PbC 518, PbC 591, Ao 115, etc.) in different parts of the country by making crosses between promising pure line varieties developed during phase I. Dr. B.P. Pal, Chaudhary Ramdhan Singh and Dr. B.S. Kadam were some of the pioneer wheat breeders of the phase II period.

Phase III : This phase consisted of the development of varieties by hybridizing Indian wheat varieties with exotic varieties (Thatcher, Chinese White, Federation, Kononso, Democrat, Gabo, Hofed, etc.). During this period, main emphasis was given for the development of disease resistant varieties. The varieties developed during this phase period were varieties of NP 700 and NP 800 series, PbC 228, PbC 253, Hy 65, Arnej 614, etc.

Simultaneously, work on the improvement of durum wheat was also started in 1930s and crosses between Indian durum selections and some exotic varieties (Arabian durum, Gaza, Egypt 8626, etc.) were made. As a result, varieties like Jay and Vijay and N 59 were evolved. According to Deodikar *et al.* (1979), some other tetraploid species were also used for improving durum wheat.

Nevertheless, no real breakthrough in the yield levels of wheat could be brought during this period.

Semidwarf wheat era : The era of semidwarf wheats in India may be considered as a golden chapter in the history of wheat in the country. The development of semidwarf wheat varieties in Mexico by a team of scientists headed by Dr. Norman E. Borlaug using Norin 10 dwarfing genes Rht-B1 (formerly Rht 1) and Rht-D1 (formerly Rht 2) was the beginning of semidwarf wheat era. Indian wheat breeders also got attracted towards this new approach of wheat breeding. As a result, large quantities of two high yielding red grained spring wheat varieties, *Sonora 64* (200 metric tonnes) and *Lerma Rojo* (50 metric tonnes), were introduced in the country during the year 1965 for extensive trials. Again a quantitity of 13000 metric tonnes of wheat was imported in 1966 for testing the performance of these varieties at farmers' fields. Although red-grained wheats are not a liking of the people of India and have a low market value here, these red-grained Mexican varieties became popular among the farming community of this country because these varieties gave very high yields as compared to the yields of Indian tall wheats. At that time, the main consideration was quantity rather than quality. Despite very high yield potential of the Mexican varieties, Indian wheat breeders were continuously searching for amber-grained semidwarf wheats. This desire was fulfilled by the release of wheat varieties like *Kalyansona* (timely-sown high yielding variety), *Sonalika* (late-sown variety), *Safed Lerma* and *Chhoti Lerma* in the year 1967. The varieties Kalyansona and Sonalika proved to be wonder wheat varieties in terms of yield potential and adaptability and, therefore, formed the basis of wheat revolution in India. Further, since these varieties had several desirable characteristics (disease resistance, higher fertilizer and irrigation response, photoinsensitivity, etc.) in addition to high yield potential, wheat production technologies in India went under a significant change. As a result, within 10 years, spectacular progress was witnessed at all the three fronts : (1) Increase in wheat production (from 10.4 to 28.3 million tonnes); (2) increase in productivity (from 8.3 to 14.1 quintals per hectare); and (3) increase in area under wheat (12.6 to 20.1 million hectares) as the cultivation of wheat spread to unconventional areas where wheat was never grown (Rao, 2001). The quantum jump in wheat production and productivity acted as catalyst for a great enthusiasm among the wheat scientists of the country. Numerous wheat scientists belonging to the Directorate of Wheat Research (DWR), agricultural institutes and agricultural universities all over the country are actively busy in bringing further improvement in various characteristics of this important cereal.

However, Dr. M.S. Swaminathan (2001) divided the evolution of wheat breeding during the twentieth century into four major phases:

Phase I (1900-1930) : This phase consisted of the *early days of Mendelian genetics*. Since Mendel's laws of inheritance were rediscovered in 1900, the scientists were able to give the genetic basis of their research findings. For example, systematic efforts were made to study the inheritance of the resistance to the three rusts (stem, leaf and stripe) of wheat. Simultaneously, scientists started to exploit the naturally occurring genetic variability present in the wheat germplasm. The most popular wheat variety NP 4 (the best quality wheat) of its time was evolved through simple selection. Soon after, the use of land races in hybridization also began. Some of the important wheat land races were *Indian G, Hard Red Calcutta* and *Etawah* (from India), *Alfredo Chaves* and *Polyssu* (from Brazil), *Daruma* (probably originated in Korea and a source of dwarfing genes), *Yaroslav Emmer* (from USSR), Turkey (from Turkey), Fife (from Poland), Rieti (from Italy) and *Zeeuwse White* (from Netherlands) (Swaminathan, 2001). The land races which have been facing the consequences of natural selection since immemorial times, can still be used to transfer specific desirable characteristics to the modern wheat varieties. During the period of phase I, more emphasis was on the resistance to wheat rusts and the improvement in the grain quality.

Phase II (1930-1960) : Dr. Swaminathan called this phase as *enlarging the base of theory and its application*. The testing for resistance to rusts and other wheat diseases continued in this period also for meeting the challenge of physiologic specialization in pathogens. Other characteristics of this phase of wheat improvement were the use of cytogenetic knowledge and tools in wheat improvement, widening the gene pool used by wheat breeders, incorporation of dwarfing genes in wheat genotypes and use of shuttle breeding system developed by Borlaug. The genes responsible for the semidwarf plant genotype were identified and incorporated in wheat genotypes. Development of Norin 10 semidwarf wheat by Japanese scientists using Daruma as the donor of the semidwarf character, was the first breakthrough in this direction. Semidwarf wheats were used by Vogel (late 1950s) to develop winter wheat variety *Gaines* and by Borlaug to develop semidwarf spring wheat. Shuttle breeding system and international testing nurseries were used for selecting photoinsensitive genotypes, increasing spectrum of resistance to stem rust and for reducing the time required to develop a new variety.

Phase III (1960-1980) : This phase may also be called as *green revolution phase* or *green revolution era*. During this period, spectacular increases in wheat production and productivity were achieved in several developing countries, especially in India and Pakistan. In addition to improvement in productivity, emphasis was also given on the stability of yield potential. Genes for slow rusting were identified and used in wheat breeding programmes. CIMMYT played a major role in developing genotypes with durable resistance. Alien gene transfers also played an important role in improving stability and widening adaptation of wheat genotypes. For example, 1BL/1RS translocation not only carries important resistance genes (Sr. 31, Lr 26, Yr 9 and Pm 8) but has also proved as a major factor for wide adaptation. This translocation has been and is being exploited extensively by Indian wheat breeders. It is present in many modern Indian wheat varieties. Crosses between wheat and *Triticum tauschii* have also given valuable results. During phase III, there was remarkable progress in interdisciplinary and international collaboration. CIMMYT may be credited for spreading diverse genetic material through international screening nurseries and trials (Rajaram and Hettel, 1994). Probably the use of CIMMYT wheat material in India was firstly made in 1962 when a few dwarf wheat strains were raised on the farm of Indian Agricultural Research Institute, New Delhi (Swaminathan, 2001). In 1963, Borlaug sent a wide range of semidwarf material after his visit to India. A national demonstration programme was started at farmers' fields in 1964 to verify the findings of the research experiments. As mentioned earlier, large quantities of hard red-grained Mexican varieties were imported in the country in 1965 and 1966. In 1967, amber-grained varieties like Kalyansona, Sonalika, Safed Lerma and Chhoti Lerma were released which, in fact, formed the basis of wheat revolution in India. Indian wheat breeders continued their efforts towards evolving new high yielding varieties like HD 2009 (Arjun), WH 147 and WL 711 which were released in 1975. These varieties were later on replaced by the variety HD 2329 (released in 1985) having greater adaptability.

Phase IV (1980-2000) : Dr. Swaminathan called this phase as the period of *transition from Mendelian to molecular breeding*. According to him, the use of sophisticated approaches to wheat breeding has played an important role during these 20 years. As a result, hybrid wheat is expected to become a commercial proposition in the near future. According to Khush and Baenziger (1998), the use of wild relatives in genetic engineering is increasing day by day. The book "*Wheat : Ecology and Physiology of Yield Determination*" edited by E.H. Satorre and G.A.Slafer (1999) contain valuable information about some critical issues in yield improvement in wheat. The progress made in the areas of functional genomics and molecular manipulation is expected to influence the future trends in wheat breeding (Briggs, 1998; McCouch, 1998). The identification of many quantitative trait loci (QTLs) may greatly help in accelerating the pace of breeding for yield in wheat.

However, a large number of wheat varieties namely, HD2329, HD2380, HD2643, HD2687, etc. by I.A.R.I., New Delhi; CPAN 3004 by DWR, Karnal; WH 283, WH 542, WH 896, etc. by CCS HAU, Hisar; PBW 154, PBW 175, PBW 226, PBW 299, PBW 343, PBW 373 etc. by PAU, Ludhiana; RAJ 3077, RAJ 3765, etc. by RAU Regional station, Durgapura; UP 2338, UP 2425 etc. by GBPUAT, Pantnagar and many other varieties by several other research centres, were developed and released during the phase IV period.

Role of All India Coordinated Wheat Improvement Project

Before 1961, wheat improvement work in India was mainly restricted to isolated work done by wheat breeders of different states. In the year 1961, a Cooperative Research Programme was initiated to promote interaction among breeders of different research centres of the country. In 1965, the same programme was converted into All India Coordinated Wheat Improvement Project (AICWIP) under the auspices of the Indian Counil of Agricultural Research (ICAR) to coordinate the wheat research activities on all India basis and to have more interaction among the scientists of different disciplines. It was just a coincidence that large quantities of Mexican varieties Sonora 64 and Lerma Rojo were imported in the country in the same year. AICWIP was given the status of Directorate of Wheat Research (DWR) in the year 1978 with its headquarters at New Delhi. In 1990, DWR was shifted to Karnal (Haryana). Based on the agroclimatic conditions prevailing in wheat growing areas and disease spectrum, the country has been divided into following six wheat zones (mega-environments):

1. **Northern Hill Zone (NHZ):** It includes hills of Jammu and Kashmir, Himachal Pradesh and Uttaranchal states.
2. **North Western Plains Zone (NWPZ) or Wheat Bowl of India:** Punjab, Haryana, Delhi, Western Uttar Pradesh and major part of Rajasthan come under this zone.
3. **North Eastern Plains Zone (NEPZ):** This zone includes Eastern Uttar Pradesh, Bihar, Jharkhand, Orissa, West Bengal, Assam and other North-Estern states.
4. **Central Zone (CZ):** It incudes Madhya Pradesh, Chhattisgarh, Gujarat states and small parts of Uttar Pradesh (Bundelkhand region) and Rajasthan (Kota and Udaipur).
5. **Peninsular zone (PZ):** Maharastra, Andhra Pradesh, Karnataka and plains of Tamil Nadu states come under this zone.
6. **Southern Hill Zone (SHZ):** Only hills of Tamil Nadu and Kerala states come under this zone.

However, the two most important zones which account for about 80 per cent of the total wheat area in India, are NWPZ and NEPZ and, therefore, the wheat production in the country is mainly dictated by the wheat production in these two zones. Of course, the two zones are considerably different in terms of agroclimatic and socio-economic conditions and also for the productivity of wheat. The realized wheat yields (less than 30 q/ha) of NEPZ are considerably lower than the potential yields and, therefore, this zone has attracted the attention of the wheat scientists.

Taking into consideration the cultural practices and the requirements of different mega-environments, three types of the production conditions have been identified to evolve varieties: (i) Irrigated timely sown; (ii) irrigated late sown; and (iii) rainfed timely sown. Twentynine centres are presently functioning under the directorate. The programme is assisted by 30 additional voluntary centres for conducting various experiments on different aspects related to breeding, pathology and agronomy. In addition, special trials are conducted under various conditions (salinity/alkalinity, high altitudes and very late conditions) to meet specific needs. Some other activities of the Indian wheat improvement programme are:

1. Growing National Genetic Stock Nursery (NGSN) for providing facility to wheat breeders of the country in their hybridization programme.
2. Planting special nurseries (Yield Component Screening Nursery, Quality Component Screening Nursery, Salinity/Alkalinity Screening Nursery, Drought and Heat Tolerance Screening Nursery, etc.) to identify desirable genotypes.
3. Planting summer nurseries at Lahaul Spiti (Himachal Pradesh) and Wellington (Tamil Nadu) for advancing generations, testing material for biotic stresses and screening material for photoinsensitivity.

4. Using shuttle breeding system for solving regional problems.

A large number of varieties (more than 300) have so far been released under the programme (Kundu *et al.*, 2005). Wheat scientists working in agricultural institutes (like I.A.R.I., New Delhi), DWR, Karnal and agricultural universities (like CCS HAU, Hisar; PAU, Lodhiana and Govind Ballabh Pant University of Agriculture and Technology, Pantnagar; CSA University, Kanpur and RAU Durgapura) all over the country are playing an important role in developing improved varieties. A list of wheat varieties currently grown in different agroclimatic zones of the country is given in Table 12.1 and source, pedigree, year of release and characteristic features of important wheat varieties grown in different wheat growing zones of the country are given in Table 12.2.

Table 12.1. Wheat varieties currently grown in different agro-climatic zones of the country

Zone	Growing conditions		
	Irrigated, timely sown	Irrigated, late sown	Rainfed, timely sown
North Western Plain Zone (NWPZ)	HD 2329, HD 2687, PBW 343, PBW 502, WH 896(D), UP 2338, WH 542, WH 912(D), WH 711, WH 283, PDW 291, WH 147 (Limited irrigation), PDW 233, Raj 3077	DBW 16, HD 2285 PBW 373, Raj 3765 UP 2425, WH 291	C 306, PBW 175 PBW 396, PBW 527
North Eastern Plain Zone (NEPZ)	HD 2733, HD 2824 HUW 468, K 9107 PBW 343	DBW 14, HUW 234 PBW 524, NW 1014 NW 2036	C 306, HUW 533 K 8027, MACS 6145, HD 2888
Central Zone (CZ)	GW 273, GW 322 HI 1077, HI 8498(D) Lok 1, WH 147	DL 788-2, GW 173, HD 2864, Lok 1 MP 4010	HI 1500, HW 2004 HI 1531 Lok 1, A-9-30-1(D) HD 4672(D), HI 8627(D)
Peninsular Zone (PZ)	DWR 162, HD 2189 Raj 4037	HI 977, NIAW 34 UP 2565	NI 5439 Bijaga Yellow (D) MACS 1967(D)

Contd.

Zone	Irrigated, Timely sown	Restricted irrigated, late sown	Rainfed Timely sown High altitude	Rainfed Early sown	Rainfed very high altitude regions, summer
Northern Hills Zone (NHZ)	HS 240, VL 738 VL 804	HS 295, HS 420 Sonalika	HS 365, HPW 42 SKW 196, Sonalika, VL 832	HS 277 VL 616 VL 829	HS 375 Sonalika
Southern Hills Zone (SHZ)	Restricted irrigated Timely sown HW 1085, HW2044 HW5001				
All Zones	Timely sown, irrigated alkalinity/salinity Kharchia65, KRL1-4, KRL-19, WH157				

Table 12.2. Source, pedigree, year of release and characteristics features of important wheat varieties grown in different wheat growing zones of the country

Variety	Source	Pedigree	Year of release	Characteristic features
C 306	CCS HAU Hisar	RGN/CSK3//2*C591/3/C217/N14//C281	1965	Tall variety of medium late maturity, released for timely sown, low fertility, rainfed condition of NWPZ and NEPZ, semi-erect with light green foliage, white parallel years with short awn, grains amber, hard, lustrous, attractive, medium with oblong shape, very good for chapati making with chapati score 8.4, sedimentation value 44 ml and protein content 10-11%
WH 147	CCS HAU Hisar	E4870/C286/C273/4/S339/PV18	1975 (Haryana) 1978	Double dwarf wheat variety of medium maturity, broad and erect leaves of light green shade, ears clavate, grains amber, hard,

Contd.

Variety	Source	Pedigree	Year of release	Characteristic features
			(Central Zone)	medium, semi-lustrous, slow ruster for brown rust, very good for chapati making, protein content 10-11%
WH 283	CCS HAU Hisar	HD 1981/Raj821	1983	Semi-dwarf variety of medium early maturity, early in heading, dark green drooping leaves, bottom leaves have tendency of yellowing, white tapering ears, smooth glumes fully awned, grains amber, bold, hard, shining, attractive, high flour recovery (74.8%), protein content >12%, very good for chapati and bread making
WH 157	CCS HAU Hisar	NP876/S308// CNO/8156	1978 (Haryana) 1989 (All zones)	Double dwarf variety of medium early maturity, dark green foliage, older leaves show a tendency of tip drying, resistant to lodging, white tapering ears, glumes with slight hairiness, fully awned, grains amber, hard, bold, tolerant to soil salinity/alkalinity conditions of all zones
WH 542	CCS HAU Hisar	JUPATCO/ BLUEJA// URES	1992	Semi-dwarf wheat variety of very high yield potential and wider adaptation, high tillering, erect with dark green short narrow leaves, strong straw, white tapering ears with short awn, grains amber, hard, medium, shining, high flour recovery, protein content 11-12%
WH 711	CCS HAU Hisar	ALD'S'/HUAC// HD2285/3/ HFW17	2002	Double dwarf wheat variety of very high yield potential and wider adaptation, high tillering, erect with dark green foliage, white tapering ears with medium awns of creamy colour, grains amber, hard, medium bold, oval shape and shining, protein content 12%
WH 896	CCS HAU Hisar	STIL'S'/YAV'S'// PEN'S'	1995	Semi-dwarf durum wheat variety of slightly late maturity, semi-erect with dark green foliage, resistant to lodging and Karnal bunt, parallel ear of white colour with long white

Contd..

Variety	Source	Pedigree	Year of release	Characteristic features
				awns, grains amber, bold, semi-hard with oblong shape, protein content 11-12%
WH 912	CCS HAU Hisar	HUI'S'/YAV'S'// FULI'S'/ALYAR 84	2002	Semi-dwarf durum wheat variety, erect growing with dark green foliage, ears fusiform with brown colour at maturity, awns long and of brown colour, grains amber, hard, bold having elongated shape
PBW 343	PAU, Ludhiana	ND/VG9144// KAL/BB/3/ YCO'S'/4/VEE# 5'S'	1996	Semi-dwarf wheat variety of very high yield potential and wide adaptability, released for timely sown, irrigated conditions of NWPZ, very high tillering ability, erect growing with dark green foliage, having tendency of yellowing during foggy weather condition, resistant to lodging, white tapering ears with smooth glume having medium awns, grains amber, hard and medium bold, protein content 11-12%
PBW 373	PAU, Ludhiana	ND/VG9144// KAL/BB/3/ YCO'S'/4/ VEE#5'S'	1997	Semi-dwarf wheat variety for late sowing, semi-erect growth habit with dark green foliage, tapering white ears, smooth glume with medium awns, grains amber, semi-hard and medium bold
PBW 502	PAU Ludhiana	WH485/PBW343 //RAJ1482	2003	Semi-dwarf wheat variety with high tillering ability, semi-erect growth habit with dark green foliage, tapering white ears, smooth glumes with medium awns, grains amber, medium bold, hard and attractive
UP 2338	GBPUAT Pantnagar	UP368/VL421// UP262	1995	Semi-dwarf wheat variety with erect growth habit with dark green foliage, tapering white ears with short awns, smooth glumes, grains amber, hard and medium bold

Contd..

Variety	Source	Pedigree	Year of release	Characteristic features
UP 2425	GBPUAT Pantnagar	HD2320/ UP2263	1999	Semi-dwarf wheat vareity for late sowings, erect growing, dark green leaves, low heat susceptibility index, grains amber, hard and medium bold, good for chapati making
UP 262	GBPUAT Pantnagar	S308/BJ 66	1978	Double dwarf wheat variety of medium maturity, erect growing habit, tapering white ears of medium length, short white awns, grains amaber, semi-hard, bold, good for chapati and bread making
DL 788-2	IARI, New Delhi	K7537/HD2160/ HD2278//L24/ K4.14	1997	Double dwarf wheat variety for late sowing, waxy plant type, semi-erect with dark green broad leaves, white tapering ears of medium size, grains amber, hard, medium bold and ovate shaped
HD 2329	IARI, New Delhi	HD1962/E4870/ 3/K65/5/SKA/6/ UP262	1985	Double dwarf wheat vareity of medium maturity, erect with dark green foliage, compact plant type, stem turns purple at maturity, brown tapering ears with brown short awns, grains amber, semi-hard, medium bold, ovate shaped and semi-lustrous
HD 2733	IARI New Delhi	ATTILA/3/TUI/ CARC//CHEN/ CHTO/4/ATTILA	2001	Semi-dwarf wheat variety for timely sowns, irrigated conditions of NEPZ, small erect green leaves, grain amber, hard, medium bold, good for chapati and bread making
HD 2687	IARI New Delhi	CPAN2009/ HD2329	1999	Semi-dwarf wheat of medium maturity, erect with dark green foliage, grain amber, hard, medium bold, good for chapati making
Sonalika	IARI New Delhi	1154.388/AN/ 3/YT54/N10B LR	1969	Early maturing, semi-dwarf wheat variety for wider adaptability, suitable for late sowings, grains amaber, semi-hard, bold and attractive

Contd.

Variety	Source	Pedigree	Year of release	Characteristic features
Raj 1482	RAU, Regional Station, Durgapura	NPO-TOB'S'/ 8156/KAL-BB	1983	Double dwarf wheat of medium maturity, grains amber, hard, medium bold, attractive, good for chapati and bread making
Raj 3077	RAU, Regional Station, Durgapura	HD2277/Raj 1482/5/BB/ INIA66'S'/ NAPO	1989	Semi-dwarf wheat of medium-early maturity, erect with dark green foliage, white tapering ears of medium size, white awns of medium size, grains amber, semi-hard, medium bold, oblong shaped, good for chapati and bread making
Raj 3765	RAU, Regional Station, Durgapura	HD2402/ VL639	1996	Semi-dwarf wheat variety for late sowings, erect growth habit, light green foliage, white ears, grains amber, semi-hard, medium bold and ovate shaped
Lok 1	Lok Bharti, Sanosra, Gujrat	S308/ S331	1982	Double dwarf, early maturing, erect growth habit, dark green foliage, white tapering ears with medium awns, grains amber, hard and very bold, very good for chapati making
NI 5439	MPKV, Regional Station NIPHAD	REP80/3* NP710	1973	Tall wheat of medium maturity, erect growth habit, white parallel ears with medium awns, grains amber, hard, medium bold, attractive, very good for chapati making, good early vigour index, high root length, drought tolerant, suitable for rainfed conditions of PZ
DWR 162	UAS, Dharwad	KVZ/BUHO// KAL/BB	1993	Semi-dwarf wheat variety of medium maturity, erect growth habit, waxy plant type, white awns of medium length, grains amber, hard and medium bold
HW 2004	IARI, Regional station, Wellington	C306*7// TR380-14#7/ 3AG14	1997	Semi-dwarf wheat, semi-erect growing, medium maturity, white clavate ears, pubescent glumes, grains amber, hard, medium bold and oblong shaped

Contd.

Variety	Source	Pedigree	Year of release	Characteristic features
HUW 468	BHU, Varanasi	CPAN1962/ TONI//LIRA'S' PRL'S'	1999	Double dwarf variety, suitable for timely sown conditions of NEPZ, erect with dark green foliage, grains amber, hard, bold, attractive, good for chapati making
K 9107	CSAUAT, Kanpur	K8101/K68	1996	Semi-dwarf wheat variety, suitable for timely sown conditions of NEPZ, erect with dark green foliage, grains amber, hard, bold, oblong shaped, very good for chapati making
VL 616	VPKAS, Almora	SKA/P46	1986	Tall wheat of slightly late maturity, erect growing, parallel ears of medium size, awn colour turns brown at maturity, grains amber, semi-hard, medium bold and ovate shaped
GW 173	Gujrat Agri. Univ. Reg. Station, Vijapur	TW275/7/6/ 10/Lok1	1994	Double dwarf vareity for late sowings of CZ conditions, erect growing, narrow leaves of light green shade, grains hard, amber and medium bold
GW 273	Gujrat Agri. Univ. Reg. Station, Vijapur	CPAN2084/ VW205	1998	Semi-dwarf wheat variety, suitable for timely sown irrigated conditions of CZ, waxy plant type, dark green leaves, grains amber, hard lustrous, very bold, good for chapati and bread making
GW 322	Gujrat Agri. Univ. Reg. Station, Vijapur	PBW173/ GW196	2002	Double dwarf wheat variety, suitable for timely sown and irrigated conditions of CZ, waxy leaves, grains amber, semi-hard, lustrous, bold, good for chapati and bread making
DBW 14	DWR, Karnal	Raj3765/ PBW343	2002	Semi-dwarf wheat variety, suitable for late sown irrigated conditions of NEPZ, heat tolerant, erect growing, grains amber, hard and medium bold, good for chapati and bread making

Contd.

Variety	Source	Pedigree	Year of release	Characteristic features
KRL I-4	CSSRI, Karnal	KHARCHIA65/ WL711	1990	Semi-dwarf wheat variety, suitable for timely sown, irrigated, alkalinity/salinity conditions of all zones, erect growing with dark green foliage, waxy plant type, long white tapering ears of medium awn length, grains amber, semi-hard, ovate, medium bold
KRL-19	CSSRI Karnal	PBW225/ KRL1-4	2000	Semi-dwarf wheat variety, suitable for timely sown, irrigated, alkalinity/salinity conditions of all zones, erect, dark green leaves, grains amber, semi-hard and medium bold
JOB 666	RAU, Jobner	K65/HD2009	1996	Semi-dwarf, semi-erect, late maturity, white tapering ears, grains amber, hard, medium bold, tolerant to salinity/alkalinity conditions of all zones
HI 977	I.A.R.I. Regional Station, Indore	GLL/AUST1161. 157/CNO/NO3/ Y50E/3*KAL	1988	Semi-dwarf wheat variety of medium early maturity, erect growing, dark green foliage, brown tapering ears with brown awns and glumes, grains amber, semi-hard, ovate, medium bold, suitable for late sown conditions of PZ, high protein cotnent (14.5%), high SDS value (65 ml) and excellent for bread making
HI 1077	I.A.R.I. Regional Station, Indore	GALLO/AUST- 11-61-157/CNO/ No66/K913	1989	Semi-dwarf wheat variety of medium maturity, semi-erect growing, waxy plant type (leaf sheath, blade, peduncle, ear), brown tapering ears with brown awn and glumes, grains amber, semi-hard, oblong, medium bold, suitable for timely sown conditions of CZ, high protein content, SDS value, good for bread and chapati making
HI 8498	I.A.R.I. Regional Station, Indore	CR'S'-GS'S'/ A-9-30-1// Raj911	1999	Double dwarf, medium early, glabrous, white ears, durum wheat variety suitable for timely sown, irrigated conditions of CZ, grain amber, hard and very bold, high protein and β-carotene

Contd.

Variety	Source	Pedigree	Year of release	Characteristic features
				content, good thermo-tolerance, good for pasta making and for export purpose
DDK 1001	University of Agril. Sciences, Dharwad	Local *diocccum* 4*// Local *dicoccum*/ Raj 1555	1997	Semi-dwarf emmer wheat (*Triticum dicoccum*) [(Schrank.) Schulb.)] for timely sown, irrigated conditions of PZ, erect growing, dark green foliage, medium late maturity, waxy leaf sheath, peduncle, ear, white parallel ears, grains red, hard, elliptical shaped and bold, good for pasta products
DDK 1009	UAS, Dharwad	NP200*4// NP200/ALTAR 84	1998	Semi-dwarf emmer wheat variety for timely sown, irrigated conditions of PZ, grains red, elongated, hard, bold, good for pasta products

New wheat genetic stocks : Under a new scheme, genetic wheat stocks possessing novel and unique plant traits of academic interest and/or economic importance have been registered with National Bureau of Plant Genetic Resources (NBPGR), New Delhi. To facilitate utilization of these genetic stocks by the wheat breeders of the country in their wheat improvement programmes, DWR, Karnal provides the seeds of registered stocks in the form of National Genetic Stock Nursery to different wheat breeding centres. The list of new wheat genetic stocks registered with NBPGR is given in Table 12.3.

Table 12.3. New wheat genetic stocks registered with NBPGR, New Delhi for some unique traits

Genetic stock	Source	Traits
DI-105	CCS HAU, Hisar	Dwarf isogenic line of C591 (Rht3 gene)
DI-9	-do-	Dwarf isogenic line of C306 (Rht1 gene)
SG-15	-do-	Duospiculum spike
SG-22	-do-	Branched spike
SG-8809	-do-	Normal 'gigas' spike with RMTs gene comples
C306M10	-do-	Non-carrier of necrotic allele Ne 1
WH423	-do-	High protein, high bread and chapati score, bold grain
WH595	-do-	Leaf and stripe rust resistant and high protein content

Contd..

Genetic stock	Source	Traits
WH712	-do-	High sedimentation value (63.6 ml)
Hindi 62	DWR, Karnal	Heat and drought tolerant
Kharchia Local	-do-	Salinity and alkalinity tolerant
Halna	-do-	Heat tolerant
Harit (M3)	-do-	Resistant to leaf blight
DBP01-16	-do-	High β-carotene content (10 ppm)
DW1001	-do-	Gamma gliadin 45 for pasta quality, high yield and resistant to Karnal bunt
Giant-3	-do-	High grains/spike, spikelets/spike, spike length, high grain filling period
FLW-2	DWR, Reg. Station Flowerdale, Shimla	Resistant to black and brown rusts (Lr24 + Lr26, Sr24 + Sr31, Yr9)
FLW-3	-do-	Resistant to black and yellow rusts (Lr26, Sr31, Yl9)
FLW-4	-do-	Resistant to black and brown rusts (Lr24, Lr26, Sr2, Sr24, Sr31, Yr9)
FLW-5	-do-	Resistant to black and brown rusts (Lr24, Lr26, Sr2, Sr24, Sr31, Yr9)
FLW-6	-do-	Resistant to brown and black rusts (Lr19, Lr24, Sr2, Sr24)
FLW-8	-do-	Resistant to brown and black rusts
Pusa 5-3	IARI, New Delhi	High protein and lysine
HD-29	-do-	Karnal bunt resistant
HD-30	-do-	-do-
RD-20 (Durum)	-do-	High protein and grain weight
ISD-215	-do-	Superior over amber grained Sonalika
PUSA-T-3336	-do-	Leaf blight resistant
HW-2002	IARI, Reg. Station Wellington	Resistant to brown and black rusts (Lr 24 & Sr 24)
HW-2031	-do-	Resistant to brown rust (Lr28)
HW-2049	-do-	Resistant to brown and black rusts (Lr19 & Sr25)
KRL-35	CSSRI, Karnal	Salinity/alkalinity and water logging tolerance
KBRL-10	PAU, Ludhiana	Karnal bunt resistant
KBRL-13	-do-	-do-
KBRL-22	-do-	-do-
ML 1194	-do-	Resistant to loose smut, Karnal bunt, brown and yellow rusts
WL 3093	-do-	-do-
WL 3203	-do-	-do-
WL 3526	-do-	-do-
WL 5634	-do-	-do-
AKAW2862-1	PDKV, Akola	Early and late heat tolerant

Problems and Objectives

Wheat-breeding problems in India may be summarized as follows :

1. After the exploitation of dwarfing genes and other desirable alien genes (through translocations like 1B/1R and other means) and the use of good management practices (fertilizer, irrigation, etc.), it is becoming increasingly difficult to evolve varieties which have a considerable superiority in yield potential over the modern high yielding wheat varieties like PBW 343, PBW 502 and WH 542.
2. The human population in India is still increasing with an alarming rate. Since wheat is the chief food crop of the country, its production has a direct effect on the food situation (shortage or surplus) of the country. So, either there should be a check on the population or there should be a proportional increase in wheat production so that population does not overtake food supply. However, to achieve a further jump in wheat productivity is not an easy task.
3. Due to several factors (importance of other crops, increased demand for construction of houses, roads, etc.), the scope of increasing area under wheat is diminishing day by day.
4. The wheat growing areas of the country greatly differ for climatic conditions, soil types, length of the crop season, attack of pathogens, etc.
5. The control of wheat diseases and weeds is becoming complex day by day. Not only the new races of pathogens are coming up, but the weed *Phalaris minor* has become a serious problem in some parts of the country since the weed plant is indistinguishable from the wheat plant before flowering.
6. A large part of the area under wheat in India is rainfed where nature rather than man's effort plays a major role in the success of the crop.
7. Even a well-irrigated and well-fertilized crop may be adversely affected by high temperature at the time of the crop maturity.

However, the objectives of wheat breeding in India, as discussed in Chapter 3, come under the three main categories : (i) Increase in the yield potential, (ii) stabilization of yield levels already achieved; and (iii) improvement in the grain quality. According to Heyne and Smith (1967), there should be a good balance between art and science in wheat breeding. No doubt, the wheat breeder should be well aware about the scientific techniques which can be helpful in bringing improvement in the wheat plant, but his knowledge about the crop and his skill, especially used at the time of visual selection of plants/lines, are also equally important. Since the breeder lives with his crop right from sowing to its harvest, he is able to take an appropriate decision about the performance of a selected line as a variety.

Increase in yield potential : As regards wheat production in India, presently we are in a happy situation as our surplus wheat stocks have reached 35 million tonnes (Nagarajan, 2004). The beginning of minimum support price system by the Government of India in 1970 was a welcome and most positive step towards encouraging farmers of the country to grow more wheat and harvest higher yields by using better management practices. Under this system, the wheat production was to be procured by the Food Corporation of India (FCI) and other wheat purchase agencies to meet the demands of public distribution system.

Grain yield is a complexly inherited character dependent upon several component traits (tiller number, plant height, spike length, number of grains per spike, 1000 grain weight, etc.). Further, though each component character is, in general, positively correlated with grain yield, but some of the component traits are negatively correlated among themselves (e.g., number of grains per spike and 1000-grain weight). Also, grain yield, in general, has low heritability as it is considerably affected by fluctuations in the environment and, therefore, direct selection for this character, manytimes, is not effective.

As mentioned earlier, the wheat growing regions of India show great variations for climatic conditions, soil types, length of crop season, etc. A large part of the area under wheat is dependent on rains. Some regions have reduced irrigation facilities. Late sown wheat which is sown after harvesting late rice or sugarcane (sometimes as late as third week of January), has to face consequences of hot winds at the time of crop maturity. Therefore, to increase wheat yield in India, it is imperative to assess the situation regionwise as well as production-condition-wise (irrigated timely sown, irrigated late sown and rainfed timely sown). For irrigated timely sown condition, all possible efforts should be made to develop hybrid wheat varieties so that maximum advantage of all three kinds of gene effects (additive, dominance and epistatic) and growing coditions (irrigation, fertilizer dose, etc.) may be taken. For irrigated late sown condition, development of heat tolerant varieties (especially for the later part of growth and development of the plant) are expected to give more yield. Similarly, for timely sown rainfed conditions, varieties which perform fairly well even with low input application, will prove best. In fact, harvesting maximum wheat yields requires the optimization of all factors influencing grain yield in this cereal, that is, not only the genetic potential of the variety but crop husbandry should also be optimized.

Since yield potential in wheat is dependent upon several genetic, pathological and ecological factors, it is not possible to exactly determine the optimum ecological requirements of any wheat variety. Similarly, there is no method available so far which can precisely tell the maximum hereditary yielding ability of any wheat variety. However, the fact remains that the use of dwarfing genes in wheat breeding has tremendously increased the yield potential of this cereal. almost similar role, though of lower magnitude, has been played by wheat-rye translocation 1B/1R in increasing yield levels of wheat in India in late 1980s and early 1990s. The wheat varieties WH542, UP2338 and PBW343 released in 1992, 1993 and 1995, respectively, have better grain yield potential than other varieties. All these three varieties carry 1B/1R translocation. More transfers of alien genes or chromosome segments from wild relatives of wheat may help in further improving the yield levels of wheat varieties. The *Triticum tauschii* genome has several genes governing desirable characteristics like discase resistance and drought tolerance. Yield potential in wheat can also be increased by increasing the extent of homozygous genomic heterosis.

Stabilization of yield levels : India is a country of diverse agroclimtic conditions and different soil types. Therefore, it is rather impossible for a wheat variety to perform uniformly under such a great diversity of conditions. In such situation development of area-specific varieties has a special significance.

Yield stability in wheat is influenced by several factors like maturity period, drought, heat, salinity, diseases and insect pests. There are advantages and disadvantages of early maturing wheat varieties. Whereas early maturity of a variety protects it from adverse climatic conditions (heat, drought, etc.) and diseases and helps in adopting a desired crop rotation, it is usually associated with low yielding ability of the genotype. However, the problem of low yield potential has been largely solved by the cultivation of early maturing but high yielding Mexican spring semi-dwarf wheat varieties. In addition, these Mexican varieties are photoinsensitive, fertilizer responsive and lodging resistant. The presence of these desirable characteristics has considerably promoted the geographical adaptation of spring wheats.

Low moisture content in the soil adversely influences the metabolism of plant and ultimately there is reduction in the grain weight, grains per spike and in the number of productive tillers per plant. Some wild relatives of wheat (e.g., *T. tauschii*) have drought tolerance genes which may be transferred to cultivated wheat through wide hybridization.

Heat stress may affect the wheat crop at any major developmental phase (vegetative, ear development, or grain growth phase) of the plant. The post-anthesis heat stress can considerably reduce the size of the grain (Sohu *et al.*, 2004). In India, this kind of stress occasionally affects the wheat crop (especially late sown crop) in the northern regions of the country.

Enough variability for heat tolerance is available in wheat germplasm which can be exploited by using conventional breeding methods or by sophisticated biotechnological tools. According to Wang *et al.* (1993), *in vitro* selection for heat tolerance is effective in wheat. This is presumably because heat tolerance is largely a cellular manifestation. Further, there is a correlation between cellular stage and whole plant stage for genotypic differences in thermo-tolerance in wheat.

About 10 million hectares of arable land in India is affected by soil salinity and sodicity (Singh and Tyagi, 1998). Distinct inter-varietal differences for salt tolerance indicate that sufficient genetic variability exists for this characteristic in the wheat germplasm. In fact, it is easy to reclaim salt affected soils for tolerant genotypes, otherwise reclaimation of these soils is a very lengthy process. Therefore, choice of suitable crop or suitable genotype of a crop for salt affected soils is one of the most critical considerations. Fortunately, wheat crop (especially some wheat varieties like Kharchia 65, KRL2-10, KRL 304, KRL 8, KRL 1-4, KRL-19, WH 157, Job 666 and KRL 9) has a good degree of tolerance to salinity. However, planned and more vigorous efforts should be made for the identification of salt tolerant genotypes.

In India, wheat crop is attacked by a number of diseases (rusts, powdery mildew, smuts and other diseases). In the past, rusts caused considerable losses in wheat crop. However, the use of broad-based resistance has significantly reduced the losses in wheat yields. But, Karnal bunt is still a serious disease of wheat in some areas of the country.

Improvement in the grain quality : Grain quality in wheat is a complex character and is determined by several characteristics like grain colour (amber or red), grain texture (soft or hard) and chemical composition of the grain (quantity and quality of protein, carbohydrate and starch content and content of other chemical constituents). The produce should also be physically pure. In addition, wheat grain quality may vary according to the intended use and consumer preferences. In India, wheat is primarily used for domestic consumption in the form of chapati, puri, parotha, tandoori, nan, etc. About 90 per cent of wheat consumption in the country is in the form of these home-made products. Therefore, chapati making quality is the chief consideration in the assessment of wheat varieties in the country. Also, efforts are being made to breed varieties for superior bread making quality.

Breeding Methodology

Breeding efforts have made a spectacular contribution towards productivity improvement in wheat in India, especially after the release of the varieties Kalyansona and Sonalika in the year 1967. These two varieties occupied large areas in the country till 1977. However, there was no significant increase in the yield level of wheat between 1975-1985 despite the release of the varieties HD 2009 and WL

711 in 1975. Release of HD 2009, WL 711 and WH 147 mainly affected the wheat yield of North Western Plains Zone (NWPZ). Another spurt in wheat yields came after the release of *Veery* lines during late 1980s and early 1990s. These lines carry 1B/1R translocation and perform better under diverse environmental conditions. The yield levels of NWPZ during this period went up to 52 quintals per hectare. However, the varieties WH 542, UP 2338 and PBW 343 (all three derived from further hybridizations with Veery genotypes and carry 1B/1R translocation) released in 1992, 1993 and 1995, respectively, have a higher yield potential (55-60 q/ha).

Breeding procedures : Among the breeding procedures, the **pedigree method** has been and is being used most extensively in wheat breeding in India. Numerous investigators and wheat breeders have applied this method to bring improvement in wheat materials. However, to make this method more efficient and useful, some modifications/refinements may be made. For example, for minimizing the adverse effect of successive selfing (fixation of linkage blocks in early generations and less chances of recombination), random crosses among selected plants in early generations may be made. Similarly, selective intermating in between selfing series may be advantageous in several ways (enhancing the process of recombination, accumulating favourable genes in the experimental material, increasing genetic variability and population mean, using hidden variability, etc.). According to Pawar *et al.* (1990b, 2000), selective intermating is effective in increasing grain yield and its component traits in wheat (Also see Chapter 4).

Bulk population breeding is relatively a slow method. However, since natural selection plays a major role in this method, the improvement achieved is longer lasting. The procedure also provides information about the survival of genotypes and genes in populations. But, there is no frequent use of this method by wheat breeders in India. Nevertheless, a combination of modified bulk method and pedigree method is proving quite useful. Pawar *et al.* (1990a) observed that simplified pedigree selection (bulking at F_3 stage of the pedigree method) proved better than or equal to pedigree method for mean performance, coefficient of variation and for number of high yielding lines retained.

The **single seed descent method** of Goulden though has several advantages (is less costly, allows to obtain the F_2 genetic spectrum in homozygous condition in the shortest possible time, minimizes the effect of natural selection on the genetic structure of the original population, is uninfluenced by the degree of heritability, is one of the best methods for advancing generations, etc.) has not been frequently used by wheat breeders in India. However, the use of one-spikelet-one-plant method or single spike selection of Qualset (1977) or multiple seed descent method of Ndondi (1987) or single head descent method of Jensen (1988) may be of greater practical utility than using traditional single seed descent method. Single head descent method is also proving better for producing nucleus seed.

Backcross method has been continuously used by wheat breeders to transfer characters controlled by a single gene or by a few genes. But, the use of this method so far has been mainly restricted to the transfer of genes resistant to diseases. However, now a days, this method is being used to develop near isogenic lines of earlier wheat varieties like C 306, Kalyansona, Sonalika, HD 2009, WL 711, WH 147, HD 2329, WH 542 and VL 421. The variety HW 2004 which is a backcross derivative line of the old variety C 306 and carries Lr 24 and Sr 24 genes, was released in 1997 for timely sown, rainfed conditions of the central zone of the country. Similarly, the variety Sonak which is a near isogenic line of Sonalika and carries Lr 24 gene was released for late sown conditions of the Haryana state in the year 1998.

Diallel selective mating system of Jensen (1970) though has a number of advantages over conventional breeding procedures used in self-fertilizing crops, has not yet found an important place in wheat breeding programme of India due to the difficulties faced by the breeders in using this procedure. In a highly self-fertilized crop like wheat, it is not easy to make large number of crosses required by the method. However, availability of genetic or cytoplasmic male sterility may help the wheat breeders in taking advantages of this method.

Multilineal breeding (usually referred as multiline breeding) has been used in India for developing some wheat varieties like KSML 3, MLKS 11 and UPKML 7406. The purpose of developing a multilineal variety which is a mixture of near-isogenic lines, is to combine resistance genes from various sources into a single agronomically superior genotype so that the new variety is homogeneous for all important agronomic characters but is genetically heterogeneous for resistance genes. However, this breeding programme has not been very successful in India.

The breeding procedure which is, at present, catching the attention of the wheat breeders most is **shuttle breeding system**. The method is not only being extensively used by CIMMYT scientists but in India also it is becoming increasingly important. Considering the agroclimatic conditions, soil types, lower wheat yields, etc. of the North Eastern Plains Zone (a major wheat producing region of the country), the Directorate of Wheat Research, Karnal started a shuttle breeding programme at CIMMYT's pattern in 1995-96 (Singh *et al.*, 2004). Taking into consideration the rice-wheat cropping system of eastern India, two research projects were formulated for developing genotypes with high yield potential, high adaptability and resistance to diseases.

The basic objective of the programme was to help the farmers of this comparatively less fortunate region of the country by evolving wheat varieties according to their requirements. Six centres (Karnal, Varanasi, Faizabad, Pusa, Shillongani and Cooch Behar) have been chosen for shuttling the breeding material. The material is tested for important characteristics like yield potential, adaptability and disease resistance. The site-specific performance of the genotypes is also taken into consideration.

The efforts made by DWR scientists are praiseworthy. They have been able to develop some promising genotypes suitable for NEPZ conditions. For example, the variety DBW 14 has been released for late sown irrigated coditions of this zone. The variety is least affected by late sown conditions, is tolerant to leaf and stripe rusts and to Karnal bunt and has good grain quality.

Induced mutagenesis : The main advantage of mutation breeding is that a character can be induced in a genotype without severely disturbing the rest of the genotype. In India, some useful mutants have been developed in wheat. For example, the wheat variety *NP 836* which was released in 1961, was developed by treating the variety NP 799 (an awnless variety) with X-rays. The mutant variety had presence of awns and was comparatively higher yielder than NP 799. Similarly, the mutant varieties *Sharbati Sonora* (released in 1967) and *Pusa Lerma* (released in 1971) were developed through gamma rays treatment from the varieties Sonora 64A and Lerma Rojo, respectively. Both the mutant varieties have improved grain colour (amber colour). There is also a report that non-necrotic genetic stock of the variety C306 (a highly adapted variety for rainfed conditions with excellent grain type but having necrotic genes which interfere in production of successful crosses) has been produced to overcome the adverse effect of necrotic genes (Rao, 2001). Induced mutagenesis can also be helpful in breaking negative correlations between component traits of yield in wheat. For example, grain weight in wheat is negatively correlated with number of grains per spike. Efforts may be made to solve this problem by keeping the value of one component trait constant and inducing genetic variability for the other trait through mutagenic treatment.

Transfer of alien genes : Since desirable genetic variability in wheat is limited, the transfer of alien favourable genes to wheat from other species is becoming increasingly important and necessary. Several wild relatives of wheat (*Triticum tauschii, Secale cereale, Agropyron* species, etc.) contain genes for disease and insect resistance, drought tolerance, high productivity, high adaptive possibilities, etc. For example, the rye chromosome fragment involved in 1BL/1RS wheat-rye translocation possesses genes for disease resistance, wide adaptation and high productivity. Advantage of 1BL/1RS translocation has also been harvested by Indian wheat breeders by developing several varieties (e.g., HUW 206, HPW 42, WH 542, UP 2338 and PBW 343, released in 1985, 1991, 1992, 1993 and 1995, respectively) carrying this translocation.

Development of hybrid varieties : By 2020, India would require about 109 million tonnes of wheat (Mahajan *et al.*, 2004). To produce this quantity of wheat, there should be another major breakthrough in wheat production and productivity in the country. The development of hybrid wheat varieties and thereby exploiting maximum degree of heterosis, may probably play a key role in achieving this goal. The advantage of inter-genomic heterosis or homozygous genomic heterosis in wheat is being regularly harvested using conventional breeding approach. However, development of hybrid varieties would facilitate exploitation of intra-genomic heterosis in the three genomes of wheat.

The efforts to develop hybrid wheat in India were initiated about four decades ago with main emphasis on three-line cytoplasmic male sterility (CMS) system. But, these efforts did not produce encouraging results (Mahajan and Nagarajan, 1998). The two-line approach using photoperiod sensitive CMS system has also not been successful, especially under long-day conditions.

Considering the drawbacks associated with CMS system and the advantages of chemical hybradizing agent (CHA) method, Directorate of Wheat Research (DWR), Karnal decided to re-address the hybrid wheat programme in 1995 with special emphasis on CHA approach. The programme was started for a target area of irrigated, high fertility and timely sown conditions of the North Western Plains Zone (the wheat bowl) of the country with four objectives : (i) Identification of parental lines showing commercial heterosis; (ii) formulation, evaluation and operationalization of chemical hybridizing agents in producing hybrids; (iii) development of reliable CMS and restorer systems; and (iv) for investigating floral biology and related diseases (Mahajan *et al.*, 1998). Presently, work is being done at five cooperative centres, namely, DWR (Karnal), IARI (New Delhi), CCS HAU (Hisar and Kaul), PAU (Ludhiana) and NCL (Pune). In addition, several other centres (ICAR and state agricultural universitires) and the private companies (MAHYCO, MONSANTO, etc.) are showing keen interest in the programme.

Among large number of chemicals tested, only five CHAs, namely CH 9701, CH 9702, CH 9708, CH 9831 and CH 9832, have been found to induce acceptable levels of male sterility (Mahajan *et al.*, 2000). According to Mahajan *et al.* (1998), CHA-induced male sterility in wheat is associated with auto-induction of floret opening, an essential condition for outcrossing. Rao *et al.* (2000) found that in CHA-induced male sterile WH 542 (a promising wheat variety), the male sterile florets open twice and thus facilitate outcrossing.

More than 1000 single cross wheat hybrids have been evaluated on large plot basis at the cooperative centres. Some of these hybrids have also been tested in multilocation hybrid wheat trials. Based on their performance, especially in terms of standard heterosis, eight hybrids (HM 9837, HM

9946, HM 9997, HM 0054, HM 00756, HM 99104, HM 99426 and HM 99495) have been short-listed at DWR. All these hybrids exhibited more than 15 per cent standard heterosis in the past few years (Mahajan *et al.*, 2004). Some hybrids showed upto 29 per cent heterosis. The DWR scientists feel that hybrid wheat programme in future should be aimed at to explore geographic and genetic diversity of parents, combine wheat quality with wheat productivity, take the farmers of the country into confidence, develop liaison with private sector, synthesize effective CHAs and to standardize seed production at commercial scale.

Breeding for disease resistance : Among wheat diseases, maximum attention has been paid by the scientists to the control of **rusts** and, as a result, a large number of resistance genes against these diseases have been identified. However, single resistance genes even from alien sources could not provide durable resistance against rusts and there may be emergence of new races of the pathogens after the resistant cultivar is extensively grown. Therefore, breeding for disease resistance is a continuous process. According to Sawhney (1995), related species of wheat are the main source of currently effective variability for resistance against rusts. However, some alien translocation stocks are becoming increasingly important as they allow concurrent transfer of resistance for two or all the three wheat rusts. The most important and most extensively used source of resistance in the development of wheat varieties all over the world is the wheat-rye translocation 1B/1R carrying Lr 26, Sr 31 and Yr 9 resistance genes. As metnioned earlier, many Indian wheat varieties carry this translocation.

Sawhney (1998) discussed the genetic basis of rust resistance in Indian wheats and emphasized the need to exploit alien genes for durable resistance. However, effective exploitation of alien genes or gene combinations involves two steps: (1) Development of a superior stock; and (2) utilization of the stock in breeding programme. Using Kalyansona as the recurrent parent in a backcross breeding programme, Sawhney and Sharma (1996) came to the conclusion that with limited backcrosses and selection of desirable rust resistant plants in each selfed and backcross generation, it was possible to develop high yielding lines equal to or better than Kalyansona. Important alien genes exploited in resistance breeding are Lr 26/Yr 9/Sr 31 (*Secale cereale*), Lr 19/Sr 25, Lr 24/Sr 24 and Sr 26 (*Agropyron elongatum*), Lr 21/Sr 21 and Lr 32 (*Triticum tauschii*) and Lr 9 (*Triticum umbellulatum*) (Sawhney, 1998). These genes have been exploited for the development of backcross derivatives of wheat varieties like Sonalika, Kalyansona and C306 and these backcross derivatives led to the development of several rust resistant varieties like *Sonali* (developed from a Sonalika backcross derivative at IARI Regional Station, Pusa and was released in 1992), *HW 2004* (from C 306 backcross derivative at IARI Regional Station, Wellington and was released in 1997) and *Sonak* (from Sonalika derivative and was released in 1998 for late sown conditions of Haryana state). The varieties Sonali, HW 2004 and Sonak, carry rust resistant genes Lr 9, Lr 24/Sr 24 and Lr 24, respectively.

Sawhney (1998) also concluded that since adult plant durable resistances controlled by Lr 34/Yr 18 and Sr 2 are linked with morphological markers, the manipulation of these genes is easy even in the presence of more effective genes.

The availability of diverse resistance genes is a pre-requisite for conferring long term resistance. Although stripe rust may cause more damage in wheat than leaf rust, but relatively less attention has been paid for the identification of diverse genes against the former rust in India (Saini *et al.*, 2004). The adult plant resistance gene Lr 34 in combination with some unidentified adult plant resistance genes, has been very useful in conferring durable resistance against leaf rust. According to Saini *et al.* (2004), scientists at PAU, Ludhiana, have been able to designate two novel adult plant leaf rust resistance genes, Lr 48 and Lr 49. The two genes are found in *Triticum aestivum* and are effective against the prevalent races from India as well as against the races from Australia and Mexico (Saini *et al.*, 2002).

Foliar blight (commonly referred to as *Helminthosporium* leaf blight or HLB in south Asia) is the major biotic constraint to wheat crop, especially in those regions where environmental conditions for growing wheat crop are less favourable (particularly eastern Uttar Pradesh, Bihar, Jharkhand and West Bengal which constitute eastern Gangetic plains of the country) and where rice-wheat crop rotation is followed (Duveiller, 2004). The disease may cause considerable yield losses (15 per cent on average). However, yield losses may vary depending on sowing time and other environmental conditions like year, site and stress conditions (Dubin and Duveiller, 2000) and the losses can be reduced by improving crop growing conditions.

Although very little information is available about the inheritance of resistance genes against foliar blight, resistance breeding has been recommended as a key approach to control this disease. Modern fungicides can effectively control this disease, but such fungicides are not easily available in most areas of the Gangetic plains. Further, the use of fungicides is not environmentally safe and is also not cost effective.

Saharan *et al.* (2004) studied phenotypic, pathogenic and molecular variation among *Fusarium* species, the causal organisms of **head scab** or **head blight** of wheat. At present, this disease is mainly confined to the humid and subhumid wheat growing areas of the world and causes considerable destruction. Although head scab of wheat is currently a disease of minor importance in India (only reported from Gurdaspur, Wellington and Arunchal Pradesh), but due to global warming in future, it may become a serious disease in this country also. *Fusarium graminearum*, reported from Arunchal Pradesh and Wellington, produces mycotoxin which adversely affects grain quality and makes the grain unfit for consumption.

Karnal bunt (partial grain smut of wheat) is a destructive disease in several parts of India, especially Haryana, Punjab, Western Uttar Pradesh, northern Rajasthan, Jammu and tarai region of Himachal Pradesh. Using indigenously developed computer softwares, Kumar *et al.* (2004) assessed the probability of risk due to Karnal bunt occurrence in central and Peninsular zones of the country. Based on climatic requirements for competition of the life cycle of *Tilletia indica* (Karnal bunt pathogen), the softwares predicted non-establishment of Karnal bunt in these two zones.

Resistance breeding is considered to be the best method for controlling Karnal bunt. After screening diverse germplasm, some promising resistant lines/varieites (HD 29, HD 30, KBRL-10, KBRL-22, K 9843, WH 283, etc.) have been identified and are being used in breeding programmes.

Nevertheless, looking at the number of diseases affecting wheat and the complex nature of these diseases, the best way of developing disease resistant wheat varieties is to combine resistances for different diseases with high yield potential and wide adaptation. The use of wheat-rye translocation 1B/1R has played a major role in achieving this goal.

Breeding for tolerance to abiotic stresses : Wheat plant is thermosensitive, a long-day plant and is best adopted to the temperate climate. However, wheat is a major crop of many tropical and subtropical regions of the world where mostly spring wheat is grown (Sohu *et al.*, 2004). In India, about 90 per cent of the wheat area is occupied by spring bread wheat. Spring wheat in India, especially in northern India, is exposed to chronic heat stress, paticularly during its grain growth phase. This post anthesis high temperature stress (PAHTS) or post anthesis heat stress (PAHS) has a larger effect on the late sown crop than on the timely sown crop. PAHS has a considerable negative effect on grain size.

Several investigators (Bagga and Rawson, 1977; Dawson and Wardlaw, 1989; Sharma, 2000; Sharma *et al.*, 2001; and others) have observed significant varietal differences for heat stress in wheat. Considering various characters, several heat tolerant varieties have been identified. These are PBW 226, Raj 3765, UP 2425, HD 2329, CPAN 3004, WH 542 and many others. Conventional breeding procedures as well as modern biotechnological tools can be used to evolve heat tolerant varieties.

Similarly, inter-varietal differences are found for drought tolerance. Veery lines and their derivatives are drought tolerant. Therefore, hybridization with these lines is an effective method for developing drought tolerant genotypes.

A large arable land (about 10 million hectares) in India is affected by soil salinity and sodicity. Therefore, development of salinity tolerant wheat genotypes is an important objective in some wheat breeding programmes in the country. Scientists at Central Soil Salinity Research Institute (CSSRI), Karnal, are doing a commendable work on this aspect. A large number of wheat genotypes have been screened for salt tolerance. Singh and Tyagi (1998) have given a list of Indian wheat varieties according to their response against salinity. Varieties Kharchia, KAL 2-10, KR 3-4, KRL 8, KRL 9, etc. fall under tolerant category; varieties WH 157, Raj 3077, KRL 1-4, etc. under medium tolerant category; and WH 542, HD 2329, WL 711, etc. in medium sensitive group.

Breeding for quality traits : In India, wheat is primarily used for domestic purposes (making chapati parotha, puri, non, tandori, etc.). Therefore, chapati making has been the main consideration during the evaluation of new wheat varieties. But now wheat varieties are being evaluated in coordinated trials for bread, chapati and biscuit making qualities. Even durum wheat which has a poor chapati making quality, was grown for this purpose in some parts of the country. However, since the people of India are becoming increasingly urbanized, the demand for instant foods and processed products is also increasing accordingly. As a result, the importance of breeding quality durums is increasing partly because the pasta industry has picked up in the domestic market and partly because of the price advantage in the international market.

Among cereals, only wheat contains gluten (one of the most intricate naturally occurring protein complexes) which makes this food crop species unique in terms of processing possibilities into different products like leavened and unleavened breads, biscuits, cakes and pastris. Although various components of wheat flour (starch, proteins, lipids, minerals, etc.) play their own role in shaping the end product, the quality of end product is mainly determined by the viscoelastic strength of the protein. But, presence of low amount of lysine (an essential amino acid) in the wheat grain is a serious problem before the wheat scientists since lysine content is negatively correlated with total protein content of the grain in wheat. However, realizing the importance of quality parameters in wheat breeding, wheat varieties in coordinated trials are being evaluated for various quality parameters. Also, efforts are being made to transfer the *triticin* (a minor protein of the wheat endosperm but rich in lysine) gene constructs to wheat through genetic engineering (Singh *et al.*, 1998). Triticin belongs to the legumin superfamily of storage proteins predominantly found in leguminous plant species and in some cereals like rice and oats (Shewry *et al.*, 1994). Barro *et al.* (1997) also came to the conclusion that functional properties of wheat can be improved by transforming wheat with high molecular weight subunit genes.

Singh et al. (2004) suggested that there is a need to develop product specific varieties through targeted quality breeding programmes since, now in India also, the demand for ready-to-eat wheat based products has risen sharply because of rapid urbanization and changing food habits. Similarly, Ram and Singh (2004) emphasized the need for identifying molecular tools and micro-level techniques for biscuit making quality of wheat since demand for biscuits has increased recently. According to them, the major areas of research for accelerating breeding for developing wheat varieties for good biscuit making quality are : (1) Identification of genotypes with higher potential for good biscuit making quality traits; (2) better knowledge regarding genetic basis of grain quality; and (3) development of small-scale tests.

Application of biometrical genetics : The use of biometrical genetic procedures can help the wheat breeders in a number of ways like detecting and estimating gene effects and components of variance, choosing parents for hybridization, determining character association and cause of heterosis, quantifying genetic parameters, enhancing efficiency of selection methods, measuring phenotypic stability and genetic divergence and classifying environments according to regional and temporal variations (Chapter 11). At least in some cases, it is possible to generalize the results (Singh and Pawar, 1998). For example, the application of tripe test cross method in wheat populations clearly indicates that additive variance plays a major role in governing quantitative characters, epistasis is an essential component for grain yield and additive gene effects are relatively more sensitive to environmental change than the dominance gene effects.

Use of biometrical genetic techniques has also helped in knowing the genetic basis of tolerance to abiotic stresses like heat, drought and soil salinity. Sohu et al. (2004) found that heat tolerance in wheat is governed by recessive alleles. However, according to Singh et al. (1998), the dominance and/or overdominance relationship of alleles conferring thermal non-responsiveness was different under different thermal environments. Genes conferring thermotolerance can also cause changes in the correlations between different characters like days to heading, number of spikelets per spike and number of grains per spike, under different natural thermal environments. Further, the thermotolerant genotypes showed good combining ability for grain yield and its component characters. Similar results were found by Sharma and Tandon (1998). According to Sharma (2001), both additive and dominance variances were important for most of the characters.

Use of biotechnological tools : Wheat molecular research in India for tagging and mapping of agronomically important quality traits was initiated in 1995. The initiative was supported by the Department of Biotechnology and scientists of six diverse groups (DBT, ICAR, CSIR, DST, SAU and SU) are working together to make the best possible use of biotechnological tools in wheat breeding (Ranjekar et al., 2004). Considering the importance of wheat end products, important grain qualitites like kernel size and hardness, grain protein content and bread making quality, were selected for improvement. Markers associated with some characteristics have been identified by Varshney et al. in 2000 and Ammi Raju et al. in 2001 (1000 grain weight), Galande et al., 2001 (grain hardness), Prasad et al. in 1999, Dholakia et al., 2001 and Singh et al., in 2001 (grain protein content) and by Ammi Raju et al. in 2002 (yellow berry tolerance). According to Prasad et al. (2003), QTL interval mapping for grain protein content was done using a framework map. In this study, 13 QTLs were identified in five environments and these QTLs were validated using near isogenic lines (NILs).

A study aimed at to assess genetic diversity in 63 Indian tetraploid wheat genotypes using ISSR and RAPD primers revealed hierarchical groupings of these genotypes. Genetic distances calculated through different coefficients showed good correlation (Pujar et al., 1999, 2002).

The pyramiding of seedling and adult plant resistance genes can greatly help in developing durable resistance against wheat rusts and pyramiding of major genes into a suitable genetic background, in turn, can be efficiently facilitated by identifying markers for resistance genes. After analyzing NILs of *Triticum speltoides* derived leaf rust restance gene Lr 28 in eight varietal backgrounds, a sequence characterized amplified region (SCAR) marker linked to Lr 28 has been identified. Also, a sequence tagged site (STS) marker linked to the gene Lr 28 has been identified (Naik et al., 1997).

Efforts are also being made under a programme jointly launched by DBT and Swiss Development Corporation to identify molecular markers linked to seedling resistance genes Lr 15 and Lr 23 and adult plant resistance genes Lr 22a and Lr 34. NILs for these genes have been developed in the background of susceptible Thatcher lines and some populations have been developed through crossing. NILs as well as populations are being used with some markers (AFLP, RAPD, ISSR, STMS and RGAs). Good markers will be selected, converted into SCAR (more repeatable and reproducible marker) and will be used in marker assisted selection (Ranjekar et al., 2004).

In addition, DBT is supporting another multi-institutional programme aimed at to the pyramiding of favourable brown rust and yellow rust resistance genes in popular Indian wheat varieties. The new lines will be tested for their suitability at farmers' field and also for their use as genetic stocks. The programme has six collaborators: (1) Directorate of Wheat Research, Karnal; (2) Indian Agricultural Research Institute, New Delhi; (3) Punjab Agricultural University, Ludhiana; (4) CCS University, Meerut; (5) National Chemical Laboratory (NCL), Pune; and (6) Agharkar Research Institute (ARI), Pune.

Tiwari et al. (2004) discussed in detail the marker assisted breeding initiatives in India. They used 62 genotypes of Advanced Varietal Trials (AVT) for their study. SCAR marker was used for detecting Lr 26/Sr 31/Yr 9 resistance genes and the molecular marker developed by Francis et al. (1995) was used for detecting wheat-rye translocation 1B/1R. Their results indicated that NWPZ (the wheat bowl of the country) comprises of maximum number of genotypes/varieties having 1B/1R translocation. According to them, this situation may be dangerous for the country if there is evolution of rust pathotypes able to match the resistance conferred by the segment of the rye chromosome.

Future Strategies

Looking at the multidimentional challenges ahead, especially rapidly increasing human population, declining resources (water, arable land, etc.) and degrading environment, it is imperative to take following steps regarding wheat breeding in India:

1. All possible efforts must be made to develop hybrid varieties in wheat and to make hybrid wheat as a viable commercial proposition. Production of hybrid varieties would allow exploitation of intra-genomic heterosis in the three wheat genomes.
2. Possibilities of growing winter wheat in some parts of the country should be explored. Winter wheats show natural flowering in some hilly places of the country (e.g., parts of Almora and Shimla). These places can be used for making winter × spring wheat crosses and combining desirable characteristics of the two types of wheat.
3. More emphasis should be given to improve wheat quality by bringing together desirable combinations of different components of wheat proteins (high molecular weight glutenin, low molecular weight glutenin and gliadin) and by increasing amount of specific essential amino acids (especially lysine content) through systematic efforts.

4. Due importance should be attached to bring improvement in durum wheat. As regards the scope for export, durum wheat is better than bread wheat. In addition to the criteria of grain yield potential and resistance to biotic and abiotic stresses, emphasis should be given for improving quality characters like freedom from yellow berry, high semolina recovery, more protein and β-carotene content.
5. Efforts should be made to increase the extent of inter-genomic heterosis by making wide crosses and transferring alien genes.
6. Complete dependence on 1B/1R translocation alone may prove dangerous in future. In fact, it is always better to avoid monoculture or even growing of varieties carrying translocations having segmental uniformity. It means that it is better to provide a plethora of varietal mosaicism rather than growing varieties carrying same translocation or translocations having segmental uniformity.
7. The use of biotechnological tools has a vast scope in the improvement of wheat. These tools/techniques should be more extensively used for screening genotypes resistant to diseases (rusts, powdery mildew, Karnal bunt, etc.) and tolerant to abiotic stresses like salinity, heat stress and drought. For improving any characteristic (heat tolerance, salinity tolerance, etc.) which is largely a cellular manifestation, selection in cell cultures may prove to be a potential method. Similarly, the use of marker aided selection has a vast potential for pyramiding resistance genes. Further, the use of novel techniques like Fluorescence *in situ* Hybridization (FISH) and Genomic *in situ* Hybridization (GISH) may play a key role for transferring desirable alien genes to wheat germplasm. For example, transfer of *triticin* gene construct to wheat from oats, rice or any leguminous species through genetic engineering may be helpful in increasing lysine content in wheat. If it is possible to successfully produce *quality protein maize* (QPM) and *golden rice* (GR), why a *high lysine wheat* cannot be developed?
8. There is a big gap between the potential yields and realized yields of wheat varieties in India. For example, in Punjab, wheat varieties have a yield potential of 70 q/ha, but the realized yield (state average) is only 42.3 q/ha (Rao, 2001). Development of suitable varieties for sub-optimal environments and regionwise optimization of input use efficiency may help in bridging the gap between potential yields and realized yields. Production of low-input wheat varieties for rainfed areas may help in reducing the cost of cultivation in these areas.

Further, wheat breeding should no more be treated as an isolated activity, rather a system-oriented research should be done since wheat is a component of several cropping systems.

Although, due to concerted efforts made by the scientists (plant breeders, geneticists, plant pathologists, agronomists, soil scientists, etc.), the Malthusian prediction was proved squarely wrong but is does not mean that this prediction will never come true if the speed of increase in human population, especially in developing countries, remains the same. We must remember the words said by Dr. N.E. Borlaug that *there is no time to relax* and the words said by Dr. M.S. Swaminathan (2001) that *there is no room for complacency*. However, only a practical plant breeder can take a right decision about the actual worth of a plant. Dr. N.E. Borlang has very rightly said: "*Plants speak but they speak in a very low voice. You must have the ears to listen to them. But if you are far away from the field and sitting in the cosy laboratory building you will not be able to hear them.*

References

Abbasi, F.H. (1949). Inheritance of resistance to stem rust and leaf rust in crosses of Premier and Kenya wheats. *Indian J. Genet.* **9**, 7-17.

Acharya, S. and Singh, V.P. (1986). Combining ability analysis of yield and related attributes in wheat under rainfed conditions. *Crop. Improv.* **13**, 104-106.

Ahmad, F. and Comeau, A. (1990). Wheat × pearlmillet hybridization : consequence and potential. *Euphytica*, **50**, 181-190.

Ahmed, K.Z. and Abdelkareem, A.A. (2005). Somaclonal variation in bread wheat II. Field performance of somaclones. *Cereal Res. Comm.* **33**, 485-492.

Ahsan, M., Wright, D. and Virk, D.S. (1996). Genetic analysis of salt tolerance in spring wheat. *Cereal Res. Comm.* **24**, 353-360.

Alesin, E.P. and Tsigrin, V.V. (1966). Physiological and biochemical reaction of spring wheats showing different degrees of resistance to black rust (in Russian). *Fiziol. Rast.* (Moscow) **13**, 99-104.

Allan, R.E. (1973). Yield of wheat hybrids of the *Triticum timopheevi* nucleo-cytoplasm system. *Proc. 4th Int. Wheat Genet. Symp.*, pp. 422-427.

Allan, R.E. (1980). Wheat. In *Hybridization of crop plants*, W.R. Fehr and H.H. Hadley (Eds.). *Am.Soc. of Agron. Inc.* Madison, Wis, pp. 709-720.

Allan, R.E. and Purdy, H.L. (1970). Reaction of F_2 seedling of several crosses of susceptible and resistant wheat selections to *Puccinia striiformis*. *Phytopathology* (Worcester) **60**, 1368-1372.

Allan, R.E. and Vogel, O.A. (1960). F_1 monosomic analysis involving a smooth awn durum wheat. *Wheat Inf. Serv.* **11**, 3-4.

Allan, R.E. and Vogel, O.A. (1965). Monosomic analysis of Red Seed Color in Wheat. *Crop Sci.* **5**, 475.

Allan, R.E., Vogel, O.A. and Purdy, L.H. (1963). Influence of stripe rust upon yields and test weights of closely related lines of wheat. *Crop Sci.* (Madison) **3**, 564-565.

Allard, R.W. (1960). *Principles of Plant Breeding*, John Wiley and Sons Inc., New York, London.

Allard, R.W. and Shands, R.G. (1954). Inheritance of resistance to stem rust and powdery mildew in cytologically stable spring wheats derived from *Triticum timopheevii*. *Phytopathology* **44**, 266-274.

Alonso, L.C. and Kimber, G. (1984). Use of restitution nuclei to introduce alien genetic variation into hexaploid wheat. *Zeit. Pflanzenzucht.* **92**, 185-189.

Amawate, J.S. and Behl, P.N. (1995). Genetical analysis of some quantitative componnet of yield in bread wheat. *Indian J. Genet.* **55**, 120-125.

Ammiraju, J.S.S., Dholakia, B.B., Jawdekar, G., Santra, D.K., Gupta, V.S., Roder, M.S., Singh, H., Lagu, M.D., Dhaliwal, H.S., Rao, V.S. and Ranjekar, P.K. (2002). Inheritance and identification of DNA marker associated with yellow berry tolerance in wheat. *Euphytica* **123**, 229-233.

Ammiraju, J.S.S., Dholakia, B.B., Santra, D.K., Singh, H., Lagu, M.D., Tamhankar, S.A., Dhaliwal, H.S., Rao, V.S., Gupta, V.S. and Ranjekar, P.K. (2001). Identification of inter-simple sequence repeat marker associated with seed size in wheat. *Theor. Appl. Genet.* **102**, 726-732.

Andreev, L. (1968). Protection against cereal rust (in Russian). *Zemledelie* (Moscow) **4**, 38-43.

Appels, R. and Moran, L.B. (1984). Molecular analysis of alien chromatin introduced into wheat. In *Gene Manipulation in Plant Improvement*, J.P. Gustafson (Ed.), 16th Stadler Genet Symp, Columbiam, Missouri.

Appleby, A.P. (1987). Weed control in wheat In; *Wheat and Wheat Improvement* 2nd edition, E.G. Heyne (Ed.), Agronomy Monograph No. 13, ASA, CSSA, SSSA, Madison, Wisconsin, USA, pp. 396-415.

Arunachalam, V. (1977). Heterosis for characters governed by two genes. *J. Genet.* **63**, 15-24.

Arunachalam, V. (1981). Genetic distance in plant breeding. *Indian J. Genet.* **41**, 226-236.

Arunachalam, V. and Bandyopadhyay, A. (1984). Limits to genetic divergence for occurrence of heterosis-experimental evidence from crop plants. *Indian J. Genet.* **44**, 548-554.

Asiedu, R., Mujeeb-Kazi, A. and Kuile, N.T. (1989). Marker assisted introgression of alien chromatin into wheat. In *Review of Advances in Plant Biotechnology*, A. Mujeeb-Kazi and L.A. Sitch (Eds.), 2nd Int. Symp. on Genetic Manipulation in crops, Mexico and Manilla, Philippines : CIMMYT and IRRI, pp. 133-144.

Athwal, D.S. (1953). Gene interaction and inheritance of resistance to stem rust of wheat. *ibid.* **13**, 91-103.

Athwal, D.S., Phul, P.S. and Minocha, J.L. (1967). Genetic male sterility in wheat. *Euphytica* **16**, 354-360.

Atkins, A.E. (1953). Effect of selection upon bulk barley populations. *Agron. Jour.* **45**, 311-314.

Aujla, S.S., Sharma, Indu and Singh, B.B. (1987). Physiologic specialization of Karnal bunt of wheat. *Indian Phytopathology* **40**(3), 333-336.

Ausemus, E.R., Mc Neal, F.H. and Schmidt, J.W. (1967). Genetics and Inheritance. In *Wheat and wheat improvement*, K.S. Quinsenberry and L.P. Reitz (Eds.), 1st Ed. American Society of Agronomy, Madison, Wisconsin, U.S.A. pp. 225-267.

Austin, R.B., Ford, M.A., Morgan, C.L., Kaminski, A. and Miller, T.E. (1984). In *Advances in Photosynthesis Research. Proc. 4th Int. Congr. Photosynthesis*, C. Sybesma (Ed.), Brussels, Belgium **4**, 103-110.

Avivi, L. (1979). *Proc. 5th Int. Wheat Genet. Symp.* Indian Society of Genetics and Plant Breeding, New Delhi, India, pp. 372-380.

Ayad, M.A.G. (1952). Inheritance studies of some qualitative and quantitative characters in Egyptian varieties of wheat. *Proc. Egypt. Acad. Sci.* **8**, 26-38.

Ayers, J.E., Southern, J.W., Roelfs, A.P. and Wilcoxson, R.D. (1981). Inheritance of slow rusting and the relationship of Sr genes to slow rusting in the wheat lines FKN. *Phytopathology* **75**, 636-643,

Babayan, V.O., Avakyan, D.C. and Babayan, R.S. (1965). Effects of X-ray treatment of different age wheat seed-grains on the viability and winterhardiness of plants (in Russian). *Ser. Biol.* (Erevan) **18**, 28-32.

Babenko, V.I. and Gevorkyan, A.M. (1967). The amino acid content of winter wheat and its change during hardening (in Russian). *Dokl. Vashnil* (Moscow) **7**, 7-10.

Bagga, A.K. and Rawson, H.M. (1977). Contrasting responses of morphologically similar wheat cultivars to temperatures appropriate to warm temperate climates with hot summers a study in controlled environment. *Aust. J. Plant Physiol.* **4**, 877-887.

Bahl, P.N. and Kohli, S.P. (1960). Inheritance of seedling resistance to some Indian races of yellow rust in crosses of *Triticum aestivum*. *Indian J. Genet.* **20**, 42-47.

Bailey, T.B., Qualset, C.O. and Cox, D.F. (1980). Predicting Heterosis in Wheat. *Crop Sci.* **20**, 339-342.

Bajaj, Y.P.S. (1978). Effect of super-low temperature on excised anthers and pollen embryos of *Atropa, Nicotina* and *Petunia*. *Phytomorphology* **28**, 171-176.

Bajaj, Y.P.S. (1990). *In vitro* production of haploids and their use in cell genetics and plant breeding. In *Biotechnology in Agriculture and Forestry Haploids in Crop Improvement*, Vol. 12, Y.P.S. Bajaj, Springer-Verlag, Berlin-Heidelberg, **12**, 3-44.

Bajaj, Y.P.S. and Mohapatra, D. (1990). Pollen embryogenesis and chromosomal varieation in anther culture on *Brassica hirta* (*Sinapsin alba* L.) (Cited by Y.P.S. Bajaj, 1990).

Bajwa, M.A., Khan, N.I. and Mazoor, U. (1985). Genetic analysis of some agronomic traits and protein in wheat. *J. Agric. Res. Pak.* **23**, 239.

Banks, P.M., Larkin, P.J., Bariana, H.S., Lagudah, E.S., Appels, R., Waterhouse, P.M., Brettel, R.I.S., Chen, X., Xu, H.J., Xin, Z.Y., Qian, Y.T., Zhou, X.M., Cheng, Z.M. and Zhou, G.H. (1995). The use of cell culture for sub chromosomal introgression of barley yellow dwarf virus resistance from *Thinopyrum intermedium* to wheat. *Genome* **38**, 395-405.

Barbero, L. and Cavalli, G. (1977). Determination of lead and copper in soft and durum wheat. *Technica Molitoria* **28**, 105.

Barlow, K.K. and Driscoll, C.J. (1981). Linkage studies involving two chromosomal sterility mutants in hexaploid wheat. *Genetics* **98**, 791-799.

Barrett, B.B. and Kidwell, K.K. (1998). AFLP-based genetic diversity assessment among wheat cultivars from the Pacific Northwest. *Crop Sci.* **38**, 1261-1271.

Barro, F., Rooke, L., Bekes, F., Gras, P., Tatham, A.S., Fido, R., Lazzeri, P.A., Shewry, P.R. and Barcelo, P. (1997). Transformation of wheat with high molecular weight subunit genes results in improved functional properties. *Nature Biotechnology* **15**, 1295-1299.

Baum, B.R. (1977). Taxonomy of the tribe *Triticeae* (Poaceae) using various numerical techniques.I. Historical perspectives, data accumulation and character analysis.*Can. J. Bot.* **55**, 1712-1740.

Baum, B.R. (1978a). Taxonomy of the tribe *Triticeae* (Poaceae) using various numerical techniques.II. Classification. *Can J. Bot.* **56**, 27-56.

Baum, B.R. (1978b). Taxonomy of the tribe *Triticeae* (Poaceae) using various numerical techniques.III. Synoptic key to genera and synopses. *Can. J. Bot.* **56**, 374-385.

Bebyakin, V.M. and Ishina, G.F. (1983). Theoretical prerequisites for selecting durum wheat for grain quality in breeding nurseries. *Doklady Vsesoyuznoi ordena Lenina Trudovogo Krasnogo Znameni Akademii Sel Skokhozyaistvennykh Nauk Imeni V.I. Lenina* **3**, 7.

Bedi, P.S., Meeta, M. and Dhiman, J.S. (1981). Effect of Karnal bunt of wheat on weight and quality of the grains. *Indian Phytopathol.* **34**(3), 330-333.

Belea, A. and Fejer, O. (1980). Evolution of wheat (*Triticum aestivum* L.) in respect to recent research. *Acta Agron. Acad. Scient. Hung.* **29**, 306-315.

Belyakov, I.I. (1968). Growth and development of root system of wheat and barley in semidesert zone. *Vest. Selhoz. Nanki* (Moscow) **13**, 31-33.

Bhagwat, S.K., Bhatia, C.R., Gopalakrishna, T., Joshna, D.C., Mitra, R.K., Narahari, P., Pawar, S.E. and Thakur, R.G. (1979). Increasing protein production in cereals and grain legumes. In *Seed protein improvement in cereals and grain legumes.* Vol. II *Proc. Int. Symp. on Seed Protein Improvement in Cereals and Grain Legumes*, Neuherberg, 4-8 Sept., 1978, IAEA, Vienna, STI/PUB/496, pp. 225-236.

Bhatia, C.R. and Swaminathan, M.S. (1963). Frequency and spectrum of mutations induced by radiations in some varieties of bread wheat. *Euphytica* **12**, 97-112.

Bhattacharya, P.K. and Shaw, M. (1967). The physiology of host parasite relations. XVIII. *Canad. J. Bot.* (Ottawa) **45**, 555-563.

Bhattacharya, P.K., Nylor, J.M. and Shaw, M. (1965). Nucleic acid and protein changes in wheat nuclein during rust infection. *Science* (Washington) **150**, 1606-1607.

Bhullar, B.S., Gill, K.S. and Mahal, G.S. (1978). Genetic analysis of protein in wheat. *Proc. of 5th Int. Wheat Genetics Symposium*, S. Ramanujam (Ed.). Indian Society of Genetics and Plant Breeding, IARI, New Delhi, pp. 613-625.

Bietz, J.A. and Rothfus, J.A. (1971). Differences in amino acid sequences of gliadin and glutenin. *Cereal Chem.* **48**, 677.

Bietz, J.A. and Wall, J.S. (1975). The effect of various extractants on the subunit composition and association of wheat glutenins. *Cereal Chem.* **52**, 145-155.

Biffen, R.H. (1905). Mendel's laws of inheritance and wheat breeding. *J. Agric. Sci.* (London) **1**, 44-48.

Biffen, R.H. (1907). Studies in the inheritance of disease resistance. *J. Agric. Sci.* **2**, 109.

Bingham, J. and Lupton, F. G.H. (1987). Production of new varieties : an integrated research approach to plant breeding. In *Wheat Breeding, Its Scientific Basis*, Lupton, FGH (Ed.), Chapman and Hall, London, pp. 487-538.

Bing-Hua, L. and Jing-yang, D. (1986). A dominant gene for male sterility in wheat. *Plant Breed.* **97**, 204-209.

Bitzer, M.J. and Fu, S.H. (1972). Heterosis and combining ability in southern soft red winter wheats. *Crop Sci.* **12**, 35-37.

Blakeslee, A.F. and Avery, A.G. (1937). Methods of inducing doubling of chromosomes in Plants. *J. Hered.* **28**, 392-411.

Bogdan, G.P. (1968). Isoelectric zones of leafs of mildew resistant wheats (in Russian). *Selhoz. Biol.* (Moscow) **3**, 779-782.

Bohorova, N. (1998). Genetic engineering : a tool for creating novel variations in wheat. In *Wheat : Research Need Beyond 2000 AD*, S. Nagarajan, G. Singh, B.S. Tyagi (Eds.), Narosa Publishing House, New Delhi, pp.137-144.

Bolton, F.E. (1968). *Plant Breeding Abstract* **40** (2684), 344.

Borlaug, N.E. (1953). New approach to the breeding of wheat varieties resistant to *Puccinia graminis tritici. Phytopathology* **43**, 467.

Borlaug, N.E. (1959). The use of multilineal or composite varieties to control airborne epidemic diseases of self-pollinated crop plants, *Proc. 1st Int. Wheat Genet. Symp.* Winniped, Canada 1958 University of Manitoba, Winnipeg, pp.12-26.

Borlaug, N.E. (1968). Wheat breeding and its impact on world food supply. 3rd Int. Wheat Genet. Symp. (Canberra) 1-36.

Borojevic, K. (1963). The effect of X-rays and thermal neutrons on some varieties of *Triticum species* (in Serbian). *Savr. Poljopr.* (Novi Sad) **11**, 181-202.

Borojevic, S. (1965). Efficiency of ten incomplete backcrosses method in wheat breeding (in Serbian) *Savr. Poljopr.* (Novisad) **13**, 403-415.

Bowden, W.M. (1959). The taxonomy and nomenclature of the wheats, barleys and ryes and their wild relatives. *Can J. Bot.* **37**, 657-684.

Bozhanova, V. and Dechev, D. (2002). Assessment of tissue culture derived durum wheat lines for somaclonal variation. *Cereal Res. Comm.* **30**, 277-284.

Bozzini, A. (1965). Sphaerococcoid, a radiation-induced mutation in *Triticum durum* Desf. Report of the FAO/IAEA tech. meeting (Rome) pp. 375-383.

Bozzini, A. and Scarascia-Mugnozza, G.T. (1968). A factor for male sterility inherited as a Mendelian recessive. *Euphytica* **17** (Suppl.) **I**, 83-86.

Bozzini, A.P. and Carluccio, F. (1973). Comparative monopentaploid analysis of 5A chromosomes of 8 lines of tetraploid wheats and of hexaploid Chinese Spring. *Genet. Agrar.* **27**, 148-163.

Bozzini, A.P. and Giorgi, B. (1971). Genetic analysis of tetraploid and hexaploid wheat by utilization of monopentploid hybrids. *Theor. Appl. Genet.* **41**, 67-74.

Bradhury, D., Gill, I.M. and McMasters, M. (1956). *Cereal Chem.*, **33**, 329-391.

Braun, H.J. (1994). Winter wheat breeding and zinc deficiency. In *Wheat Breeding at CIMMYT*, S. Rajaram and G.P.Hettel (Eds.). Commemorating 50 years of Research in Mexico for Global Wheat Improvement. Wheat Special Report No. 29, CIMMYT, Mexico, D.F.pp.60-67.

Braun, H.J., Pfeiffer, W.H. and Pollmer, W.G. (1992). Environments for selecting widely adapted spring wheat. *Crop Sci.* **32**, 1420-1427.

Breakwell, E.J.and Hutton, E.M. (1939). Cereal breeding and variety trials at Roseworthy college 1937-38. *J. Agric. S.A.* **42**, 632-641.

Brennan, J.P., Warham, E.J., Harnandez, J., Byerlee, D. and Coronel, F. (1990). Economic losses from Karnal bunt in Mexico. CIMMYT *Economic Working Paper* 90/02, p.56.

Brennan, P.S. (1975). General resistance in wheat to stem rust (*Puccinia graminis* Pers. f. sp. *tritici* Erikss. and Henn). Ph.D. Thesis, University of Saskatchewan, Saskatoon, Saskatchewan, p.141.

Brezhnev, D.D. (1977). The utilization of world plant gene pool of the U.S.S.R. in distant hybridization in plant breeding. In *Interspecific hybridization in plant breeding*. Proc. 8th Cong. E. Sanchez-Monge and F. Garcia-Olmedo (Eds.) EUCARPIA, Madrid.

Briggle, L.W. (1963). Heterosis in wheat - a review. *Crop Sci.* **3**, 407-412.

Briggle, L.W., Cox, E.L. and Hayes, R.M. (1967). Performance of a spring wheat hybrid, F_2, F_3 and parent varieties at five population levels. *Crop Sci.* **7**, 465-470.

Briggs, S.P. (1998). Plant genomics : More than food for thought. *Proc. Natl. Acad. Sci.USA*, **95**, 1986-1988.

Brock, R.D. (1977). When to use mutations in plant breeding. In *Manual on mutation breeding*. 2nd ed. IAEA, Vienna. STI/DOC/10/119, pp.213-219

Brooking, I.R. and Kirby, E.J.M. (1981). Interrelationships between stem and ear development in winter wheat : the effects of a Norin 10 dwarfing gene, Gai/Rht_2. *J. Agric. Sci.* **97**, 373-381.

Brown, J.F. and Sharp, E.L. (1969). Interaction of minor host genes for resistance to *Puccinia striiformis* with changing temperature regime. *Phytopath.* (Worcester) **59**, 999-1001.

Brown, J.F., Shipton, W.A. and White, N.H. (1966). The relationship between hypersensitive tissue and resistance in wheat seedlings infected with *Puccinia graminis tritici*. *Ann. Appl. Biol.* **58**, 279-290.

Browning, J.A. and Frey, K.J. (1969). Multiline cultivars as a means of disease control. *Annu. Rev. Phytopathol.* **7**, 355-382.

Bruce, A.B. (1910). The Mendelian theory of heredity and the augmentation of vigour. *Science* **32**, 627-628.

Bruns, R. and Peterson, J. (1998). Yield and stability factors associated with hybrid wheat. In *Wheat Prospects for Global Improvement*, H.J. Braun *et al.* (Eds.), Kluwer, Academic Pub. (Proc. 5th Int. Wheat Conf., Ankara, Turkey), pp. 23-27.

Bucio-Alanis, L. (1966). Envoirnmental and genotype-environmental components of variability.I. Inbred lines. *Heredity* **21**, 387-397.

Bucio-Alanis, L. and Hill, j. (1966). Environmental and genotype-environmental components of variability.II. Heterozygotes. *Heredity* **21**, 399-405.

Bucio-Alanis, L., Perkins, J.M. and Jinks, J.L. (1969). Environmental and genotype-environmental components of variability V. Segregating generations. *Heredity* **24**, 115-127.

Busch, R.H., Lucken, K.A. and Frohberg, R.C. (1971). F_1 hybrids versus random F_5 line performance and estimates of genetic effects in spring wheat. *Crop Sci.* **11**, 357-361.

Bushnell, W.R. (1964). Respiration of microsamples excised from single rust colonies. *Plant Physiol.* (Kutztown) **39**, 63-69.

Caldwell, K.A. and Kasarda, D.D. (1978). Assessment of genomic and species relationships in *Triticum* and *Aegilops* by PAGE and by differential staining of seed albumins and globulins. *Theor. Appl. Genet.* **52**, 273-280.

Caldwell, R.M., Roberts, J.J. and Eyal, Z. (1970). General (slow rusting) resistance to *Puccinia recondita* f. sp. *tritici* in winter and spring wheats. *Phytopathology* **60**, 1287.

Cavalli, L.L. (1952). An analysis of linkage in quantitative inheritance. In *Quantitative Inheritance*, E.C.R. Reeve and C.H. Waddington (Eds.), HMSO, London, pp. 135-144.

Ceccarelli, S. (1989). Wide adaptation : How wide? *Euphytica* **40**, 197-205.

Chahalan, C. and Law, C.N. (1979). The genetical control of cold resistance and vernalisation requirement in wheat. *Heredity* **42**, 125-132.

Chakravarti, B.P. (1968a). Attempts to alter infection process and aggressiveness for *Puccinia graminis* var *tritici*. *Phytopath* (Worcester) **56**, 223-229.

Chakravarti, B.P. (1968b). Behaviour of haustoria of *Puccinia graminis* var. *tritici* in some resistant wheats. *Indian Phytopath* (New Delhi) **21**, 86-91.

Chang, M., Fry, J.F., Pang, S., Zhou, H., Hironaka, C.M., Dunan, D.R., Conner, T.W. and Wan, Y. (1997). Genetic transformation of wheat by *Agrobacterium tumefaciens Plant Physiology* **115**, 971-980.

Chang, T.T., Li, C.C. and Tagumpay, O. (1973). *Bot. Bull. Acad. Sin.* **14**, 83-93.

Chapman, G.P. (1987). The tapetum. *Int. Rev. Cytol.* **107**, 111-125.

Chapman, V., Miller, T.E. and Riley, R. (1976). Equivalence of the A-genome of bread wheat and that of *Triticum uraru*. *Genet. Res. Camb.* **27**, 69-76.

Chavan, J.K. and Adsule, R.N. (1985). Evaluation of nutritive value of wheat. In *Quality of Wheat and Wheat Products*. D.K. Salunkhe, Kadam, S.S. and Austin, A. (Eds.), Metropolitan Book Co. (P) Ltd., New Delhi, pp. 21-34.

Chen, P.D., Tsujimoto, H. and Gill, B.S. (1994). Transfer of Ph^1 gene promoting homoeologous pairing from *Triticum speltoides* into common wheat and their utilization in alien genetic introgression. *Theor. Appl. Genet.*

Chen, T.H.H., Lazar, M.D., Scoles, G.J., Gusta, L.V. and Kartha, K.K. (1987). Somaclonal variation in population of winter wheat. *J. Plant Physiol.* **130**, 27-36.

Chinoy, J.J. (1962). Physiology of drought resistance in wheat. IV. *Fyton (Vicente Lopes)* **19**, 5-10.

Chinoy, J.J. (1966). Physiology of drought resistance in wheat V. *Fyton (Vicente Lopez)* **19**, 11-20.

Chopra, V.L. and Swaminathan, M.S. (1966). Mutagenic efficiency of individual and combined treatments of ethyl-methane- sulfonate and hydroxylamine in emmer wheat. *Indian J. Genet.* **26**, 59-62.

Chopra, V.L., Jain, S.K. and Swaminathan, M.S. (1960). Studies on the chemical induction and pollen sterility in some crop plants. *Indian J. Genet.* **20**, 188.

Chugh, A., Mahalakshmi, A., Singh, Vikrant and Khurana, P. (2004). A non-tissue culture approach for green line transformation of Indian bread wheat. (Cited by Khurana *et al.*, 2004).

CIMMYT (1976). The CIMMYT wheat training manual (Rev. February, 1976). Int. Maize and Wheat Improvement Ctr., Mexico 6, D.F.

Clausen, M., Kranter, R., Schachermayr, G., Potrykus, I. and Sautter, C. (2000). Antifungal activity of a virally encoded protein in transgenic wheat. *Nature Biotechnol.* **18**, 446-449.

Comeau, A., Plourde, A., St-Pierre, C.A. and Nadeau, P. (1988). Production of doubled haploid wheat lines by wheat × maize hybridization. *Genome* **30**, 482.

Costillo, A.M. and Cistue, L. (1993). Production of gynogenetic haploids of *Hordeum vulgare* L. *Plant Cell Rep.*, **12**, 139.

Cox, T.S. (1991). The contribution of introduced germplasm to the development of U.S. wheat cultivars. In *Use of Plant Introductions in Cultivar Development*, Part 1, CSSA Special Publication No. 17, pp. 25-47.

Cox, T.S. and Hatchett, J.H. (1994). Hessian fly resistance gene H26 transferred from diploid goat grass to common wheat. *Crop Sci.* **34**, 958-960.

Cox, T.S., Harrell, L.G., Chen, P. and Gill, B.S. (1991). Reproductive behaviour of hexaploid/diploid wheat hybrids. *Plant Breeding* **107**, 105-118.

Cox, T.S., Raupp, W.J. and Gill, B.S. (1993). Leaf rust resistance genes Lr 41, Lr 42 and Lr 43 transferred from *Triticum tauschii* to common wheat. *Crop Sci.* **34**, 339-343.

Cregan, P.B. and Busch, R.H. (1978). Heterosis, inbreeding and line performance in crosses of adapted spring wheats. *Crop Sci.* **18**, 247-251.

Cukadar, B., Pena, R.J. and Van Ginkel, M. (2001). Yield potential and bread making quality of bread wheat hybrids produced using Genesis, a chemical hybridizing agent. In *Wheat in a Global Environment*, Z. Bedo and L. Lang (Eds.), Kluwer Academic Publishers, Dordrecht-Boston-London, pp. 541-550.

Cukadar, B., van Ginkel, M., Dunphy, D. and Rajaram, S. (1998). Hybrid Wheat Research at CIMMYT using Genesis Hybridizing Agnet. In *Hybrid Wheat* - A New Crop Going to Farmers. Z. Aimin and Tiecheng, H. (Eds.), The Proceedings of 1st International Workshop on Hybrid Wheat. China Agricultural University Press, Beizing, China, pp. 31-36.

Daly, J.M. and Mrupka, L.R. (1962). Effect of *Puccinia graminis tritici* on organic acid content of wheat leaves. *Plant Physiol.* (Kutztown) **37**, 277-282.

D'Amato, F. and Scarascia, G.T. (1962). Types and frequencies of chlorophyll mutations in durum wheat induced by radiations and chemicals. *Radiat. Bot.* (London) **2**, 217-239.

Damisch, W. (1970). Uber die Entstehung des Kornertrages bei Getreide. *Albrecht-Thaer-Arch. (Berlin)* **14**, 169-179.

Daniel, G., Baumann, A. and Schmucker, S. (2005). Production of wheat doubled haploids (*Triticum aestivum* L.) by wheat × maize crosses using colchicine enriched medium for embryo regeneration. *Cereal Res. Comm.* **33**, 461-468.

Das, B.V. (1954). Study of the inheritance of reaction to stem rust in certain wheat crosses. Thesis, I.A.R.I., New Delhi.

Das, M.K., Rajaram, S., Mundt, C.C. and Kronstad, W.E. (1992). Inheritance of slow-rusting resistance to leaf rust in wheat. *Crop Sci.* **32**, 1452-1456.

Dasgupta, T. and Mondal, A.B. (1988). Diallel analysis in wheat. *Indian J. Genet.* **48**, 167-170.

Davenport, C.B. (1908). Degeneration, albinism and inbreeding, *Science* **28**, 454-455.

Dawson, I.A. and Wardlaw, I.F. (1989). The tolerance of wheat to high temperatures during reproductive growth III. Booting to anthesis. *Aust. J. Agric. Res.* **40**, 965-980.

de Buyser, J., Henry, Y., Lonnet, P., Hertzog, R. and Hespel, A. (1987). "Florin" : A doubled haploid wheat variety developed by the anther culture method. *Plant Breed.* **98**, 53-56.

de Kock, M. (1972). The actions of gamma irradiations and N-methyl-N nitrosomea in plants. Ph.D. diss. Washing ton stat. Univ.

De Vries, A. Ph. (1971). Flowering biology of wheat, particularly in view of hybrid seed production- A review. *Euphytica*, **20**, 152-170.

De Vries, A. Ph. (1972). Some aspects of cross-pollination in wheat (*Triticum aestivum* L.) I. Pollen concentration in the field as influenced by variety, diurnal pattern, weather conditions and level as compared to the height of the pollen donor. *Euphytica* **21**, 185-203.

De Vries, A. Ph. (1973). Some aspects of cross-pollination in wheat (*Triticum aestivum* L.) 2. Anther extrusion and ear and plant flowering pattern and duration. *Euphytica* **22**, 445-456.

De Vries, A. Ph. (1974a). Some aspects of cross-pollination in wheat (*Triticum aestivum* L.) 3. Anther length and number of pollen grains per anther. *Euphytica* **23**, 11-19.

De Vries, A. Ph. (1974b). Some aspects of cross-pollination in wheat (*Triticum aestivum*) 4. Seed set on male sterile plants as influenced by distance from the pollen source, pollinator, male sterile ratio and width of the male sterile strip, *Euphytica* **23**, 601-622.

Deghais, M. and Auriau, P. (1993). Comparison between pedigree, modified bulk and single seed descent methods of selection on grain yield in wheat under semi-arid conditions. *Annals-de-I-Institute-National-de-la-Recherche-Agronomique-de-Tunisie* **66**, 1-17.

Delibes, A., Sanchez-Monge, R. and Garcia-Olmedo, F. (1977). Biochemical and cytological studies of genetic transfer from the M^v genome of *Aegilops ventricosa* into hexaploid wheat: A progress report. In Interspecific hybridization in plant breeding, E. Sanchez-Monge and F. Garcia-Olmedo (Ed.), *Proc. 8th Congr.* Eucarpia, Madrid, pp. 81-89.

Dell'Aquila, A., Colaprico, G., Taranto, G. and Carella, G. (1983). Endosperm changes in developing and germinating *T. aestivum, T. turgidum* and *T. monococcum* seeds. *Cereal Res. Comm.* **11**, 107-113.

den Nijis, A.P.M. and van Dijik, G.E. (1993). Apomixis. In *Plant Breeding Principles and Prospects*. M.D. Hayward, N.O. Bosemark and I. Romagosa (Eds.), Chapman and Hall, London, pp. 229-245.

Dennell, R.W. (1973a). *Proc. Prehist. Soc.,* **39**, 75-99.

Dennell, R.W. (1973b). The phylogenesis of *Triticum dicoccum* a reconsideration. *Econ. Bot.* **27**, 329-331.

Deodikar, G.B., Patil, V.P. and Rao, V.S.P. (1979). Breeding for Indian *durum* and *dicoccum* wheats by interspecific and intergeneric hybridization with 4n *Triticum* speices. *Indian J. Genet.* **39**, 114-125.

Devos, K.M. and Gale, M.D. (1993). Extended genetic maps of the homoeologous group 3 chromosomes of wheat, rye and barley. *Theor. Appl. Genet.* **85**, 649-652.

Dhaliwal, A.S., Mares, D.J. and Marshall, D.R. (1987). Effect of 1B/1R chromosome translocation on milling and quality characteristics of bread wheats. *Cereal. Chem.* **64**, 72-76.

Dhayal, L.S., Sastry, E.V.D. and Jakhar, M.L. (2003). The genetic architecture of yield and its component traits in bread wheat grown under saline and normal environments. *Indian J. Genet.* **63**, 335-336.

Dhiman, J.S. (1982). Epidemiology of Karnal bunt of wheat in Punjab. Ph.D. Thesis, Punjab Agricultural University, Ludhiana, Punjab.

Dhiman, K.C., Dawa, Tashi and Dawa, T. (1999). Genetic architecture of yield traits in bread wheat. *Crop Improv.* **26**, 193-197.

Dhindsa, G.S. and Anand, S.C. (1973). Effect of spacing on heterosis in wheat. *Ind. J. Agric. Sci.* **43**, 177-180.

Dhindsa, G.S. and Bains, K.S. (1986). Genotype × environment interaction for some morpho-physiological characters in triple test cross progenies of wheat. *Crop Improv.* **13**, 168-171.

Dholakia, B.B., Ammiraju, J.S.S., Santra, D.K., Singh, H., Katti, M.V., Lagu, M.D., Tamhankar, S.A., Rao, V.S., Gupta, V.S., Dhaliwal, H.S. and Ranjekar, P.K. (2001). Molecular makrer analysis of protein content using PCR based DNA markers in wheat. *Biochemical Genetics* **39** (9/10), 325-328.

Dobrinin, M.G. 1969. Root system of grasses and its role in the trend of yield (in Russian). *Izd. Kolos* (Leningrad), 181-254.

Donald, C.M. (1968). The design of a wheat genotype. 3rd Int. Wheat Genet. Symp. (Canberra) 377-378.

Donchev, N. (1967). Age resistance of some soft wheat varieties to races 21, 77 and 122 of wheat brown rust, *P. recondita* Rob. et. Desm. f. sp. *tritici* (Erikss). *P. triticina* (Erikss) (in Bulgarian). *Rastienev Nauki* (Sofia) **4**, 3-11.

Donini, B., Scrascia-Mugnozza, G.T. and D'Amato, F. (1964). Effect of chronic gamma irradiation in durum and bread wheat. *Radiat. Bot.* (oxford-London) **4**, 387-393.

Donini, B.G., Scarascia-Mugnozza, G.T. and D'Amato, D. (1968). Genetic effects of chronic gamma irradiation in durum wheat. *Radiat. Bot.* (Oxford-Londcn), **8**, 49-58.

Doodson, J.K., Manners, J.G. and Myers, A. (1964). Some effects of yellow rust (*Puccinia striiformis*) on the growth and yield of a spring wheat. *Ann. Bot.* (Oxford-London) **28**, 459-472.

Dorofeev, V.F. (1972). *Bull. Appl. Bot. Genet. Pl. Breeding*, Lening **47**, 3-202.

Dorofeev, V.F. and Korovina, O.N. (1979). *Flora of Cultivated Plants.I. Wheat, Kolos, Leningrad.*

Dorsey, E. (1936). Induced Polyploidy in Wheat and Rye. *J. Hered.* **25**, 155-160.

Dosba, F. and Doussinault, G. (1977). Introduction into wheat of the resistance to eyespot in *Aegilops ventricosa*. In *Interspecific hybridization in plant breeding*, E. Sanchez-Monge and F. Garcia-Olemedo (Ed.). *Proc. 8th Cong. Eucarpia*, Madrid. pp. 99-107.

Doussinault, G., Delibes, A., Sanchez-Monge, R. and Garciaolmedo, F. (1983). Transfer of a dominant gene for resistance to eyespot disease from a wild grass to hexaploid wheat. *Nature* (London) **303**, 698-700.

Driscoll, C.J. (1972). XXZ system of producing hybrid wheat. *Crop Sci.* **12**, 516.

Driscoll, C.J. (1973). Minor genes affecting homoeologous pairing in hybrids between wheat and related genera. *Genetics* **74**, 66 (Abstr.).

Driscoll, C.J. (1977). Registration of cornerstone male sterile wheat germplasm. *Crop Sci.* **17**, 190.

Driscoll, C.J. (1983). Third compendium of wheat-alien chromosome lines. Suppl. Proc. 6th Int. wheat Genet. Symp., Kyoto, Japan, Wite Agricultural Institute, University of Adelaide, Australia.

Driscoll, C.J. (1984). Semi-dwarf mutants in Triticale and wheat breeding. In *Semi-dwarf cereal mutants and their use in cross-breeding.* Vol.II. *Proc. Res. Coord. Meet on Evaluation of Semi-dwarf Cereal Mutants for Cros: Breeding.* Davis, C.A. 30 Aug.-3 Sept. 1982. IAEA, Vienna, TECDOC-307, pp. 101-110.

Driscoll, C.J. (1985). Modified XYZ system of producing hybrid wheat. *Crop Sci.* **25**, 1115.

Dubin, H.J. and Duveiller, E. (2002). *Helminthosporium* leaf blight of wheat : Integrated control and prospects for the future. In *Proceedings of the Int. Conf. on Integrated Plant Disease Management for Sustainable Agriculture*, Indian Phytopathological Society, New Delhi, India, 10-15, Nov. 1997, Mitra *et al.* (Eds.), **1**, 575-579.

Dubinin, N.P. (1969). Classification of chromosome permutational damage. *Proc. XII. Int. Congr. Genet.* (Tokyo) pp. 79-92.

Duveiller, E. (2004). *Helminthosporium* leaf blight of wheat : a biotic constraint in warmer areas. In *Wheat : Technologies for Warmers Areas*, V.S. Rao, G. Singh and S.C. Misra (Eds.), Anamaya Publishers, New Delhi, pp. 219-227.

Dvorak, J. (1976). The relationship between the genome of *Triticum urartu* and the A and G genomes of *Triticum aestivum. Can. J. Genet. Cytol.* **18**, 371-377.

Dvorak, J. (1977). Transfer of leaf rust resistance from *Aegilops speltoides* to *Triticum aestivum. Can. J. Genet. Cytol.* **19**, 133-141.

Dvorak, J. (1988). Cytogenetical and molecular inferences about the evolution of wheat. In *Proc. 7th Int. wheat Genet. Symp.*, T.E. Miller and H.M.D. Koebner (Eds.), pp.187-192.

Dvorak, J. and Knott, D.R. (1974). Disomic and ditelocentric additions of diploid *Agropyron elongatum* chromosomes to *Triticum aestivum. Can. J. Genet. Cytol.* **16**, 399-417.

Dvorak, J., Resta, P. and Kota, R.S. (1990). Molecular evidence on the origin of wheat chromosome 4A and 4B. *Genome*, **33**, 30-39.

Dwivedi, A.N., Pawar, I.S. and Madan, Shashi (2002). Studies on variability parameters and character association among yield and quality attributing traits in wheat. *Haryana Agric. Univ. J. Res.* **32**, 77-80.

Dyck, P.L. and Kerber, E.R. (1970). Inheritance in hexaploid wheat of leaf rust resistance and other characters derived from *Aegilops squarrosa. Can. J. Genet. Cytol.* **12**, 175-180.

Eapen, S. and Rao, P.S. (1984). Spontaneous and induced variation in tissue cultures and regenerated plants of bread wheat. In *Plant Tissue Culture and its Agricultural Applications*, L.A. Withers and P.G. Alderson (Eds.), Butterworths, London, pp. 461-467.

East, E.M. (1908). Inbreeding in corn. *Rept. Connecticut Agric. Exp. Sta. for 1907*, **11**, 419-429.

Eavis, R.M., Batchelor, S.E., Murray, F. and Walker, K.C. (1996). Hybrid breeding of wheat, barley and rye : Development to date and future prospects. *Res. Rev.* 35, London, Home-Grown Cereals Authority.

Eberhart, S.A. and Russell, W.A. (1966). Stability parameters for comparing varieties. *Crop Sci.* **6**, 36-40.

Edwards, I.B., Thompson, W.G. and Pingree, D.W. (1980). *Ann. Wheat Newsl.* **26**, 36-37.

Edwards, L.H. and Williams, N.D. (1966). Mutagenic and chromosomal effects of X-rays and alkylating chemicals on *Triticum durum* Desf. "Dakota". *Crop Sci.* (Madison) **6**, 271-272.

Edwards, L.H., Williams, N.D., Gough, F.J. and Lebsock, K.L. (1969). A chemically induced mutation for stem rust resistance in little club wheat. *Crop Sci.* **9**, 838, 839.

Eiges, N.S., Lapehenko, G.D., Ivanov, J.A. and Vaisfely, L.I. (1971). Winter wheat mutants produced by ethylenimin and breeding work carried on with them (in Russian). *Prakt. Him. Mut.* (Moscow) 32-45.

Einaghy, M.A. and Linko, P. (1962). The role of 4-glucosyl-2, 4-dihydroxy-7 methoxy-1, 4-benzoxazin-3-one in resistance of wheat to stem rust. *Physiol. Plant* (Copenhagen) **15**, 764-771.

Einaghy, M.A. and Shaw, M. (1966). Correlation between resistance to stem rust and the concentration of a glucoside in wheat. *Nature* (London), **210**, 417-418.

El Nadi, A.J. (1969). Efficiency of water use by irrigated wheat in the Sudan. *J. Agric. Sci.* (Cambridge) **73**, 261-266.

El-Hennaury, M.A. (1996). Heterosis and combining ability in diallel crosses of eight bread wheat varieties. *Bulletin of Faculty of Agriculture*, **47**, 379.

Endo, T.R. (1979). *Wheat Infor. Serv.* **50**, 24-28.

Endo, T.R. (1988). Chromosome mutation induced by gametocidal chromosomes in common wheat. In *Proc. 7th Int. Wheat Genet. Symp.*, T.E. Miller and R.M.D. Koebner (Eds.), Cambridge, England, pp. 259-265.

Endo, T.R. (1990). Gametocidal chromosomes and their induction of chromosome mutation in wheat. *Jpn. J. Genet.* **65**, 135-152.

Endo, T.R. and Katayama, Y. (1979). *Wheat Infor. Serv.* **47/48**, 32-35.

Endo, T.R. and Tsunewaki, K. (1975). Sterility of common wheat with *Aegilops triuncialis* Cytoplasm. *J. Hered.* **66**, 13-18.

Evans, D.A., Sharp, W.R. and Medina-Filho, H.P. (1984). Somaclonal and gametoclonal variation. *Am. J. Bot.* **71**, 759-774.

Evans, L.T. and Rawson, H.M. (1970). Photosynthesis and Respiration by the flag leaf and components of the ear during grain development in wheat. *Aust. J. Biol. Sci.*, **23**, 245-254.

Evans, L.T., Bingham, J., Jackson, P. and Sutherland, J. (1972). *Ann. appl. Biol.* **70**, 67-76.

Falk, D.E. and Kasha, K.J. (1981). Comparison of the crossability of rye (*Secale cereale*) and *Hordeum bulbosum* in wheat (*Triticum aestivum*). *Can. J. Genet. Cytol.* **23**, 81-88.

Falk, D.E. and Kasha, K.J. (1983). Genetic studies of the crossability of hexaploid wheat with rye and *Hordeum bulbosum*. *Theor. Appl. Genet.* **64**, 303-307.

Farooq, S., Shah, T.M. and Iqbal, N. (1990). Variation in crossability among intergeneric hybrids of wheat and salt tolerant accessions of three *Aegilops species*. *Cereal Res. Comm.* **18**, 335-338.

Farsky, I. (1961). Water requirement of spring cereals (in Slovak) *Vysk. Ust. Zavl. Hosp.* (Bratislava) 18-53.

Feldman, M. (1966). Identification of unpaired chromosomes in F_1 hybrids involving *Triticum aestivum* and *T. timopheevii*. *Can. J. Genet. Cytol.* **8**: 144-151.

Feldman, M. (1968). Regulation of somatic association and meiotic pairing in common wheat. In *Proc. 3rd Int. Wheat Genet. Symp.*, K.W. Finlay and K.W. Shepherd (Eds.), Canberra, Australia 5-9 August. Australian Academy of Science, Canberra, pp. 31-40..

Feldman, M. (1979). New evidence on the origin of the B-genome of wheat p.120-132. In *Proc. 5th Int. Wheat Genet. Symp.*, S. Ramanujam (ed.), New Delhi, India. 23-28 Feb., 1978. Indian Soc. Genet. Plant Breeding, I.A.R.I., New Delhi.

Feldman, M. (1988). Cytogenetics and molecular approaches to alien gene transfer in wheat. In *Proc. 7th Int. Wheat Genet. Symp.*, T.E. Miller and R.M.D. Koebner (Eds.), Cambridge, England, pp. 23-32.

Feldman, M. (2001). The origin of cultivated wheat. In *The World Wheat Book*, A. Bonjean and W. Angus (Eds.), Lavoisier Publishing, Paris, pp. 3-56.

Feldman, M. and Kislev, M. (1977) *Aegilops searsii*, a new source of section *Sitopsis* (Platystachys). *Israel J. Bot.* **26**, 190-201.

Feldman, M. and Mello-Sampayo, T. (1967). Suppression of homoeologous pairing in hybrids of polyploid wheats × *Triticum speltoides. Can. J. Genet. Cytol.* **9**, 307-313.

Feldman, M. and Sears, E.R. (1981). The wild gene resources of wheat. *Scient. Am.* **244**, 98-109.

Fida-Mohammad, Humaira-Daniel, Khurana-Shahzad and Hamayoon-Khan (2001). Heritability estimates for yield and its components in wheat. *Sarhad J. Agri.* **17**(2), 227-234.

Finlay, K.W. and Wilkinson, G.N. (1963). The analysis of adaptation in plant breeding programme. *Aust. J. Agric. Res.* **14**, 742-754.

Finney, K.F. (1978). Genetically high protein hard winter wheat. *Bakers Dig.* **52**(3), 32-35.

Flavell, R.B. and Smith, D.B. (1976). Nucleotide sequence organization in the wheat genome. *Heredity* **37**, 231-252.

Florell, V.H. (1931). *J. Agric. Res.* **42**, 341-362.

Fonseca, S. and Patternson, F.L. (1968). Hybrid vigor in a seven-parent diallel cross in common winter wheat (*Triticum aestivum* L.). *Crop Sci.* **8**, 85-88.

Fonstein, L.M. (1963). On the effect of gamma irradiation of wheat seed on the radio-resistance of the progeny of the treated plants (in Russian) *Dokl. Akad. Nauk. SSSR* (Moscow) **153**, 933-935.

Francis, H.A., Leitch, A.R. and Koebner, R.M.D. (1995). Conversion of RAPD-generated PCR product, containing a novel dispersed repetitive element, into a fast and robust assay for the presence of rye chromatin in wheat. *Theor. Appl. Genet.* **90**, 636-642.

Freeman, G.H. and Perkins, J.M. (1971). Environmental and genotype-environmental components of variability. VIII. Relations between genotypes grown in different environments and measures of these environments. *Heredity* **27**, 15-23.

Frey, K.J., Browning, J.A. and Simons, M.D. (1975). Multiline cultivars of autogamous crop plants. *SABRAO J.* **7**, 113-123.

Fric, F. and Fuchs, W.H. (1970). Veranderingen der Aktivitat einiger enzyme in Weizenblatt in Abhangigkeit Von der temperaturlabilen Vertraglichkeit fur *Puccinia graminis tritici. Phytopath. Z.* (Berlin) **67**, 161-174.

Friebe, B., Jiang, J., Gill, B.S. and Dyck, P.L. (1993). Radiation induced nonhomoeologous wheat-*Agropyron intermedium* chromosomal translocations conferring resistance to leaf rust. *Theor. Appl. Genet.* **86**, 141-149.

Friebe, B., Raupp, W.J. and Gill, B.S. (2001). Alien genes in wheat improvement. In *Wheat in a Global Environment*, Z. Bedo and L. Lang (Eds.) Kluwer Academic Publishers, pp. 709-720.

Friebe, B., Zeller, F.J., Mukai, Y., Forster, B.P., Bartos, P. and Mc Intosh, R.A. (1992). Characterization of rust resistance wheat-*Agropyron intermedium* derivatives by C-banding, *in situ* hydrization and isozyme analysis. *Theor. Appl. Genet.* **83**, 775-782.

Fritz, S.E. and Lukaszewski, A.J. (1989). Pollen longevity in wheat, rye and triticale. *Plant Breed.* **102**, 31-34.

Fuentes-Davila, G., Rajaram, S. and Singh, G. (1995). Inheritance of resistance to Karnal bunt (*Tilletia indica* Mitra) in bread wheat. *Plant Breeding*, **114**, 250-252.

Fukasawa, H. (1953). Studies on restoration and substitution of nucleus (genome) in *Aegilotriticum* I. Appearance of male sterile durum in substitution cross. *Cytologia* **18**, 167-175.

Fukasawa, H. (1957). Studies on restoration and substitution of nucleus (genome) in *Aegilotricum*. IV. Genome exchange between *durum* and *ovata* cytoplasm and its theoretical consideration for male sterility.

Fukasawa, H. (1958). Fertility restoration of cytoplasmic male sterile emmer wheat. *Wheat Inf. Serv.* **7**, 21.

Fukasawa, H. (1959). Nucleus substitution and restoration by means of successive backcrosses in wheat and its related genus *Aegilops*. *Jpn. J. Bot.* **17**, 55-91.

Galachalova, Z.N. and Skurina, A.M. (1963). Growth process of wheats on the effect of X-ray applied to kernels of different water content (in Russian). *Izd. Akad. Nauk SSSR* (Moscow) pp. 83-88.

Galande, A.A., Tiwari, R., Ammiraju, J.S.S., Santra, D.K., Lagu, M.D., Rao, V.S., Gupta, V.S., Misra, B.K., Nagarajan, S. and Ranjekar, P.K. (2001). Genetic analysis of kernel hardness in bread wheat using PCR based markers. *Theor. Appl. Genet.* **103**, 601-606.

Gale, M.D. and Law, C.N. (1977). Plant Breeding Inst. Annual Report 1976, pp. 21-34.

Gale, M.D. and Miller, T.E. (1987). The introduction of alien genetic variation into wheat. In: *Wheat Breeding-Its Scientific Basis,* F.G.H. Lupton (Ed.). Chapman and Hall, pp. 173-210.

Gale, M.D., Salter, A.M. and Angus, W.J. (1987). IAEA Publication.

Galili, G. and Feldman, M. (1984). Mapping of glutenin and gliadin genes located on chromosome 1B of common wheat. *Molec. Gen. Genet.* **193**, 293-298.

Gallais, A. (1989). Lines versus hybrids – the choice of the optimum type of variety. *Science for Plant Breeding*. Proc. XII Cong. EWCARPIA, February 27-March 4, 1989, pp. 69-80.

Gallun, R.L. and Khush, G.S. (1980). In *Breeding Plants Resistant to Insects*, F.G. Maxwell and P.R. Jennings (Eds.), Wiley, New York, pp. 62-85.

Gaul, H. and Astviet, K. (1966). Induced variability of culm length in different genotypes of hexaploid wheat following X-irradiation and EMS treatment. *Savrem. Poljopr.* **14**, 253-276.

Gavinlertvatana, S. and Wilcoxson, R.D. (1978). Inheritance of slow rusting of spring wheat by *Puccinia recondita* f. sp. *tritici* and host parasite relationship. *Trans. Br. Mycol. Soc.* **71**, 413-418.

Gerechter-Amitai, Z.K. and Stubbs, R.W. (1970). A valuable source of yellow rust resistance in Israeli populations of wild emmer, *Triticum dicoccoides* Koern. *Euphytica* (Wageningen) **19**, 12-21.

Gerlach, W.L., Appels, R., Dennis, E.S. and Peacock, W.J. (1978). Evolution and analysis of wheat genomes using highly repeated DNA sequences. In *Proc. 5th Int. Wheat Genet. Symp.*, S. Ramanujan (Ed.), New Delhi, India 23-28 Fen. 1978. Indian Soc. Genet. Plant Breeding, IARI, New Delhi. pp.81-91.

Ghiasi, H. and Lucken, K.A. (1982). Agronomic and male fertility restoration characteristics of wheat restorer lines with *Aegilops speltoides* and *Triticum timopheevii* cytoplasms. *Crop Sci.* **22**, 527-530.

Ghiasi, H., Lucken, K.A. and Hammond, J.J. (1982). Selection procedures for developing fertility restorer lines in wheat. *Crop Sci.* **22**, 523-527.

Ghosh, Suva, Sikka, S.M. and Rao, M.V. (1958). Inheritance studies in wheat. IV. Inheritance of rust resistance and other characters. *Indian J. Genet.* **18**, 142-162.

Gilbert, S.K. (1963). Chemical mutagenesis in small grains. *Diss. Abstr.* (Michigan) **24**, 1350-1351.

Gilchrist, L.I. (1994). Research on septoria diseases at CIMMYT. In Guide to the CIMMYT Wheat Crop Protection Subprogram. E.E. Saari and G.P. Hettel (Eds.), CIMMYT Wheat Special Report No. 24, CIMMYT, D.F., Mexico, pp. 42-47.

Gill, B.S. and Kimber, G. 1974. A Giemsa C-banding technique for cereal chromosomes. *Cereal Res. Commun.* **2**, 87-94.

Gill, B.S. and Raupp, W.J. (1987). Direct gene transfers from *Aegilops squarrosa* L. to hexaploid wheat. *Crop Sci.* **27**, 445-450.

Gill, K.S., Bhullar, G.S., Bhatia, A. and Pannu, D.S. (1980). Combining ability in durum wheat. *P.A.U. J. Res.* **17**, 243-247.

Gill, K.S., Nanda, G.S., Singh, G. and Sehgal, K.L. (1979). Inheritance of grain number, grain size, protein content and grain yield in two spring and winter wheat crosses. *SABRAO J.* **11**, 1.

Gill, K.S., Nanda, G.S., Singh, G. and Aujla, S.S. (1979). Multilines in wheat–A review. *Indian J. Genet.* **39**, 30-37.

Gill, K.S., Sharma, Indu and Aujla, S.S. (1993). Karnal bunt and Wheat Production. Punjab Agricultural University, Ludhiana (Punjab) p. 153.

Giorgi, B. (1978). *Mut. Breed. Newsl.* **11**, 4-5.

Goodchild, N.A. and Boyd, W.J.R. (1975). Regional and temporal variations in wheat yield in Western Australia and their implications in plant breeding. *Aust. J. agric. Res.* **26**, 209-217.

Gopal, S.K., Sekhon, S., Bajaj, K.L., Saigal, R.P. and Singh, H. (1988). Effect of Karnal bunt disease on the milling, rheological and nutritional properties of wheat : studies on some chemical constituents and biological effects. *J. Food. Sci.* **53**, 1560-1562.

Goud, J.V. (1967a). Induced mutations in bread wheat. *Indian J. Genet.* **27**, 40-55.

Goud, J.V. (1967b). Induced polygenic mutations in hexaploid wheats. *Radiat. Bot.* **7**, 321-331.

Goujon, C. and Ingold, M. (1967). *C.R. Hebd. Seances Acad. Sci. Ser. D.* **264**, 334-336.

Goulden, C.H. (1941). Problems in plant selection, *Proc. 7th Intn. Genet. Cong.* (1939) Edinbugh pp. 132-133.

Grafius, J.E. (1964). A geometry for plant breeding. *Crop Sci.* (Madison) **4**, 241-246.

Grama, A. and Gerechter-Amitai, Z.K. (1974). Inheritance of resistance to stripe rust in crosses between wild emmer (*Triticum dicoccoides*) and cultivated tetraploid and hexaploid wheats. II. *Triticum aestivum. Euphytica* **23**, 393-398.

Grebener, H. (1964). Untersuchungen uber den Wasser haushalt verschieden dureresistenter sommergetreidesorten. *Z. Acker. u Pflbau* (Berlin-Hamburg) **119**, 138-148.

Griffing, B. (1956). Concept of general and specific combining ability in relation to diallel crossing systems. *Aust. J. Biol. Sci.* **9**, 463-493.

Grinvald, C., Diaconu, P. and Banu, M. (1967). Effect of radiation on wheat in the years of treatment (in Romanian). *Sericicultura (Bucuresti)* **34**, 47-58.

Grivet, L. and Noyer, J.L. (2003). Biochemical and molecular markers. In *Genetic Diversity of Cultivated Tropical Plants*, P. Hamon, Seguin, M., Perrier, X. and Glaszmann, J.C. (Eds.), Science Publishers, Inc. Enfield (NH), Plymouth, U.K., pp. 1-29.

Grunberg, A.M., Costa, J.M. and Kratochvil, R.J. (2001). Amplified fragment length polymorphism in a selected sample of soft red winter wheat. *Cereal Res. Comm.* **29**, 251-258.

Gruneberg, H. (1952). Genetical studies on the skeleton of the mouse.IV. Quasi-continuous variations. *J. Genet.* **51**, 95-114.

Gubareva, N.K., Gavrilijuk, J.P., Peneva, T.I. and Konarev, A.V. (1975). Rep. All Union N.I. Vavilov Inst. Pl. Industry, Leningrad.

Guidet, F., Rogowsky, P., Taylor, C., Song, W. and Langridge, P. (1991). Cloning and characterization of a new rye specific repeated sequence. *Genome* **34**, 81-87.

Gulkayan, V.O., Gulyam, A.A. and Tamanyan, K.G. (1971). Transmission of straw firmness in wheat hybrids (in Russian) *Bil. Zh. Armenii* (Erevan) **24**, 3-13.

Gustafson, J.P., Curtis, B.C. and Yougman, V.E. (1970). A chlorotic mutation in wheat. *Crop. Sci.* (Madison) **10**, 665-667.

Gyawali, K.K., Qualset, C.O. and Yamazaki, W.T. (1968). Estimates of heterosis and combining ability in winter wheat. *Crop Sci.* **8**, 322-324.

Haaring, R. (1962). Mutationsauslosung durch chemikalien bei Weizen.III. *Z. Pflzucht. (Berlin)* **48**, 117-142.

Hadlaczky, G. and Belea, A. (1975). C-banding in wheat evolutionary cytogenotics. *Pl. Sci. Lett.* **4**, 185-188.

Hagberg, G. and Hagberg, A. (1980). High frequency of spontaneous haploids in the progeny of an induced mutation in barley. *Hereditas* **93**, 341.

Hagberg, G. and Hagberg, A. (1981). Haploid initiator gene barley. In *Barley Genetics* IV. *Proc. of the 4th Int. Barley Genet. Symp.* M.J.C. Asher, Ed. Edinburgh, U.K., pp. 686-689.

Halloran, G.M. (1981). Grain yield and protein relationships in a wheat cross. *Crop Sci.* **21**, 699-701.

Hanawalt, P.C. (1972). Repair of genetic material in living cells. *Endeavour* (London) **31**, 83-87.

Hanchinal, R.R. and Goud, J.V. (1982). Seed setting and germination of AB-genome monosomic lines of PbC591×Bijaga Yellow and their backcross generations in wheat. *Wheat Inf. Serv.* **55**, 15-21.

Hanis, M., Knytl, V. and Jech, Z. (1969). The inducing of mutants resistant to yellow rust in the wintrer wheat variety Diana. I. (in Czech.). *Gen. Slecht.* (Praha) **5**, 257-262.

Harlan, H.V. and Martini, M.L. (1929). A composite hybrid mixture. *J. Amer. Soc. Agron.* **21**, 487-490.

Harlan, H.V., Martin, M.L. and Stevens, H. (1940). A study of methods in barley breeding, *US Dept. Agric. Tech. Bull.* **720**, 26.

Harrington, J.B. (1937). The mass-pedigree method in the hybridization improvement of cereals. *Jour. Amer. Soc. Agron.* **29**, 379-384.

Harwood, W.A., Bean, S.J., Chen, D.F., Mullineanx, P.M. and Snape, J.W. (1994). Transformation studies in *Hordeum vulgare* using a highly regenerable microspore system. *Euphytica* **85**, 113-118.

Hassan-Khan, A. (1973). Radiation induced high protein mutant strain of wheat. *Fourth Int. Wheat Genet. Symp.* (Missouri) pp. 273-281.

Hatchett, J.H., Starks, K.J. and Webster, J.A. (1987). Insect and mite pests of wheat. In *Wheat and Wheat Improvement*, E.G. Heyne (Ed.), 2nd Ed. Agronomy Monograph No. 13. *Amer. Soc. Agron.* Madison, WI, USA, pp. 625-675.

Hayes, H.K., Parber, J.H. and Kurtzweil, C. (1920). Genetics of rust resistance in crosses of varieties of *Triticum vulgare* with varieties of *T. durum* and *T. dicoccum. J. Agric. Res.* **19**, 523-542.

Hayman, B.I. (1954). The theory and analysis of diallel crosses. *Genetics* **39**, 789-809.

Hayman, B.I. (1958). The separation of epistatic from additive and dominance variation in generation means. *Heredity* **12**, 371-390.

Hayward, C.F. (1975). *Proc. 2nd Int. Winter Wheat Conf.*, pp. 84-104.

He, Zhonghu (1998). Current status of Wheat Breeding in China. In *Hybrid Wheat - A New Crop Going to Farmer*, Z. Aimin and H. Tiecheng, (Eds.), China Agricultural University Press, Beijing, China, pp. 1-8.

Heitefuss, R. (1964). Veranderungen im Gehalt an Ribonucleinsaure in Weizenpflanzen unterschiedlicher und temperaturgesteuerter Resistenz gegen *Puccinia graminis tritici Z. Pfl. Krank.* (Stuttgart) **71**, 154-158.

Helback, H. (1959). Domestication of food plants in the old world. *Science* **130**, 365-372.

Helback, H. (1969). *Pre-history and Human Ecology of Deh Luran Plain*, F. Hole, K.V. Flannery and J.A. Neely (Eds.), Univ. Michigan Museum Anthropology Memoirs I, Ann Arbor, pp. 244-383.

Hendrix, J.W., Jones, J.W. and Schmitt, C.G. (1965b). Influence of stripe rust and mechanical defoliation at various stages of host development on growth and wheat yield. *St. Univ. Inst. Agric. Sci. Tech. Bull.* (Washington) 18.

Henriksen, G.B. and Pope, W.K. (1971). Additive resistance to stripe rust in wheat. *Crop Sci.* (Madison) **11**, 825-827.

Henry, Y. and De Buyser, J. (1981). Float culture of wheat anthers. *Theor. Appl. Genet.* **60**, 77-90.

Hermelin, T. (1984). Induction and selection of protein mutants in spring wheat at the IAEA Seibersdorf Laboratory. In *Cereal Grain Protein Improvement. Proc. of Final Res. Coord. Meet for cereal Grain Protein Improvement*, Vienna, Austria, 6-10 Dec., 1982, IAEA, Vienna, STI/PUB/664, pp. 17-24.

Hewstone, M.C. (1997). Los cambios geneticos of agronomicos que incrementaron el rendimiento de trigo on chile. *Explorando altos rendimientos de trigo* Oct. 20-23, 1997. La Estanzuela, Uruguay, INIA and CIMMYT.

Heyne, E.G. and Smith, G.S. (1967). Wheat Breeding. In *Wheat and Wheat Improvement*, K.S. Quisenberry (Ed.), Agronomy Monograph. American Society of Agronomy Madison, Wisconsin, USA, **13**, 269-306.

Hill, M., Witsenboer, H., Zabeau, M., Vos, P., Kesseli, R. and Michelmore, R. (1996). PCR-based fingerprinting using AFLPs as a tool for studying genetic relationships in *Lactuca* spp. *Theor. Appl. Genet.* **93**, 1202-1210.

Hillman, G.C. (1972). *Papers in Economic History,* E.S. Higgs (Ed.), Cambridge University Press, pp. 182-188.

Hopf, M. (1969). *The Domestication and Exploitation of Plants and Animals.* P.J.Ucko and G.W. Dumbleby (Eds.), Duckworth, London, pp.355-360.

Hoshikawa, K. (1960). Studies on the reopened floret in wheat. *Proc. Crop Sci. Soc. Jpn.* **29**, 103-106.

Howard, A. and Howard, G.L.C. (1910). *Wheat in India : its production, varieties and improvement.* Thacker Spink & Co., Calcutta, pp. 128.

Howard, A. and Howard, G.L.C. (1912). On the inheritance of some characters in wheat. I. *Mem. Dep. Agric. India, Bot. Ser.* **5**, 1-47.

Howard, A. and Howard, G.L.C. (1915). On the inheritance of some characters in wheat.II. *ibid.* **7**, 273-285.

Howard, A. and Howard, G.L.C. (1928). The improvement of Indian Wheat. A brief summary of investigation carried out at Pusa from 1905 to 1924 including an account of the Pusa hybrids. *Bull. Pusa Agric. Res. Inst.*, pp.171-226.

Hsu, P. and Walton, P.D. (1971). Relationship between yield and its components and structures above the flag leaf node in spring wheat. *Crop Sci.* **11**, 190-193.

Hu, D.F., Yuan, Z.D., Tang, Y.L. and Liu, J.P. (1986). Jinghua No. 1 a winter what variety derived from pollen sporophyte. *Scientia Sinica Series* BXXIX, pp. 733-745.

Hu, H. (1986). Wheat : Improvement through anther culture : In *Biotechnology in Agriculture and Forestry*, Y.P.S. Bajaj (Ed.), Vol. 2, Crop I. Springer-Berlin Heidelberg, New York, Tokyo, pp. 55-72.

Hu, H. (1997). *In vitro* induced haploids in wheat. *In vitro Haploid Production in Higher Plants*, S. Jain, S. Sopory and R. Veilleux (Eds.), pp. 73-97.

Hu, Han, Hsi, T., Tseng, C., Quyang, T. and Ching, C. (1978). Application of anther culture to crop plants. In *Frontiers of plant tissue culture calgary*, T.A. Thorpe (Ed.), Canada, pp. 123-130.

Huang, S.S., Li, W.L., Xu, J. and Xu, C.P. (1991). *Acta Agronomica Sinica* **17**, 81-87.

Huang, T.C. (1990). Research on hybrid wheat. BAU Press, Beijing.

Hughes, W.G. and Bodden, J.J. (1977). Single gene for restoration of cytoplasmic male sterility in wheat and its implication in breeding of restorer lines. *Theor. Appl. Genet.* **50**, 129-135.

Hughes, W.G., Bennett, M.D., Bodden, J.J. and Galanopoulon, S. (1974). *Ann. Appl. Biol.* **76**, 243-252.

Huhn, M. (1979). Beitrage zur Erfassung der phanotypischen Stabilitat. I. Vorschlag einiger auf Ranginformationen beruhenden stabilitas parameter. *EDP in Medicine and Biology* **10**, 112-117.

Hyde, B.B. (1953). Addition of Individual Haynaldia Villosa chromosomes to Hexaploid Wheat. *Am. J. Bot.* **40**, 174-182.

Ikeguchi, S., Hasegawa, A., Oyamada, Y., Toriyama, K. and Tsunewaki, K. (1994). Basic studies on hybrid wheat breeding utilizing *Aegilops kotschyi* cytoplasms. Proceedings of the Japan-Russia Workshop Sapporo on Low Temperature and Physiology and Breeding of Northern Crops, Japan, p.77.

Iljin, W.S. (1929). Der Einfluss der Standortfenchtigkeit ouf den osmotischen Wert bei Pflanzen. *Planta* (Berlin) **7**, 45-58.

Ingold, M. (1968). Male fertility restorer systems in wheat. *Euphytica* **17**, (Suppl.) **1**, 69-74.

Islam, A.K.M.R., Shepherd, K.W. and Sparrow, D.H.B. (1975). Addition of individual barley chromosomes to wheat. *Proc. 3rd Int. Barley Genet. Symp.*, Garching, West Germany, Karl Thunig, Munchen, pp. 260-270.

Islam, A.K.M.R., Shepherd, K.W. and Sparrow, D.H.B. (1978). Production and characterization of wheat-barley addition lines. In *Proc. 5th IWGS*, New Delhi, India, pp. 365-371.

Jaaska, V. and Jaaska, U. (1980).Anaerobic Induction of Alcohol Dehydrogenase Isoenzymes in tetraploid wheats and their diploid relatives. *Biochemic Und Physiologie Der Pflanzen* **175**, 570-577.

Jackson, E.A., Holt, L.M. and Payne, P.I. (1985). *Genet. Res. Camb.* **46**, 11-17.

Jakubziner, M.M. (1970). Evaluation of drought resistance of the world sortiment of spring wheats. (in Russian) *Kolos* (Moscow) 44-55.

Jan, C.C. and Qualset, C.O. (1973). Genetic male sterility in wheat (*Triticum aestivum* L.)–reproductive characteristics and possible use in hybrid wheat breeding. *Hilgardia*, **45**, 153-171.

Jatasra, D.S. and Paroda, R.S. (1983). Combining ability studies in wheat. *Haryana Agric. Univ. J. Res.* **13**, 49-54.

Jatasra, D.S., Solanki, K.R., Singh, D.P. and Yadav, J.S. (1978). Gene action for grain protein in wheat. *Cereal Res. Comm.* **6**, 273.

Jayasekara, N.E.M. and Jinks, J.L. (1976). Effects of gene dispersion on estimates of components of generation means and variances. *Heredity* **36**, 31-40.

Jensen, N.F. (1952). Intra-varietal diversification in oat breeding. *Agron. J.* **44**, 30-34.

Jensen, N.F. (1970). A diallel selective mating system for cereal breeding. *Crop Sci.* **10**, 629-635.

Jensen, N.F. (1978). Composite breeding methods and the DSM system in cereals. *Crop Sci.* **18**, 622-626.

Jensen, N.F. (1988). *Plant Breeding Methodology*. John Wiley & Sons, Inc., New York.

Jensen, N.F. and Kent, G.C. (1963). New approach to an old problem in oat production. *Farm Res.* **29**, 4-5.

Jha, H.N. and Ram, A. (1968). A note on correlation and partial regression studies between yield and yield attributing characters in wheat. *Indian J. Agron.* (New Delhi) **13**, 200-202.

Jiang, J., Chen, P., Friebe, B., Raupp, W.J. and Gill, B.S. (1993). Alloplasmic wheat *Elymus ciliaris* chromosome addition lines. *Genome* **36**, 327-333.

Jiang, J., Friebe, B. and Gill, B.S. (1994). Chromosome painting of Amigo wheat. *Theor. Appl. Genet.* **89**, 811-813.

Jiang, J., Friebe, B., Dhaliwal, H.S., Martin, T.J. and Gill, B.S. (1993). Molecular cytogenetic analysis of *Agropyron elongatum* chromatin in wheat germplasm specifying resistance to wheat streak mosaic virus. *Theor. Appl. Genet.* **86**, 41-48.

Jinks, J.L. (1981). The genetic framework of plant breeding. *Phil. Trans. R. Soc. Lond.* **B192**, 407-419.

Jinks, J.L. (1983). Biometrical genetics of heterosis. In *Heterosis, Reappraisal of Theory and Practice*, R. Frankel (Ed.), Springer-Verlag, pp. 1-46.

Jinks, J.L. and Jones, R.M. (1958). Estimation of components of heterosis. *Genetics* **43**, 223-234.

Jinks, J.L. and Pooni, H.S. (1986). Description and illustration of the practical application of biometrical genetics to plant breeding. *Proc. 6th Meeting EUCARPIA Section Biometrics in Plant Breeding*. University of Birmingham, pp. 1-20.

Jizhong, W., Jianguo, X., Sifa, S., Gang, F., Qijun, Z. and Yunlin, H. (2001). New technique of "JIN AO LIN" chemical hybridization and application of wheat hybridization. In *Wheat in a Global Environment*, Z. Bedo and L. Lang (Eds.), Kluwer Academic Publishers, pp. 551-553.

Joarder, O.I., Islam, S.N., Uddin, M.M. and Eunus, A.M. (1982). Analysis of some quantitative characters from all possible reciprocal crosses between a set of parental lines of wheat. *Indian J. agric. Sci.* **52**, 801-808.

Joffe, A. and Small, J.G.C. (1964). The effect of periods of water stress on the growth and tillering of wheat and oats under controlled conditions. *Fyton (Vicente Lopez)* **21**, 69-76.

Johnson, B.L. (1975). Identification of the apparent B-genome donor of wheat. *Can. J. Genet. Cytol.* **17**, 21-39.

Johnson, B.L., Brannaman, B.L. and Zschile jr, F.P. (1968). Protein and enzyme changes in wheat leaves following infection with *Puccinia recondita*. *Phytopath.* (Worcester) **58**, 578-583.

Johnson, B.L., Schafer, J.F. and Leopold, A.C. (1966). Nutrient mobilization in leaves by *Puccinia recondita*. *Phytopath.* (Baltimore) **56**, 799-803.

Johnson, B.L., Zscheile jr, F.P. and Brannaman, B.L. (1967). Effect of *Puccinia recondita* infection on the RNA composition of wheat leaves. *Phytopath.* (Worcester), **57**, 632-638.

Johnson, R. (1988). Durable resistance to yellow (stripe) rust in wheat and its implications in plant breeding. In *Breeding strategies for Resistance to the Rusts of Wheat*. N.W. Simmonds and S. Rajaram (Eds.), CIMMYT, Mexico, pp. 63-75.

Johnson, R. and Lupton, F.G.H. (1987). Breeding for disease resistance. In *Wheat Breeding : Its Scientific Basis*, F.G.H. Lupton (Eds.), Chapman and Hall, London, U.K., pp. 369-424.

Johnson, V.A. (1977). *Farm Seed Conf. Am. Seed Trade Assoc.*, **23rd**, pp. 27-34.

Johnson, V.A. (1978). *Cereal Foods World* **23**, 84-86.

Johnson, V.A. and Schmidt, J.W. (1968). Hybrid Wheat. *Advances in Agronomy*, **20**, 199-233.

Johnson, V.A., Biever, K.J., Hannold, A., Schmidt, J.W. (1966). Inheritance of plant height, yield of grain, and other plant seed characteristics in a cross of hard winter wheat. *Crop Sci.* **6**, 336-338.

Johnson, V.A., Mattern, P.J., Schmidt, J.W. and Stroike, J.E. (1973). Genetic advances in wheat protein quantity and composition. *Proceedings of the 4th Int. Wheat Genetics Symposium*, E.R. Sears and L.M.S. Sears (Eds.), University of Missouri, Columbia Aug. 6-11, 1973, pp. 547-556.

Johnson, V.A., Schmidt, J.W. and Mekasha, W. (1966). Comparison of yield components and agronomic characteristics of four winter wheat varieties differing in plant height. *Agron. J.* **58**, 438-441.

Johnston, R.A., Quick, J.S. and Hammond, J.J. (1983). Inheritance of semolina colour in six durum wheat crosses. *Crop Sci.* **23**, 607-610.

Jones, R.M. and Mather, K. (1958). Interaction of genotype and environment in continuous variation. II. Analysis. *Biometrics* **14**, 489-498.

Joppa, L.R. (1987). Aneuploid analysis in tetraploid wheat. In *Wheat and Wheat Improvement*, Second Edition, E.G. Heyne (Ed.), American Society of Agronomy, Inc, Crop Science Society of America, Inc, Soil Science Society of America, Inc, Madison, Wisconsin, USA, pp. 256-267.

Joppa, L.R. and Williams, N.D. (1979). A disomic-5-D nullisomic-5B substitution line of durum wheat. *Crop Sci.* **19**, 509-511.

Joppa, L.R. and Williams, N.D. (1983). The Langdon durum D-genome disomic substitutions: Development, characteristics and uses. *Agron. Abstr. American Society of Agronomy*, Madison, WI, p. 68.

Joppa, L.R., Khan, K. and Williams, N.D. (1983). Chromosomal location of genes for gliadin polypeptides of durum wheat (*Triticum turgidum* L.). *Theor. Appl. Genet.* **64**, 289-293.

Joppa, L.R., Timian, R.G. and Williams, N.D. (1980). Inheritance of resistance to greenbug toxicity in an amphiploid of *Triticum turgidum–T. tauschii*. *Crop Sci.* **20**, 343-344.

Jordaan, J.P. (1996). Hybrid wheat : Advances and Challenges. In *Increasing Yield Potential in Wheat : Breaking the Barriers*, M.P. Reynolds, S. Rajaram and A. Mc Nab, (Eds.), Mexico, D.F., CIMMYT, pp. 66-75.

Joshi, A.B. and Dhawan, N.L. (1966). Genetic improvement in yield with special reference to self-fertilizing crops. *Indian J. Genet.* **26**, 101-113.

Joshi, B.C. and Singh, D. (1979). Introduction of alien variation into bread wheat. In *Proc. 15th Int. Wheat Genet. Symp.*, S. Ramanujam (Ed.), New Delhi, India, pp. 342-348.

Joshi, L.M., Singh, D.V., Srivastava, K.D. and Wilcoxson, R.D. (1983). Karnal bunt, a minor disease that is now a threat to wheat. *The Botanical Review* **49**(4), 309-330.

Jost, M. (1979). Int. Wheat Restorer Germplasm Screening Nur., 2nd, pp. 1-64.

Jost, M. (1980). Int. Wheat Restorer Germplasm Screening Nur. 3rd, pp. 1-67.

Jost, M. (1981). Int. Wheat Restorer Germplasm Screening Nur. 4th, pp. 1-41.

Jost, M. and Hayward, C.F. (1980). F_1 hybrid versus 32 selected F_7 lines performance of common winter wheat (*Triticum aestivum* spp. *vulgare*). *Theor. Appl. Genet.* **57**, 177-180.

Kadam, B.S. (1936). Genetics of the *Bansi* wheat of the Bombay-Deccan and a synthetic *Khapli*. I. *Proc. Indian Acad. Sci.* **B.4**, 357-369.

Kadam, B.S. and Nazareth, B. (1931). Inheritance of awn colour in wheat. *Indian J. agric. Sci.* **1**, 663-670.

Kao, F.T. (1965). Genetic effects of recurrent irradiation in diploid, tetraploid and hexaploid *Triticum* species. *Diss. Abstr. (Ann Arbor)* **26**, 638-639.

Kar, G.N., Chakrabarti, S.N. and Prasad, A.B. (1978). Improvement of bread wheat through mutation breeding. *Wheat Newsl.* **24**, 62-63.

Karam, S.N. (1958). Inheritance of plant height, date of heading and tillering in three wheat crosses. *Diss. Abstr.* (Ann Arbor) 647.

Kasha, K.J. and Kao, K.N. (1970). High frequency haploid production in barley. *Nature* **225**, 874-876.

Kaul, A.K. (1969). Tests for quality in early generation P-wheat. *Indian J. Genet.* **29**, 348-352.

Kaul, R.D. (1969). Relations between water status and yield of some wheat varieties. *Z. Pflzucht.* (Berlin) **62**, 145-154.

Keeble, F. and Pellew, C. (1910). The mode of inheritance of stature and of time of flowering in peas. *J. Genet.* **1**, 47-56.

Keller, W.A., Armstrong, K.C. and de La roche, A.I. (1983). The production and utilization of microspore derived haploids in Brassica crops. In *Plant Cell Cultures in Plant Improvement*, S.K.Sen and K.L. Giles (Eds.), Plenum, New York, pp. 169-183.

Kema, G.H.J., Sayoud, R., Annone, J.G. and Van Sillhout, C.H. (1996). Genetic variation for virulence in the wheat. *Mycosphaerella graminicola* pathosystem. I. Interaction between pathogen isolates and host cultures. *Phytopathology* **86**, 200-201.

Kerber, E.R. (1983). Suppression of rust resistance in amphiloids of *Triticum*. *Proc. 6th Int. Wheat Genet. Symp.,* Kyoto, Japan, 28 Nov.- 3 Dec.Plant Germpalsm Inst. Fac. Agric. Kyoto University, Kyoto, pp. 813-817.

Kerber, E.R. and Dyck, P.L. (1969). Inheritance in hexaploid wheat of leaf rust resistance and other characters derived from *Aegilops squarrosa*. *Can. J. Genet. Cytol.* **11**, 639-647.

Kerber, E.R. and Dyck, P.L. (1973). Inheritance of stem rust resistance transferred from diploid wheat (*Triticum monococcum*) to tetraploid and hexaploid wheat and chromosome location of the gene involved. *Can. J. Genet. Cytol.* **15**, 397-409.

Kerber, E.R. and Green, G.J. (1980). Suppression of stem rust resistance in hexaploid wheat cv. Canthatch by chromosome 7DL. *Can. J. Bot.* **58**, 1347-1350.

Ketata, H., Edwards, L.H. and Smith, E.L. (1976). Inheritance of eight agronomic characters in a winter wheat cross. *Crop Sci.* **16**, 19-22.

Ketata, H., Smith, E.L., Edwards, L.H. and McNew, R.W. (1976). Detection of epistatic, additive and dominance variation in winter wheat. *Crop Sci.* **16**, 1-4.

Khadr, F.H. (1970). Variation and covariation of seed weight and its components in wheat following irradiation, EMS and hybridization. *Theor. Appl. Genet.* **40**, 280-285.

Khadr, F.H. (1971). Variability and covariability for plant height, heading date and seed weight in wheat crosses. *Theor. Appl. Genet.* **41**, 100-103.

Khanna, H.K. and Daggard, G.E. (2003). *Agrobacterium tumefaciens*-mediated transformation of wheat using a superbinary vector and a polyamine-supplemented regeneration medium. *Plant Cell Reports* **21**, 429-436.

Khurana, J., Chugh, A. and Khurana, P. (2002). Regeneration from mature and immature embryos and transient gene expression via *Agrobacterium*-mediated transformation in emmer wheat. *Indian J. Exp. Biol.* **40**, 1295-1303.

Khurana, P., Mahalakshmi, A., Patnaik, D., Chugh, A., Vishnudasan, D. and Singh, V. (2004). Regeneration and genetic transformation studies in Indian Bread, Pasta and Emmer Wheats. In *Wheat : Technologies for Warmer areas*, V.S. Rao, G. Singh, S.C. Misra (Eds.). Anamaya Publishers, New Delhi, pp.152-157.

Khurana, V., Singh, R.K. and Munjal, G. (1983). Combining ability of brown rust resistant stock of wheat for yield attributes. *Indian J. Genet.* **43**, 106-108.

Khush, G.S. and Baenziger, P.S. (1998). Crop Improvement : Emerging Trends in Rice and Wheat Crop Productivity and Sustainability - Shaping the Future. *Proceedings of 2nd Int. Crop Sci. Congress*, V.L. Chopra, R.B.Singh and R. Varma (Eds.), pp. 113-125.

Kibirige-Sebunya, I. and Knott, D.R. (1983). Transfer of stem rust resistance to wheat from an *Agropyron* chromosome having a gametocidal effect. *Can. J. Genet. Cytol.* **25**, 215-221.

Kihara, H. (1919). Uber cytologische studien bei einige Getreidearten. I. Species-Bastarde des Weizens und Weizenroggen-Bastarde. *Bot. Mag. Tokyo* **32**, 17-38.

Kihara, H. (1924). Cytologische und genetische studien bei wichtigen getreidearten mit besonderer Rucksicht auf das Verhanen der chromosomen und die Steriliat in den Bastasrden Mem. Coll. Sci., Kyoto Imp. Univ., **B**, 1-200.

Kihara, H. (1944). Discovery of the DD-analyser, one of the ancestors of *Vulgare* wheat. *Agric. Hort.* (Tokyo) **19**, 889-890.

Kihara, H. (1951). Substitution of nucleus and its effects on genome manifestation. *Cytologia*, **16**, 177.

Kihara, H. (1954). Considerations on the evolution and distribution of *Aegilops species* based on the analyser method. *Cytologia* **19**, 336-357.

Kihara, H. (1958a). Fertility and morphological variation in the substitution and restoration backcrosses of the hybrids. *Triticum vulgare × Aegilops caudata. Proc. Tenth Intern. Cong. Genet.* **2**, 142-171.

Kihara, H. (1958b). Forty years after the discovery of right chromosome numbers of the genus *Triticum. Wheat Inform. Serv.,* Kyoto, Japan No. **7**, 1-2.

Kihara, H. (1959). Fertility and morphological variation in the substitution and restoration backcrosses of the hybrids, *Triticum vulgare × Aegilops caudata. Proc. X Int. Cong. Gen.* Univ. Toronto Press, **1**, 142-171.

Kihara, H. and Katayama, Y. (1931). Genomanalyse bee *Triticum* and *Aegilops* III. Zur Entstehungsweise eines neven konstanten oktoploiden. *Aegitotricum Cytologia* **2**, 234-255.

Kihara, H. and Kondo, N. (1943). *Seiken Ziho* **2**, 24-42.

Kihara, H. and Tanaka, M. (1970). *Wheat Infor. Serv.* **30**, 1-2.

Kihara, H. and Tsunewaki, K. (1960). Production of polyploid wheat by nitrous oxide. *Proc. Jap. Acad.* **36**, 658-663.

Kihara, H. and Tsunewaki, K. (1961). *Seiken Jiho* **12**, 1-10.

Kihara, H. and Tsunewaki, K. (1962). Use of an alien cytoplasm as a new method of producing haploids. *Jpn. J. Genet.* **37**, 310-313.

Kihara, H. and Tsunewaki, K. (1963). Comparative genetics in wheat. *J. Indian Bot. Soc., Maheshwari Comm.* **42A**, 83-101.

Kimber, G. (1967). The addition of the chromosomes of *Aegilops umbellulata* to *Triticum aestivum* (var. Chinese Spring). *Genet. Res. Camb.* **9**, 111-114.

Kimber, G. (1973). The relationship of the S-genome diploids to polyploid wheat. *Proc. Nat. Acad. Sci.* (USA) **69**, 912-915.

Kimber, G. (1984). Technique selection for the introduction of alien variation in wheat. *Z. Pflanzenzuecht.* **92**, 15-21.

Kimber, G. and Athwal, R.S. (1972). A reassessment of the course of evolution of wheat. *Proc. Natn. Acad. Sci. USA* **69**, 912-915.

Kimber, G. and Feldman, M. (1987). Wild wheat. An introduction. Special Report 353, College of Agriculture, Univ. of Missouri, Columbia, USA.

Kimber, G. and Sears, E.R. (1983). Assignment of genome symbols in the Triticeae. In *Proc. 6th Int. Wheat Symp.*, S. Sakamoto (Ed.), Kyoto, Kyoto, Japan, pp.1195-1196.

Kimber, G. and Sears, E.R. (1987). Evolution in the genus *Triticum* and the origin of cultivated wheat. In *Wheat and Wheat Improvement*, E.G. Heyne (Ed.), 2nd Edition, American Society of Agronomy Madison, Wisconsin, U.S.A.

Kimber, G., Pignone, D. and Sallee, P.J. (1983). The relationship of the M and M^u genomes of *Triticum*. *Can. J. Genet. Cytol.* **25**, 509-512.

Kiraly, Z. (1968). Physiology of plant disease resistance (in Hungarian), Akademiai Kiado Budapest, p.138.

Kiraly, Z. and Farkas, G.L. (1962). Relation between phenol metabolism and stem rust resistance in wheat. *Phytopathology* (Baltimore) **52**, 657-664.

Kis, A. (1963). In Lelley, J. and Mandy, GY. Wheat. (in Hungarian) Budapest, 230p.

Klechovskii, V.M., Evdokimova, T.P. and Zhulikova, A.E. (1962). Influence of irradiation on the composition of deoxyribonucleic acid (DNA) in plants (in Russian). *Dokl. TSHA* (Moscow) **79**, 235-242.

Knott, D.R. (1979a). Selection for yield in wheat breeding. *Euphytica* **28**, 37-40.

Knott, D.R. (1979b). The transfer of genes for rust resistance to wheat from related species. *In*: *Proc. 5th Int. Wheat Genet. Symp.*, S. Ramanujam (Ed.), India, pp.354-357.

Knott, D.R. (1987). The application of breeding procedures to wheat. In *Wheat and Wheat Improvement* (2nd Edition) Agronomy Monograph No. 13, E.G. Heyne (Ed.), *Am. Soc. Agron, Crop Sci. Soc., Am. and Soil Sci. Soc. Am.*, Madison, WI.

Knott, D.R. (1988). Using polygenic resistance to breed for stem rust resistance in wheat. In *Breeding Strategies for Resistance to the Rusts of Wheat* N.W. Simmonds and S. Rajaram (Eds.), CiMMYT, Mexico, pp. 39-47.

Knott, D.R. (1989). *The Wheat Rusts : Breeding for Resistance*. Springir-Verlag, p.201.

Knott, D.R. and Hughes, G.R. (1974). Studies on stem and leaf rust resistance in wheat. Ind. Mutatins of f. sied. res. in crop plants. *Int. At. En. Ag.* (Vienna), pp. 35-43.

Knott, D.R. and Kumar, J. (1975). Comparison of early generation yield testing and a single seed descent procedure in wheat breeding. *Crop Sci.* **15**, 295-299.

Kobayshi, M. and Tsunewaki, K. (1980). Haploid induction and its genetic mechanism in alloplasmic common wheat. *J. Hered.* **71**, 9-14.

Koebner, R.M.D. and Shepherd, K.W. (1985). Induction of recombination between rye chromosome 1RL and wheat chromosomes. *Theor. Appl. Genet.* **71**, 208-215.

Koebner, R.M.D. and Shepherd, K.W. (1988). Isolation and agronomic assessment of allosyndetric recombinants derived from wheat/rye translocation IDL.1RL carrying reduced amount of rye chromatin. *In*: *Proc. 7th Int. Wheat Genet. Symp*, T.E. Miller & R.M.D. Koebner (Eds.), Cambridge, England, pp. 343-348.

Kofoid, K.D. (1991). Selection for seed set in a wheat population treated with a chemical hybridizing agent. *Crop Sci.* **31**, 277-281.

Konzak, C.F. (1966). Development of genetic method for wheat improvement. *Mut. in Pl. Breed.* (Vienna) IAEA, pp. 173-175.

Konzak, C.F. (1973). Using mutagens and mutations in wheat breeding and genetics research. Fourth Int. Wheat Genet. Symp., (Missouri), pp. 275-281.

Konzak, C.F. (1981). Induced mutations for genetic analysis and improvement of wheat. In *Induced mutations - a tool in crop plant research. Proc. Symp. on Induced Mutations as a Tool for crop Improvement*, Vienna, Austria 9-13 March, IAEA, Vienna, STI/PUB/591, pp. 469-488.

Konzak, C.F. (1984). Role of induced mutations. In *Crop Breeding: A Contemporary basis*. P.B. Vose and S.G. Blixt (Eds.), Pergamon Press, New Delhi, pp.216-292.

Konzak, C.F. (1986). Genetic analysis, genetic improvement, and evaluation of induced semi-dwarf mutants in wheat. In *Evaluation of semi-dwarf cereal mutants for cross breeding. Proc. 4th FAO/IAEA Res. Coord. Meet.* Casaccia, Rome, Italy. 16-20 Dec. 1985, IAEA, Vienna.

Konzak, C.F. (1987). Mutations and mutation breeding. In *Wheat and Wheat Improvement (2nd Ed.)* Agronmy Monograph No. 13, E.G. Heyne (Ed.), American Society of Agronomy, Inc., Crop Science Society of America, Inc. Soil Science Society of America, Inc. Madison, Wisconsin, USA, pp. 428-443

Konzak, C.F., Kleinhofs, A. and Ullrich, S.E. (1984). Induced mutations in seed propagated crops. In *Plant Breeding reviews*. J. Janick (Ed.), AVI Publishing Co., Westport, CT, **2**, 13-72.

Konzak, C.F., Wilson, M.R. and Franks, P.A. (1984). Progress in the evaluation, use in breeding and genetic analysis of semidwarf mutants of wheat, In *Semi-dwarf cereal mutants and their use in cross-breeding*. Vol.II. *Proc. of Res. Coord. Meet. on Evaluation of Semi-dwarf Cereal Mutants for Cross Breeding*. Davis, California, 30 Aug.-3 Sept., 1982, IAEA, Vienna TECDOC 307, pp.39-50.

Korotkova, A.P. (1972). Using of experimental mutagenesis in wheat improvement (in Russia). *Selek. Semenov.* (Moscow) **37**, 35-36.

Kota, R.S. and Dvorak, J. (1985). A rapid technique for substituting alien chromosomes into *Triticum aestivum* and determining their homoeology. *Can. J. Genet. Cytol.* **27**, 559-558.

Kozhusko, N.N. (1961). Effect of gamma radiation in different plant development periods (in Russian). *Sb. Trud. Asp. Molod. Nauc. Sotr.* (Leningrad) **2/6**, 317-321.

Kozhusko, N.N. and Volkova, A.M. (1971). Laboratory estimation of drought resistance of new spring wheat varieties. (in Russian). *Vest. Sel'hoz. Nanki* (Moscow) **16**, 70-73.

Krishnawat, B.R.S. and Sharma, S.P. (1998). Genetic variability in wheat under irrigated and moisture stress conditions. *Crop Res.* **16**, 314.

Kronstad, W.E. and Foote, W.H. (1964). *Crop Sci.* **4**, 616-619.

Krstev, K. (1964). "A" coenzyme in leaf rust infected wheat leafs (in Bulgarian). *Nauk Tr. Viss. Selsk. Inst. "V. Kolarov"* (Plovdiv) **13**, 221-224.

Krupnov, V.A. (1971). *Genetika* (Moscow) **7**, 159-174.

Kuckuck, H. (1979). *Wheat Infor. Serv.* **50**, 1-5.

Kulshreshtha, V.P. (1985). History and ethnobotany of wheat in India. *J. Agric. Trad. ed. de Bot Appl.* **XXXII**, 67-71.

Kumar, J. (1973). Early generation selection and a comparison of two breeding methods in wheat (*T. aestivum* L.), Ph.D. Thesis, University of Saskatchewan, Saskatoon.

Kumar, J., Sharma, A.K., Singh, R.P., Saharan, M.S. and Nagarajan, S. (2004). Can Karnal bunt be ever a risk for wheat cultivation in warmer areas of India. In *Wheat Technologies for Warmers Areas*, V.S. Rao, G. Singh and S.C. Misra (Eds.), Anamaya Publishers, New Delhi, pp. 264-271.

Kumashiro, T. and Oinuma, T. (1985). Comparison of genetic variability among anther-derived and ovule-derived doubled haploid lines of tobacco. *Jpn. J. Breed.* **35**, 301.

Kundu, Sushila, JagShoran and Chatrath, R. (2005). A compendium of wheat (*Triticum* L.) varieties. Technical Bulletin No. 7, Directorate of Wheat Research, Karnal, p.20.

Kuspira, J. and Millis, L.A. (1967). Cytogenetical analysis of tetraploid wheats using hexaploid aneuploids. *Can. J. Genet. Cytol.* **9**, 79-86.

Kuspira, J. and Unrau, J. (1957). Genetic analysis of certain characters in common wheat using whole chromosome substitution lines. *Can. J. Pl. Sci.* **37**, 300-326.

Lacadena, J.R. (1974). Spontaneous and induced parthenogenesis and androgenesis. In *Haploids and Higher Plants, Proc. of the 1st Int. Symp.* K.J. Kasha (Ed.), University of Guelph, Guelph, Ontario, pp. 13-32.

Lacadena, J.R., Cermeno, M.C., Qrellana, J. and Santoz, J.L. (1984). Evidence for wheat-rye nucleolar competition (amphiplasty) in triticale by silver-staining procedure. *Theor. Appl. Genet.* **67**, 207-213.

Lagudah, E.S., Appels, R. and McNeil, D. (1991). The Nor-D-3 locus of *Triticum tauschii*: natural variation and linkage markers in chromosome 5. *Genome* **34**, 387-395.

Langer, R.H.M. (1967). Physiological approaches to yield determination in wheat and barley. *Fld. Crop Abstr.* (London) **20**, 101-106.

Lapitan, N.L.V., Sears, R.G. and Gill, B.S. (1984). Translocations and other karyotypic structural changes in wheat × rye hybrids regenerated from tissue culture. *Theor. Appl. Genet.* **68**, 547-554.

Lapitan, N.L.V., Sears, R.G., Rayburn, A.L. and Gill, B.S. (1986). Wheat-rye translocations. *J. Heredity* **77**, 415-419.

Lapoujade, P., Ecochard, R. and Sarrafi, A. (1991). Inheritance of semolina colour in six durum wheat crosses. *Crop Sci.* **23**, 607.

Larik, A.S., Siddiqui, K.A., Hafiz, H.M.I. and Arain, M.H. (1984). Evaluation of wheat mutants for days to maturity. *Wheat Inf. Serv.* **58**, 22-24.

Larkin, P. J., Ryan, S., Brettell, R. and Scowcroft, W. (1984). Heritable somaclonal variation in wheat. *Theor. Appl. Genet.* **81**, 581-588.

Larkin, P.J. and Scowcroft, W.R. (1981). Somaclonal variation-a novel source of variability from cell cultures for crop improvement. *Theor. Appl. Genet.* **60**, 197-214.

Larkin, P.J., Banks, P.M., Lagudah, E.S., Appels, R., Chen, X., Xin, Z.Y., Ohm, H.W. and McIntosh, R.A. (1995). Disomic *Thinopyrum intermedium* addition lines in wheat with barley yellow dwarf virus resistance and with rust resistance. *Genome* **38**, 385-394.

Larson, R.I. and Mac Donald, M.D. (1963). Inheritance of the type of solid stem in golden Ball (*T. durum*) III. *Canad. J. Gen. Cytol.* (Ottawa) **5**, 437-444.

Laurie, D.A. (1989). The frequency of fertilization in what × pearl millet crosses. *Genome* **32**:1063-1067.

Laurie, D.A. and Bennett, M.D. (1986). Wheat × maize hybridization. *Can. J. Genet. Cytol.* **28**, 313-316.

Laurie, D.A. and Bennett, M.D. (1987). The effect of the crossability loci Kr1 and Kr 2 on fertilization frequency in hexaploid wheat × maize crosses. *Theor. Appl. Genet.* **73**, 403-409.

Laurie, D.A. and Bennett, M.D. (1988). The production of haploid wheat plants from wheat × maize crosses. *Theor. Appl. Genet.* **76**, 393-397.

Laurie, D.A., O'donoughur, L.S. and Bennett, M.D. (1990). Wheat × maize and other wide sexual hybrids : Their potentiality for crop improvement and genetic manipulations. In *Genetic Manipulation in Plant Improvement II.* J.P. Gustaffson (Ed.), *Proc. 19th Stadler Genet. Symp.* Plenum Press, New York, *Theor. Appl. Genet.* **76**, 393-397.

Law, C.N. (1966). The location of genetic factors affecting a quantitative character in wheat. *Genetics* (Austin) **53**, 487-498.

Law, C.N. and Chapman, V. (1974). EWAC Newsl. No. 4, 8-9.

Law, C.N. and Krattiger, A. (1987). *J. Sci. Fd. and Agric.*

Law, C.N., Gaines, R.C., Johnson, R. and Worland, A.J. (1978). The application of aneuploid technique to a study of stripe rust resistance in wheat. In *Proc. 5th Int. Wheat Genet. Symp.* S. Ramanujam (Ed.), New Delhi, 1978, Indian Soc.Genet. and Plant Breeding, pp. 427-436

Law, C.N., Sutka, J. and Worland, A.J. (1978). A genetic study of day-length response in wheat. *Heredity* **41**, 185-191.

Law, C.N., Worland, A.J., Chapman, V. and Miller, T.E. (1977). Interspecific hybridization in plant breeding. *Proc. 8th EUCARPIA Congr.* Madrid, Spain, pp. 73-80.

Law, J. and Stoskopf, N.C. (1973). Further observation on ethaphon (ethrel) as a tool for developing hybrid cereals. *Can J. Plant Sci.* **53**, 765.

Lazzeri, P. and Shewry, P. (1993). Biotechnology of cereals. *In : Biotechnology and Genetic Engineering* **11**, 79-145.

Le, H.T., Armstrong, K.C. and Miki, B. (1989). Detection of rye DNA in wheat-rye hybrids and wheat translocation stocks using total genomic DNA as a probe. *Plant Mol. Biol. Reporter* **7**, 150-158.

Leaver, C.J. (1989). Structure and functionof the mitochondical genome in relation to cytoplasmic male sterility. *Vortr. Pflanzenzuchtg* **16**, 379-390.

Leaver, C.J., Isaac, P.G., Small, I.D., Bailey-Serres, J., Liddell, A.D. and Hawkesford, M.J. (1988). Mitochondrial genome diversity and cytoplasmic male sterility in higher plants. *Philos Trans. R. Soc. Lond.* **B319**, 165-176.

Leighty, C.E. and Sando, W.J. (1924).The blooming of wheat flowers. *J. Agril. Res.* **27**, 231-244.

Leighty, C.E. and Taylor, J.W. (1924). "Hairy Neck" wheat segregates from wheat-rye hybrids. *J. Agric. Res.* **28**, 567-576.

Lelley, J. (1964a). Investigations with new wheat breeding methods (in Hungarian) *Diss.* MTA 1-302.

Lelley, J. (1964b). New technology of single seed seeding in wheat for wheat breeding purposes. *Polnohosp (Bratislava)* **10**, 693-699.

Lelley, J. (1976). *Wheat Breeding : Theory and Practice.* Akademiai Kiado, Budapest (Hungary).

Lenton, J.R. and Gale, M.D. (1987). *Proc. Fourth Int. Symp. on Pre-harvest sprouting in cereals,* D.J. Mares (Ed.), Port Macquarie, Australia, pp. 253-264.

Lenton, J.R., Hedden, P. and Gale, M.D. (1987). In *Hormone Action in Plant Development—A critical Appraisal*, G.V. Hoad, J.R. Lenton, M.B. Jackson and R.K. Atkin (Eds.), Butterworths, London.

Leonard, K.J. (1969). Genetic equilibria in host-pathogen systems. *Phytopathol.* **59**, 1858-1863.

Levitt, J. (1956). The hardiness of plants. *Advances in Agronomy* **6**, Acad. Press, New York, 278.

Levy, A.A. and Feldman, M. (2002). The impact of polyploidy on grass genome evolution. *Plant Physiol.* **130**, 1587-1593.

Lewellen, R.T. (1967). Interaction of genes and environment conditioning inheritance of stripe rust resistance of wheat. *Diss. Abstr.* (Ann Arbor) **28**, 1799.

Lewellen, R.T., Sharp, E.L. and Hehn, E.R. (1967). Major and minor genes in wheat for resistance to *Puccinia striiformis* and their responses to temperature. *Can. J. Bot.* (Ottawa) **45**, 2155-2172.

Li, C.C. (1975). *Chung-hua Nung Hsueh Hui Pao (J. Agric. Assoc. China)*, **92**, 41-56.

Li, X.L., Ren, Y.H., Zhang, N.S. and Li, G.L. (1982). A preliminary study on heterosis and combining ability in hybrid wheat with *Triticum timopheevi* cytplasm. *Hereditas*, China **4**, 21-24.

Liang, G.H. and McHughen, A. (1987). Novel approaches in wheat improvement. In *Wheat and Wheat Improvement* 2nd edn., E.G. Heyne (Ed.), Agronomy Monograph No. 13, American Society of Agronomy, Inc., Crop Science Society of America, Inc, Soil Science Society of America Inc., Madison, Wisconsin, USA, pp. 472-506.

Liang, G.H., Sangduen, N., Heyne, E.G. and Sears, R.G. (1982). Polyploid production through anther culture in common wheat. *J. Hered.* **73**, 360-364.

Liang, G.H., Wang, R.C., Niblett, C.L. and Heyne, E.G. (1979). Registration of B-6-37-1 wheat germplasm. *Crop Sci.* **19**, 421.

Lin, J.J. and Kuo, J. (1995). AFLPTM : A novel PCR-based assay for plant and bacterial DNA fingerprinting. *Focus* **17**, 66-70.

Lin, J.J., Kuo, J., Ma, J., Saunders, J.A., Beard, H.S., Macdonald, M.H., Kenworthy, W., Ude, G.N. and Matthews (1996). Identification of molecular markers in soybean comparing RFLP, RAPD and AFLP DNA mapping techniques. *Plant Molecular Biology Reporter* **14**, 156-169.

Livers, R.W. (1964). Fertility restoration and its inheritance in male-sterile wheat. *Science*, **144**, 420.

Livers, R.W. and Heyne, E.G. (1968). Hybrid vigour in hard red winter wheat. *Proc. 3rd Int. Wheat Genet. Symp.* pp. 431-436.

Livne, A. (1964a). Photosynthesis of healthy and rust-affected bean and wheat plants. *Diss. Abstr.* (Michigan) **24**, 3047.

Livne, A. (1964b). Photosynthesis in healthy and rust-affected plants. *Plant Physiol.* (Lancester **39**, 614-621.

Loegering, W.Q. and Sears, E.R. (1963). Distorted inheritance of stem-rust resistance of Timstein caused by a pollen-killing gene. *Can. J. Genet.* and *Cytol.* **5**, 65-72.

Longwell, J.H., Jr. and Sears, E.R. (1963). Nullisomics in tetraploid wheat. *Am. Nat.* **97**, 401-403.

Lonts, V. (1983). Modes of gene action and heritability of economically useful characters in wheat. *Genetica Zerenovykh* (USSR), p.299.

Loo, S. and Xu, Z.H. (1986). Rice : Anther culture for rice improvement in China. In *Biotechnology in Agriculture and Forestry*, Y.P.S. Bajaj (Ed.), Vol.2., Crop 1. Springer-Berlin Heidelberg, New York, Tokyo, pp. 139-156.

Lorenz, K. and Loewe, R. (1977). Mineral composition of U.S. and Canadian Wheats and Wheat blends. *J. Agric. Food Chem.* **25**, 806.

Love, A. (1984). Conspectus of the *Triticeae. Feddes Report* **95**, 426-521.

Lucken, K.A. (1973). Comparative use of cytoplasmic male sterility-fertility restoration systems in hybrid-wheat breeding. *Proceedings of the Fourth Int.Wheat Genet. Symp., Columbia*, pp. 361-366.

Lucken, K.A. (1982). *Am. Soc. Agron. Publ. Wheat Yields.*

Lucken, K.A. (1987). Hybrid wheat. In *Wheat and What Improvement*, E.G. Heyne (Ed), Agronomy Monograph 13: ASA CSSA and SSSA Madison, Wisconsin, pp. 444-452.

Lucken, K.A. and Johnson, K.D. (1988). Hybrid Wheat Status and Outlook. *Proceedings of Int. Symp. on Hybrid Rice*, 255, Changsha, China, pp. 243-255.

Lucken, K.A. and Maan, S.S. (1967). *Agron. Abstr.* **14**,

Lunderstadt, J. and Fuchs, W.H. (1968). Hexokinaz Aktivitat an rostinfiziert en Weizenkeim Blattern. *Z. Physiol.* (Stuttgart) **59**, 445-456.

Luo, M.C., Yen, C. and Yang, J.L. (1992). Crossability percentage of bread wheat landraces from Sichuan Province, China with rye. *Euphytica* **61**, 1-7.

Lupton, F.G.H. and Macer, R.C.F. (1962). *Trans. Br. Mycol. Soc.* **45**, 21-45.

Lupton, F.G.H. and Whitehouse, R.N.H. (1957). Studies on the breeding of self-pollinated cereals. *Euphytica* **6**, 169-184.

Lupton, F.G.H., Bingham, J., Blackman, J.A., Angus, W.J., Jackson, P.J., Oliver, R.H., Kirby, A. and Taylor, M. (1980). Nuclear factor for male sterility. *Ann. Rep. Plant Breed. Institutre Cambridge* **1979**, 21.

Lupton, F.S. (1966a). The use of physiological characters in breeding for yield in wheat. *Qual. Pl. Mat. Veg.* (Den Haag) **13**, 375-376.

Lupton, F.S. (1966b). Translocation by photosynthetic assimilates in wheat. *Ann. Appl. Biol.* (London) **57**, 355-364.

Lupton, F.S. and Macer, R.C. (1962). In heritance of resistance of yellow rust in seven varieties of wheat. *Trans. Br. Mycol. Soc.* (London) **45**, 21-45.

Lupton, F.S. and Pinthus, M.J. (1969). Carbohydrate translocation from small tillers to spike-producing shoots in wheat. *Nature* (London) **221**, 483-484.

Ma, Z.Q. and Sorrells, M.E. (1995). Genetic analysis of fertility restoration in wheat using restriction fragment length polymorphism. *Crop Sci.* **35**, 1137-1143.

Maan, S.S. (1973). Cytoplasmic variability in *Triticinae*. *Proc. 8th Int. Wheat Genet. Symp.*, Columbia, pp. 367-373.

Maan, S.S. (1975). Exclusive Preferential Transmission of an alien chromosome in common wheat. *Crop Sci.* **15**, 287-292.

Maan, S.S. and Lucken, K.A. (1968). Cytoplasmic male sterility and fertility restoration in *Triticum aestivum* L. In : *Proc. 3rd Int. Wheat Genet. Symp.*, Australia, pp. 135-140.

Maan, S.S. and Lucken, K.A. (1971). Male sterile wheat with rye cytoplasm. Restoration of male fertility and plant vigour. *J. Hered.* **62**, 353-355.

Maan, S.S. and Lucken, K.A. (1972). Interacting male sterility-male fertility restoration systems for hybrid wheat research. *Crop Sci.* **12**, 360-364.

Maan, S.S. and McCracken, E.W. (1968). Meiotic instability of common wheat strains derived from *Triticum timopheevi* Zhuk. crosses. *Euphytica* **17**, 445-450.

Mac Key, J. (1954). Breeding of oats, Handbuch fur Pflanzenzuchtung **2**, 512-517.

Mac Key, J. (1956). Mutation breeding in Europe. In *Genetics in Plant Breeding. Brookhaven Symp. in Biol. No. 9*, Upton, NY 21-23 May. Associated Universities, Inc., Upton, New York, pp. 141-156.

Mac Key, J. (1963). Species relationship in *Triticum*. In *Proc. 2nd Int. Wheat Genet. Symp. (Lund)* 1965. *Hereditas,* Suppl. **2**, 237-276.

Mac Key, J. (1967). Physical and chemical mutagenesis in relation to ploidy level. In *Induzlerte Mutationin und ihre Nutzung*, H. Stubble *et al.* (Ed.), Erwin Bauer-Gedacht-nisvorlesungen IV, Gatersleben, 19-24 June, 1966, Akademie-Verlag, Berlin, pp. 185-197.

Mac Key, J. (1981). Mutations as means for analyzing polyploid systems. In *Induced Mutations-A tool for crop plant research. Proc. of Int. Symp. on Induced Mutations as a Tool for Crop Plant Improvement,* Vienna, Austria, 9-13 March, IAEA, Vienna, ST1/PUB/591.pp. 143-151.

Mac Ritchie, F. (1981). Flour lipids : Theoretical aspects and functional properties. *Cereal Chem.,* **58**, 156.

Macer, R.C.F. (1963). The formal and monosomic genetic analysis of stripe rust resistance in wheat. *Proc. 2nd Int. Wheat Genet. Symp.* (Lund) 2m 127-143.

Madan, Shashi, Rana, R.K. and Pawar, I.S. (2004). Evaluation of wheat varieties for quality characteristics. *Natnl. J. Pl. Improv.* **6**, 38-41.

Maddock, S.E., Lancaster, V.A., Risiott, R. and Franklin, J. (1983). Plant regeneration from cultured immature embryos and inflorescences of 25 cultivars of wheat. *J. Exp. Bot.* **34**, 915-926.

Mahajan, V. and Nagarajan, S. (1998). Opportunities in Hybrid Wheat - A review. *PINSA* **B64** : 51-58.

Mahajan, V. and Nagarajan, S. (2001). Hybrid wheat evaluation by raised bed fixed plot drill. ICAR Newsletter (*A Science and Technology Newsletter*) **7** (2), 19.

Mahajan, V., Ganga Rao, NVPR and Nagarajan,S. (2004). Recent progress of hybrid wheat research in India. In *Wheat : Technologies for Warmers Areas*, V.S. Rao, G. Singh and S.C. Misra (Eds.), Anamaya Publishers, New Delhi, pp. 75-78.

Mahajan, V., Nagarajan, S., Deshpande, V.H. and Kelker, R.G. (2000). Screening chemical hybridizing agent for development of hybrid wheat. *Curr. Sci.* **78**, 235-236.

Mahajan, V., Nagarajan, S., Deshpande, V.H. and Singh, K. (1998). Chemical hybridising agent for hybrid wheat production. ICAR Newsletter (*A Science and Technology Newsletter*) **4** (4), 12.

Mahalakshmi, A., Chugh, A. and Khurana, P. (2000). Exogenous uptake via cellular permeabilization and expression of foreign gene in wheat zygotic embryos. *Plant Biotech.* **17**, 235-240.

Mahalakshmi, A., Khurana, J.P. and Khurana, P. (2003). Rapid induction of somatic embryogenesis in leaf base explants of wheat. *Plant Biotech.* **20**, 267-273.

Maia, N. (1967). C.R. Seanc. Acad. d' Agric. Fr., **53**, 149-154.

Mandloi, K.C., Rao, M.V. and Austin, A. (1974). Inheritance of two baking quality characteristics in common wheat. *Indian J. Genet.* **34**(A): 646.

Mandloi, K.C., Rao, M.V. and Joshi, A.B. (1974). Protein inheritance in a common wheat. *Indian J. Genet.* **34**(A), 642.

Manocha, M.S. and Shaw, M. (1966). The physiology of host-parasite relatins. XVI. *Can. J. Bot.* (Ottawa) **44**, 669-673.

Marino, C.L., Nelson, J.C., Lu, Y.H., Sorrels, M.E., Leroy, P., Tuleen, N.A., Lopes, C.R. and Hart, G.E. (1996). Molecular genetic maps of the group 6 chromosomes of hexaploid wheat (*Triticum aestivum* L. em. Thell). *Genome* **39**, 359-366.

Martens, J.W., Seaman, W.L. and Atkinson, T.G. (1984). Diseases of field crops in Canada. Canadian Phytopathological Society, Harrow, Ont.

Martin, J.M., Talbert, L.E., Lanning, S.P. and Blake, N.K. (1975). Hybrid performance in wheat as related to the parental diversity. *Crop Sci.* **35**, 104-108.

Martin, T.J., Harvey, T.L. and Hatchett, J.H. (1982). Registration of green bug and Hessian fly resistant wheat germplasm. *Crop. Sci.,* **22**, 1089.

Martinez-Gonzalez, J.M.S. (1979). Slow rusting to *Puccinia graminis* f. sp. *tritici* in Era wheat. Ph.D. thesis. University of Minnesota. St. Paul. p. 53.

Martinez-Gonzalez, J.M.S., Wileoxson, R.D., Stuthman, D.D., McVey, D.V. and Busch, R.H. (1983). Genetic factors conditioning slow rusting in Era wheat. *Phytopathology* **73**, 247-249.

Martini, G. and Bozzini, A. (1965). Analysis of a sticky mutant induced by radiation in the hard wheat Capelli (in Italian) *Genet.Agr.* (Pavia) **19**, 184-194.

Mascrenhas, J.P. (1990). Gene activity during pollen development. *Ann. Rev. Plant Physiol. Plant Mol. Biol.* **41**, 317-338.

Mather, K. (1949). *Biometrical Genetics* (First Edition). Menthuen, London.

Mather, K. and Jinks, J.L. (1982). *Biometrical Genetics*, (3rd ed.), Chapman and Hall.

Mather, K. and Jones, R.M. (1958). Interaction of genotype and environment in continuous variation.I. Description. *Biometrics* **14**, 343-359.

Matsumura, S. (1964). Differences in RBE of gamma rays and fast neutrons in the polyploid wheat series. *Jap. J. Genet.* (Tokyo) **2-3**, 86-90.

Matsumura, S. (1966). Radiation genetics in wheat. IX. *Rad. Bot.* (Oxford) **6**, 275-283.

Mattern, P.P.J., Morris, R., Schmidt, J.W. and Johnson, V.A. (1973). Location of genes for kernel properties in the wheat variety "Cheyenne" using chromosome substitution lines. 4th Int. Wheat Genet. Symp. (Missouri) 703-707.

Mattern, P.P.J., Schmidt, J.W. and Johnson, V.A. (1970). Screening for high lysine content in wheat. *Cereal Sci. Today* **15**, 409.

Maystrenko, O.I. (1976). *Genetika*, USSR, **12**, 5-15 (Cited in Plant Breed. Abstr., 47 (9205), 784.

Mc Clung, A.M. and Cantrell, R.G. (1986). Inheritance of glume colour and gluten strength in durum wheat. *Euphytica* **35**, 885.

Mc Couch, S. (1998). Toward a plant genomics initiative : Thoughts on the value of cross-species and cross-genera comparisons in the grasses. *Proc. Natl. Acad.Sci. USA*, **95**, 1983-1985.

Mc Fadden, E.S. and Sears, E.R. (1946). The origin of *Triticum spelta* and its free-threshing hexaploid relatives. *J. Hered.* **37**, 107-116.

Mc Guire, P.E. and Dvorak, J. (1981). High salt tolerance potential in wheat grasses. *Crop Sci.* **21**, 702-705.

Mc Intosh, R.A. (1973). A catalogue of gene symbols for wheat. 4th Int. Wheat Genet. Symp. Missouri), pp. 893-937.

Mc Intosh, R.A. (1978). Breeding for resistance to powdery mildew in the temperate cereals. In *The Powdery Mildews*, D.M. Spencer (Ed.), Academic Press, London, pp. 237-257.

Mc Intosh, R.A. (1988). The role of specific genes in breeding for durable stem rust resistance in wheat and triticale. In *Breeding Strategies for Resistance to the Rusts of Wheat*, N.W. Simmonds and S. Rajaram IEds.), CIMMYT, Mexico, pp. 1-9.

Mc Intosh, R.A. and Gyarfas, J. (1971). *Triticum timopheevii* as a source of resistance to wheat stem rust. *Z. Pflanzenzuecht.* **66**, 240-248.

Mehdi, V., Joshi, L.M. and Abrol, Y.P. (1973). Studies on chapati making quality (vi) Effect of wheat grains with bunts on the quality of chapaties. *Bulletin of Grain Technol.* **11**(3), 195-197.

Mellaart, J. (1975). The Neolithic of the Near East, Thomas and Hudson.

Mello-Sampayo, T. (1968). Homoeologous chromosome pairing in pentaploid hybrids of wheat. In *Proc. 3rd Int. Wheat Genet. Symp.*, K.W. Finlay and K.W. Shepherd (Eds.), Canberra, Australia, 5-9 August. Australian Academy of Science, Canberra, pp. 179-184.

Mello-Sampayo, T. (1971). Genetic regulation of meiotic chromosome pairing by chromosome 3D of *Triticum aestivum. Nature New Biol.* **230**, 22-23.

Mello-Sampayo, T. (1972). Promotion of homologous pairing in hybrids of *T. aestivum* × *Ae. longissima. Genet. Iber.* (Madrid).

Mello-Sampayo, T. and Canas, A.P. (1973). Suppressors of meiotic chromosome pairing in common wheat, In *Proc. 4th Int. Wheat Genet. Symp.*, E.R. Sears and L.M.S. Sears (Eds.), Columbia, MO 6-11 August, Univ. of Missouri, Columbia, pp. 709-713.

Merkle, O.G. and Starks, K.J. (1985). Resistance of wheat to yellow sugarcane aphid (*Homoptera: Aphididae*). *J. Econ. Entomol.* **78**, 127-128.

Metzger, J.R. and Silbaugh, B.A. (1970a). Location of genes for seed coat color in hexaploid wheat, *Triticum aestivum* L. *Crop Sci.* **10**, 495-496.

Metzger, J.R. and Silbaugh, B.A. (1970b). Inheritance of resistance to stripe rust and its Association with brown glume color in *Triticum aestivum* L., P.I. 178383. *Crop Sci.* **10**, 567-568.

Micke, A. and Donini, B. (1982). Use of induced mutations for the improvement of seed propagated crops. In *Induced Variability in Plant Breeding. Proc. Int. Symp. Sect.* Mutation and Polyploidy. Wageningen, The Netherlands. pp.2-9.

Mijo, K. (1962). For high and constant average yields of wheat (in Serbian) *Jug. Savet. Centar*, 47-53.

Milica, C.I. and Juncu, A.H. (1968). The response to drought during different growth periods of winter wheat varieties and lines cultivated in Romania (in Romanian). *Probl. Agric.* (Bucuresti) **20**, 9-18.

Milkova, Venetsiya, R., Ivanov, P.I. and Todorov, I. (2003). Intensification of the breeding process in wheat by using *in vitro* methods and characterization of the new developed genotypes. *Cereal Res. Comm.* **31**, 355-361.

Miller, J.F. (1970). M.S. Thesis, Univ. of Nebraska, Lincoln.

Miller, J.F., Rogers, K.J. and Lucken, K.A. (1974). Male-sterile wheat seed production in North Dakota. *Crop Sci.* **14**, 702-705.

Miller, T.E. (1983). In *Kew Chromosome Conferance II*. P.E. Bradham and M.D. Bennett (Eds.), George Allen and Unwin, Hemel Hempstead, pp. 173-182.

Miller, T.E. (1984). *Can. J. Genet. Cytol.* **26**, 578-589.

Miller, T.E. (1987). Systematics and evolution. In *Wheat Breeding : its scientific basis*, F.G.H. Lupton (Ed.), Chapman and Hall, U.K. pp.1-30.

Miller, T.E., Hutchinson, J. and Chapman, V. (1982). Investigation of a preferentially transmitted *Aegilops sharonensis* chromosome in wheat. *Theor. Appl. Genet.* **61**, 27-33.

Mitra, M. (1931). A new bunt on wheat in India. *Annals of Appl. Biol.* **18**, 178-179.

Mochizuki, A. (1968). The monosomics of durum wheat. In *Proc. 3rd Int. Wheat Genet. Symp.*, K.W. Finlay and K.W. Shepherd (Ed.), Canberra, Australia, 5-9 August. Australian Academy of Science, Canberra. pp.310-315.

Mochizuki, A. (1970). The monosomics of durum wheat. In Sears, E.R. *Ann. Rev. Genet.* **3**,

Monneveux, P., Reynolds, M.P., Zaharieva, M. and Mujeeb-Kazi, A. (2003). Effect of T 1BL.1RS chromosome translocation on bread wheat grain yield and physiological related traits in a warm environment. *Cereal Res. Comm.* **31**, 371-378.

Moore, G., Gale, M.D., Kurata, N. and Flavell, R.W. (1993). Molecular analysis of small grain cereal genomes : current status and prospects. *Biotechnology,* **11**, 584-589.

Morgan, C.L., Austin, R.B., Ford, M.A., Bingham, J., Angus, W.J. and Chowdhury, S. (1989). An evaluation of F_1 hybrid winter wheat genotypes produced using a chemical hybridizing agent. *J. agric. Sci. Camb.* **112**, 143-149.

Morris, R. (1962-1973). Chromosome locations of gene for wheat characters. *Ann. Wheat Newsletter* (Kansas), IX-XIX.

Morris, R. and Sears, E.R. (1967). The Cytogenetics of Wheat and Its Relatives. In *Wheat and Wheat Improvement*, K.S. Quisenberry and L.P. Reitz (Eds.), American Society Agronomy, pp. 19-87.

Morrison, R.A. and Evans, D.A. (1987). Gametoclonal variation. *Plant Breed. Rev.* **5**, 359.

Morrison, R.A. and Evans, D.A. (1988). Haploid plants from tissue cultures : new plant varieties in a shortest time frame. *Biotechnology* **6**, 684.

Mujeeb-Kazi, A. (1995). Interspecific crosses: hybrid production and utilization. *In Utilizing Wild Grass Biodiversity in Wheat Improvement : 15 years of wide cross research at CIMMYT*, A. Mujeeb-kazi and G.P. Hettel (Eds.). CIMMYT Research Report No. 2, Mexico, DF, CIMMYT, pp. 14-21.

Mujeeb-Kazi, A. and Asiedu, R. (1990). Wide hybridization–Potential of alein genetic transfers for *Triticum aestivum* improvement. In *Biotechnology in Agriculture and Forestry*, 13, Y.P.S. Bajaj (Ed.), Springer-Verleg, Berlin, pp. 111-127.

Mujeeb-Kazi, A. and Hettel, G.P. (1995). Utilizing Wild Grass Biodiversity in Wheat Improvement: 15 years of Wide Cross Research at CIMMYT. CIMMYT Research Report No. 2, Mexico, D.F., CIMMYT.

Mujeeb-Kazi, A., Kuile, N.T., Waskom, R. and Nabors, M.W. (1995). Applications of tissue culture in wheat wide crosses. In *Utilizing Wild Grass Biodiversity in Wheat Improvement* (Eds.), A. Mujeeb-Kazi and G.P. Hettel (Eds.), CIMMYT Research Report No. 2, Mexico, DF, Mexico, pp.66-75.

Mujeeb-Kazi, A., Riera-Lizarazu, O. and William, M.D.H.M. (1995). Production of polyhaploid wheat plants using maize and *Tripsacum*. In *Utilizing Wild Grass Biodiversity in Wheat Improvement*, A. Mujeeb-Kazi and G.P. Hettel (Eds.), CIMMYT Research Report No. 2, Mexico, DF, Mesico, pp. 47-65.

Mujeeb-Kazi, A., Roldan, S., Suh, D.Y., Sitch, L.A. and Farooq, S. (1987). Production and cytogenetic analysis of hybrids between *Triticum aestivum* and some caespitose *Agropyron* speices. *Genome* **29**, 537-553.

Mujeeb-Kazi, A., Roldan, S., Suh, D.Y., Ter-Kuile, N. and Farooq, S. (1989). Production and cytogenetics of *Triticum aestivum* L. hybrids with some rhizomatous *Agropyron species*. *Theor. Appl. Genet.* **77**, 162-168.

Mujica, F.L., Antonelli, E.F. and Cenoz, H.P. (1972). Induced mutant of the wheat variety sinvalecho MA and reaction of lines originating from its crossing (in Italian). *Ind. Mut. and Plant Improvement* (Vienna) IAEA, pp. 355-363.

Mukai, Y. (1981). Genetic studies of the wheat haploids induced by alien cytoplasms. Mem. Osaka Kyoiki Univ., Ser. III, **30**, 31-55.

Mukai, Y. and Tsunewaki, K. (1979). Basic studies on hybrid wheat breeding VIII. A new male sterility fertility restoration system in common wheat utilizing the cytoplasm of *Aegilops kotschyi* and *Aegilops variabilis*. *Theor. Appl. Genet.* **54**, 153-160.

Mukai, Y., Friebe, B., Hatchett, J.H., Yamamoto, M. and Gill, B.S. (1993). Molecular cytogenetic analysis of radiation induced wheat-rye terminal and intercalary chromosomal translocations and detection of rye chromatin specifying resistance to Hessian fly. *Chromosome* **102**, 88-95.

Murai, K. (1997a). Genetic analysis of fertility restoration against photoperiod-sensitive cytoplasmic male sterility in *Triticum aestivum* cv. Norin 61. *Plant Breed.* **116**, 592-594.

Murai, K. (1997b). Effect of *Aegilops crassa* cytoplasm on the agronomic characters in photoperiod sensitive CMS Wheat lines and F_1 hybrids. *Breed. Sci.* **47**, 321-326.

Murai, K. (1998). F_1 seed production efficiency by using photoperiod sensitive cytoplasmic male sterility and performance of F_1 hybrid lines in wheat. *Breed. Sci.* **48**, 35-40.

Murai, K. and Tsunewaki, K. (1993). Photoperiod-sensitive cytoplasmic male sterility in wheat with *Ae. Crassa* cytoplasm. *Euphytica* **67**, 41-48.

Murai, K. and Tsunewaki, K. (1994). Genetic analysis on the fertility restoration by *Triticum aestivum* cv. Chinese Spring against photoperiod-sensitive cytoplasmic male sterility. *Jpn. J. Genet.* **69**, 195-202.

Murashige, T. and Skoog, F. (1962). A revised medium for rapid growth and bioassays with tobacco tissue culture. *Physiol. Plant.* **15**, 473-497.

Murty, G.S. and Lakhani, L.B. (1958). Genetic studies in crosses between *aestivum* varieties and the durum wheat, Gaza. *Indian J. Genet.* **18**, 163-177.

Nagarajan, S. (2004). Opportunities and strategies to make Indian wheat globally competitive. In *Wheat : Technologies for Warmer Areas*, V.S. Rao, G. Singh and S.C. Misra (Eds.), Anamaya Publishers, New Delhi, pp. 11-23.

Naik, S.S., Gill, K.S., Prakash Rao, V.S., Gupta, V.S., Tamhankar, S.A., Pujar, S., Gill, B.S. and Ranjekar, P.K. (1997). Identification of STS marker linked to the *Aegilops speltoides*- derived leaf rust resistance gene Lr 28 in wheat. *Theor. Appl. Genet.* **97**, 536-540.

Nair, S., Kumar, A., Srivastva, M.N. and Mohan, M. (1990). PCR-based DNA markers linked to a gall midge resistance gene, Gmut, has potential for marker aided selection in rice. *Theor. Appl. Genet.* **92**, 660-665.

Nanda, G.S. and Singh, G. (1989). Genetic analysis of yield and its component characters in bread wheat. *SABRAO J.* **21**, 123-134.

Nanda, G.S., Singh, G. and Tiwana, S.S. (1990). A comparison of triple test cross and model fitting analysis in two spring wheat crosses. *Indian J. Genet.* **50**, 369-372.

Nanda, G.S., Singh, P. and Gill, K.S. (1982). Epistatic, additive and dominance variation in a triple test cross of bread wheat. *Theor. Appl. Genet.* **62**, 49-52.

Nanda, G.S., Singh, P. and Gill, K.S. (1983). Estimating epistasis through triple test cross in wheat. *Indian J. Genet.* **43**, 160-163.

Nassar, R. and Huhn, M. (1987). Studies on estimation of phenotypic stability : Test of significance for non-parametric measures of phenotypic stability. *Biometrics,* **43**, 45-53.

Nath, J., Hanzel, J.J., Thompson, J.P. and Mc Nay, J.W. (1984). Additional evidence implicating *Triticum searsii* as the B-genome donor to wheat. *Biochem. Genet.* **22**, 37-50.

Nath, J., McNay, J.W., Paroda, C.M. and Gulati, S.C. (1983). Implication of *Triticum searsii* as the B-genome donor to wheat using DNA hybridization. *Biochem. Genet.* **21**, 745-760.

Ndondi, R.V. (1987). Comparison of the single seed descent (SSD) method, the multiple seed descent (MSD) method and the bulk population method for yield and protein improvement in wheat. *Fifth Regional Wheat Workshop* October 5-10, 1987, Antsirabe, Madagascar.

Nelson, J.C., Sorrells, M.E., Van Deynze, A.E., Lu, Y.H., Atkinson, M., Bernard, M., Faris, J.D. and Anderson, J.A. (1995). Molecular mapping of wheat : major genes and rearrangements in homoeologous groups 4,5 and 7. *Genetics* **141**, 721-731.

Nettevich, E.D. and Naumov, A.A. (1970). The genetic characteristics of fertility restoration in wheat forms with cytoplasmic male sterility. *Plant Breed. Abstr.* **43**, 4865.

Nilson-Ehle, H. (1908). *Kreuzunguntersuchungen an Hafer und Weizen.* Lund Univ. *Arsskrift.* **5**, 1-122.

Noronha-Wagner, M. and Mello-Sampayo, T. (1966). Aneuploids in durum wheat. In *Proc. 2nd Int. Wheat Genet. Symp.*, Mac Key (Ed.). Lund, Sweden, 18-24 August, Hereditas (Suppl.) **2**, pp.395-408.

Nunn, J.R., Louis, J.D. and Kimball, K.L. (1971). *Br. J. Anaesth.* **43**, 524-530.

Nyquist, W.E. (1962). Differential fertilization in the inheritance of stem rust resistance in hybrids involving a common wheat strain derived from *Triticum timopheevii. Genetics,* **47**, 1109-1124.

Oehler, E. and Ingold, M. (1966). New cases of male sterility and new restorer source in *Triticum aestivum. Wheat Inf. Serv.* (Kyoto) **22**, 1-3.

Oerke, F.C., Dehne, H.W., Schonbeck, F. and Weber, A. (1994). Crop production and crop protection. Amsterdam, Elsevier Science.

Ohkawa, Y., Suenaga, K. and Ogawa, T. (1992). Production of hexapoloid wheat plants through pollination of sorghum pollen. *Japanese J. Breed.* **42** : 891-894.

Ohm, H.W., Sharma, H.C., Patterson, F.L., Rateliffe, R.H. and Obanni, M. (1995). Linkage relationships among genes on wheat chromosome 5A that condition resistance to Hessian fly. *Crop Sci.* **35**, 1603-1607.

Ohno, S. (1970). Evolution by gene duplication Springer-Verlag, Berlin, 160p.

Okamoto, M. (1957). Asynaptic effect of chromosome V. *Wheat Inf. Serv.* **5**, 6.

O' Mara, J.G. (1940). Cytogenetic studies on *Triticale* I. A method for determining the effects of individual *Secale* chromosomes on *Triticum*. *Genetics* **25**, 401-408.

O'Mara, J.G. (1947). The substitution of a specific *Secale cereale* chromosome for a specific *Triticum vulgare* chromosome. *Genetics* **32**, 99-100.

Omara, M.K., El-Defrawy, M.M., Tammam, A.M. and Kassem, A.A.F. (2004). Genetic control of preanthesis attributes of wheat plant and their associations with yield under heat stress. *Assiut. J. Agril. Sci.* **35(4)**, 97-115.

Ooart, A.J.P. (1944). Tijdschr. Plziekt. **1**, 73-106 (Abstract, 1946, *Rev. Appl. Mycol.*, **25**, 160-161.

Ooart, A.J.P. (1963). *Neth. J. Pl. Pathol.* **69**, 104-109.

Osmanzai, M., Raja Ram, S. and Knapp, E.B. (1987). Breeding for moisture stressed areas. *Proc. Int. Workshop on Drought Tolerance in Winter Cereals* held at Capri, Italy from Oct. 27-31, 1985, pp. 151-161.

Ostrowska, A. (1964). Effect of small doses of gamma irradiation on some cultivated plants (in Polish). *Roczn. Nank. Koln. Soc. Rosl.* (Warszawa) **89**, 77-99.

Oury, F.X., Pichon, M. and Rousset (1993). Une comparaison entre 2 methodes d'haplodiploidisation chez ble tendre : 1 androgenese in vitro et le croisement interspecifique avec mats. *Agronomie* **13**, 95-103.

Ozias-Akins, P. and Vasil, I.K. (1982). Plant regeneration from cultured immature embryos and inflorescences of *Triticum aestivum* L. (Wheat) : Evidence for somatic embryogenesis. *Protoplasma*, **100**, 95-105.

Pal, B.P. (1951). Wheat breeding investigations at the I.A.R.I. *J. Indian Bot. Soc.* **30**, 1-13.

Pal, B.P., Sikka, S.M. and Rao, M.V. (1956). Inheritance studies in wheat. *Indian J. Genet.* **16**, 32-46.

Palenzoni, D.L. (1961). Effects of high doses of X-rays on seedling growth in wheats of different ploidy. Eff. of ion. rad. on seeds (Vienna) *IAEA* pp. 533-542.

Panayotov, I. (1980). New cytoplasmic male sterility sources in common wheat, their genetical and breeding considerations. *Theor. Appl. Genet.* **56**, 153-160.

Panayotov, I. and Gotsov, K. (1973). Interactions between nucleus of *Triticum aestivum* L. and cytoplasms of certain species of *Triticum* and *Aegilops*. Proc. 4th Int. Wheat Genet. Symp. 1973, Columbia, pp. 381-383.

Pande, M.K., Atale, S.B., Patel, M.C., Golhar, S.R. and Peshattiwar, P.D. (1998). Comparison of single seed descent and pedigree selection method in durum wheat. *Annals of Plant Physiology* **12**, 153-155.

Pandey, K.K. and Phung, M. (1982). 'Hertwig Effect' in plants : induced parthenogenesis through the use of irradiated pollen. *Theor. Appl. Genet.* **62**, 295-300.

Paran, I. and Michelmore, R.W. (1993). Development of reliable PCR-based markers linked to downy mildew resistance genes in lettuce. *Theor. Appl. Genet.* **85**, 985-993.

Parlevliet, J.E. (1979). Components of resistance that reduce the rate of epidemic development. *Annu. Rev. Phytopathol.* **17**, 203-222.

Parlevliet, J.E. (1988). Strategies for the utilization of partial resistance for the control of cereal rusts. In *Breeding Strategies for Resistance to Rusts of Wheat*, N.W. Simmonds and S. Rajaram (Eds.), CIMMYT, Mexico, D.F. pp. 48-62.

Parodi, P.C. and Nebreda, I.M. (1982a). *Triticum aestivum. Carolina Mutat. Breed. Newsl.* **19**, 18.

Parodi, P.C. and Nebreda, I.M. (1982b). Testing, cross-breeding, induction and nutritional evaluation of wheat and triticale mutants. In *Induced mutants for cereal grain protein improvement. Proc. Res. Coord. Meet.* Nicosia, Cyprus, 21-25 Apr. 1980, IAEA, Vienna, TEC Doc-259.pp. 31-52.

Pathak, G.N. (1940). Studies in the cytology of cereals. *J. Genet.* **39**, 437-467.

Patnaik, D. and Khurana, P. (2001). Wheat Biotechnology : A mini review. *Electronic Journal of Biotechnology* **4**, 1-29 (Available on line at http://www.ejb.org/content/vol.4/Issue 2/Full/4/).

Patnaik, D. and Khurana, P. (2003). Genetic transformation of Indian bread (*Triticum aestivum*) and pasta (*Triticum durum*) wheat by particle bombardment of mature embryo-derived calli. *BMC Plant Biol.* **3**, 5-17.

Patnaik, D., Vishnudashan, D. and Khurana, P. (2002). *Agrobacterium*-mediated transformation of mature embryos of *Triticum aestivum* and *Triticum durum* (Submitted).

Pauk, J., Kertesz, Z., Beke, B., Bona, L., Csosz, M. and Matuz, J. (1995). New winter wheat variety "GK Delibab" developed via combining conventional breeding and *in vitro* androgenesis. *Cereal Res. Comm.* **23**, 251-256.

Paul, S., Wachira, F.M., Powell, W. and Waugh, R. (1997). Diversity and genetic differentiation among populations of Indian and Kenyan tea (*Camellia sinensis* L.O. Kuntze) revealed by AFLP markers. *Theor. Appl. Genet.* **94**, 255-263.

Pawar, I.S. (2000). Hybrid wheat : Present status and probable future. Presented at 6th International Wheat Conference, Budapest, Hungary, June 4-9, 2000.

Pawar, I.S. and Singh, S. (1991). An evaluation of genetic variability maintained by three selection procedures in wheat. *Haryana agric. Univ. J. Res.* **21**, 46-49.

Pawar, I.S., Paroda, R.S. and Singh, S. (1986). A comparison of pedigree selection, single seed descent and bulk method in two wehat crosses. *Crop Improv.* **13**, 34-37.

Pawar, I.S., Paroda, R.S. and Singh, S. (1987). A comparison of range and phenotypic coefficient of variation in selected and unselected populations of two wheat crosses. *Seeds and Farms* **13**, 37-39.

Pawar, I.S., Paroda, R.S. and Singh, S. (1988). Gene effects for six metric traits in four spring wheat crosses. *Indian J. Genet.* **48**, 195-199.

Pawar, I.S., Paroda, R.S. and Singh, S. (1989). Study of heritability and genetic advance in three wheat populations. *Bangladesh J. Agric. Res.* **14**(1), 24-26.

Pawar, I.S., Paroda, R.S., Yunus, M. and Singh, S. (1985a). A comparison of three selection methods in two wheat crosses. *Indian J. Genet.* **45**, 345-353.

Pawar, I.S., Paroda, R.S., Singh, S. and Yunus, M. (1985b). Evaluation of early generation selection in two wheat crosses. *Seeds and Farms* **11**, 77-80.

Pawar, I.S., Redhu, A.S. and Singh, I. (2003). Emerging trends in hybrid wheat breeding. *Natnl. J. Pl. Improv.* **5**, 1-6.

Pawar, I.S., Redhu, A.S., Singh, I. and Yunus, M. (2001). Effectiveness of selection procedures in wheat breeding. *Haryana agric. Univ. J. Res.* **31**, 119-121.

Pawar, I.S., Redhu, A.S., Yunus, M. and Singh, I. (2000). Evaluation of selective intermated populations for yield and its component traits in wheat. *Haryana agric. Univ. J. Res.* **30**, 137-139.

Pawar, I.S., Sarmah, P. and Yunus, M. (1999). Test of failure of additive-dominance model in wheat triple test cross data. *Haryana agric. Univ. J. Res.* **29**, 43-45.

Pawar, I.S., Singh, I. and Singh, S. (1990). Traditional versus simplified pedigree selection in wheat. *Haryana agric. Univ. J. Res.* **20**, 134-138.

Pawar, I.S., Singh, S. and Yunus, M. (1990). Studies on selective intermating in bread wheat. *Crop Improv.* **17**, 68-69.

Pawar, I.S., Singh, S., Paroda, R.S. and Singh, I. (1988). An analysis of generation means for yield and its component traits in bread wheat. *Indian J. Genet.* **48**, 317-319.

Pawar, I.S., Yunus, M. and Singh, V.P. (1996). A study of interaction of additive, dominance and epistatic gene effects with environment in wheat. *Haryana Agric. Univ. J. Res.* **26**, 17-21.

Pawar, I.S., Yunus, M., Karwasra, S.S. and Sarmah Prabalee (1997). Use of single spike selection procedure in wheat improvement. *Haryana agric. Univ. J. Res.* **27**, 167-169.

Pawar, I.S., Yunus, M., Singh, S. and Singh, V.P. (1994a). A comparison of genetic variability generated by five selection procedures in wheat. *Haryana agric. Univ. J. Res.* **24**, 170-175.

Pawar, I.S., Yunus, M., Singh, S. and Singh, V.P. (1994b). Detection of additive, dominance and epistatic variation in wheat using triple test cross method. *Indian J. Genet.* **54**, 275-280.

Payne, P.I. (1987). Genetics of wheat storage proteins and the effect of allelic variation on bread making quality. *Ann. Rev. Plant Physiol.* **38**, 141-153.

Payne, P.I., Holt, L.M., Lawrence, G.H. and Law, C.N. (1982). The genetics of gliadin and glutenin, the major storage proteins of the wheat endosperm. *Qual. Plant Foods Hum. Nutr.* **31**, 229-241.

Payne, P.I., Holt, L.M., Worland, A.J. and Law, C.N. (1982). Structural and genetical studies on the HMW subunits of wheat glutenin.3. Telocentric mapping of the subunit genes on the long arms of the homoeologous group I chromosomes. *Theor. Appl. Genet.* **63**, 129-138.

Payne, P.I., Jackson, E.A., Holt, L.M. and Law, C.N. (1984). Genetic linkage between endosperm storage protein genes on each of the short arms of chromosomes 1A and 1B in wheat. *Theor. Appl. Genet.* **67**, 235-243.

Pena, R.J. (1996). Combining high yield potential and grain quality in wheat. In *Increasing Yield Potential in Wheat : Breeding the Barriers*, M.P. Reymolds, S. Rajaram, A. McNab (Eds.), Mexico, DF, CIMMYT.

Pena, R.J., Amaya, A., Rajaram, S. and Mujeeb-Kazi, A. (1990). Variation in quality characteristics associated with some spring 1B/1R translocation wheats. *J. Cereal Sci.* **12**, 105-112.

Percival, J. (1921). *The Wheat Plant-A Monograph*. Duckworth & Co., London, 463pp.

Perkins, J.M. and Jinks, J.L. (1968). Environmental and genotype-environmental components of variability. IV. Non-linear interactions for multiple inbred lines. *Heredity,* **23**, 525-535.

Peruansky, J.V. and Peruanskaya, O.N. (1965). Relation between resistance of wheat to infection with stem rusts and its content of glucosides (in Russian). *Agrobiologia* (Moscow) **156**, 913-915.

Peterson, C.J., Moffatt, J.M. and Erickson, J.R. (1997). Yield stability of hybrids vs. pureline hard winter wheats in regional performance trials. *Crop Sci.* **37**, 116-120.

Pfeiffer, E., Jager, K. and Reisener, H.J. (1969). Untersuchungen uber stoff wech selbezie-hungen Zwischen Parasit und wirt an Beispiel von *Puccinia graminis* var. *tritici* auf Weizen. *Planta* (Berlin) **85**, 194-201.

Picard, E., Hours, C., Gregoire, S., Phan, T.H. and Mennier, I.P. (1987). Significant improvement of androgenetic haploid and doubled haploid induction from wheat plants treated with chemical hybridization agent. *Theor. Appl. Genet.* **74**, 289-297.

Pickett, A.A. (1993). Hybrid wheat-results and problems. *Adv. Pl. Br.* **15**: Paul Parey Sc. Publ., Berlin.

Pickett, A.A. (1998). Wheat. In : *Hybrid Cultivar.* Development. S.S. Banga and S.K.Banga (Eds.), Narosa Publishing House, New Delhi, pp. 257-281.

Pickett, A.A. and Galwey, N.W. (1997). A further evaluation of hybrid wheat. *Plant Varieties and Seeds* **10**, 15-32.

Piech, J. and Evans, L.E. (1979). *Z. Pflanzenzuchtg* **82**, 212-217.

Pink, D.A., Bennett, F.G.A., Caten, C.E. and Law, C.N. (1983). Correlated effects of homoeologous group 5 chromosomes upon infection of wheat by yellow rust and powdery mildew. *Z. Pflanzenzuecht.* **91**, 278-294.

Pinthus, M.J. (1967). Spread of the root system as indicator for evaluating lodging resistance of wheat. *Crop Sci.* (Madison), **7**, 107-110.

Pinthus, M.J. (1972). A suggested method to estimate the economic value of plant breeding programmes. *Z. Pflzucht.* **68**, 258-260.

Pinthus, M.J. (1987). Yield, grain weight and height relationships in two random samples of early semi-dwarf genotypes of samples of spring wheat. *Plant Breed.* **98**, 34-40.

Pinthus, M.J. and Millet, E. (1978). Interactions among number of spikelots, number of grains and grain weight in the spikes of wheat (*Triticum aestivum* L.). *Ann. Bot.* **42**, 839-848.

Plourde, A., Fedak, G., St-Pierre, C.A. and Comeau, A. (1990). A novel intergeneric hybrid in the Triticeae : *Triticum aestivum* × *Psathyrostachys juncea*. *Theor. Appl. Genet.* **79**, 45-48.

Poehlman, J.M. and Sleper, D.A. (1995). *Breeding Field Crops* (4th edn.), Panima Publishing Corporation, New Delhi, Bangalore.

Pogna, N.E., Redaelli, R., Dachkevitch, T., Curioni, A. and Dal Belin Peruffo, A. (1994). Genetics of wheat quality and its improvement by conventional and biotechnological breeding. *In Wheat: Production, Properties and Quality*, W. Bushuk and V.F Rasper (Eds.), Chapman and Hall, London, pp. 205-224.

Pollmer (1957). In Balint, A. 1966. Breeding agronomic plants. (in Hungarian) Mezogazdasagi Konyvkiado, Budapest, 398.

Pooni, H.S. and Jinks, J.L. (1981). The true nature of non-allelic interactions in *Nicotiana rustica* revealed by association crosses. *Heredity* **47**, 253-258.

Porter, K.B. and Weise, A.F. (1961). Evaluation of certain chemicals as selective gametocides for wheat. *Crop Sci.* **1**, 381-382.

Prakash, V. (2005). Gene effects and interaction analysis for yield and quantitative traits in bread wheat under normal and terminal heat stress conditions. *Crop. Improv.* **32**, 20-25.

Prakash, V. and Joshi, P. (2003). Genetic analysis of yield and its components in different environments in wheat. *Indian J. Genet.* **63**, 341-342.

Prasad, K.D., Haque, M.F. and Ganguli, D.K. (1998). Heterosis studies for yield and its components in bread wheat. *Indian J. Genet.* **58**, 97.

Prasad, M., Kumar, N., Kulwal, P.L., Roder, M.S., Balyan, H.S., Dhaliwal, H.S. and Gupta, P.K. (2003). QTL analysis for grain protein content using SSR markers and validation studies using NILs in bread wheat. *Theor. Appl. Genet.* **106**, 659-667.

Prasad, M., Varshney, R.K., Kumar, A., Balyan, H.S., Sharma, P.C., Edmards, K.J., Singh, H., Dhaliwal, H.S., Roy, J.K. and Gupta, P.K. (1999). A microsatellite marker associated with a QTL for grain protein content on chromosome arm 2DL of bread wheat. *Theor. Appl. Genet.* **99**, 341-345.

Prasad, R.B. (1959). Inheritacne of field resistance to rusts and certain other characters in certain intervarietal crosses of *Triticum aestivum* L. Thesis, IARI, New Delhi.

Prasad, R.B. and Rao, M.V. (1960). Inheritance studies in wheat VII. Inheritance of field reaction to stem rust and certain other characters in crosses of common wheat. *Indian J. agric. Sci.* **30**, 196-215.

Prikryl, K. (1962). Influence of dynamics of tillering on yield of winter wheat (in Czech). *Rost. Vyr.* (Praha) **8**, 11-12.

Protsenko, D.F., Smatko, I.G. and Rubanyuk, E.A. (1968). Drought resistance of winter wheat in connection with amino acid composition (in Russian). *Fiziol. Rast.* (Moscow) **15**, 680-687.

Puchov, Y.M. and Zhirov, E.G. (1978). *World Sci. News,* India, **15**, 17-22.

Pugsley, A.T. and Oram, R.N. (1959). Genic male sterility in wheat. *Aust. Plant Breed Genet. Newsl.* **14**, 15-16.

Pujar, S., Tamhankar, S.A., Gupta, V.S., Rao, V.S. and Ranjekar, P.K. (2002). Applicability of ISSR markers to assess genetic variability in Indian tetraploid wheat and their comparison with RAPD makrers. *Biochemical Genetics* **40** (1/2), 63-69.

Pujar, S., Tamhankar, S.A., Rao, V.S., Gupta, V.S., Naik, S. and Ranjekar, P.K. (1999). Arbitrarily primed-PCR based diversity assessment reflects hierarchical groupings of Indian tetraploid wheat genotypes. *Theor. Appl. Genet.* **99**, 868-876.

Purdy, L.H. (1965). Flag smut of wheat. *Bot. Rev.* **31**, 565-606.

Pyatigin, A.V. and Smihov, V.F. (1967). Lodging of winter wheat under conditions of irrigation (in Russian). *Vest. Sel. hoz. Nauki* (Moscow) **12**, 57-60.

Qi, X. and Lindhout, P. (1997). Development of AFLP markers in barley. *Mol. Gen. Genet.* **254**, 330-336.

Qian, C.M., Wu, A. and Liang, G.H. (1986). Effects of low temperatures and genotypes on pollen development in wheat. *Crop Sci.* **26**, 43-46.

Qualset, C.O. (1977). Population management for efficient method of breeding and genetic conservation. Plant Breeding Papers. 3rd Int. Congr. Soc. for the Advancement of Breeding Researches in Asia and Oceania (SABRAO). *Aust. Plant Breeding Cong.,* Canberra, Feb. 1977.

Quick, W.A. and Shaw, M. (1964). The physiology of host parasite relations XIV. *Can. J. Bot. (Ottawa),* **42**, 1531-1540.

Quick, W.A. and Shaw, M. (1966). The physiology of host-parasite relations. XVII. *Can. J. Bot.* (Ottawa) **44**, 77-78.

Qureshi, J.A., Hucl, P. and Kartha, K.K. (1992). Is somaclonal variation a reliable tool for spring wheat improvement? *Euphytica* **60**, 221-228.

Rabinovich, S.V. (1998). Importance of wheat-rye translocations for breeding modern cultivars of *Triticum aestivum* L. In *Wheat: Prospects for Global Improvement*, H.J. Braun *et al.* (Eds.) Kluwer Academic Publishers, Dordrecht, Boston, London, pp. 401-418.

Rachinski, T.A. (1971). Inheritance of height and ear productivity in soft wheat hybrids (in Bulgarian). *Gen. Sel.* (Sofia) **4**, 369-380.

Rai, R.K. and Stoskopf, N.C. (1974). Morphological and cyto-histological expression of male sterility (*Triticum timopheevi* cytoplasm) in common wheat. *Z. Pflanzenzuecht* **71**, pp. 307-318.

Raine, R., Singh, R.B. and Sharma, G.S. (1979). Combining ability for grain quality in spring wheat. *Indian J. Genet.* **39**, 225.

Rajaram, S. and Braun, H.J. (2001). Half a century of international wheat breeding. In *Wheat Taxonomy:the Legacy of John Percival*, P.D.S. Caligari and P.E. Brandham (Eds.). *Proceedings of the Percival Symposium : Wheat-Yesterday, Today and Tomorrow,* The Linnean Society of London, pp. 137-162.

Rajaram, S. and Hettel, G.P. (1995). Wheat Breeding at CIMMYT : Commemorating 50 years of Research in Mexico for Global Wheat Improvement. Wheat Special Report No. 29, Mexico, DF, CIMMYT, Ciudad Obregon, Sonora, Mexico, p.162.

Rajaram, S. and Luig, N.H. (1972). The genetic basis for low coefficient of infection to stem rust in common wheat. *Euphytica* **21**, 363-376.

Rajaram, S. and Van Ginkel, M. (1995). Wheat breeding methodology, international perspectives. *Proceedings of the 20th Hard Red Winter Wheat Workers Workshop*, Oklahoma City, USA.

Rajaram, S., Mann, C.E., Ortiz-Ferrara, G. and Mujeeb-Kazi, A. (1983). Adaptation, stability and high yield potential of certain 1B/1R CIMMYT wheats. *Proc. 6th Int. Wheat Genetics Symposium*, S. Sakomoto (Ed.), Kyoto Japan, pp. 613-621.

Rajaram, S., Singh, R.P. and Torres, E. (1988). Current CIMMYT approach in breeding wheat for rust resistance. *In : Breeding Strategies for Resistance to the Rusts of Wheat*, N.W. Simmonds and S. Rajaram (Eds.), CIMMYT, Mexico, pp. 101-118.

Rajaram, S., Singh, R.P. and Van Ginkel, M. (1995). CIMMYT's approach to breeding for durable disease resistance in bread wheat : A global perspective. *In Genetic Research and Education : Current Trends and the Next Fifty Years*. B. Sharma et al. (Eds.), Indian Society of Genetics and Plant Breeding, New Delhi, pp. 325-338.

Ram, S. and Singh, R. (2004). Identification of molecular tools and micro-level techniques for biscuit making quality of wheat. In *Wheat Technologies for Warmer Areas*, V.S. Rao, G. Singh and S.C. Misra (Eds.), Anamaya Publishers, New Delhi, pp. 100-109.

Ramage, R.T. (1977). Varietal improvement of wheat through male sterile facilitated recurrent selection, *ASPAC Food and Fertilizer Technology Ctr. Tech. Bull.* **36**, 6.

Ramage, R.T. (1980). Genetic methods to breed salt tolerance in plants. In *Genetic Engineering of Osmoregulation*, D.W. Rains, Valentine, R.C. and Hollander, A. (Eds.). Plenum, N.Y., pp.311-318.

Rana, R.S. and Swaminathan, M.S. (1967). Relationship between chimeras and mutations induced by ^{60}Co gamma rays and 2 Mev fast neutrons at specific loci in bread wheats. *Radiat. Bot.* (Oxford) **7**, 543-548.

Randhawa, M.S. (1980). A History of Agriculture in India. Indian Council of Agricultural Research, New Delhi, India, **1**, 1-288.

Ranjekar, P.K., Dhaliwal, H.S., Rao, V.S., Gupta, V.S. and Tiwari, R. (1998). Molecular biology approaches to wheat improvement in India-Present Status and Future Strategies. *In Wheat : Research Need Beyond 2000 AD* , S. Nagarajan, G. Singh, B.S. Tyagi (Eds.), Narosa Publishing House, New Delhi, pp. 145-159.

Ranjekar, P.K., Dholakia, B.B., Pujar, S., Lagu, M. and Gupta, V. (2004). Molecular biology of wheat: Challenges and opportunities. In *Wheat Technologies for Warmer Areas*, V.S. Rao, G. Singh and S.C. Misra (Eds.), Anamaya Publishers, New Delhi, pp. 116-123.

Rao, M.V. (1969). Alteration in the rate and spectrum of chlorophyll mutations induced by ethyl methane sulphonate in wheat. *Curr. Sci.* (Bangalore) **38**, 22-23.

Rao, M.V., Somayajulu, P.L.N. and Ahire, S.G. (1962). Inheritance studies in wheat XV. *Indian J. Genet.* (New Delhi), **22**, 187-191.

Rao, N.V.P.R.G., Mahajan, V. and Nagarajan, S. (2000). Effect of chemical hybridizing agent on floret opening and seed set in wheat. *Indian J. Agric. Sci.* **70**, 689-690.

Rao, V.S. (2001). Wheat. In *Breeding Field Crops : Theory and Practice*. V.L. Chopra (Ed.). Oxford and IBH Publishing Co. Pvt. Ltd., New Delhi, pp. 87-146.

Ratnalikar, V.P. and Singh, V.S. (1998). Role of industry in promoting hybrids in self-pollinated crops. In *Wheat Research Needs Beyond 2000 AD,* S. Nagarajann, G. Singh and B.S. Tyagi (Ed.), Narosa Publishing House, New Delhi, p.392.

Reddi, M.V., Heyne, E.G. and Liang, G.H.L. (1969). Heritabilities and interrelationships of shortness and other agronomic characters in F_3 and F_4 generations of two wheat crosses. *Crop Sci.* **9**, 222-225.

Rees, R.G., Thompson, J.P. and Mayer, R.J. (1979). Slow rusting and tolerance to rusts in wheat.I. The progress and effects of epidemics of *Puccinia graminis tritici* in selected wheat cultivars. *Aust. J. Agric. Res.* **30**, 403-419.

Richey, F.D. (1927). Tne convergent improvement of selfed lines of corn. *Amer. Nat.* **61**, 430-449.

Riera-Lizarazu, O. and Mujeeb-Kazi, A. (1993). Polyhaploid production in the *Triticeae* : Wheat × *Tripsacum* crosses. *Crop Sci.* **33**, 973-976.

Riley, R. (1965). Cytogenetics and Plant Breeding. In *Proc. XI. Intern. Congr. Genet.* 1963, **3**, 681-688.

Riley, R. (1966). Cytogenetics and Wheat Breeding. *Contemp. Agric.* **11-12**, 107-117.

Riley, R. and Chapman, V. (1958a). Genetic control of the cytologically diploid behaviour of hexaploid wheat. *Nature* (London) **182**, 713-715.

Riley, R. and Chapman, V. (1958b). The production and phenotypes of wheat-rye chromosome addition lines. *Heredity*, **12**, 301-315.

Riley, R. and Chapman, V. (1960). The D genome of hexaploid wheat. *Wheat Infor. Serv.* **11**, 18-19.

Riley, R. and Chapman, V. (1967a). Effect of 5BS in supressing the expression of altered dosage of 5BL on meiotic chromosome pairing in *Triticum aestivum. Nature* (London) **216**, 60-62.

Riley, R. and Chapman, V. (1967b). Inheritacne in wheat of crossability with rye. *Genet. Res.* **9**, 259-267.

Riley, R. and Macer, R.C.F. (1966). The chromosomal distribution of the genetic resistance of rye to wheat pathogens. *Can. J. Genet. Cytol.* (Ottawa) **8**, 640-653.

Riley, R., Chapman, V. and Johnson, R. (1968a). Introduction of yellow rust resistance of *Aegilops comosa* into wheat by genetically induced homologous recombination. *Nature* (London) **217**, 383-384.

Riley, R., Chapman, V. and Johnson, R. (1968b). The incorporation of alien disease resistance in wheat by genetic interference with the regulation of meiotic chromosome synapsis. *Genet. Res.* (London) **12**, 199-219.

Riley, R., Chapman, V., Young, R.M. and Belfield, A.M. (1966). Control of meiotic chromosome pairing by the chromosomes of homeologous group 5 of *Triticum aestivum. Nature* (London) **212**, 1475-1477.

Riley, R., Unrau, J. and Chapman, V. (1958). Evidence on the origin of the B-genome of wheat. *J. Hered.* **49**, 91-98.

Rimpau, W. (1891). Kreuzungsprodukte landwirtschaftlicher Kulturpflanzen, *Landwirtschaftl,* Jahrb **20**, 335-371.

Rodriguez, R., Quinones, M.A., Borlaug, N.E. and Narvaez, I. (1967). Hybrid wheats : their development and food potential, CIMMYT, Mexico, *Res. Bull.* p.3,

Roelfs, A.P. (1988). Resistance to leaf rust and stem rust in wheat. In *Breeding Strategies for Resistance to the Rusts of Wheat*, N.W. Simmonds and S. Rajaram (Eds.), CIMMYT, Mexico, pp. 10-22.

Roelfs, A.P., Singh, R.P. and Saari, E.E. (1992). Rust Diseases of Wheat:Concepts and Methods of Disease Management, CIMMYT, Mexico, D.F.

Rogowsky, P.M., Guidet, F.L.Y., Langridge, P., Shepherd, K.W. and Koebner, R.M.W. (1991). Isolation and characterization of wheat rye recombinants involving chromosome aun 1DS of wheat. *Theor. Appl. Genet.* **82**, 537-544.

Rohringer, R., Fuchs, A., Lunderstadt, J. and Samborski, D.J. (1967). Metabolism of aromatic compounds in healthy and rust infected primary leaves of wheat. *Can. J. Bot.* (Ottawa) **45**, 863-889.

Rosen, H.R. (1949). Oat parentage and procedure for combining resistance to crown rust including race 45 and *Helminthosporium* blight. *Phytopathol.* **39**, 20.

Rosenquist, C.E. (1927). An improved method of producing F_1 hybrid seeds of wheat and barley. *J. Am. Soc. Agron.* **19**, 968-971.

Rowell, P.L. and Miller, D.G. (1974). Effect of 2-chloroethyl-phosphonic acid (ethephon) on female fertility of two wheat varieties. *Crop Sci.* **14**, 31-34.

Rudnoy, Sz., Paldi, E., Bratek, Z., Szego, D., Racz, I. and Lasztity, D. (2004). ITS Region in hexaploid bread wheat and its supposed progenitors. *Cereal Res. Comm.* **32**, 423-428.

Rybalka, A.I. and Sozinov, A.A. (1979). *Tsitol. Genet.* **13**, 276-286.

Sadasivaiah, R.S., Orshinsky, B.R. and Kozub, G.C. (1999). Production of wheat haploids using anther culture and wheat × maize hybridization techniques. *Cereal Res. Comm.* **27**, 33-40.

Sage, G.C.M. (1976). Nucleo-cytoplasmic relationships in wheat. *Adv. Agron.* **28**, 267-300.

Saharan, M.S., Kumar, J., Tiwari, R., Nagrajan, S., Sharma, S. and Priyamvada (2004). Phenotypic, pathogenic and molecular variation among *Fusarium* spp., the causal agents of Head Scab of wheat. In *Wheat : Technologies for Warmers Areas*, V.S. Rao, G. Singh and S.C. Misra (Eds.). Anamaya Publishers, New Delhi, pp. 254-263.

Saini, R.G., Bansal, U.K., Kaur, L., Khanna, R., Singh, H., Kaur, S., Sharma, A.K., Sharma, A., Kaur, H. and Kaur, M. (2004). Genes for adult plant leaf rust and stripe rust resistance in breed wheat against races from the Indian sub-continent. In *Wheat : Technologies for Warmers Areas*, V.S. Rao, G. Singh and S.C. Misra (Eds.). Anamaya Publishers, New Delhi, pp. 228-233.

Saini, R.G., Kaur, M., Singh, B., Sharma, S., Nanda, G.S., Nayar, S.K., Gupta, A.K. and Nagarajan, S. (2002). Lr 48 and Lr 49 novel hypersensitive adult plant leaf rust resistance genes in wheat (*Triticum aestivum* L.). *Euphytica* 124, 365-370.

Sakamoto, S. (1973). Patterns of phylogenetic differentiation in the tribe Triticeae. *Seiken Ziho* 24, 11-31.

Sakamura, T. (1918). Kurze Mitteilung uber die chromosomenzahlen und die Verwandtschaftsverhaltnisse der Triticum-*Arten. Bot. Mag.* 32, 151-154.

Salcheva, G. and Gramatikova, H. (1965). Certain changes in the free sugar and nitrogen metabolism in the course of hardening and freezing of winter wheat. (in Bulgarian). *Rast. Nauki* (Sofia) 2, 25-36.

Salcheva, G., Pavlov, G.P. and Gramatikova, H. (1964). Effect of light supply and light quality on the winter hardiness of winter wheat (in Bulgarian). *Rast. Nauki* (Sofia) 1, 17-28.

San, Noeum, L.H. and Ahmadi, N. (1983). Variability of doubled haploids from *in vitro* androgenesis and gynogenesis. In *Variability in Plants Regenerated from Tissue Culture*, E. Earle and Y. Demarly (Eds.), Praeger, New York, p.273.

Sanchez, A.C., Brar, D.S., Huang, N., Li, Z. and Khush, G.S. (2000). Sequence tagged site marker assisted selection for three bacterial blight resistance genes in rice. *Crop Sci.* 40, 792-797.

Santarius, K. and Heber, W. (1972). Physiological and biochemical aspects of frost damage and winter hardiness in higher plants. *Coll. Winter Hardiness* (Martonvasar) 7-29.

Sarkar, P. and Stebbins, G.L. (1956). Morphological evidence concerning the origin of the B-genome of wheat. *Am. J. Bot.* 43, 297-304.

Sarmah, P. and Pawar, I.S. (2000). Genetic architecture of some wheat crosses through triple test cross method. *Natnl. J. Pl. Improv.* 2, 45-48.

Sarmah, P., Pawar, I.S., Yunus, M. and Sharma, S.C. (1997). Genotype × environment interaction analysis of some triple test cross families in bread wheat. *Haryana agric. Univ. J. Res.* 127, 117-120.

Sarrafi, A., Ecochard, R. and Grignac, P. (1989). Genetic variability for some grain quality characters in tetraploid wheats. *Plant Varieties and Seeds*, 2, 163-169.

Sasakuma, T. and Maan, S.S. (1978). Male sterility fertility restoration systems in *Triticum durum*. *Can J. Genet. Cytol.* 20, 389-398.

Sautter, C. (2004). Wheat transformation : Opportunities and challenges. In *Wheat : Technologies for Warmer Areas*, V.S. Rao, G. Singh, S.C. Misra, (Eds.), Anamaya Publishers, New Delhi, pp.146-151.

Savchenko, M.G., Lastovich, G.S., Belous, V.C. and Sea, L.V. (1971). Pollen sterility of induced mutants of winter soft wheat, *T. aestivum* L. by ionizing irradiation (in Russian). *Eksp. Mut. Ser. Rsl.* (Kiev) 95-104.

Savidan, Y.H. (1992). Progress in research on apomixis and its transfer to major grain crops. In *Reproductive Biology and Plant Breeding*, C. Dumas, Datteey, A. Gallais (Eds.), Springer-Berlin, Heidelberg, New Delhi, pp. 269-279.

Savin, V.N. (1963). Effect of grain treatment by low rate gamma irradiation (Co-60) on the growth of plants (in Russian). *Pr. Obl. Zemj. Sel. Kult. Izd. Akad. Nank. SSR* (Moscow) pp.190-193.

Savov, P.G. (1969). The effect of gamma rays on variability of different wheat varieties and their hybrids (in Bulgaria) *Genet. Selek.* (Sofia) **2**, 477-490.

Sawhney, R.N. (1995). Genetics of wheat rusts interaction. *Plant Breed. Revs.* **13**, 293-343.

Sawhney, R.N. (1998). Genetic basis of rust resistance in Indian Wheats and the need to harness alien genes for durability. In *Wheat : Research Needs Beyond 2000 AD*, S. Nagarajan, G.S. Singh and B.S. Tyagi (Eds.), Narosa Publishing House, New Delhi, pp. 161-175.

Sawhney, R.N. and Sharma, J.B. (1996). Introgression of diverse genes for resistance to rusts into an improved wheat variety Kalyansona. *Genetica* **97**, 255-261.

Sax, K. (1918). The behaviour of the chromosomes in fertilization. *Genetics.* **3**, 309.

Sax, K. (1922). Sterility in wheat hybrids II chromosome behaviour in partially sterile hybrids. *Genetics* **7**, 513-552.

Sayre, K.D., Rajaram, S. and Fischer, R.A. (1997). Yield potential progress in short bread wheats in northwest Mexico. *Crop Sci.*, **37**, 36-42.

Scarth, R. and Law, C.N. (1984). *Z. Pflanzenzuchtg* **92**, 140-150.

Schaeffer, G.W., Baenziger, P.S. and Worley, J. (1979). Haploid plant development from anthers and *in vitro* embryo cultures of wheat. *Crop Sci.* **19**, 696-702.

Schmalz, H. (1962). Makromutationen bei Sommergerste und Sommerloizen. *Zuchter* (Berlin-Gottingen) **32**, 133-146.

Schmid, J. and Keller, E.R. (1986). Effect of a gametocide on the induction of haploids in *Triticum aestivum*. In *Genetic Manipulation in Plant Breeding*, W. Horn, C.J. Jensen, W. Odenbach and O. Schieder (Eds.), de Gruyter, Berlin, pp. 347-349.

Schmidt, J.W. and Johnson, V.A. (1966). Inheritance of the sphaerococcum effect in tetraploid wheat. *Wheat Inform. Serv.* (Kyoto) **22**, 5-6.

Schmidt, J.W., Johnson, V.A., Morris, M.R. and Mattern, P.J. (1971). *Seiken Jiho,* **22**, 113-118.

Schwinn, F.J. and Dahmen, H. (1973). Beobachtung zum Infections vorgang bei *Erysiphe graminis* D.C. *Phytopat. Z.* (Berlin) **77**(1), 89-92.

Scossiroli, R. (1962). Application of ionising raps for raising genetic variability of cultivated plants (in Italian) I. *Georgofil* (Firenze) **9**, 44-64.

Scossiroli, R., Palenzona, D. and Rusmini, R. (1961). Radiation experiments of *Triticum durum* and *Triticum vulgare*. Eff. of ion. rad. on seeds (Vienna) *IAEA*, 373-386.

Sears, E.R. (1939). Cytogenetic studies with polyploid species of wheat. I. Chromosomal aberrations in the progeny of a haploid of *Triticum vulgare*. *Genetics* **24**, 509-523.

Sears, E.R. (1941). Chromosome pairing and fertility in hybrids and amphidiploids in the *Triticinae*. *Missouri Agri. Exp. Sta. Res. Bull.* **337**, 20.

Sears, E.R. (1944). Cytogenetic studies with polyploid species of wheat.II. Additional chromosomal aberrations in *Triticum vulgare. ibid*, **29**, 232-246.

Sears, E.R. (1948). The cytology and genetics of wheats and their relatives. *Adv. Genet.* **2**, 239-270.

Sears, E.R. (1954a). *Res. Bull.* 572, University of Missouri, Columbia, Missouri, USA.

Sears, E.R. (1954b). The aneuploids of common wheat. *Res. Bull. Univ. Miss. agric. Exp. Sta.* **572**, 58.

Sears, E.R. (1956a). The B genome of *Triticum. Wheat Inform. Serv.* **4**, 8-10.

Sears, E.R. (1956b). The transfer of leaf rust resistance from *Aegilops umbellulata* to wheat. *Brookhaven Symp. Biol.* **9**, 1-21.

Sears, E.R. (1959). The aneuploids of common wheat. *Proc. First Int. Wheat. Genet. Symp.* **1958**, 221-229.

Sears, E.R. (1966). Nullisomic-tetrasomic combination in hexaploid wheat. In *Chromosome manipulation in plant genetics*, R. Riley and K.R. Lewis (Eds.), Oliver & Boyd, London, pp.29-45.

Sears, E.R. (1972). Chromosome engineering in wheat. *Stadler Genet. Symp.* **4**, 23-38.

Sears, E.R. (1973). *Agropyron*-wheat transfers induced by homoeologous pairing. In *4th Int. Wheat Genet. Symp., Univ. of Missouri, Columbia*, pp. 191-199.

Sears, E.R. (1977). An induced mutant with homoeologous pairing in wheat. *Can J. Genet. Cytol.* **19**, 585-593.

Sears, E.R. (1981). Transfer of alien genetic material to wheat. In *Wheat Science Today and Tomorrow*, L.T. Evans and W.J. Peacock (Ed.), Cambridge University Press, Cambridge, pp. 75-89.

Sears, E.R. (1982). A wheat mutation conditioning an intermediate level of homoeologous chromosome pairing. *Can. J. Genet. Cytol.* **24**, 715-719.

Sears, E.R. (1984). Mutations in wheat that raise the level of meiotic chromosome pairing. In *Gene manipulation of plant improvement*, J.P. Gustafson (Ed.), 16th stadler Genet. Symp., Plenum Press, New York, pp. 296-300.

Sears, E.R. and Okamoto, M. (1956). Genetic and structural relationships of non-homologous chromosomes in wheat. In *Proc. Int. Genet. Symp.*, Tokyo, Cytologia Suppl. pp.332-335.

Sears, E.R., Loegering, W.Q., Kimber, G., Sears, L.M.S., Chang, T.D. and Larson, J. (1973). Cytogenetics studies in wheat. *Ann. Wheat Newsletter* (Kansan) **19**, 105-106.

Semenko, N.I. (1968). Susceptibility of specimens in the VIR World Collection of wheat to stem rust (in Russian). *Vest. Sel'hoz. Nauki* (Moscow) **13**, 34-39.

Sen, S. and Joshi, M. G. (1955). Inheritance of resistance to black rust in wheat. *Indian J. Genet.* **15**, 36-46.

Shands, H. and Kimber, G. (1973). Reallocation of the genomes of *Triticum timopheevii* Zhuk. In *Proc. 4th Int. Wheat Genet. Symp.*, E.R.Sears and L.M.S. Sears (Eds.), Univ. Missouri, Columbia, MO 6-11 Aug. 1973. pp.101-108.

Shaner, G. (1987). Wheat Diseases. In *Wheat and Wheat Improvement 2nd*, E.G. Heyne (Ed.), amer. Soc.Agron. Madison, Wisc., USA, pp. 508-624.

Shaowen, Y. and Shan, R. (1980). Studies on the VE-type male sterility of wheat. *Acta Genetica Sinica* **7**, 26-35.

Sharma, D. and Knott, D.R. (1964). The inheritance of seed weight in a wheat cross. *Can. J. Genet. Cytol.* **6**, 419-425.

Sharma, H., Ohm, H., Goulart, L., Lister, R., Appels, R. and Benlhabib, O. (1995). Introgression and characterization of barley yellow dwarf virus resistance from *Thinopyrum intermedium* into wheat. *Genome* **38**, 406-413.

Sharma, H., Yang, Y. and Ohm (2002). An assessment of doubled haploid production in soft red winter wheat by wheat × corn wide crosses. *Cereal Res. Comm.* **30**, 269-275.

Sharma, H.C., Waines, J.G. and Foster, K.W. (1981). Variability in primitive and wild wheats for useful genetic characters. *Crop Sci.* **21**, 555-559.

Sharma, J.C. and Ahmad, Z. (1980). Genetic architecture for some traits in spring wheat. *Indian J. agric. Sci.* **50**, 457-461.

Sharma, R.K. and Tandon, J.P. (1998). Effect of heat stress on heterosis for some physiological characters in wheat. *Agric. Sci. Digest* **18**, 165-167.

Sharma, S. (2000). Genetic variation and response to selection for heat stress. during reproductive phase in bread wheat. M.Sc. Thesis, Punjab Agricultural University, Ludhiana, India.

Sharma, S., Sohu, V.S. and Dhindsa, G.S. (2001). Genetic variation for foliar traits in wheat varieties exposed to different thermal regimes. *Hundred Years of Post-Mendelian Genetics and Plant Breeding : Retrospect and Prospects*. Symp. Proc. M.C. Kharkwal and R.B. Mehra (Eds.), New Delhi, p. 165.

Sharma, S.K. and Singh, R.K. (1982). Diallel analysis for combining ability over environments in wheat. *Haryana agril. Univ. J. Res.* **12**, 675-678.

Sharma, S.N. and Sain, R.S. (2002). Inheritance of tillers per plant in durum wheat. *Indian J. Genet.* **62**, 101-103.

Sharman, B.C. (1958). Purple pericarp : A monofactorial dominant in tetraploid wheats. *Nature* **181**, 929.

Sharp, E.L. and Volin, R.B. (1970). Additive genes in wheat conditioning resistance to stripe rust. *Phytopathology*, **53**, 1239-1240.

Shebeski, L.H. (1971). *Inf. Bull. Near East Cereal Improv. Prod. Proj.* **8**, 1-7.

Shekhawat, U.S., Bhardwaj, R.P. and Prakash, V. (2000). Gene action for yield and its components in wheat. *Indian J. agric. Res.* **34**, 176-178.

Shewry, P.R., Tatam, A.S., Halford, N.G., Barker, J.H.A., Hanneppel, U., Gallois, P., Thomas, M. and Kries, M. (1994). Opportunities for manipulating the seed protein composition of wheat and barley in order to improve quality. *Transgenic Res.* **3**, 3-12.

Shull, G.H. (1908). The composition of field maize. *Rept. Amer. Breeder's Assoc.* **4**, 296-301.

Shu-Wen, Y. and Tsing-Tsi, C. (1964). On the effect of drought hardening at seedling stage of wheat plants and its physiological basis. *Zuowu xuebao* (Peking) **3**, 169-181.

Siddiqui, K.A. and Haahr, V. (1971). Different reactions of wheat mutants to a systemic fungicide. *Naturwiss.* (Berlin-Heidelberg) **58**, 415-416.

Sigurbjornsson, B. (1972). Breeding with natural and induced variability. In *Induced mutations and plant improvement. Proc. of Latin american Study Group Meet on Induced Mutations and Plant Improvement,* Buenos Aires 16-20 Nov., 1979. IAEA, Vienna, STI/PUB/297, pp. 3-5, 526-544.

Sikka, S.M. and Jain, K.B.L. (1959). Inheritance of leaf blotching in an intervarietal cross of *Triticum aestivum* L. *Curr. Sci.* **28**, 191-192.

Sikka, S.M. and Maini, N.S. (1962). Correlation studies in some Punjab wheats. *Indian J. Genet.* (New Delhi) **22**, 181-186.

Sikka, S.M. and Rao, M.V. (1957). Inheritance studies in wheat II. *Indian J. Genet.* **17**, 7-18.

Sikka, S.M. and Rao, M.V. (1958). Inheritance studies in wheat III. Inheritance of field reaction to black rust. *ibid* **18**, 34-40.

Sikka, S.M., Makhija, O.P. and Rao, M.V. (1961a). Inheritance studies in wheat. XI. Inheritance of seedling reactin to physiologic race 75 and biotype 42B of *Puccinia graminis tritici* Erikss. and Henn. in some intervarietal crosses of *Triticum aestivum* L. *Indian J. agric. Sci.* **31**, 23-28.

Sikka, S.M., Makhija, O.P. and Rao, M.V. (1961b). Inheritance studies in wheat. XII. Inheritance of seedling reaction to physiologic races 15 and 21 of *Puccinia graminis tritici* Erikss. and Henn. in some intervarietal crosses of *Triticum aestivum* L. *ibid* **31**, 103-107.

Sikka, S.M., Rao, M.V. and Ahluwalia, M. (1960). Inheritance studies in wheat. X. Inheritance of field reaction to rusts and other characters. *ibid* **30**, 223-232.

Simeone, R.A., Blanco, A. and Giorgi, B. (1983). The primary trisomics of durum wheat (*Triticum durum* desf.) In *Proc. 6th Int. Wheat Genet. Symp.*, S. Sakamoto (Ed.), Kyoto, Japan, 28 November-3 December. Plant Germplasm Institute, Fac. Agric., Kyoto University. pp.1103-1107.

Simmonds, D.H., Burlow, K.K. and Wrigley, C.W. (1973). The biochemical basis of grain hardness in wheat. *Cereal Chem.* **50**, 553.

Simpson, G.M. (1968). Association between grain yield per plant and photosynthetic area above the flag-leaf node in wheat. *Can. J. Plant Sci.* (Ottawa) **48**, 253-260.

Singh, A.M., Mishra, B.K., Ahlawat, A.K. and Deveshwar, J.J. (2004). Development of bread wheat genotypes with superior bread making quality. In *Wheat : Technologies for Warmer Areas*, V.S. Rao, G. Singh and S.C. Misra (Eds.), Anamaya Publishers, New Delhi, pp. 110-115.

Singh, D. (1980). A note on the Karnal bunt infection on the vigour of wheat seed. *Seed Res.* **8**(1) : 81-82.

Singh, G., Bhullar, G.S. and Gill, K.S. (1986). Genetic control of grain yield and its related traits in bread wheat. *Theor. Appl. Genet.* **72**, 536-540.

Singh, G., Bhullar, G.S. and Gill, K.S. (1988). Inheritance of yield and its components in an intervarietal cross of bread wheat. *Crop Improv.* **15**, 200-202.

Singh, G., Chatrath, R., Singh, G.P. and Jagshoran (2004). Shuttle breeding approach for wider adaptability and disease resistance in wheat. In *Wheat Technologies for Warmer Areas*, V.S. Rao, g. Singh and S.C. Misra (Eds.), Anamaya Publishers, New Delhi, pp. 24-35.

Singh, G., Nanda, G.S. and Gill, K.S. (1984). Inheritance of yield and its components in five crosses of spring wheat. *Indian J. agric. Sci.* **54**, 943-949.

Singh, H., Prasad, M., Varshney, R.K., Roy, J.K., Balyan, H.S., Dhaliwal, H.S. and Gupta, P.K. (2001). STMS markers for grain protein content and their validation using near isogenic lines in bread wheat. *Plant Breed.* **120**, 273-278.

Singh, H.B., Anderson, E. and Pal, B.P. (1957). Studies in the genetics of *Triticum vavilovi* Jakub. *Agron. J.* **49**, 4-11.

Singh, I. and Pawar, I.S. (2000). Effects of epistasis on the estimates of additive and dominance components and their interactions with environment in bread wheat. *Natnl. J. Pl. Improv.* **2**, 93-94.

Singh, I., Chowdhury, R.K., Pawar, I.S. and Singh, S. (1987). A comparative study of three selection procedures in bread wheat. *Wheat Information Service* **65**, 16-18.

Singh, I., Paroda, R.S. and Singh, S. (1985). Estimation of additive and dominance components through triple test cross in wheat. *J. agric. Sci. Camb.* **105**, 123-128.

Singh, I., Paroda, R.S. and Singh, S. (1986a). Genotype × environment interaction analysis of TTC progenies for some metric traits in wheat. *Crop Improv.* **13**, 117-121.

Singh, I., Paroda, R.S. and Singh, S. (1986b). Relative efficiency of diallel, partial diallel and triple test cross designs for studying genetic architecture of some traits in wheat. *Indian J. Genet.*, **46**, 530-540.

Singh, I., Pawar, I.S. and Singh, S. (1988). Detection of additive, dominance and epistatic components of genetic variation for some metric traits in wheat. *Genet.Agr.* **42**, 371-378.

Singh, I., Pawar, I.S. and Singh, S. (1989). Detection of genotype×environment interaction in spring wheat through triple test cross analysis. *Crop Improv.* **16**, 34-37.

Singh, I., Pawar, I.S. and Singh, S. (1991). Genetic variation in wheat varieties. *Haryana agric. Univ. J. Res.* **21**, 153-154.

Singh, I., Pawar, I.S. and Singh, S. (1995). A study of components of genetic variation and genotype × environment interaction in selfed wheat tripe test cross families. *Indian J. Genet.* **55**, 324-329.

Singh, K.B. and Singh, J.K. (1971). Potentialities of heterosis breeding in wheat. *Euphytica* **20**, 586-590.

Singh, K.N. and Tyagi, N.K. (1998). Genetic improvement of suppressive/salt affected soils. In *Wheat : Research Needs Beyond* 2000 AD, S. Nagarajan, G. Singh and B.S. Tyagi (Eds.), Narosa Publishing House, New Delhi, pp. 199-207.

Singh, M.P. (1969). Some radiation induced changes at "Q" locus in bread wheat. *Caryologia (Firenze)* **22**, 119-126.

Singh, M.P. and Swaminathan, M.S. (1959). Monosomic analysis in bread wheat. III. Identification of chromosomes carrying genes for resistance to two races of yellow rust in Cometa Klein. *Indian J. Genet.* **19**, 171-175.

Singh, N.K., Larosa, P.C., Nelson, D., Iraki, N., Carpita, P.M., Hasegawa, P.M. and Bressan, R.A. (1989). Reduced growth rate and changes in cell wall proteins of plant cells adapted to NaCl. In *Environmental Stress in Plants : Biochemical and Physiochemical Mechanism*, J.H. Cherry (Ed.). Springer-Verlag, Berlin, pp. 174-194.

Singh, N.K., Sailesh, G., Kumar, A., Sarita, Puri, N., Singh, D.T., Garg, G.K., Nayal, S., Gaur, A.K. and Srinivas, B. (1998). Improvement in the nutritional quality of wheat through genetic engineering. In *Genetics and Biotechnology in Crop Improvement*, P.K. Gupta *et al.* (Eds.). Rastogi Publications Meerut, India, pp. 158-168.

Singh, R.P. (1992a). Genetic association of leaf rust resistance gene Lr 34 with adult plant resistance to stripe rust in bread wheat. *Phytopathology* **82**, 835-838.

Singh, R.P. (1992b). Genetic association between gene Lr 34 for leaf rust resistance and leaf tip necrosis in bread wheats. *Crop Sci.* **32**, 874-878.

Singh, R.P., Burnett, P.A., Albarran, M. and Rajaram, S. (1993). Bdvl : A gene for tolerance to barley yellow dwarf virus in bread wheats. *Crop Sci.* **33**, 231-234.

Singh, R.P., Payne, T.S. and Rajaram, S. (1991). Characterization of variability and relationship among components of partial resistance to leaf rust in CIMMYT bread wheats. *Theor. Appl. Genet.* **82**, 674-680.

Singh, S. (1979). Relative efficiency of north carolian design I and II and standard design III in three wheat crosses. *Theor. Appl. Genet.* **54**, 33-35.

Singh, S. (1980). Detection of components of genetic variation and genotype × environment interaction in spring wheat. *J. agric. Sci. Camb.* **95**, 67-72.

Singh, S. (1981). Single tester triple test cross analysis in spring wheat. *Theor. Appl. Genet.* **59**, 247-249.

Singh, S. (1990). Bias caused by epistasis in the estimates of additive and dominance components and their interactions with environment in wheat. *Indian J. Genet.* **50**, 157-160.

Singh, S. and Dahiya, M.S. (1984). Detection and estimation of components of genetic variation and genotype × environment interaction in three wheat crosses. *J. agric. Sci. Camb.* **103**, 543-547.

Singh, S. and Pawar, I.S. (1998). Recent advances in breeding of self-pollinated crops. In *Genetics and Biotechnology in crop improvement*, P.K. Gupta, S.P.Singh, H.S. Balyan, P.C. Sharma and B. Ramesh (Eds.), Rastogi Publications, Meerut. pp. 255-275.

Singh, S. and Pawar, I.S. (2005). *Theory and Application of Biometrical Genetics*. CBS Publishers and Distributors, New Delhi.

Singh, S. and Pawar, I.S. (2006). *Genetic Basis and Methods of Plant Breeding*. CBS Publishers and Distributors, New Delhi.

Singh, S. and Singh, R.B. (1976). Triple test cross analysis in two wheat crosses. *Heredity* **37**, 173-177.

Singh, S. and Singh, R.B. (1978). A study of gene effects in three wheat crosses. *J. agric. Sci. Camb.* **91**, 9-12.

Singh, S., Kumar, S., Pawar, I.S. and Singh, I. (1992). Detection and estimation of additive and dominance components and their interaction with sowing date in presence and absence of epistasis in wheat. *Haryana agric. Univ. J. Res.* **22**, 165-169.

Singh, S., Sethi, G.S. and Chaudhary, H.K. (2004). Differential responsiveness of winter and spring wheat genotypes to maize mediated production of haploids. *Cereal Res. Comm.* **32**, 201-207.

Singh, S., Yunus, M. and Paroda, R.S. (1984). Detection of epistasis in a cross of bread wheat. *Indian J. agric. Sci.* **54**, 250-252.

Skovmand, B., Roelfs, A.P. and Wilcoxson, R.D. (1978). The relationship between slow-rusting and some genes specific for stem rust resistance in wheat. *Phytopathology* **68**, 491-499.

Skovmand, B., Wilcoxon, R.D., Shearer, B.L. and Stucker, R.E. (1978). Inheritance of slow rusting to stem rust in wheat. *Euphytica* **27**, 95-107.

Skvarnikov, P.K. (1963). The effect of seed storage at high temperatures and under increased oxygen pressure on the mutagenic effect of gamma rays (in Russian) *Cytologia* (Moscow) **5**, 535-545.

Skvarnikov, P.K., Moegun, V.V., Boreiko, V.S. and Sickar, V.I. (1971). Sensibility of winter wheat to chemical mutagens and gamma irradiation (in Russian) *Eksp. Mut. Sel. Rosl.* (Kiev.), pp. 74-87.

Slafer, G.A. and Andrale, F.H. (1991). Changes in the physiological attributes of dry matter economy of bread wheat through genetic improvement of grain yield potential of different regions of the world. *Euphytica* **58**, 37-49.

Smith, E.L. (1987). A review of plant breeding strategies for rainfed areas. *Proc. Int. Workshop on Drought Tolerance in Winter Cereals* held at Capri, Italy from Oct. 27-31, 1985, pp. 79-87.

Smith, E.L., Schlehuber, A.M., Young, H.C. and Edwards, L.H. (1968). Registration of Agent Wheat. *Crop Sci.* **8**, 511-512.

Snape, J.W. (1982). Predicting the frequencies of transgressive segregants for yield and yield components in wheat. *Theor. Appl. Genet.* **62**, 127-134.

Snape, J.W. (1996). The contribution of new biotechnologies to wheat breeding. In *Increasing Yield Potential in Wheat : Breeding the Barriers*, M.P. heynolds, S. Rajaram and A. McNab (Eds.), Mexico, DF : CIMMYT. pp. 167-181.

Snape, J.W. and Parker, B.B. (1985). The genetical basis of heterosis for yield in wheat. *Annu. Rep. Plant Breed. Inst.* Cambridge 1984, 73-74.

Snape, J.W., Chapman, V., Moss, J., Blanchard, C.E. and Miller, T.E. (1979). The crossabilities of wheat varieties with *Hordeum bulbosum. Heredity* **42**, 291-298.

Snape, J.W., Flavell, R.B., O'Dell, M., Hughes, W.G. and Payne, P.I. (1985). Intrachromosomal mapping of nucleolar organiser region relative to three marker loci on chromosome 1B of wheat (*Triticum aestivum* L.). *Theor. Appl. Genet.* **69**, 263-270.

Snape, J.W., Law, C.N. and Worland, A.J. (1975). A method for the detection of epistasis in chromosome substitution lines of hexaploid wheat. *Heredity* **34**, 297-303.

Snape, J.W., Law, C.N. and Worland, A.J. (1976). Chromosome variation for loci controlling ear emergence time on chromosome 5A of wheat. *Heredity* **37**, 335-340.

Snape, J.W., Law, C.N., Parkar, B.B. and Worland, A.J. (1985). Genetic analysis of chromosome 5A of wheat and its influence on important agronomic characters. *Theor. Appl. Genet.* **71**, 518-526.

Sneep, J. (1977). Selection for yield in early generations of self-fertilizing crops. *Euphytica* **26**, 27-30.

Sneep, J., Murty, B.R. and Utz, H.F. (1979). Current breeding methods. In *Plant Breeding Perspectives*, J. Sneep and A.J.T. Hendriksen (Eds.), Centre for Agricultural Publishing and Documentation Wageningen, Netherlands, pp. 104-233.

Sobko, T.I. (1984). *J. Agric. Sci.* (Kiev.) **N7(320)**, 78-80.

Sohu, V.S., Sharma, S. and Mavi, G.S. (2004). Breeding for terminal heat tolerance in wheat. In *Wheat : Technologies for Warmers Areas*, V.S. Rao, G. Singh and S.C. Misra (Eds.). Anamaya Publishers, New Delhi, pp. 64-74.

Solari, R. and Favret, E.A. (1968). Genetic control of protein constitution in wheat endosperm and its implication on induced mutagenesis. In : *Mutations in Plant Breeding II. Proc of Res. Coord. Meet* on the use of Induced Mutations in Plant Breeding. Vienna, Austria 11-15 Sept. 1967, IAEA, Vienna, STI/PWB/182, pp. 219-231.

Southern, J.W. (1978). The stability of the slow rusting character in nine spring wheat cultivars to five races of *Puccinia graminis tritici* in four Minnesota environments. Ph.D. Thesis, University of Minnesota, St. Paul. p.162.

Sprague, G.F. (1983). Heterosis in maize. Theory and Practice. In *Heterosis : A Reappraisal of Theory and Practice*, R. Frankel (Ed.), Springer Verlag, pp. 47-70.

Sprague, R. (1936). Relative susceptibility of certain species of Gramineae to *Cercosporella herpotrichoides. J. Agric. Res.* **53**, 659-670.

Srivastava, J.P. and Ram, H.H. (1974). Considerations on improvement in grain quality characters in wheat. *Indian J. Genet.* **34A**, 610-620.

Srivastava, P.S.L. and Arunachalam, V. (1977). Heterosis as a function of genetic divergence in triticale. *Z. Pflanzenzuehtg* **78**, 269-275.

Srivastava, R.B., Paroda, R.S., Sharma, S.C. and Yunus, M. (1989). Genetic variability and advance under four selection procedures in wheat pedigree breeding programme. *Theor. Appl. Genet.* **77**, 516-520.

Srivastava, R.B., Sharma, S.C. and Yunus, M. (1992). Additive and non-additive gene effects for yield and yield components in two crosses of wheat. *Indian J. Genet.* **52**, 297-301.

Srivastva, R.B., Luthra, O.P., Singh, D. and Goyal, K.C. (1981). Genetic architecture of yield, harvest index and related traits in wheat. *Cereal Res. Comm.* **9**, 31-37.

Starr, C., Smith, D.B., Blackman, J.A. and Gill, A.A. (1983). *Analyt. Proc. R. Soc. Chem.* **20**, 72-74.

Sun, P.L., Shands, H.L. and Forsberg, R.A. (1972). Inheritance of kernel weight in six spring wheat crosses. *Crop Sci.* **12**, 1-5.

Sunderland, N. and Roberts, M. (1977). New Approach to pollen culture. *Nature* (London), **270**, 236-238.

Suneson, C.A. (1956). An evolutionary plant breeding method. *Agron. J.* **48**, 188-190.

Suneson, C.A. (1960). Genetic diversity a protection against plant diseases and insects. *Agron. J.* **52**, 319-321.

Suneson, C.A. (1962). Use of Pugsley's sterile wheat in cross breeding. *Crop Sci.* **2**, 534-553.

Sutka, J. (1977). The association of genes for purple coleoptile with chromosomes of the wheat variety Mironovskaye 808. *Euphytica* **26**, 475-479.

Sutka, J. (1981). Genetic studies of frost resistance in wheat. *Theor. Appl. Genet.* **59**, 145-152.

Sutka, J. and Kovacs, G. (1987). Chromosomal location of dwarfing gene Rht 12 in wheat. *Euphytica.* **36**, 521-523.

Swaminathan, M.S. (1977). In *Genetics and Wheat Improvement*, A.K.Gupta (Ed.). Oxford and IBH, New Delhi, pp. 3-20.

Swaminathan, M.S. (2001). A century of Mendelian breeding : Impact on wheat. In *Wheat in a Global Environment*, Z. Bedo and L. Lang (Eds.). Kluwer Academic Publishers, Dordrecht., Netherlands, pp. 5-21.

Swamainathan, M.S. and Rao, M.V. (1961). *Wheat Infor. Serv.* **13**, 9-11.

Swaminathan, M.S., Chopra, V.L. and Bhaskaran, S. (1962). Chromosome aberrations and the frequency and spectrum of mutations induced by ethylmethane sulphonate in barley and wheat. *Indian J. Genet.* **22**, 192-207.

Swaminathan, M.S., Chopra, V.L. and Sastry, R.K. (1966). Expression and stability of an induced mutation for ear branching in bread wheat. *Curr. Sci.* (Bangalore) **35**, 91-92.

Swaminathan, M.S., Kohli, S.P. and Anderson, R.G. (1966). Sonora 64 : an early dwarf wheat with high yield. *Indian Farming* **16**, 4-6.

Symes, K.J. (1965). The inheritance of grain hardness in wheat as measured by the particle size index. *Aust. J. Agric. Res.* **16**, 113-123.

Tandon, J.P. (1993). Wheat cultivation, research organization and production technology in the hot dry regions of India. In *Wheat in Heat stressed Environments : Irrigated, Dry Areas and Rice-Wheat Farming Systems*, D.A. Saunders and G.P. Hettel (Eds.), Mexico, DF : CIMMYT, pp. 17-23.

Tavcar, R. (1962). Useful mutations obtained by irradiation in some wheat species (in Serbian). *Arh. Poljopr. Nauke* (Beograd) **15**, 20-30.

Tavcar, R. (1965). Gamma-ray irradiation of seed of wheat, barley and inbreds of maize and the formation of some useful point mutations. *Rep. of the FAO/IAEA Tech. meeting* (Rome), 159-174.

Tee, T.S. (1971). Comparison of single seed descent and bulk population breeding methods and evaluation of single seed selection in wheat (*T. aestivum* L.), thesis University of California, Davis.

Tee, T.S. and Qualset, C.O. (1975). Bulk population in wheat breeding-Comparison of single seed descent and random bulk methods. *Euphytica* **24**, 393-405.

Tesemma, T. and Mitiku, M. (1992). Production constraints of durum wheat in Ethiopia and use of Ethiopian durum wheat landrace varieties in breeding. In *Durum Wheats : Challenges and opportunities*. Wheat Special Report No. 9, S.Rajaram, E.E. Saari and G.P. Hettel (Eds.), CIMMYT, Mexico, DF, Mexico, pp. 49-57.

Thakral, S.K., Luthra, O.P., Behl, R.K. and Dhindsa, K.S. (1986). Combining ability analysis for grain protein content and quality traits in wheat. *Annals Biology* **2**, 136.

Tiwari, R. (2005). Tackling rust resistance in Indian wheat through molecular marker aided selection. Presented at 44th All India Wheat and Barley workers' Meet held at Univ. of Agril. Sciences, Dharwar, Karnatka (August 27-30, 2005), p.5.

Tiwari, R., Singh, R., Priyamvada, Datta, D., JagShoran and Nagarajan, S. (2004). Marker assisted breeding initiatives in India. In *Wheat Technologies for Warmers Areas*, V.S. Rao, G. Singh and S.C. Misra (Eds.). Anamaya Publishers, New Delhi, pp. 138-145.

Toenniessen, G. (1993). Progress and prospects for using biotechnology in plant breeding. In *Biotechnology in Agriculture*, C.B. You *et al.* (Ed.), Kluwer Academic Publishers.

Toman, F.R. and Pauli, A.W. (1964). Changes in nitrate reductase activity and contents of nitrate and nitrite during hardening and dehardening of crowns of wheat. *Crop. Sci.* **4**, 356-359.

Troughton, A. (1962). The roots of temperate cereals, wheat, barley, oats and rye. *Hurley, CAB, Mimeo*, **2**, 62-91.

Trunova, T.I. (1965). Role of light and heat conditions in hardening winter wheats and the importance of oligosaccharides from the point of view of winter hardiness (in Russian). *Fiziol. Rast.* (Moscow) **2**, 85-93.

Trunova, T.I. (1970). Accumulation of sugars in the plant chloroplasts during the frost hardening of winter wheat (in Russian) *Fiziol. Rast.* (Moscow) **17**, 902-906.

Trupp, C.R. (1976). Fertility restoration in soft winter wheat hybrids. *Crop Sci.* **16**, 453-456.

Tschabold, E.E., Heim, D.R., Beck, J.R., Wright, F.L., Rainey, D.P., Terando, N.H. and Schwer, J.F. (1988). LY 195259 : New Chemical hybridizing agent for wheat. *Crop Sci.* **28**, 583-588.

Tschermak, E. and Bleier, H. (1926). *Ber. Dt. Bot. Gesell.* **44**, 110-132.

Tsigrin, V.V. and Alesin, E.P. (1965). Oxidation of phenols in leaf homogenizates of two wheat varieties showing different degrees of resistance to cereal stem rust (in Russian). *Fiziol. Rast.* (Moscow) **12**, 653-657.

Tsigrin, V.V. and Rozum, L.V. (1969). The change of phenol metabolism in stem rust infected spring wheat (in Russian). *Fiziol. Rast.* (Moscow) **16**, 330-335.

Tsuchiya, T. and Larter, E.N. (1968). Direct synthesis of *Triticale* from colchicine-doubled parents. *Canadian J. Genet. Cytol.* **10**, 770.

Tsujimoto, H. and Nodo, K. (1988). Chromosome breakage in wheat induced by the gametocidal gene of *Aegilops triuncialis* L.: Its utilization for wheat genetics and breeding. In *Proc. 7th Int. Wheat. Genet. Symp.*, T.E. Miller and R.M.D. Koebner (Eds.), Cambridge, England, pp. 455-460.

Tsunewaki, K. (1966). Comparative gene analysis of common wheat and its ancestral species.III. Glume hairiness. *Genetics* **53**, 303-311.

Tsunewaki, K., Endo, T.R. and Mukai, Y. (1974). Further discovery of alien cytoplasms inducing haplaoids and twins in common wheat. *Theor. Appl. Genet.* **45**, 104-109.

Tsunewaki, K., Endo, T.R., Kobayashi,M., Mukai, Y. and Panayotov, I. (1980). Genetic diversity of the cytoplasm in *Triticum* and *Aegilops*. Japan Society for the Promotion of Science, Tokyo.

Tsunewaki, K., Mukai, Y. and Endo, T.R. (1980). Genetic Diversity of the Cytoplasm in *Triticum* and *Aegilops*, K. Tsunewaki (Ed.), Japanese Society for Promoting Science, pp. 159-209.

Tsunewaki, K., Mukai, Y., Endo, T.R., Tsuji, S. and Murata, M. (1976). Genetic diversity of the cytoplasm in *Triticum* and *Aegilops*. VI. Distribution of the haploid-inducing cytoplasm. *Jpn. J. Genet.* **51**, 193-200.

Tyamkova, L.A. (1966). The influence of proline on the reistivity of wheat plants to drought. *Dokl. Bolg. Akad. Nauk.* (Sofia) **19**, 847-850.

Udagawa, T. and Oda, K. (1967a). Influences of environmental factors on lodging of wheat and barley plants. 2nd Proc. Crop Sci.Soc. (Tokyo) **36**, 198-205.

Uglov, P.D. and Volkova, A.M. (1970). Varietal differences in hot-resistance in spring wheat (in Russian). *Tr. Prikl. Bot. Gen. Sel.* (Leningrad) **41**, 98-102.

Upadhya, M.D. and Swaminathan, M.S. (1965). Studies on the origin of *Triticum zhukovskyi* and on the mechanism regulating chromosome pairing in *Triticum*. *Indian J. Genet.* **25**, 1-13.

Upadhya, M.D. and Swaminathan, M.S. (1967). Mechanisms regulating chromosome pairing in *Triticum*. *Biol Zentralbl.* **87** (Suppl.), 239-255.

Upadhya, M.D. and Swaminathan, M.S. (1969). Systematic mutations induced by ethyl methane sulphonate in *Triticum pyramidale*. *Indian J. Genet.* **29**, 338-341.

Urich, M.A. and Heyne, E.G. (1968). Genetic instability of Ottawa wheat (*T. aestivum* L.). *Crop Sci.* **8**, 740-743.

Ushiyama, T., Shimizu, T. and Kuwabara, T. (1991). High frequency of haploid production of wheat through intergeneric cross with Teosinte. *Japanese J. Breed.* **41**, 353-357.

Valeev, A.Z. (1967). The valuation of frost resistance of germinating wheat and rye seeds (In Russian) *Sel'hoz. Biol.* (Moscow) **2**, 308-311.

Valentine, J. (1984). Accelarated pedigree selection : an alternative to individual plant selection in the normal pedigree breeding method in the self-pollinated cereals. *Euphytica* **33**, 943-951.

Valkoun, J., Dostal, J. and Kucerova, D. (1990). *Triticum* × *Aegilops* hybrids through embryo culture. In *Biotechnology in Agriculture and Forestry,* Y.P.S. Bajaj (Ed.), Wheat, Springer-Verlag, Berlin, Heidelberg, **13**, 152-166.

Van Deynze, A.E., Dubcovsky, J., Gill, K.S., Nelson, J.C., Sorrells, M.E., Dvorak, J., Gill, B.S., Lagudah, E.S., McCouch, S.R. and Appels, R. (1995). Molecular genetic maps for group I chromosomes of Triticeae species and their relation to chromosomes in rice and oat. *Genome* **38**, 45-59.

Van Ginkel, M., Calhoun, D.S., Gebeyehou, G., Miranda, A., Tian-you, C., Pargas Lara, R., Trethowan, R.M., Sayre, K., Crossa, J. and Rajaram, S. (1995). Plant traits related to yield of wheat in early, late or continuous drought conditions. *Euphytica* **100**, 109-121.

Van Zeist, W. (1972). *Helinium* **12**, 3-19.

Van Zeist, W. and Bakker-Heeres, J.A.H. (1979). *Palaeorient* **5**, 61-167.

Varenitsa, E.T. and Zimina, T.K. (1976). Heterosis in soft winter wheat (*T. aestivum* L.) under conditions of the non-chernozem zone of the U.S.S.R. In *: Heterosis in Plant Breeding, Proc. 7th Congress of EUCARPIA,* A. Janossy and F.G.H. Lupton (Eds.), Elsevier, Amsterdam, pp. 283-288.

Varshney, R.K., Prasad, M., Roy, J.K., Kumar, N., Singh, H., Dhaliwal, H.S., Balyan, H.S. and Gupta, P.K. (2000). Identification of 8 chromosomes and a microsatellite marker on IAS associated with QTL for grain weight in bread wheat. *Theor. Appl. Genet.* **100**, 1290-1294.

Vasil, V., Castillo, A., Fromm, M. and Vasil, I. (1992). Herbicide resistant fertile transgenic wheat plants obtained by microprojectile bombardment of regenerable embryogenic callus. *Biotechnology* **10**, 667-675.

Vasileva, I.M., Lebedeava, L.A. and Rafikova, F.M. (1964). Interactions between water, carbohydrate, and nitrogen metabolism in winter wheat in connection with winter hardiness (in Russian). *Fiziol Rast* (Moscow) **11**, 879-905.

Vavilov, N.I. (1926). Studies on the origin of cultivated wheats. *Bull. Appl. Bot. Genet. Plant Breed.* **16**, 1-248.

Verma, S.S. and Yunus, M. (1986). Role of epistasis in the analysis of genetic component of variance in bread wheat. *Indian J. agric. Sci.* **56**, 687-689.

Villareal, R.L. (1995). Expanding the genetic base of CIMMYT bread wheat germplasm. In *Wheat Breeding at CIMMYT, S. Rajaram S. and G. Hettel* (Eds.), Commemorating 50 years of research in Mexico for global wheat improvement. *Wheat Special Report No. 29*, Mexico, CIMMYT, pp. 16-21.

Villareal, R.L., Mujeeb-Kazi, A. and Pena, R. (1999). Agronomic performance and quality characteristics of tissue culture-derived lines of spring wheat cultivar Pavon. *Cereal Res. Comm.* **27**, 41-48.

Villareal, R.L., Mujeeb-Kazi, A., Rajaram, S. and Del Toro, E. (1990). *Triticum durum* × *Triticum tauschii* synthetic hexaploid wheats-New germplasm for wheat breeding. Symp. on Plant Breeding in the 1990s, N. Carolina State Univ., Raleigh, NC, USA, Dept. of Crop Sci., Res. Rep. No. 130, p.80.

Virk, D.S., Virk, P.S. and Aulakh, H.S. (1989). Detection of additive, dominance and epistasis variation using single testers analysis in bread wheat. *Indian J. Genet.* **49**, 213-217.

Virmani, S.S. and Edwards, I.B. (1983). Current status and future prospects for breeding hybrid rice and wheat. *Adv. Agro.* **36**, 145-213.

Vishnu, M. (1974). Palaeobotanical evidence in India. In *Evolutionary Studies in World Crops*, J.B. Hutchinson (Ed.). Cambridge University Press.

Vlasyuk, P.A., Procenko, D.F. and Smatko, I.G. (1970). Nature of drought resistance of winter wheat varieties (in Russian) *Kolos* (Moscow) 33-34.

Vlasyuk, P.A., Procenko, D.F. and Smatko, I.G. (1971). Characteristics of metabolism of winter wheat in connection with water supply (in Russian) *Izd. Nauka* (Moscow) 161-168.

Volodin, V.G. (1966). Influence of irradiating wheat for several consecutive generations on changes in mutability (in Russian) *Tr. MOTP Otd. Biol.* (Moscow) **23**, 92-96.

Vozvozov, I. (1969). Results of X irradiation of wheat (in Bulgarian) I. *Nac. Konf. PO. Izuch. na Joniz. Lochite* (Sofia), pp. 137-154.

Wagenaar, E.B. (1961). Studies on the genome constitution of *Triticum timopheevi* Zhuk I. Evidence for genetic control of meiotic irregularities in tetraploid hybrids. *Can. J. Genet. Cytol.* **3**, 47-60.

Walia, D.P., Dawa, T. and Plaha, P. (1994). Genetics of yield components in spring wheat. *Cereal Res. Comm.* **22**, 185-186.

Wall, A.M., Riley, R. and Chapman, V. (1971). Wheat mutants permitting homoeologous meiotic chromosome pairing. *Genet. Res. Cambridge* **18**, 311-328.

Wall, A.M., Riley, R. and Gale, M.D. (1971). The position of a locus on chromosome 5B of *Triticum aestivum* affecting homoeologous meiotic pairing. *Genet. Res.* **18** : 329-339.

Walton, P.D. (1971). Heterosis in spring wheat. *Crop Sci.* **11**, 422-424.

Wang, J.K., Ginkel, M.V., Podlich, D., Ye, G.Y., Trethowan, R., Pfeiffer, W., Delacy, I.H., Cooper, M. and Rajaram, S. (2003). Comparison of two breeding strategies by computer simulation. *Crop Sci.* **43**, 1764-1773.

Wang, L.Q., Zhu, H.R., Guan, Q.L. and Rong, J.K. (1986). Production of *Triticum aestivum* (6x)–*Hordeum bulbosum* (4x) alien disomic lines and the introgression of resistance genes (WYMV) from *H.bulbosum* to bread wheat. *Barley Genetics,* pp.359-368.

Wang, W.C., Shang, X.M., Yucel, M. and Nguyen, H.T. (1993). Selection of cultured wheat cell for tolerance to high temperature stress. *Crop Sci.* **33**, 315-320.

Wang, Y., Zhang, A., Nie, X. and Zhou, X. (1998). Preliminary studies on photoperiod-sensitive cytoplasmic male sterility and fertility restoration in *Triticum aestivum.* In *Hybrid Wheat-A new Crop going to Farmer* Zhang Aimin & Huang Tiecheng (Eds.), China Agril. University Press, Beijing, China, pp. 143-157.

Webster, J.A., Smith, Jr. D.H. and Hoxie, R.P. (1982). Effect of cereal leaf beetle on the yields of resistant and susceptible winter wheat. *Crop Sci.* **22**, 836-840.

Weibel, R.O. (1958). In : Balint, A. 1966 : Breeding of agricultural plants (in Hungarian) Mezogazdasagi Kiado, Budapest.

Weiss, M.G. (1949). Soybeans. *Adv. in Agron.* **1**, 77-157.

Wells, D.G. and Lay, C.L. (1970). Hybrid Vigor in Hard Red Spring Wheat Crosses. *Crop Sci.* **10**, 220-223.

Welsh, J.R. and McClelland, M. (1990). Fingerprinting genomes using PCR with arbitrary primers. *Nuclei acid Res.* **18**, 7213-7218.

Welsh, J.R., Keim, D.L., Pirasteh, B. and Richards, R.D. (1973). *Proc. 4th Int. Wheat Genet. Symp.,* Columbia, USA, pp. 879-884.

Wenholz, H., Pridham, J.T., Vears, C.K. and Curteis, W.M. (1940). Wheat varieties in Australia. II. *Agric. Gaz.* N.S.W. **51**, 605-610.

Whittington, W.J. (1970). Root Growth. Butter worths London, **15**, 450.

Widner, J.N. and Lebsock, K.L. (1973). Combining ability in Durum wheat : I. Agronomic characteristics. *Crop Sci.,***13**, 164-167.

Wienhues, F. (1968). Long-term yield analyses of heterosis in wheat and barley:variability of heterosis, fixation of heterosis. *Euphytica* **17** (Suppl. I), pp. 49-62.

Wiese, M.V. (1987). Compendium of wheat diseases, 2nd edition, American Phytopathological Society, St. Paul, M.N., USA.

Wilcoxson, R.D. (1981). Genetics of slow rusting in cereals. *Phytopathology* **71(a)**, 989-993.

William, M.D.H.M. and Mujeeb-Kazi, A. (1995a). Applications of biochemical makrers in wheat wide cross. In *Utilizing Wild Grass Biodiversity in Wheat Improvement*, A. Mujeeb-kazi and G.P. Hettel (Eds.), CIMMYT Research Report No. 2. Mexico, D.F. CIMMYT, pp. 76-92.

William, M.D.H.M. and Mujeeb-Kazi, A. (1995b). Applications of Molecular markers in wheat wide crosses. In *Utilizing Wild Grass Biodiversity in Wheat Improvement*, A. Mujeeb-Kazi and G.P. Hettel (Eds.), CIMMYT Research Report No. 2, Mexico, DF, Mexico, pp.93-101.

Williams, J.K.G., Kubelik, A.R., Livak, K.J., Rafalski, J.A. and Tingey, S.V. (1990). DNA polymorphism amplified by arbitrary primers are useful as genetic markers. *Nucleic acids Res.* **18**, 6531-6535.

Wilson, J.A. (1968). Problems in hybrid wheat breeding. *Euphytica* **17** (Suppl.) **1**, 13-33.

Wilson, J.A. and Ross, W.M. (1962). Male sterility interaction of *Triticum aestivum* and *Triticum timopheevii* cytoplasm. *Wheat Infor. Ser.* **14**, 29-31.

Wilson, J.A., Wilson, P. and Schmidt, H.J. (1980). Full-dwarf × Semi-dwarf hybrid wheat. *Proc. 3rd Int. Wheat Conf.* Madrid, Spain, pp. 210-214.

Wilson, P. and Driscoll, C.J. (1983). Hybrid Wheat. In *Heterosis : Reappraisal of Theory and Practice. Monogr. Theor. Appl. Genet.* Vol. 6. R. Frankel (Ed.), Springer, Berlin, Heidelberg, New York, pp. 94-123.

Woloschuk, C.M. and Mc Hughen, A. (1984). Variant wheat regenerants. IAPTC (Canada). 1st Plant Genetic Engineering Workshop. Saskatoon. Sark. Canada (Abstr.).

Wright, G.M. and Thomas, G.A. (1976). An evaluation of the single seed descent method of breeding, *New Zealand Wheat Rev.* **13**, 46-49.

Wrigley, C.W. and Shepherd, K.W. (1973). Electrofocusing of wheat grain esterase from wheat genotypes. *Ann. NY Acad. Sci.* **209**, 154-162.

Xie, D.X., Devos, K.M., Moore, G. and Gale, M.D. (1993). RFLP-based genetic maps of the homoeologous group 5 chromosomes of bread wheat. *Theor. Appl. Genet.* **87**, 70-74.

Xu, Naiyu (1995). Preliminary studies on photoperiod-sensitive cytoplasmic male sterility in wheat. *J. Wuhan Univ. Natural Science Edition,* **41**, 218-222.

Yadav, M.S. and Singh, I. (1988). Combining ability analysis over environments in spring wheat. *Wheat Infor. Serv.* **67**, 21-24.

Yadav, R. and Behl, R.K. (2002). Genetics of morpho-physiological characters and grain yield in wheat. *Natnl. J. Pl. Improv.* **4**, 26-29.

Yadav, S.P. and Murty, B.R. (1976). Heterosis and combining ability in crosses of different height categories in bread wheat. *Indian J. Genet.* **36**, 184-196.

Yamagata, H. (1981). Fruits and perspectives of mutation breeding. In *Progress in mutation breeding.* 20th Gamma Field Symposium, Ohimaya, Ibaraki, Japan, 16-17, July 1981, pp. 11-49

Yang, H.Y. and Zhou, C. (1982). *In vitro* induction of haploid plants from unpollinated ovaries and ovules. *Theor. Appl. Genet.* **63**, 97-104.

Yang, H.Y. and Zhou, C. (1990). *In vitro* gynogenesis. In *Plant Tissue Culture : Applications and Limitations,* S.S. Bhojwani, S.S. (Ed.), Elsevier, New York.

Yen, C., Dai, D.Q. and Luo, M.C. (1986). The high compatibility resources of wheat for generic hybridization among *Secale* and *Aegilops*. Proc. Int. Triticale Symp., pp. 42-52.

Yeo, A.R. and Flowers, T.J. (1989). Selection for physiological characters-examples from breeding for salt tolerance. In *Plant Under Stress*. H.G. Jones, T.J. Flowers and M.B. Jones (Eds.). Cambridge University Press, Cambridge, pp. 217-234.

Yirgou, D. and Caldwell, R.M. (1968). Stomatal penetration of wheat seedlings by stem and leaf rust in relation of effects of carbon dioxide, light and stomatal aperture. *Phytopath.* (Worcester) **58**, 500-507.

Yonezawa, K. and Yamagata, H. (1981). *Japan J. Breed.* **31**, 35-42.

Yoshizo, K. (1968). Study on the effects of ^{60}Co-gamma rays irradiation on the growth and yield of crops. *Mem. Tokyo Univ. Agric.* (Tokyo) **12**, 37-124.

Youssefian, S. (1986). Ph.D. Thesis, University of Cambridge.

Zabeau, M. and Vos, P. (1993). Selective restriction fragment amplification : A general method for DNA fingerprints. European Patent Application Publication 0534858AI.

Zevan, A.C. (1978). The prehistoric spread of wheat in Asia. In *Proc. 5th Int. Wheat Genet. Symp.*, New Delhi, India, S. Ramanujam (Ed.), pp. 103-107.

Zevan, A.C. (1980). The spread of wheat over the old world since the neolithicum as indicated by its genotype for hybrid necrosis. *J. d Agric. Trad. et. bot. Appl.* **27**, 19-53.

Zeven, A.C. (1968). Cross-pollination and sources of restorer genes in wheat and a semi-hybrid variety. *Euphytica* **17**, (Suppl.1), pp. 75-81.

Zeven, A.C. (1987). Crossability percentage of some 1400 bread wheat varieties and lines with rye. *Euphytica* **36**, 299-319.

Zhang, A. and Huang, T. (1998). Progress of Hybrid Wheat Breeding in China. In *Hybrid Wheat– A New Crop Going to Farmers*, Zhang Aimin and Huang, Tie Cheng (Eds.), Proceeding of 1st Int. Workshop on Hybrid Wheat. China Agril. University Press, Beijing, China, pp. 9-14.

Zhang, A., Xiuling, N., Dongcheng, L. and Xiaoli, G. (2001). Advances of hybrid wheat breeding in China. *Cereal Res. Comm.* **29**, 343-350.

Zhang, H.B. and Dvorak, J. (1989). Isolation of repeated DNA sequences from *Lophopyrum elongatum* for detection of *Lophopyrum chromatin* in wheat genomes. *Genome* **33**, 283-293.

Zhang, H.B. and Dvorak, J. (1990). Characterization and distribution of an interspersed repeated nucleotide sequence from *Lophopyrum elongatum* and mapping of a segregation-distortion factor with it. *Genome* **33**, 927-936.

Zhang, X., Li, Z. and Chen, S. (1992). Production and identification of three 4 Ag (4D) substitution lines of *Triticum aestivum–Agropyron* : relative transmission rate of alien chromosomes. *Theor. Appl. Genet.* **83**, 707-714.

Zheng, Y., Luo, M., Yen, C. and Yang, J. (1992). Chromosome location of a new crossability gene in common wheat. *Wheat Infor. Serv.* **75**, 36-40.

Zhu, Z.C., Wu, H.S., An, W.K. and Liu, Z.Y. (1981). Induction of haploid plantlets from unpollinated ovaries of *Triticum aestivum* cultured *in vitro*. *Acta Genet. Sin.* **8**, 386-390.

Zlobina, E.S. (1970). Cytophysiological diagnostics of the depth of dormany and frost resistance in winter wheat (in Russian). *Biologia* (Moscow) **5**, 21-25.

Zohary, D. and Feldman, M. (1962). Hybridization between amphidiploids and the evolution of the polyploids in the wheat (*Aegilops-Triticum*) group. *Evolution* **16**, 44-61.

Zohary, D., Harlan, J.R. and Vardi, A. (1969). The wild diploid progenitors of wheat and their breeding value. *Euphytica* **18**, 58-65.

Zoz, N.N. (1965). Variability of wheat induced by chemical mutagens (in Russian) *IZv. Akad. Nauk. Sec. Biol.* SSSR (Moscow) **3**, 423-437.

Zoz, N.N. (1971). Characteristics of some chemical mutagens and the mutation breeding (in Russian). *Prak. Him. Mt.* (Moscow) pp. 7-12.

Zoz, N.N. and Makarova, S.I. (1964). Variability in wheat induced by chemical mutagens in the first generation after treatment (in Russian). *Dokl. Akad. Nauk. SSSR* (Moscow) **159**, 195-197.

Zoz, N.N. and Makarova, S.I. (1965a). Mutation in wheat induced by chemical mutagens (in Russian). *Dokl. Akad. Nank* SSSR (Moscow) **163**, 224-226.

Zoz, N.N. and Makarova, S.I. (1965b). Hereditary changes of winter wheat induced by chemical mutagens (in Russian). *Bull. Isp. Pri.* (Moscow) **70**, 124-125.

Subject Index

Adaptive characters 34, 35
Addition lines 108
Adventitious roots 70
AFLPs 133
Aids to selection 74
Albumin 179
Alien cytoplasm technique 126
Alien translocations 109-115
Allelopathy 170
Alternaria leaf blight 167
Aluminium toxicity 66
Androgenesis 119
Aneuploidy 25-30
Anther colour 34
Anther culture 119
Anther size 34
Anthesis 70
Anthocyanin pigmentation of the rachis 34
Aphids 169
Apogamy 121
Apomixis 150
Approach method 72
Awn arrangement 32
Awn colour 32

Awn shedding 32
Awned mutants 96
Awning 31

Backcross method 79, 216
    Variants 81
Biochemical markers 130
Bulbosum method 122
Bulk method 77, 85, 86, 216
    Variants 77, 78

Cereal cyst nematode 167
Cereal leaf beetle 170
Chemical hybridizing agents (CHAs) 148
Choice of parents 74, 191
Clean crop approach 83
Cold hardiness 63
Coleoptile colour 34
Common bunt 165
Convergent improvement method 81
Cuckoo chromosomes 101

Days to heading 52
Diallel selective mating system 81, 217

Dirty crop approach 83
Diseases 64
Disease resistance 35, 155-168, 219
Double fertilization 73
Drought tolerance 60, 171
Dwarf mutants 94

Ear allignment 31
Ear shape 31
Earlinss 95
Early generation testing 74
English grain aphid 169

Fertility and sterility 34
Fertilization 72
Flag smut 65, 166
Flour stability 67
Flour stiffness 67
Flour strength 67
Foot rot 65
Fusarium root rot 167

Gametoclonal variation 127
Gene pyramiding 163
General resistance 159
Genome elimination technique 122
Genomic *in situ* hybridization (GISH) 114
Globulin 179
Glume beak 33
Glume colour 32
Glume hairiness 32
Glume shoulder 33
Gluten 1, 179
Glutenins, 179
Grain colour 33, 96

Grain lustre 33
Grains per spike 41, 46
Grain shape 33
Grain shattering 65
Grain storage progeins 38
Grain texture 33, 67, 178, 181-183
Grain weight 41, 44, 178
Grain yield 41, 43
Grasshoppers 170
Greenbug 169
Gynogenesis 121

Hardening 161
Harvest index 53
Head blight 167
Head scab 64, 167
Hectolitre weight 182
Helminthosporium leaf blight (HLB) 166
Hill bunt 65
Homeoalleles 31
Homozygous genomic heterosis 23, 139, 141

Ideotype concept 58
Inflorescence 70
In situ hybridization (ISH) 114
Insect pests 65, 168
Intermittent backcrossing 81

Karnal bunt 65, 164

Leaf blight 65
Leaf blotching 34
Lodging resistance 62, 173
Loose smut 64, 166

Subject Index

Male-sterile facilitated recurrent selection 95
Maturity period 41, 60
Megagametogenesis 73
Megasporogenesis 73
Microgametogenesis 73
Microsporogenesis 72
Modified backcross method 81
Modified bulk method 78
Modified mass method 78
Modified pedigree method 85
Molecular markers 132
Multiline breeding 82, 217
Multiple non-recurrent parent backcrossing 81
Multiple recurrent parent backcrossing 81
Multiple seed dcescent (MSD) method 79, 86
Mutagen-induced disease resistance 95
Mutation recombination-breeding 88

Nature of heterosis 138
New wheat genetic stocks 211

Ovule culture 121

Parthenogenesis 121
Pedigree method 75, 85, 216
    Variants 77
Phalaris minor 170
Photoperiodism 35
Plant canopy 96
Plant height 38, 42, 50
Pollen lethality 34
Pollination 70
Powdery mildew 64, 163
Preharvest sprouting 66
Primary gene pool 104

Protein content 42, 179, 182, 185
Protein quantity and quality 96, 179

Qualitative characters 31-40
Quantitative characters 40-53
Quasi-continuous variation 30

RAPDs 133
RFLPs 132
Rht genes 39, 40, 94
Root 69
Rusts 64, 155
    Leaf rust 36, 156
    Stem rust 36, 157
    Stripe rust 37, 159

Secondary gene pool 104
Sedimentation value 182
Selected bulk method 85
Semidwarf wheat era 199
Seminal roots 69
Septoria tritici blotch 167
Shuttle breeding system 59, 83, 217
Single seed descent (SSD) method 78, 85, 86, 216
Sink-source relationship 57
Slow rusting 160
Spike length 41, 47
Spikes per plant 41
Spikelets per spike 41, 48
Stem 69
Stem colour 34
Substitution lines 108
Syngamy 73
Synthetic hexaploids 99, 108

Tertiary gene pool 104
Tillering capacity 70
Tiller number 49
Total biomass 42
Totipotency 119
Transpiration coefficient 61
Triple fusion 73
Triplet band proteins 38
Twirl pollination method 72

Vernalization 34

Winter-hardiness 35

XYZ system 148